MACMILLAN CONNECTIONS READING PROGRAM

TAPESTRIES

SENIOR AUTHORS

Virginia A. Arnold   Carl B. Smith

AUTHORS

James Flood   Diane Lapp

LITERATURE CONSULTANTS

Joan I. Glazer   Margaret H. Lippert

Macmillan/McGraw-Hill School Publishing Company

New York   Chicago   Columbus

Parts of this work were published in earlier editions of CONNECTIONS. This work is also published in individual volumes under the titles *Voices, Ventures, Voyages,* and *Viewpoints.*

Macmillan/McGraw-Hill School Division
866 Third Avenue
New York, New York 10022

Printed in the United States of America

ISBN 0-02-178723-9

9 8 7 6 5 4 3 2 1

ACKNOWLEDGMENTS

The publisher gratefully acknowledges permission to reprint the following copyrighted material:

"Balloon Trip" is from BALLOON TRIP: A Sketch Book by Huck Scarry. Copyright © 1983 by Huck Scarry. Published by Prentice-Hall, Inc., Englewood Cliffs, N.J. and reprinted with their permission.

"The Bayeux Tapestry" is from THE BAYEUX TAPESTRY by Norman Denny and Josephine Filmer-Sankey. Reprinted by permission of Collins Publishers, London.

"The Best of the Books" contains art from the following books: THE MOUSE AND THE MOTORCYCLE by Beverly Cleary, illustrated by Louis Darling. Copyright © 1965 by Beverly Cleary. RALPH S. MOUSE by Beverly Cleary, illustrated by Paul O. Zelinsky. Copyright © 1982 by Beverly Cleary. DEAR MR. HENSHAW by Beverly Cleary, illustrated by Paul O. Zelinsky. Copyright © 1983 by Beverly Cleary. Used by permission of William Morrow & Company. JULIE OF THE WOLVES by Jean Craighead George. Pictures by John Schoenherr. Illustration copyright © 1972 by John Schoenherr. Reprinted by permission of Harper & Row, Publishers, Inc. and Hamish Hamilton Ltd. BRIDGE TO TERABITHIA by Katherine Paterson. Illustrations by Donna Diamond (Thomas Y. Crowell). Copyright © 1977 by Katherine Paterson. Reprinted by permission of Harper & Row, Publishers, Inc. and Victor Gollancz, London. CHARLOTTE'S WEB by E. B. White. Pictures by Garth Williams. Copyright 1952 by E. B. White. Illustrations copyright renewed 1980 by Garth Williams. Reprinted by permission of Harper & Row, Publishers, Inc. WHERE THE WILD THINGS ARE by Maurice Sendak. Copyright © 1963 by Maurice Sendak. Reprinted by permission of Harper & Row, Publishers, Inc. and The Bodley Head, Ltd., London. SNOW WHITE AND THE SEVEN DWARFS translated by Randall Jarrell, illustrations by Nancy Ekholm Burkett. Copyright © 1972 by Nancy Ekholm Burkett. Reproduced by permission of Farrar, Straus and Giroux, Inc. M. C. HIGGINS, THE GREAT by Virginia Hamilton, jacket illustration by Jim McMullan. New York: Macmillan Publishing Company, 1974. Used by permission. A VISIT TO WILLIAM BLAKE'S INN by Nancy Willard, illustrations by Alice Provensen and Martin Provensen. Illustrations copyright © 1981 by Alice Provensen and Martin Provensen. Reprinted by permission of Harcourt Brace Jovanovich, Inc. THE SNOWY DAY by Ezra Jack Keats. Copyright © 1962 by Ezra Jack Keats reprinted by permission of Viking Penguin Inc. and The Bodley Head, Ltd., London. MADELINE'S RESCUE by Ludwig Bemelmans. Copyright 1951, 1953 by Ludwig Bemelmans, renewed © 1979, 1981 by Madeleine Bemelmans and Barbara Marciano. Reprinted by permission of Viking Penguin Inc.

"The Borrowers Aloft" is from THE BORROWERS ALOFT by Mary Norton. Copyright © 1961 by Mary Norton. Reprinted by permission of Harcourt Brace Jovanovich, Inc. and Hughes Massie Ltd.

"Buying Pencils" is from WHEN HITLER STOLE PINK RABBIT by Judith Kerr. Copyright © 1971 by Judith Kerr. Reprinted by permission of Coward-McCann and William Collins Sons & Co., Ltd., London.

"Robin Hood and the Stranger," originally titled "Robin Hood Meets Maid Marian in Sherwood Forest" is from ROBIN HOOD edited by George Cockburn Harvey. Copyright 1923, 1951 by John C. Winston Co. Reprinted by permission of Henry Holt and Company.

"Saint George and the Dragon" is from SAINT GEORGE AND THE DRAGON retold by Margaret Hodges and illustrated by Trina Schart Hyman. Text copyright © 1984 by Margaret Hodges, illustrations copyright © 1984 by Trina Schart Hyman. By permission of Little, Brown and Company.

"Serendipity" is from IT DOESN'T ALWAYS HAVE TO RHYME by Eve Merriam. Copyright © 1964 by Eve Merriam. All rights reserved. Reprinted by permission of Marian Reiner for the author.

"Shackleton's Epic Voyage" is from SHACKLETON'S EPIC VOYAGE by Michael Brown. Reprinted by permission of the British publishers, Hamish Hamilton Ltd.

"The Training of a Knight" is an adaptation of pp. 126–131 from THE STORY OF KNIGHTS AND ARMOR by Ernest E. Tucker. Copyright © 1961 by Ernest E. Tucker. By permission of Lothrop, Lee & Shepard Books (A Division of William Morrow & Company).

"Travel" is from COLLECTED POEMS by Edna St. Vincent Millay. Copyright 1921, 1948 by Edna St. Vincent Millay, published by Harper & Row, Publishers, Inc. Reprinted by permission of Norma Millay Ellis, Literary Executor.

"Voyage to Freedom" is from CAPTAIN OF THE PLANTER by Dorothy Sterling. Copyright © 1958, published by Doubleday & Company, Inc. Reprinted by permission of the author.

"What Do You Mean by *Average*?" is from WHAT DO YOU MEAN BY 'AVERAGE'? by Elizabeth James and Carol Barkin. Copyright © Elizabeth James and Carol Barkin and reprinted with their permission.

"A Wrinkle in Time" is an excerpt from A WRINKLE IN TIME by Madeleine L'Engle. Copyright © 1962 by Madeleine L'Engle Franklin. Reprinted by permission of Farrar, Straus and Giroux, Inc. and Lescher and Lescher Ltd.

"The Writing Lessons" is from MAMA'S BANK ACCOUNT by Kathryn Forbes. Copyright 1943 by Kathryn Forbes; renewed 1971 by Richard E. McLean and Robert M. McLean. Reprinted by permission of Harcourt Brace Jovanovich, Inc. and Curtis Brown, Ltd.

Cover Design: Suzanne Duranceau

Feature Logos and Medallion Logos: Eva Vagreti Cockrille

Unit Openers: Dennis Potokar

ILLUSTRATION CREDITS: Sal Murdocca, 7–16; Laurie McGraw, 18–28; John Hatzakis, 29, 135, 211, 249, 323, 407, 465; Joel Snyder, 31, 45, 103, 189, 326, 341; Gerry Sevier, 34–41; Burt Groedell, 42–43, Alan Neider, 46–55; Jerry Pinkney, 58–70; Julie Downing, 72–84; Barbara Maslen, 85; Linda Solovic, 88–95; Lane Yerkes, 96–101; Joseph Veno, 106–123; Donna Ward, 136–159; Isidre Mones, 162–175; Kenneth Dewey, 178–185; David Johnston, 186–187, Logeron, 190–199; Hima Pamoedjo, 200; Ron LeHew, 212–231; Richard Hooks, 236–248; Bernadette Lau, 272–280; Laurie Jordan, 281; Tim Hildebrandt, 282–303; Roger and Linda Garland, 306–322; Fred W. Thomas, 328–338; Steve Madson, 339; Vera Rosenberry, 342–352; Wendy Popp, 354–367, Frederic Marvin, 392–406; Richard Hull, 408–422; Mario Stasolla, 450–464; Mac Evans, 470–477, Jack Brusca, 478–479; Eldon Doty, 498–510; Franklin Hammond, 511; Robert Jackson, 514–523; Christiane Bauregard, 539; Jerry Harston, 540–551; Frederic Winkowski, 556–571; Alex Bloch, 572–591; Joel Snyder, 593–624.

PHOTO CREDITS: © Clara Aich, 88 to 94. Reprinted by permission of the American Library Association, 126, 127R, 131BL, 133BL. ART RESOURCE: © Giraudon "with special authorization of the City of Bayeux," 201 to 209. THE BETTMANN ARCHIVE, INC.: 535L. BLACK STAR: © Robert Lackenbach, 530 to 531. © Fay Foto Service, Inc., 267. © Joel Gordon, 552. Photo © Michael Holford/Courtesy the Trustees of the British Museum, 530R. © Jim Kalett/Courtesy Houghton Mifflin Company, 353. © Candid Lang, 132R. © Jane Latta, 532L, R. The Louvre, 535R, 536. THE METROPOLITAN MUSEUM OF ART, Harris Brisbane Dick Fund, 1931 (31.60.4), 530L (detail), 533 (detail), 534R; Bequest of Laura Frances Hearn, 1917 (17.101), 537, Rogers Fund, 1913 (13.173.59), 534L. PHOTOUNIQUE: © R. Hamilton Smith, 423. © Marilyn Stafford, 71. UPI/ BETTMANN NEWSPHOTOS: 497. © Jill Paton Walsh, 128T. WOODFIN CAMP & ASSOCIATES: © Adam Woolfitt, 528 to 529.

Contents

Introducing Level 12

VOICES

Beneath the rule of men entirely great,
The pen is mightier than the sword.

Edward Bulwer-Lytton

UNIT 1

Language is the most powerful tool we have for reaching out to others. We can use it to express our feelings, to spread our ideas, and even to establish peace. The stories in this unit can help you understand the problems of learning another language. You will also learn about how people use all kinds of writing to voice their thoughts. How do you share your own voice?

BUYING PENCILS

JUDITH KERR

Anna and her brother Max were happy growing up in Berlin, Germany. Then Adolf Hitler rose to power. Soon Papa's newspaper editorials against the Nazis made it dangerous for the family to stay in Germany. Leaving everything behind them, they fled their homeland in 1933. They became refugees, living first in Switzerland, then in Paris, France.

In this excerpt from When Hitler Stole Pink Rabbit, *which is based on the author's own life, Anna and her family have just come to Paris.*

When Anna woke up in the morning it was bright daylight. Through a gap in the yellow curtains she could see a patch of windy sky above the rooftops. There was a smell of cooking and a clicking sound which she could not at first identify, until she realized that it was Papa typing in the room next door. Max's bed was empty. He must have crept out while she was still asleep. She got up and wandered out into the hall without dressing. Mama and Grete must have been busy, for all the luggage had been cleared away and through the open door she could see that Mama's bed had been turned back into a sofa. Then Mama herself appeared from the dining room.

"There you are, my darling," she said. "Come and have some breakfast, even though it's nearly lunch-time."

Max was already installed at the dining room table, drinking milky coffee and pulling pieces off a long and incredibly thin loaf of bread.

"It's called a baguette,"[1] explained Mama, "that means a stick"—which was exactly what it looked like.

Anna tried some and found it delicious. There was a red oilcloth on the table which made the cups and plates look very pretty, and the room was warm in spite of the blustery November day outside.

"It's nice here," said Anna. "We wouldn't have been able to have breakfast in our pajamas at the Gasthof Zwirn."[2]

"It's a bit small," said Mama. "But we'll manage."

---

1. **baguette** (ba get′)
2. **Gasthof Zwirn** (gast′ hōf tsvirn′): the hotel where the family had stayed while they were in Switzerland.

Max stretched himself and yawned. "It's nice having our own place."

There was something more that was nice. Anna could not at first think what it was. She looked at Mama pouring coffee and at Max tilting back his chair as he had been told a hundred times not to. Through the thin walls she could hear Papa's typewriter.

"I don't really mind where we are," she said as it came to her,—"as long as we're all together."

In the afternoon Papa took them out. They went on the Underground, which was called the Metro and had a peculiar smell. Anna rather liked it. They saw the Eiffel Tower[3] (but did not go up it because it would have cost too much) and the place where Napoleon[4] was buried, and at last the Arc de Triomphe[5] which was quite near home. By this time it was getting late, but Max noticed that you could go up to the top and that it was quite cheap, probably because it was not nearly as high as the Eiffel Tower—so they went.

No one else wanted to go to the top of the Arc de Triomphe on this cold, dark afternoon and the elevator was empty. When Anna stepped out at the top she was met by an icy blast of wind and a prickle of raindrops and she wondered whether it had been a good idea to come. Then she looked down. It was as though she were standing at the center of a huge sparkling star. Its rays stretched out in all directions and each one was a road lined with lights. When she looked closer she could see other lights which were cars and buses

---

3. **Eiffel** (ī′ fəl) **Tower:** an iron tower built by A.G. Eiffel for the 1889 Exposition. The top can be reached by elevator.
4. **Napoleon** (nə pō′ lē ən): French military leader, and emperor of France.
5. **Arc de Triomphe** (ärk′ də trē *onf′*): famous landmark in Paris. It is a monument to the Unknown Soldier.

crawling along the roads, and immediately below they formed a bright ring circling the Arc de Triomphe itself. In the distance were the dim shapes of domes and spires and the twinkling spot which was the top of the Eiffel Tower.

"Isn't it beautiful?" said Papa. "Isn't this a beautiful city?"

Anna looked at Papa. His overcoat had lost a button and the wind was blowing through it, but Papa did not seem to notice.

"Beautiful," said Anna.

It was nice to get back to the warm apartment. Grete had helped Mama with supper and it was ready in good time.

"Have you learned any French yet?" asked Mama.

"Of course not," said Grete before anyone else could answer. "It takes months."

But Anna and Max found that they had picked up quite a few words just from listening to Papa and other people. They could say *oui* and *non* and *merci* and *au*

revoir and *bonsoir Madame*, and Max was particularly proud of *trois billets, s'il vous plaît*[6] which was what Papa had said when he bought tickets for the Metro.

"Well, you'll know a lot more soon," said Mama. "I've arranged for a lady to come and give you French lessons, and she's starting tomorrow afternoon."

The lady's name was Mademoiselle[7] Martel and the following morning Anna and Max tried to collect everything they would need for her lesson. Papa lent them an old French dictionary and Mama found them some paper to write on. The only thing neither of them had was a pencil.

"You'll have to go and buy some," said Mama. "There's a shop at the corner of the street."

"But we can't speak French!" cried Anna.

"Nonsense," said Mama. "Take the dictionary with you. I'll give you a franc each and you can keep the change."

"What's the French for pencil?" asked Max.

"*Un crayon*,"[8] said Mama. Her voice did not sound as French as Papa's but she knew quite a lot of words. "Now off you go—quickly."

By the time they had traveled down in the lift by themselves—and it was Anna's turn to press the button—Anna felt quite bold about the enterprise, and her courage did not falter even when she found that

---

6. ***oui*** (wē): yes.
non (non): no.
merci (mär sē'): thank you.
au revoir (ō rə vwär'): good-bye.
bonsoir Madame (bon swär' mə dam'): good evening, Madame.
trois billets, s'il vous plaît (twa bē yā' sē vü plā'): three tickets, please.
7. ***mademoiselle*** (mad ə moi zel'): miss.
8. ***un crayon*** (un krā on'): a pencil.

the shop was rather grand and sold more office equipment than stationery. Clutching the dictionary under her arm she marched through the door ahead of Max and said in ringing tones, "*Bonsoir Madame!*"

The owner of the shop looked astonished and Max nudged her.

"That's not a *Madame*—that's a *Monsieur*,"[9] he whispered. "And I think *bonsoir* means good evening."

"Oh!" said Anna.

9. ***Monsieur*** (mə siu′): mister.

But the man who owned the shop did not seem to mind. He smiled and said something in French which they could not understand. They smiled back.

Then Anna said hopefully, "*Un crayon*," and Max added, "*S'il vous plaît*."

The man smiled again, searched in a cardboard box behind the counter and produced a beautiful red pencil which he handed to Anna.

She was so amazed at her success that she forgot to say "*Merci*" and just stood there with the pencil in her hand. This was easy!

Then Max said, "*Un crayon*," because he needed one too.

"*Oui, oui*," said the man, smiling and nodding and pointing to the pencil in Anna's hand. He agreed with Max that it was a pencil.

"*Non*!" said Max. "*Un crayon!*" He sought about for a way to explain. "*Un crayon,*" he cried, pointing to himself. "*Un crayon!*"

Anna giggled because it looked as though Max were introducing himself.

"Aah!" said the man. He took another pencil out of the box and handed it to Max with a little bow.

"*Merci*," said Max, much relieved. He gave the man the two francs and waited for the change. After a while it appeared that there wasn't any. Anna was very disappointed. It would have been nice to have some money.

"Let's ask him if he has any other pencils," she whispered. "They might be cheaper."

"We can't!" said Max.

"Well, let's just try," said Anna who was sometimes very pigheaded. "Look up the French for 'other.'"

Max leafed through the dictionary while the man watched him curiously. At last he found it. "It's '*autre*,'"[10] he said.

Anna smiled brightly and held out her pencil to the man. "*Un autre crayon*?" she said.

"*Oui, oui*," said the man after a moment's hesitation. He gave her another pencil from the box. Now she had two.

"*Non*," said Anna, handing one of the pencils back to him. His smile was getting a bit frozen. "*Un autre crayon* . . ."—she made a face and a shape with her fingers to suggest something infinitely small and unimportant.

The man stared at her to see if she was going to do anything else. Then he shrugged his shoulders and said something hopeless in French.

"Come on!" said Max, pink with embarrassment.

"No!" said Anna. "Give me the dictionary!" She turned the pages feverishly. At last she found it. Cheap . . . *bon-marché*.[11]

"*Un bon-marché crayon!*" she cried triumphantly, startling two ladies who were examining a typewriter. "*Un bon-marché crayon, s'il vous plaît!*"

The man looked very tired. He found another cardboard box and took from it a thinner blue pencil. He gave it to Anna who nodded and gave him back the red one. Then the man gave her twenty centimes[12] change. Then he looked questioningly at Max.

---

10. ***autre*** (ō′ trə): other; ***un autre*** (ən ō′ trə): another.
11. ***bon-marché*** (bon mär shā′): cheap.
12. ***centimes*** (san tēmz′): French coins. They are similar in value to pennies.

"*Oui!*" said Anna excitedly. "*Un autre bon-marché crayon!*" and the procedure was repeated with Max's pencil.

"*Merci,*" said Max.

The man just nodded. He seemed worn out.

"We've got twenty centimes each," said Anna. "Think of what we'll be able to buy with that!"

"I don't think it's very much," said Max.

"Still, it's better than nothing," said Anna. She wanted to show the man that she was grateful, so as they went out of the shop she smiled at him again and said, "*Bonsoir Madame!*"

Thinking and Writing About the Selection

1. Why were Anna and her family in Paris?
2. Anna compared standing on the top of the Arc de Triomphe to standing at the center of a huge sparkling star. How were the two things similar?
3. How did Anna and Max's shopping trip turn out? Did they get a bargain? Would they have done better keeping the first pencils the man sold them?
4. Write five phrases that you think would be most useful to a person who is just beginning to learn English.

Applying the Key Skill
Synonyms and Antonyms

Write synonyms for the underlined words in Part A. Write antonyms for the underlined words in Part B.

A. 1. Anna and Max tried to <u>collect</u> everything they would need for Mademoiselle Martel's <u>lesson</u>.

2. By the time they had traveled down in the <u>lift</u>, Anna felt quite <u>bold</u> about the enterprise.

3. The owner of the shop looked <u>astonished</u>.

B. 1. "<u>Merci</u>," said Max, much <u>relieved</u>.

2. "Well, let's just try," said Anna who was sometimes very <u>pigheaded</u>.

3. She made a face and a shape with her fingers to suggest something <u>infinitely</u> <u>small</u> and <u>unimportant</u>.

LANGUAGE ACTIVITY

IN OTHER WORDS

When Anna and Max found themselves in Paris, they realized that they would have to learn French if they wanted to get along. You might find that it is easier for you to learn either German or French than it was for Anna and Max to learn French. Let's see why.

German and French belong to different language groups. German is classified as a Teutonic (tü ton′ ik), or Germanic, language—a group that also includes Dutch and Danish. French is a Romance language. Romance languages, which also include Spanish and Italian, are based on Latin, the language of ancient Rome.

English is classified as a Germanic language. After Germanic words, the most important words in English are those of Latin origin. They have come from Latin directly or through one of the Romance languages, in particular French. The chart below lists just a few common English words and their equivalents in French and German.

English	French	German
pencil	crayon	Bleistift
red	rouge	rot
blue	bleu	blau
other	autre	ander
house	maison	Haus
street	rue	Strasse
come	venir	kommen
go	aller	gehen
music	musique	Musik
book	livre	Buch

SKILLS ACTIVITY

DICTIONARY

In "Buying Pencils," Anna and Max used a special kind of dictionary to find the French words they needed to know. The kinds of dictionaries we ordinarily use don't tell us the French words for English words, but they do tell us a lot of other things about words.

A **dictionary** is a book of information about words. The words in a dictionary are listed in alphabetical order. The dictionary shows you how to spell and pronounce words, and gives word meanings. Many dictionaries have other useful information about words, too. They tell the parts of speech of words, show examples of correct usage, and give word origins.

In order for the dictionary to be helpful to you, you must know how to use it. Refer to the sample dictionary page on the next page as you read about the dictionary features listed below. If you become familiar with how to use a dictionary, you will be able to find the word information you want quickly and easily.

Guide words are the first and last entry words on a dictionary page. *Pen* is the first entry on the sample page, and *pendent* is the last. The other entry words that appear on the page fall alphabetically between *pen* and *pendent*.

An **entry word** is printed in boldface, or heavy, type and is divided into syllables by dots. Not all forms of a word appear as entry words. For example, to find out about *penciling*, you must look under the base word *pencil*.

The pronunciation of a word is given in parentheses following the entry. The special symbols used to show you how to pronounce the word are explained at the bottom of the page in the **pronunciation key**. Accent marks indicate which syllable or syllables to stress. A heavy mark (ʹ) is used for primary stress, and a lighter one (ʹ) for secondary stress.

Parts of speech are indicated by abbreviations. The following abbreviations are used for the different parts of speech.

n. noun	*adj.* adjective
v. verb	*adv.* adverb
pron. pronoun	*prep.* preposition

The **definition** is the meaning of the word. Many words have more than one definition. These are usually labeled 1, 2, 3, and so forth.

A **sample sentence** is an example of how the word is used. It can help you understand the meaning of the word and how to use it correctly.

The history of a word, or its **etymology**, is given in brackets following the definitions and sample sentences. The words from which the English entry word comes are printed in italic type. The names of the languages for these words and the explanations of the words are printed in roman type.

guide words

entry word

part of speech

pronunciation

etymology

sample sentence

definition

pen/pendent

pen[1] (pen) *n.* **1.** any of various instruments for writing or drawing with ink. **2.** detachable metal point of certain pens. **3.** fountain pen. **4.** ball-point pen. **5.** pen regarded as a means of expression or instrument of authorship: *The pen is mightier than the sword.* **6.** writer; author. —*v.* **penned, pen·ning.** to write with or as with a pen: *to pen a letter.* [Old French *penne* quill, feather pen for writing, from Latin *penna* feather; because the earliest pens were made from feathers.]

pen[2] (pen) *n.* **1.** small enclosure used to confine animals. **2.** animals confined in such an enclosure. **3.** any of various small or relatively small enclosures, such as a playpen. —*v.* **penned** or **pent, pen·ning.** to confine in or as in a pen. [Old English *penn* fold.[2]]

pe·nal (pē′ nəl) *adj.* **1.** of or relating to legal punishment: *penal laws.* **2.** punishable: *a penal offense.* [Latin *poenālis* relating to punishment, from *poena* punishment, from Greek *poinē* penalty.]

pe·nal·ize (pē′ nəl īz′) **pe·nal·ized, pe·nal·iz·ing.** *v.* **1.** to subject to a penalty or punishment: *Team members will be penalized for lateness.* **2.** to put at a disadvantage: *Her lack of education penalized her in the business world.*

pen·al·ty (pen′ əl tē) *n., pl.* **pen·al·ties. 1.** punishment for violating a law. **2.** sum of money to be paid as punishment for violation committed; fine. **3.** *Sports.* disadvantage or punishment imposed on a player or team for breaking a rule. [Medieval Latin *poenalitas* punishment. See PENAL.]

pen·cil (pen′ səl) *n.* **1.** marking, drawing, or writing implement usually consisting of graphite in a case of wood, metal, or plastic. **2.** something like a pencil in shapes or use, esp. having cosmetic or medicinal use, as an eyebrow pencil. **3.** style or technique in drawing. —*v.* **pen·ciled, pen·cil·ing.** [Old French *pincel* painter's brush, going back to Latin *pencillus* little tail, painter's brush which resembled a little tail.]

pen·dant (pen′ dənt) *n.* **1.** piece of jewelry that is suspended from a necklace or bracelet. **2.** ornament often highly decorated, hanging down from a roof or ceiling. [Old French *pendant*, present participle of *pendre* to hang, going back to Latin *pendēre* to hang.]

pen·dent (pen′ dənt) *adj.* **1.** suspended; hanging. **2.** jutting out; overhanging. **3.** undecided or unsettled. [Latin *pendēns*, present participle of *pendēre* to hang.]

> at; āpe; cär; dāre; end; mē; tėrm; it; īce; hot; ōld; fôrk; up; pu̇t; rüle; cūte; oil; out; sing; thin; th̲is; hw in white; zh in treasure. The symbol ə stands for the sound of a in about, e in taken, i in pencil, o in lemon, and u in circus.

pronunciation key

ACTIVITY Use the sample dictionary page to answer the questions below. Write the answers on your paper.

1. How many syllables does the word *penalize* have? Which syllable receives primary stress?
2. What word in the pronunciation key has the same vowel sound as the vowel in the first syllable of *penal*?
3. What words in the pronunciation key have the same vowel sound as the vowel in the second syllable of *penalize*?
4. As what parts of speech can the word *pencil* be used?
5. To what languages can the word *pen* be traced?
6. What is the part of speech of each underlined word as it is used in the sentence?
   a. The farmer constructed a <u>pen</u> from old crates.
   b. The <u>pendant</u> was a brilliant red ruby.
   c. The guard was <u>penalized</u> for fouling the center.
   d. The <u>pendent</u> chandelier rocked back and forth during the earthquake.
7. What is the meaning of the underlined word as it is used in the sentence?
   a. The <u>penalty</u> for speeding is more than fifty dollars in our town.
   b. The sheep were <u>penned</u> close to the barn.
   c. The <u>penal</u> code clearly describes the <u>penalties</u> for robbery.
   d. Monica carefully removed and cleaned each <u>pen</u> before she began to draw.
8. How might the etymology of <u>penal</u> help you to remember its meanings?

Are you able to speak several languages? Did you know that the English language has many words that come from other languages? Words are changing in meaning, too.

THE MELTING POT

HOWARD GREENFELD

Our English language is constantly growing and changing as words are borrowed from other languages, new words are coined, and old words take on new meanings. The vocabulary we use today can best be described as a melting pot. The term itself is defined as a country or city in which people of various races or nationalities are brought together and assimilated. Leafing through a good dictionary and looking up the derivations of our everyday words, we find ample proof that our language itself is a melting pot. It has brought together words from an enormous number of tongues, left them as they were or adapted them, and successfully assimilated them.

Words From Other Languages

We use words every day that come to us not only from Latin or German or French, but also from such exotic tongues as Tamil, Arawak, Sanskrit, and Turkish. The average person is probably unaware of it, but the shelves of the local supermarket are filled with items whose names are derived from these and many other languages.

Bread is Old Norse in origin, ***rye*** and ***pumpernickel*** come from the German, and ***bagel*** comes from the Yiddish. ***Salt*** and ***eggs*** are Old Norse, but the ***bacon*** to accompany the eggs comes from the French, while ***coffee*** is Arabic, and ***tea*** is Chinese. ***Toast*** is French, but the ***butter*** we put on it comes from the Latin, and the ***marmalade*** we might use is Portuguese in origin.

Yogurt is Turkish, and ***ginger*** comes from the Sanskrit. And barbecue sauce? That seemingly American word ***barbecue*** comes from

Arawak, the language of the people who come from the Greater Antilles.[1] ***Sauce*** comes from the French, who are known for their sauces. ***Spaghetti***, of course, comes from the Italian, but it is found on many an American ***menu*** (that's French) and ***cole slaw*** and ***cookies*** are Dutch in origin. ***Sauerkraut*** and ***pretzels*** are originally German, so it's not surprising that we often find them in the ***delicatessen*** (a German word). ***Potato*** comes from the Spanish; ***tapioca***, ***squash***, and ***pecan*** are words we've acquired from the American Indians; and ***curry*** comes from the Tamil, a language of southern India and northern and eastern Sri Lanka.[2]

All of these words are now so much a part of the English language that they are completely accepted as English, but it must be remembered that their origins are foreign.

Changing Meanings

Our language has never stood still. English has also grown and evolved because many words have changed in meaning through the centuries.

---

1. **Greater Antilles** (an til′ ēz): group of islands including Cuba and Puerto Rico.
2. **Sri Lanka** (srē län′ kə): an island in the Indian Ocean, southeast of India.

The word ***hybrid*** is a colorful example. Today it means something of mixed origin, but this word, which came from the Latin, once meant the offspring of a tame sow and a wild boar. And before that, in Greek, it meant arrogance or ruthlessness.

Zest is another interesting example. Borrowed from the French, it entered our language in the seventeenth century and at first meant lemon or orange peel. What originally gave additional flavor only to food or drink grew in meaning, until this flavor—or enjoyment—was applied to every phase of life. Today we have a zest for learning, and traveling adds zest to our lives.

There are very many more examples of words which mean one thing today and meant other things in the past. A ***pest*** today is a nag or nuisance, a troublesome person. But originally this word, which came from the French ***peste***, was something far more serious, since it meant an epidemic, usually the bubonic plague. It wasn't merely irritating, as is today's pest; it was deadly.

Sleuth is another word that has changed in meaning. Today's sleuth is a detective, but originally a ***sloth***, an Old Norse word, was a track or a trail. The word came into Middle English as ***sleuth***, meaning the track of an animal or person. In a short time, it was used only in

compounds such as ***sleuthdog***, meaning a dog trained to follow a track. In Scotland, a ***sleuth-hound*** was a kind of bloodhound used to seek out criminals. In the nineteenth century, Americans began to call detectives "sleuthhounds," and in time the term was shortened to ***sleuth***.

Students of language have placed changes in word meaning in four categories. One category includes words that have narrowed in meaning, in which a general term has developed into a specific one. For example, ***meat*** once meant any food; ***deer*** was a general term for any animal; a ***wife*** was any woman, not necessarily a married one.

The second category is the opposite of this—words that have widened in meaning, a specific term having developed into a more general one. A ***butcher*** was once no more than a slaughterer of goats, and a ***place*** was no more than a wide street or open square.

A number of words, too, acquired broader meanings when the English language came into contact with American soil. In England, a ***rock*** had been a large mass of mineral material; in America, the term was applied to small stones as well. In England, a ***barn*** was a place in which to store nothing but crops; in America, it became a place to keep cattle as well. And the word ***mad***, which meant insane in England, came to mean not only that, but angry as well when brought to America.

The other two categories include words whose meanings have either been lowered or elevated in status. For example, a ***villain*** was once a serf or peasant and not someone evil. To call someone ***puny*** today is an insult compared to the earlier meaning of the word which was "younger." These are examples of words which have been lowered in meaning.

Other words have been elevated or enhanced in meaning. Today's ***pioneer*** is a person of courage and vision; a pioneer was once nothing more than a common infantry soldier who specialized in digging trenches. ***Nice*** is a rather weak and vague adjective today, but it is certainly complimentary; yet in the past it has meant ignorant, then foolish, then shy, and finally discriminating, before its current definition as agreeable or pleasant. A ***banquet*** was once not the huge and festive meal it is today; it was merely a light refreshment served between meals.

Words From Names

A study of word origins teaches us, too, that many of our words came from proper nouns—from the names of people who have achieved a certain fame, from the names of gods, and from the names of places.

For example, there was the case of Nicolas Chauvin (shō vän′), a very patriotic man. A soldier in Napoleon's army, he loved his leader and his country. He was so devoted to them that all people who showed excessive love for their country became known as chauvinists. Today ***chauvinist*** also refers to people who believe their group is superior to others.

Gods also have provided us with common nouns. Atlas was one of the giants of Greek mythology, whose duty was to hold up the sky. A Flemish mapmaker published a book of maps in the sixteenth century with a drawing of Atlas on the title page. He titled this collection of maps Atlas and before long an ***atlas*** was any book of maps. ***Panic*** is another example, a word derived from the ancient Greek god Pan who instilled fear and terror into those who saw him.

Places, too, are the sources for many common nouns. The word ***attic*** comes from the region of ancient Greece called Attica, and its elegant architectural style known as Attic. A ***milliner*** was originally a person who sold goods from the Italian city of Milan.

Chauvinist, ***atlas***, ***panic***, ***attic***—these and other words are but a few examples of the ways in which human ingenuity has led to the enrichment of the English language.

Thinking and Writing About the Selection

1. Give an example of a word whose meaning has changed over time. What did the word mean in earlier days? What does it mean today?
2. Why do you think so many of our language's borrowed words are names of foods?
3. The brand name for a new product sometimes becomes the commonly used word for the object. Can you think of an example of this happening? Why do you think this happens?
4. Suppose your name were to become a common noun or adjective. What would you like it to mean?

Applying the Key Skill

Summarize

Imagine that you have been asked to present a speech to a group of chefs. Your topic is "Word Stew in a Melting Pot." To prepare for your speech, reread the section called "Words From Other Languages."

List the most important idea of the first paragraph. You can use this idea to introduce your speech. Then choose interesting examples from the next two paragraphs to explain your main idea. Finally, write one or two sentences to sum up your speech. Include the information you want your audience to remember.

PTARMIGAN

O Ptarmigan, O ptarmigan,
O ptarmigan: pt
is such a funny way to start
a name. Don't you agree?
You've never had pneumonia,
though you live among the Lapps
and Eskimos inhabiting
those ice-cold ptops of maps.
There's no one here to tell me
how you ptolerate that name!
It saddens me to think that
someone like me was to blame.
Some ancient Gael? It wasn't. No,
his word was *tarmachan*.
The Greek for feather? *pteron*; but
did Greeks know how you fan
your feathered feet to walk on snow?
You wouldn't walk on ptar;
and, anyway, the Greeks lived south
and never got that far.
Some day I guess, I'll travel north
and ask a caribou
or reindeer; How's your pterritory?
Got a Pt-V ptoo?

David McCord

SKILLS ACTIVITY

SUFFIXES

Suffixes are word parts that are added to the ends of base words to form new words. Suffixes are very useful because they help us make words that are one part of speech from words that are another part of speech. Look at the example below.

safe	**+**	**ty**	**=**	**safety**
(adjective)	+	(suffix)	=	(noun)

The suffixes below are used to make nouns from adjectives.

-ity, -ty = state, condition, or quality of being

Some suffixes make adjectives from other words. The suffixes below are examples.

-able, -ible = able or capable of being; worthy of being; likely to; able to cause

-ic, -ical = of or relating to; being or like

pass	**+**	**able**	**=**	**passable**
(verb)	+	(suffix)	=	(adjective)
atom	**+**	**ic**	**=**	**atomic**
(noun)	+	(suffix)	=	(adjective)

Other suffixes can be used to form nouns *and* adjectives.

-al, -ial = of or relating to; act, process, or result of

arrive	**+**	**al**	**=**	**arrival**
(verb)	+	(suffix)	=	(noun)
origin	**+**	**al**	**=**	**original**
(noun)	+	(suffix)	=	(adjective)

When adding suffixes to base words, remember that the spelling of the base words may change. Here are a few rules.

1. A final *y* may change to *i*. (deny + able = deniable)
2. A final *e* may be dropped. (sane + ity = sanity)
3. Vowels may be dropped. (clear + ity = clarity
4. Consonants may be changed. (defend + ible = defensible)
5. Letters may be added. (act + al = actual)
6. A final *e* may change to *i*. (race + al = racial)

ACTIVITY A Add a noun suffix to the word in parentheses to form a noun that will fit the blank in the sentence. Write the words on your paper.

1. Arnold blamed his own ____ for the mistake. (stupid)
2. Our request for admission was met with ____. (deny)
3. Betsy's poster won the prize for ____. (original)
4. It's a ____ to have snow in June. (rare)
5. "Thank you for your ____ in contributing to our campaign fund," said the woman. (generous)

ACTIVITY B Read each definition below. Then write the adjective whose meaning is given.

1. Of or relating to the face
2. Capable of being divided
3. Of or relating to the theater
4. Act, process, or result of surviving
5. Of or relating to an office
6. Being, or like, a magnet
7. Likely to perish
8. Able to cause pity
9. Of or relating to medicine
10. Of or relating to logic

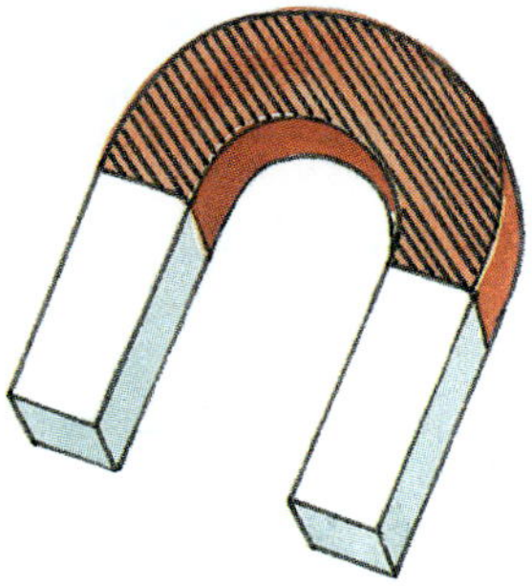

GRANDMOTHER'S ICEBERG

MARY ELLEN CHASE

Eliza Ann Westcott grew up in Maine more than one hundred years ago. When she was nineteen she married a sea captain named Melatiah Chase, and went on his voyages with him. In later years, she told her grandchildren about her many adventures. One story they never tired of hearing was her iceberg story.

One of these grandchildren, Mary Ellen Chase, became a writer when she grew up. In this excerpt from *A Walk on an Iceberg*, she tells the story the way she heard it from her grandmother.

There are icebergs and icebergs, of course, which means only that there are all kinds of icebergs. I have seen many of them myself in voyages across the Atlantic. Some of them look like vast islands of ice and snow; other, smaller ones look like huge castles or cathedrals. Some of them are white and crusty, while others are clear and shining. Once in the North Atlantic I saw an iceberg that looked just like a clear, shining ship, pale green in color and brilliant in the sunlight. It was lovely.

My grandmother's iceberg was so large that it might well

have been a great island or even a big slice of a continent. She and my grandfather sighted it one early spring morning on their way to the port of Riga (rē′ gə), now a part of the Soviet Union.

"I don't think I ever saw such a huge iceberg in all my years at sea," my grandfather said. "Upon my word, it might be even a country."

"Just right for a walk on it," my grandmother said. "It's so big and snowy and crusty that I'm sure it's quite safe for a walk. And the side facing us slopes down to the water and looks just right for a landing."

"You just forget any such silly notion as that," my grandfather said. "You just put it straight out of your head!"

"Well, I won't," said my grandmother.

Now, my grandmother would certainly have *had* to forget her silly notion, whether she wanted to forget it or not, had it not been for a young man who just happened to be making that special voyage on my grandfather's ship. This young man's name was Kemper Swift, and he had been for four years to Harvard College. He was a scientist, and he had shipped with my grandfather because he wanted to study all manner of things about the sea—its currents, the things that lived in it, its weather, and all its many moods. He kept a big journal in his cabin and he was forever writing down things on its pages. He was learning untold things, he said, and when he saw that huge iceberg, he became quite as excited as my grandmother.

"I'll never have another chance like this, sir," he said to my grandfather. (He said this politely, for he was a very

polite young man; besides, my grandfather was captain of the ship, and he was always addressed as *sir* by everyone on board, except of course, my grandmother.) "I've just *got* to get on that berg and study it.

"And I'll take you along with me," he told my grandmother. "All we need is a boat; and if you insist, sir, we'll take along a couple of sailors. There isn't one bit of danger on a berg the size of that one."

"You're both crazy," my grandfather said. "I never heard of such nonsense!"

"Well, you're hearing it now," my grandmother said. "Get the boat ready, Kemper, and we'll start off right away."

So with my grandfather fretting and fuming—and scared, of course, as well—off they went. They took three sailors with them instead of two. Kemper Swift said they would be just about as much use as nothing at all, except that they could row the boat, which would give him plenty of time to write in his notebook and see everything there was to see.

The iceberg did slope down to the water in one place instead of rising high above it. Kemper Swift told the sailors to make for that place, where they could make an easy and safe landing, and the sailors did. And before my grandmother had time to realize it, they were actually on that iceberg and climbing up its side over the ice and crushed snow. It was so huge that they couldn't begin to see the entire size of it.

"My word!" Kemper Swift said. "It's more than an island. It might be a good-sized piece of the coast of Maine. It really might."

The walking wasn't very easy, my grandmother said, but they moved along. And the iceberg really did seem like a slice of the mainland, for there were sea-gulls upon it and some odd birds that even Kemper Swift didn't know and about which he wrote down notes for the big journal in his cabin. There were seals, too, which flopped about in fright when they saw people approaching them.

"Poor beasts!" Kemper Swift said. "I wonder how long they have to live, and just where they'll swim to when this old berg breaks up, if it ever does break up."

But the most exciting thing happened after they had trudged along for just a few minutes—so exciting that the very thought of it made shivers run up and down our spines.

"Get along quickly, Grand-mother!" my brother John used to cry. "It isn't gulls or seals we want to hear about. It's that poor man!"

"I'm coming to him right now," my grandmother would say. "That poor, poor man! Shall I ever forget him? No! I surely never shall!"

They saw that man, my grandmother said at last, after they had plowed their way

through a good bit more snow and ice. Of course, at first they couldn't believe their eyes! Still, there he was, a real man on that iceberg! At first he was so scared to see them that he ran away from them. Then he came stumbling back toward them. He was in rags and tatters, my grandmother said, and so thin that his very bones stuck out.

"Don't forget a word about what he looked like!" my brother John always cried to her. "Don't forget a single word, Grandmother!"

"I won't," my grandmother said. "His legs were just like pieces of sticks, just like—well, just like nothing at all. His face was covered with hair, and this hair fell down over what was left of an old, ragged, red coat he had on."

"Don't forget his eyes, or his nose, or the way he kept falling down," I used to cry here.

"I won't," my grandmother said. "Just give me time. His eyes looked just like great burnt holes in his poor face. They were full of terror, too, as though he were looking at ghosts. His nose rose up like a sharp knife, and he kept falling down like a lot of sticks or jackstraws or toothpicks, and then putting himself together again."

"Don't forget his language!" my sister Edith always said here. "Don't forget how he tried to make Kemper Swift and you understand him!"

"Give me time," my grandmother said. "Just give me time. I won't forget a single thing. First of all, the three sailors ran and grabbed him so he couldn't get away. They said it was just like trying to hold on to a bundle of slats or like seizing a lot of sharp bones. When they first seized him, he tried to beat them off and get away. His fingers felt just like so many sharp nails, they said. Then, after he found he couldn't get away, he just grew limp and began to shake and shudder.

"They asked him who he was, of course, and what in the world he was doing on an iceberg. But he only screamed at them in some strange tongue, and then he was crying and sobbing as though he were about to fall entirely apart again. He was just stark crazy—mad—the sailors said. At first he was crazy from astonishment; and then he was crazy from fear; and at last

he was crazy from relief and hope. And he was crazy all the time from loneliness and hunger and from not knowing where he was or what might happen to him."

"Now's when you always tell about the way Kemper Swift knew how to talk with him," my brother John reminded my grandmother, for he didn't want to miss a single word.

"I'm just coming to that," my grandmother said. "Kemper Swift bent over that poor, ragged bag of bones, who by now had fallen on the ice and snow, and began to try to talk to him in what seemed to me a dozen different tongues. I thought I

had never heard so many strange sounds coming out of anyone's mouth, and remember, I've heard any number of strange tongues in all my journeyings."

"Now's the time you tell us we should learn languages," my sister Edith said.

"I'm going to right now," my grandmother said. "I won't forget that, for it is *most important*. When you children grow up and go away to schools and colleges, you just must learn languages. It's wrong to know only your own language and no other at all. There isn't one chance in ten million that you'll ever walk on an iceberg the way I did; but you might well meet some poor lost souls in Boston or New York or New Orleans or Chicago or San Francisco who can't speak a word that you can understand to tell you who they are and what they want. So you must learn German and French and Italian and Spanish and any other language that you may have the chance to learn. It's a disgrace that most people in our country don't know any language but their own. It's a disgrace, I say, and don't you forget it!"

"We won't, Grandmother," I always said here, for she looked really so fierce that I was almost scared of her. "We won't forget, *ever*, and we *will* learn languages. We will!"

"Go on about Kemper Swift!" my brother John begged then, for John wasn't at all concerned about studying languages years later on in his life. He was still, in his mind, right on that iceberg.

"I'm coming to him, bless him!" my grandmother said. "He was a scientist at Harvard College, and he had studied languages so that he could

read more about scientific matters. For, he told me once, much that is written about science is written in tongues other than just plain English.

"Well, Kemper Swift, what did he do but discover that this poor man, this castaway, could speak German. German was his native tongue, you see; and once he discovered that Kemper Swift could talk with him, tears just rolled down his poor, thin, blistered face, he was so glad. *'Gott in Himmel!'* (got in him′ əl), he kept saying over and over, *'Mein* (mīn) *Gott in Himmel!'* which means—"

"I know," my brother John always cried here. "I know! It means 'My God in heaven!'"

"Yes, it does," my grandmother said. "But, please, don't interrupt me. Whose story is this, I'd like to know? Kemper Swift asked him how in the world he got on that iceberg, and when, and where, and a lot of other questions in the German language. And the man said that he had been out on the ice many days earlier, hunting for seals just a few miles from his home in the northern part of Germany and that when he started to go back home, what did he find but a sea of water between him and the land! In other words," my grandmother said gravely,

"that great sheet of ice had just broken away from the land, and there he was, caught on it, a prisoner who knew his awful sentence."

We always shivered with fear at this point while she repeated her frightening words, and after we had shivered all we could stand, one of us always begged her to go on. "Now finish it, Grandmother. Now tell us how it came out."

"Well," my grandmother said, "those three sailors all stood around, wondering at Kemper Swift; for of course they couldn't speak a word but their Coast-of-Maine lingo, just like you children now, though it will be different with you when you are grown up. But when Kemper Swift told them all that poor man had suffered, they just gathered him up like a bundle of sticks and took him down to our boat.

"And our walk on that iceberg ended right then and there," my grandmother concluded. "The one thought we all shared was to get that poor soul to our ship, where we could give him hot food and cold water and a good warm bed. That's just what we did. And when your grandfather saw us coming back safe and sound, he thanked God and went to the ship's ladder over the side. He helped that poor man on board, even though he couldn't believe his very eyes!

"We sailed quite a way out of our course to drop him in Germany near the town where he had lived; and according to Kemper Swift, he kept saying over and over that we were angels from heaven, sent by God himself.

"And that's my story of my walk on an iceberg," my grandmother finished, with not a little pride in her voice.

Thinking and Writing About the Selection

1. How did the narrator of the story find out about the man on the iceberg?
2. Why did Kemper Swift want to walk on the iceberg? Why did Grandmother want to walk on it?
3. If no one in the group had been able to speak German, how might they have communicated with the man on the iceberg?
4. Do you agree with Grandmother that it is important to learn another language? Why or why not?

Applying the Key Skill

Sequence of Events

Rewrite the following sentences about "Grandmother's Iceberg" in the order in which they happened.

Mary Ellen Chase wrote a book based on her grandmother's experiences.
Kemper Swift persuaded Captain Chase to allow him to explore the iceberg.
The ice broke and floated away, stranding the man on the iceberg.
Eliza Ann Westcott married Captain Melatiah Chase.
Captain Chase's ship went out of its way to take the man to his home.
A man had been hunting for seals a few miles from his home in northern Germany.
On their way to Riga, the Captain and his wife spotted a giant iceberg.
Mrs. Westcott told her grandchildren about the man on the iceberg.

SKILLS ACTIVITY

SUMMARIZE

A **summary** is a brief account. You may sometimes be asked to summarize a paragraph, several paragraphs, or even an entire selection. When you do this, you should think about the important information, facts, or ideas that are presented. Your summary should be in your own words and should include only the most important information.

Read the paragraphs below from "Grandmother's Iceberg." Think about how you would summarize them.

> So with my grandfather fretting and fuming—and scared, of course, as well—off they went. They took three sailors with them instead of two. Kemper Swift said they would be just about as much use as nothing at all, except that they could row the boat, which would give him plenty of time to write in his notebook and see everything there was to see.
>
> The iceberg did slope down to the water in one place instead of rising high above it. Kemper Swift told the sailors to make for that place, where they could make an easy and safe landing, and the sailors did. And before my grandmother had time to realize it, they were actually on that iceberg and climbing up its side over the ice and crushed snow. It was so huge that they couldn't begin to see the entire size of it.

To summarize these two paragraphs, you should first find the main idea of the first paragraph: *Grandmother and Kemper Swift set off for the iceberg in a boat.* Now find the main idea of the second paragraph: *Grandmother and Kemper*

Swift landed on the iceberg and were soon climbing up its side over the ice. If you combine the main idea of each paragraph, you will have a summary of both of them: *Soon after setting out for the iceberg in a boat, Grandmother and Kemper Swift landed there and began climbing up its side over the ice.*

ACTIVITY Read the two paragraphs below from "Grandmother's Iceberg." Then write a summary of the paragraphs on your paper.

> "Kemper Swift discovered that this poor man, this castaway, could speak German. German was his native tongue, you see; and once he discovered that Kemper Swift could talk with him, tears just rolled down his poor, thin, blistered face, he was so glad. *Gott in Himmel!* he kept saying over and over, *Mein Gott in Himmel!*
>
> "Kemper Swift asked him how in the world he got on that iceberg, and when, and where, and a lot of other questions in the German language. And the man said that he had been out on the ice many days earlier, hunting for seals just a few miles from his home in the northern part of Germany, and that when he started to go back home, what did he find but a sea of water between him and the land! In other words," my grandmother said gravely, "that great sheet of ice had just broken away from the land, and there he was, caught on it, a prisoner who knew his awful sentence."

MUKASA
JOHN NAGENDA

Do you remember your first day at school? Were you curious and excited as well as a little scared? When did you begin to understand the mysteries of our language? When did you first know that the marks on paper were letters and words?

This story is set in Uganda in the early 1940s. Like most of the people in his small village, Mukasa's family had little money. It was more difficult for them to pay for an education, than it was for people who lived in larger villages or in the towns. They were also more tied to a traditional way of life.

Like the other boys of the village, Mukasa spent his days tending his father's goats. Few families in the village could afford to send their children to school. But by carefully putting away money and borrowing from relatives, Mukasa's mother had managed to collect enough to pay his school fees. Finally the great day arrived for him to start school.

Mukasa was a little too early. He stood in the road by the entrance to the school compound and wondered what to do while he waited. Perhaps after all he should have come with Namata's two sons as their mother had suggested. But they were so much older than he, and besides, they never talked to him. He was convinced they looked down on him.

The school compound was built around a rectangle, with buildings on three sides. The fourth side was open to the road that went past. On the other side of the road was the football field, and the masters' houses stood among the trees behind it. The football field at present was knee-high in grass and the crossbar of one of the goalposts had fallen down.

About now I would be far away with the goats and my friends, doing things I know how to do, thought Mukasa, as he walked slowly into the compound. There were already about a hundred children there, most of them moving confidently around in groups, obviously glad to see each other again after the holidays. Mukasa envied them their assurance. They made him feel that they belonged to a world altogether their own. He continued walking forward but he would much rather have turned and fled. He reached into his bag and felt the envelope with the money and told himself that he had as much a right to be there as anybody, and with that things looked a little bit better.

It was easy to pick out the newcomers. In the bustle and noise, they stood out as if they had been drenched with water. It was amazing that he had not yet seen a single face he knew.

More and more schoolchildren were arriving and the noise was increasing. Already a couple of fights

had broken out. Mukasa was standing by one of the buildings, the newest-looking one, and on an impulse he decided to go in. He opened the door, its hinges creaking, and walked in. And stopped.

All the shutters were closed, and the only light came from the opened door. Mukasa looked at a confusion of desks and benches, all obviously as they had been at the start of the holidays. He noticed the blackboard and did not know what it was. There was a powerful smell in the room, of damp and above all of bats and something else which he could not place, but which later he learned was the smell of chalk. It seemed to bite at his nostrils.

There was a strangeness about it all. But what really made Mukasa pause was a feeling of a presence in the room. It was as if the empty room were occupied, as if the desks were full. For a moment he had the sharp impression that something was going on although it could not be seen, like an invisible ghost, and then the feeling was gone. It is the presence of Learning, Mukasa thought wonderingly, almost frightened, the idea filling his head.

He hurriedly left the room.

A voice beside him shouted, "You! Did somebody ask you to leave that door open?"

Mukasa saw a big boy towering over him.

"No, sir," he said.

"Well, close it, newcomer. And keep out of rooms that have nothing to do with you. That room is Class Six."

Mukasa closed the door. And then a bell rang and the noise of the schoolchildren started dying down. Everybody was rushing toward one of the end buildings. Mukasa joined them.

Mukasa's teacher, Miss Nanteza, said, "How many of you know anything about reading and writing? Put up your hands."

Mukasa saw to his surprise that one of the boys put his hand up. He was the only one. Mukasa had not thought it was possible to learn these things before you came to school. The boy had a rather pleased look on his face which Mukasa found annoying. He also noticed that the boy's uniform looked smarter than his own.

Miss Nanteza said, "All right, Kalanzi. Anybody else?"

Later Mukasa found out that Kalanzi was Miss Nanteza's second cousin. Kalanzi's parents were the richest people for miles around, and in fact they had had Miss Nanteza give him lessons before he started school.

Miss Nanteza said, "If you all pay attention, most of you won't find it very difficult to follow what I am going to teach you."

Slates were passed around, together with funny-looking sticklike objects which left a mark when you scratched the slates with them.

Miss Nanteza started with the alphabet. She wrote a letter on the blackboard and said it out loud. The class said it after her and scratched its likeness on their slates. Then after about five letters, Miss Nanteza had everything wiped off. When that was done, she wrote the letters down again and asked what each was.

Up went Kalanzi's hand immediately. After the second time she told him that until the rest of the class had caught up with him, she would not call on him to answer. The whole class laughed loudly at this, but Mukasa, although he too laughed, felt a little sorry for Kalanzi; after all, it wasn't his fault that he already knew the answer.

As for himself, he was having a wonderful time. He had often wondered whether he would find it difficult to learn. At home if he was told something he always remembered it; indeed on some occasions he had annoyed his parents by remembering things which they would have preferred forgotten. But he had thought that school learning might be different. Now he discovered that once the teacher had written a letter and said it out loud, and once he had written it down himself, it seemed to stick in his mind. And what's more, it seemed to make sense in itself so that the way it looked gave it a character of its own.

Before coming to school, Mukasa had from time to time seen old pieces of paper with writing on them; for example, the shopkeeper sometimes used them for packaging. But every time Mukasa had looked closely at the writing, all he could think of were swarming little insects. Now it was as if Miss Nanteza gave sound and meaning to them.

Miss Nanteza filled the blackboard with more and more letters and then a few words, and it seemed to Mukasa as if a treasure chest were being opened up and offered to him. As if by magic, what had been an empty space on the wall was now covered, right before him, by all manner of exciting and mysterious things. If this was what learning was about, he was going to love it.

When Miss Nanteza rubbed the letters off, the dust of the chalk drifted over the whole class and to Mukasa even the somewhat biting sensation he felt in his nose was full of excitement.

He wished Miss Nanteza would move more quickly. By now he had almost forgotten about the others in the class. It was as if everything the teacher said was for him alone.

Every time Miss Nanteza asked a question, almost before she had completed it, Mukasa's hand shot up. But after a time he noticed that she would leave his hand up and look straight past him, and ask the question of someone who didn't even understand it, and in the meantime, his own upraised arm would be getting unbearably heavy. He heard one or two snickers from some of the class whenever this happened. On one occasion he caught Kalanzi openly laughing at him. Then finally just before the end of the day, when Mukasa stood up to answer yet another question, someone hit him on the back of the head with a piece of chalk.

"Who did that?" shouted the teacher.

Nobody answered. Mukasa had looked around quickly and he had seen who had thrown the chalk. Usually he wouldn't have told, but by now he was so fed up that before he knew it he had blurted out, "It was that nasty boy over there in the back row!"

"Come here Mutahi," Miss Nanteza ordered.

The boy came forward slowly to receive his punishment. The look Mutahi gave Mukasa as he walked back to his seat was ferocious.

After school Mukasa was walking past the staff room when he heard his teacher's voice. Something made him stop and listen.

He could hardly believe his ears: ". . . a real firecracker. His name is Mukasa, . . . probably too good for his class!"

Mukasa was still floating on air from that remark when he turned a corner. Mutahi was waiting.

It was only a brief fight before someone separated them, but it was long enough for Mukasa to know that he would have had no chance of winning.

It didn't matter. There wasn't a thing on this wonderful evening that could for long detract from his happiness and he was almost singing as he ran home to tell his family all about it.

After the second day of classes he could write his name. When he had written it he looked at it for a long time. It seemed to be his name more than ever before, and he thought it even looked like him.

He walked home with his name tucked away inside his exercise book.

"Look, look," he said, trying to appear calm and collected. "That's my name and I wrote it myself; with my own hand!"

He passed the book around.

"Now is that not something?" his mother exclaimed. She was looking at the writing as if she half expected it to come to life and shake her by the hand.

Arithmetic came next. They started off by learning to count, and then to add one small number to another, and to subtract. All this they did using piles of stones.

Arithmetic made Mukasa feel as if the inside of his head were jumping up and down. He could hardly wait to check that his answers were correct. After you had decided that two and three was five, and then had used two lots of stones and proved that you were right, it made you feel as if there wasn't anything in the world you couldn't do.

It seemed so simple and yet it took so many days for the class to get the hang of it that Mukasa was amazed. He couldn't understand why the faces of so many in the class lengthened at the beginning of each period.

All the teaching was in Mukasa's own language and would be so for the next four years. But after that everything would be taught entirely in English. It was important to make an early start, so in the

English lesson Miss Nanteza started off by teaching the names of things—chairs and tables and ears and teeth. Mukasa discovered that he either remembered them afterward or not; beyond that, English so far did not hold the magic of arithmetic or of reading and writing.

One day Miss Nanteza decided to ask the pupils to come forward and write their names on the blackboard. Mukasa had for long envied her her right to use the blackboard. He put up his hand at once, but Miss Nanteza ignored it. She chose Mutahi instead, and Mukasa, disappointed though he was, nearly burst into laughter when he saw Mutahi's face.

When Mutahi left to return to his seat, the blackboard had on it an indecipherable scrawl of which you might just make out the first letter. The whole effort looked as if it was merely waiting to fall over; indeed some of it seemed already to have done so.

By the time Miss Nanteza turned to Mukasa, he had become so impatient that he was nearly standing up. He almost ran to the blackboard.

He started to write his name. Writing on the blackboard had always looked so easy when Miss Nanteza did it. But now Mukasa found that the chalk refused to make the kind of smooth flowing lines he had expected. He had wanted to write his name more beautifully than anybody else could.

When he finished, there was his name, and anyone who could read could read it: MUKASA.

"Very good," Miss Nanteza said.

But Mukasa looked at his name on the blackboard and he felt like bursting into tears. It looked mean and lifeless and it had sloped badly down the board. Besides which, the letters didn't match in size and their lines were shaky. He felt the blackboard had betrayed him.

And yet of all those who wrote, only Kalanzi came out better, and only just.

Mukasa thought to himself, "What you try to do and what comes out are two different things!" He was very relieved when the blackboard was cleaned.

Author's Note

If you went to Mukasa's village today you would notice changes. For a start, the outside world has made more of an impact upon it. This is the result of better communications, and also because so many of the villagers have been to the towns, mainly to search for work. And of those who have never left the village, quite a few possess radio sets and know about other parts of the country and beyond.

As for going to school, the chances are much better today; in Mukasa's village there are fewer children who would now look forward only to a life of tending goats. But it is still true that many who go to school today might go for just a couple of years before they are overtaken by a lack of fees or classroom space. So although Mukasa would find it easier to go to school, unless he were very lucky, the horizons which schooling could open to him would remain as far off as ever.

Thinking and Writing About the Selection

1. What would Mukasa be doing if he hadn't gone to school?
2. Why did Kalanzi know about reading and writing even though he had never been to school before?
3. Why do you think Mutahi threw the chalk at Mukasa?
4. What was the most interesting or memorable day you ever had in school? What do you remember about it? Write a paragraph telling about your experience.

Applying the Key Skill

Sequence of Events

The following incomplete sentences are about events in "Mukasa." Complete each sentence with the words *before*, *after*, or *as*. Then write the complete sentences on your paper.

1. Mukasa felt he was in the presence of Learning even ____ his first lesson began.
2. Miss Nanteza taught her class the alphabet ____ she introduced them to numbers.
3. Mutahi and Mukasa got into a fight ____ the first day of classes.
4. Mukasa learned how to write his name ____ he had completed the first week of school.
5. Mukasa began to learn English ____ he learned to read and write in his own language.

JOHN NAGENDA

"What is an African writer? Personally, I think it's someone who lives in Africa and who writes on matters which are also universal in the final instance, but which have got an African slant."

John Nagenda was born in 1938 in Gahini, Uganda, where his father was a missionary. He attended a school very much like the one in "Mukasa."

While in college, Nagenda edited the university literary magazine, *Penpoint*, and graduated with honors in English in 1962—the same year that Uganda gained its independence from Great Britain. Since then, he has been a radio and magazine critic and an editor for a publishing company. His main interest, however, is in writing poems and stories.

As an African writer, Nagenda has faced the dilemma which all writers who grow up in former colonies must face: In what language shall I express myself—my original tongue, or the language of the foreign settlers? John Nagenda uses English, but he has also said that African writers should begin to use their own languages, which can be better understood by the great majority of the population in the writer's own country.

More to Read *Pan-African Short Stories*, edited by Neville Denny; *Origin East Africa*, edited by David Cook

The Writing Lessons

Kathryn Forbes

Times were hard when Katrin was growing up in San Francisco more than seventy years ago. Papa worked hard and Mama took in boarders and was careful with every penny. Somehow the family managed. But Katrin had a dream, and one day she thought she found a way to make her dream come true.

We had our first boarder in the new house. Her name was Miss Durant, and she was a telephone operator who worked at night. We saw very little of her.

Miss Durant was a great reader. Her room was piled with magazines, and once she gave me a box of them to throw away. She had put string around the box, but instead of throwing the magazines away, I'd taken them up to my attic.

The family still hadn't got used to the big house. Mama loved the spacious kitchen and large dining room. She and Papa had got a dining-room table that would seat twenty people. And every Saturday, we'd go to the secondhand stores on McAllister Street and pick up chairs. Mama had her eye on a big brass bed and a carpet. Soon now we'd have another room furnished. Then we would get a couple more boarders.

There was a cubbyhole underneath the stairs, right off the first-floor hall. This my sister Christine took over and decorated with her three leather cushions, and Uncle Chris's old chair. She wouldn't let any of us in without a special invitation.

Not to be outdone, I took over the attic. It was big and drafty. I called it my "study," and loved every foot of its bareness. I boasted that *my* attic had a *door* and a *key* that locked. (It locked if you had pliers to help turn the rusty mechanism.)

For the very first time in my life I had a place all my own. And for the first time in my life I heard rain falling directly onto a roof. My attic skylight could be lifted up and held in place with a heavy piece of firewood. I would perch on the sill

and dream long dreams. Or I would read the magazines that Miss Durant had given me to throw away.

The stories within were the most exciting I had ever read. Even the advertisements were good.

"DO YOU WANT TO BECOME A WRITER?" it asked in large clear type. And continued: "WRITING SECRETS. This Complete Course in Motion Picture, Novel, Short Story, Poetry, Drama, Pageantry, and Newspaper Technique yours for only $7.00! USED BY ALL FAMOUS AUTHORS."

Why, how *wonderful*, I thought. So that's how it was done? If one only had seven dollars one could become a Famous Author overnight. Think of the money one could make! Money for Mama, for Papa, for Nels. Why, we could even go right down to one of the big furniture stores and order brand-new furniture for all the rooms. All at one time! For that matter, Mama wouldn't have to run a boardinghouse anymore. With all the money that I could make, none of the family would have to do any work at all.

At school, Miss Scanlon would tap on her desk with her pencil. "Girls," she would say. "Girls, we have a Famous Author in our midst. Stand up, Kathryn."

And the girls would clap, and they would quarrel among themselves as to which one would walk with me at recess.

I sighed. It could all come true too, if by some miracle I could just get this magic course. But with only seventeen cents—

Something about the finer print caught my eye. "Yours for five days' free trial," it said. "If you are not satisfied with the course at the end of five days, return at absolutely no cost to yourself."

My goodness! Here was a golden opportunity. With trembling hands, I clipped the coupon. I got out the fancy letter paper Aunt Trina had given me the Christmas before.

I tried hard to make the letter sound grown-up and Famous Authorish.

"I have had," I wrote, "some success with my Writing Endeavors." (Well, hadn't I always had an *A* in composition?) "But now," I continued, "I wish to turn to the Broader Fields of Motion Picture, Novels, and Drama."

Two of my precious seventeen cents went for a stamp. The rest I invested in the largest notebook I could find. Five days were, after all, only five days, and I would have to copy the precious secrets in a hurry.

I planned to keep a bowl of warm water by my side as I wrote, so that I could bathe my aching fingers. Wasn't that what Mr. Edgar Allan Poe* did when his hands got cramped from writing? I was willing to suffer for my art.

No longer did Mama have to call me three times before I tumbled out of bed. I was the first one up in the morning now, and I haunted the front steps, watching for the mailman.

"Something is wrong with you, Katrin?" Mama looked worried.

"Oh, *no*, Mama."

In my heart, I knew that Mama would not approve of what I had done. She would think that sending for the course without planning to pay for it would be dishonest. To copy the precious secrets and then send the course back—that would be

---

* **Edgar Allan Poe:** nineteenth-century American writer and poet.

wrong. I couldn't see that it was any different from going down to the big department stores and saying to the saleslady, "I'm just looking, thank you." That's what Aunt Jenny did all the time.

I badgered the poor postman mercilessly. "When would I get my package?" He was so kind. He figured it all out for me on the back of an envelope. Six days going—six days coming—say two days for a little leeway—well, twelve days would be his guess.

I thanked him. And it was so important, I told him, that the package be delivered in the morning. Since in the afternoons I had to be in school, and since I didn't want the family to know. "It's a sort of present," I said, "for them all. A big surprise."

The postman nodded understandingly and assured me that the important package would be delivered to me personally, and in the morning.

The postman's twelve days stretched to fifteen, to twenty. Still the eagerly awaited package failed to arrive.

Then, just as I was ready to give up hope the package arrived. Mama had taken Baby Kaaren and gone over to Aunt Jenny's, and I was alone with my joy. I dashed up to my attic, my heart thudding with anticipation. With nervous fingers, I opened the package. My Open Sesame to Success!

There were seven gray little pamphlets.

Eagerly I skimmed through them, hunting for the Secret Technique of Famous Authors. But the long, involved paragraphs were difficult to understand; the print was small and faded, and the text abounded with unfamiliar words.

I was dismayed, but still hopeful. I borrowed my brother Nels's dictionary, but it didn't help much. Maybe I would understand them better some other time. Tomorrow. Yes, I promised myself, tomorrow I would read them thoroughly. Tomorrow, I would start copying off the precious secrets.

But one tomorrow after another marched by, and I did not get back to the pamphlets. Other interesting things were going on.

In truth, I had completely forgotten about the "How to Become a Famous Author" course until I received a letter from New York.

"We remind you," they said, "that your remittance of $7.00 has not been received. Since you kept the course over the five-day trial period, the amount is now due and payable." Hoping to hear from me, they were sincerely mine.

Oh, how could I have kept the pamphlets too long? The calendar assured me that I had. Exactly sixteen days too long.

Where was I to ever get *seven whole dollars*? I, whose father worked hard and long, whose mother was taking in boarders to help support us? Panic-stricken, I rushed to my friend Carmelita. What was I going to *do*?

"You might," she suggested, "get children to take care of after school."

Our usual pay was ten cents a child. Feverishly I added and subtracted. How could I take care of seventy children within the thirty-day limit the New York people had given me?

Still Carmelita and I asked neighbors to let us take care of their children. Meanwhile, long, official letters kept coming addressed to me. Each letter more sternly worded. I became more and more frightened.

It was Carmelita who finally brought the first ray of hope into my darkness. She had found a newspaper that was offering a fifty-dollar first prize for the best essay on Americanism. Not only that, we read, but it also offered a second prize of twenty dollars and three prizes of ten dollars each.

"You see?" Carmelita comforted. "With the fine course, you are sure to win one of the prizes."

I sobbed with relief. *Of course*! Very probably I'd win the first prize. My goodness, I'd have forty-three dollars left over.

We read on. The contest closed in nine days.

On the closing day of the contest, we skated all the way downtown to the *Examiner* Building to deposit the essay. We weren't going to trust any

post office or mailbox. Besides, we had no money for stamps.

We discovered two neighbors who had the *Examiner* delivered to their doors. We took turns sneaking their paper and following news of the judging of the contest.

Finally, those welcome words, "See tomorrow's *Examiner* for the list of the essay winners."

Carmelita and I were huddled on the neighbor's steps when the paper boy came by. We waited until he was out of sight, then tore open the newspaper.

Carmelita's shaking finger traced down the page. First Prize Winner—Second Prize Winner—Third Prize Winner. My name wasn't there! Fourth—Fifth—We looked at each other with frightened eyes and started reading again. Ah—my name!

I had got forty-fifth Honorable Mention.

But no prize.

Carmelita blew her nose while I rubbed my eyes hard.

"I didn't study the course hard enough," I said.

I had finally reached the end of my rope. I said a long farewell to Carmelita and went into the house to find Mama. I coaxed her upstairs to my attic, and told her everything.

"It means so much to you, Katrin, this writing?" Mama questioned me gently.

"Oh, Mama, yes!" I cried.

"The stories, Katrin, you like to make them up?"

I sobbed loudly. Some day, I assured her, I would write great books. "It is something within me, Mama. Right here!" I pounded on my chest dramatically.

Mama picked up the little gray pamphlets. "It is here, then, how to do these great things you plan?"

Right there, I assured her. All I had to do was study 'em.

"We will find the money," Mama said.

And when I threw myself into her arms in gratefulness, she patted my back soothingly.

The rest of the family, however, were not so understanding.

Nels gave me a disgusted look and Christine said right out loud that I was getting away with murder. But Mama had Papa send away the seven-dollar money order. She clipped out the Honorable Mention column in the *Examiner* to show my name to Aunt Jenny.

Each night, Mama asked me how I was getting along with my study of the writing course. Each night I assured her that I was learning more and more.

Then it was report-card time. I had never in my life got anything lower than an *A*, so I didn't even bother to open the envelope. I just carried it home to Mama.

We were alone in the kitchen, and while she was looking at my card, I broke off a piece of freshly baked fladbröd. Mama made a funny little sound. I looked up. She was staring at my card.

"A red letter *F*," she said slowly. "That is bad?"

"Bad?" I said. "My goodness, Mama, that's the very worst mark you can get. That's *failure*. Who got an *F*?"

"You did," Mama said. "In Composition."

I stared with horror at the mark. *Composition—F?* That book report I'd failed to turn in—

Desperately, I tried to make excuses, but Mama wouldn't listen.

“Katrin,” she said severely. “That writing course we pay the seven dollars for—you march right upstairs and get it.”

I marched. In a hurry. Returning, I laid the pamphlets on the table.

“Now,” Mama said sternly, “you will sit down and copy off every one of the lessons.”

“All of them?” I wailed.

Mama nodded. “Every word.”

“But, Mama, it will take me *forever*!”

“Then,” Mama was firm, “then you had better get started.”

So I did.

Thinking and Writing About the Selection

1. How did Katrin find out about the writing lessons?
2. What was her plan for using the lessons?
3. Do you think Mama should have paid the seven dollars for the lessons? What else might she have done?
4. How do you think writers learn how to write? What prepares them to become writers?

Applying the Key Skill

Predict Outcomes

Use complete sentences to answer the following questions about "The Writing Lessons."

1. What did Katrin predict would happen once she became a famous author?
2. What information did the postman use to make his prediction about when Katrin would receive the writing lessons?
3. Carmelita told Katrin about the newspaper essay contest and the prizes offered. What prize did Katrin predict she would win? How do you know?
4. Why didn't Katrin open her report card before she gave it to her mother? What did Katrin predict her grades would be? Why?
5. Do you think Mama will make Katrin copy *all* of the writing lessons? What makes you think she will or she won't?

Faded Tools

Give me a pen,
and I shall write.
But give me a voice
and I cannot speak.
This pen of mine is:
my voice with which to speak,
my emotion with which to feel,
and my thought with which to dream.
To others this pen
is but a writing tool
until one day
the ink fades.
But, what happens to
my words,
my feelings,
and my dreams?
Yes, they too
fade deep inside me—
lost into that part of me
that wishes so much to be heard.

Vanessa Alimario

WRITING ACTIVITY

BUSINESS LETTER

Prewrite

Many people, like Katrin in "The Writing Lessons," order books, records, and other merchandise from advertisements. Sometimes, like Katrin, they get the merchandise as ordered—even though they may not like it. Other times, they may not receive the merchandise, it may be damaged, or the wrong merchandise may have been sent. What other examples of complaints could people have about their orders?

When such things happen, people should write a letter of complaint to the company from whom they ordered their merchandise. You are going to practice writing a letter of complaint. You may use the following information or write about something that really happened to you.

> Sally Tucker ordered a set of records called *Exercise for Health* on June 27, 1986, from an advertisement in the monthly magazine *Teenage Life.* When she received the records on July 15, 1986, they were damaged. She returned them the next day. She has never received a new set of records, but she has received bills in July, August, and September. What should Sally say in her letter of complaint?

Think about these ideas as you plan your letter.

1. What is your exact complaint?
2. What facts will you include?
3. What specific action do you want taken? Sally, for example, might like to cancel the order or demand a new set of records.

Write

A letter of complaint is a business letter. Check your language textbook for the correct form of a business letter.

1. Write the heading, inside address, and greeting.
2. The first paragraph should state your complaint as the main idea. Write the facts supporting your complaint in chronological order, that is, time order.
3. The second paragraph should suggest what action you would like to be taken and when.
4. Write the closing and signature of your letter.
5. Try to use Vocabulary Treasures in your letter.
6. Now write the first draft of your business letter.

VOCABULARY TREASURES

anticipation	dismayed
confidently	sincerely

Revise

Read your letter. Have a friend read it, too. Think about this checklist as you revise.

1. Could your reader easily indentify your complaint by reading the first sentence of your letter?
2. Did you report all the facts about the complaint? Did you write them in chronological order? If you left out a fact or date, add it now.
3. Will your reader know exactly what action you want taken about the complaint? Be specific.
4. Did you include all the correct information for the parts of your business letter?
5. Now rewrite your letter of complaint to share.

LETTERS MAKE THINGS HAPPEN

With just a pen, some paper, an envelope, and a few cents for postage, you can find answers to your questions or speak your mind to a newspaper read by thousands. Let your voice be heard.

It's fun to send a letter to a friend, and even more fun to receive one in return. But have you ever thought of all the other things you could do by letter? Perhaps you've been thrilled with something you bought or received as a gift. Maybe you've been upset by a television program, or needed information for a school report. Did you write a letter?

GETTING INFORMATION

How do you get answers to your questions? Often you'll find what you need to know

by talking to people, or you'll turn to books, magazines, or newspapers. Sometimes these methods don't work or don't give you up-to-date information. Then you might try writing a letter.

Many publishers of encyclopedias have a research service available to owners of their encyclopedia. If the answer to your question is not in the encyclopedia, the research department may be able to help you.

Some specialty magazines will answer questions on their topic or refer you to previous articles they have published. Address your letter to the editor.

Most libraries have a reference librarian who can suggest books for you to consult. Of course, it's quickest to ask in person at your school or local library, but you may want to write to a university library, a state historical library, another state library, or the Library of Congress. (Send your letter to Washington, DC 20540.)

Perhaps your question should be directed to a museum. There are thousands of museums across the country, ranging from tiny local museums to the huge Smithsonian Institution in Washington, D.C. You'll discover there are art museums, music museums, antique car museums, and professional sports museums, to name a few. You can also ask your librarian to help you locate the names and addresses of museums that might answer your question.

The public relations departments of large companies are good sources of information. Some of the larger companies may have produced books on your topic and will be glad to send them to you. Send your questions about cars to a car manufacturer, write to a sewing machine company with

questions about sewing. You can often find the address of a company on the package of one of its products or in a magazine or newspaper advertisement.

An excellent source of information is the U.S. Government Printing Office, which issues hundreds of booklets and pamphlets. Write to:

Superintendent of Documents
U.S. Government Printing
Office
Washington, DC 20402

and ask to be sent a copy of the catalog, *U.S. Government Books*. The catalog contains descriptions of almost one thousand of the most popular books published by the U.S. Government. There are books on all sorts of subjects, from computers to weather.

One catalog could not possibly list all of the 15,000 different books, pamphlets, and posters available from the Superintendent of Documents. So if you have a special area of interest, such as stamps or camping, you should ask for a copy of the *Subject Bibliography Index*. This is a listing of 240 separate catalogs available for specific subject areas.

Another helpful booklet listing free and inexpensive government publications is *Consumer Information*. Order your copy from:

Consumer Information Center
P.O. Box 100
Pueblo, CO 81002

If you cannot find the information you need in these government publications, try writing to the government agency that deals with your topic. For example, write to the National

Aeronautics and Space Administration (NASA) to ask for information about space flights. Send a letter to the National Oceanographic and Atmospheric Administration to ask questions about the weather and about oceanographic research.

If you'd like information on good books to read, send letters and self-addressed, stamped envelopes to

American Library Association
Children's Service Division
50 East Huron Street
Chicago, IL 60611

Children's Book Council
67 Irving Place
New York, NY 10003

Be sure to tell both organizations how old you are and what kinds of books you like to read. They will send you booklists or tell you how to order them.

People, companies, and government agencies will be glad

to send you catalogs, brochures, pamphlets, and information. All it takes is a letter from you.

GIVING YOUR OPINION

Most magazines carry a "Letters to the Editor" column. People usually write to magazines to comment on an article that appeared in the magazine. People writing to newspapers may comment on the coverage of the news, as well as give their opinions on the hot dogs served at the county fair or the money spent on fireworks for the Fourth of July celebration.

Do you have an opinion on a local or national event? Why do you feel the way you do? Does this event involve you? What action should be taken? Can you back up your opinion with facts? Can you send the editor of the local paper a letter explaining your feelings?

Find an article that makes you feel good and write a letter explaining your feelings. Why do you like the article? Do you agree with the writer's opinion? Is the writer truthful? Is the article about something you'd like to do? Is it a true story with a happy ending? How do you think other people would react to the article?

Now find a magazine or newspaper article that makes you angry. Write a letter to the editor. Explain what you find disturbing. Is it the tone or opinion of the writer? Is the writer deliberately expressing an opinion? Does this writer have the facts straight? Or are you bothered by the event or action reported in the article? Could something have been done to prevent the event or action? Has the situation been corrected? What would you do to fix things?

When you write your letter to the editor, you don't have to mention all you know about your topic. Remember to be informative and to the point. Don't wait too long to write. Not all letters are used, but perhaps yours will be printed.

Letters to radio and television stations get results, too. Programs are sometimes added and dropped according to what people say about them. Of course, one unfavorable letter about a program will not lead to its cancellation. But station managers do care about what

people think of programs. Your comments are important for planning future programming and will be kept on file for the Federal Communications Commission to read when reviewing the station's license renewal.

Letters to station managers can be about one program you see or hear, or the letters can discuss all the programs on that particular station.

You'll find the addresses for local radio and television stations in your telephone book. If the station is in another town or if you have a cable television hookup, your librarian may be able to help you locate the addresses.

Most television programs are not produced by your local station, but by the major networks. In addition to writing the local station, you may want to write to the network. Do you feel there is too much violence on television? Do you watch the Saturday morning cartoons? Do you enjoy the after-school movie specials? Are there other types of programs you'd like to see? If you have comments to make, write.

Is there a person you think should be honored with a state or national holiday? Is there a law you think should be passed? These are topics you might want to write to your senator or congressperson about. Your parent, teacher or librarian can tell you the names. Send your letters to:

(Name of Senator)
Senate Office Building
Washington, DC 20510

(Name of Representative)
House of Representatives
Office Building
Washington, DC 20515

Be sure to explain clearly what you think should be done and why you feel that way. Your representatives will be

glad to hear your opinion, and you will probably receive an answer.

DOING BUSINESS

You can use letters to transact business. You can order a green felt hat, complain about

a mystery book with pages missing, ask questions about how your record player works, or praise the manufacturer of your new jogging shoes.

Pick an item you've purchased recently. How well does it work? Do you have suggestions for improving it? Write a letter to the company describing what you like and don't like about the item.

Ask a parent or teacher to help you identify the companies in your town that are active in sponsoring civic affairs. For example, a bank may sponsor a marathon run, or a gas station may support city parks. Write a letter of appreciation.

Learn about the positions that various companies take on important issues. What does your local power company have to say about nuclear energy? What is a national paper company doing about forest preservation? Write a letter giving your opinion.

Look at the appearance of some local businesses. Is there one that plants brightly colored flowers every spring or that has done something unusual to spruce up the neighborhood? Write and tell the company you appreciate its efforts.

Letters to businesses get results. If you have a complaint or a problem, managers try to solve it. And if you send a letter of praise, they'll be delighted to hear from you.

Thinking and Writing About the Selection

1. What kinds of information would you find in the *Subject Bibliography Index* published by the U. S. Government Printing Office?
2. Name two kinds of business letters described in the selection that you might need to write. Explain why you might write such letters.
3. Why do people write letters to the editor of a newspaper or magazine? Why do many people enjoy reading the letters?
4. Choose one of the addresses listed in the selection and write a letter to the group or agency requesting specific information about something that interests you.

Applying the Key Skill
Persuasion and Propaganda

Use the information in "Letters Make Things Happen" to complete two of the following activities.

1. Write an ad or commercial encouraging students in your class to write to the American Library Association or the Children's Book Council requesting information about recommended books. Try to include a catchy slogan in your ad or commercial.
2. What information could you use to persuade someone that writing a letter to a radio or television station in order to express an opinion about programming is not a waste of time?
3. What points or ideas would you include in a letter to try to persuade a local business to join in the Clean Up Main Street Campaign? List your ideas in order to show which you think are the most persuasive.

Do you remember the song about those unusual gifts—drummers drumming and lords a-leaping, calling birds and swimming swans? Manghanita Kempadoo, an eleven-year-old author, imagined what it would be like to *really* receive such gifts. Her story is told through letters, and her characters include Lord Gilbert, the gift giver, and Lady Katherine Huntington, the letter writer.

Letters of Thanks

by Manghanita Kempadoo

Huntington Hall
December 25th, 1895.

Dear Lord Gilbert,

How delighted I was to receive that dear little partridge in the pear tree. Whenever I look at him I shall remember you, but he does look rather lonely and cold. Maybe he would be better off with a muffler!

Oh, thank you so much for such a thoughtful gift.

Yours lovingly,

Katherine Huntington.

Huntington Hall
December 26th, 1895.

Dear Lord Gilbert,

The two turtle doves arrived safely and are cooing in the pear tree with the partridge.

My head gardener is building a new dove cote as the old one is not quite suitable for them.

The partridge still looks lonely, though I cannot think why!

Yours thankfully,

Katherine Huntington.

Huntington Hall
December 27th, 1895.

Dear Lord Gilbert,

How enchanting the three French hens are! Do they really come from France? The turtle doves are quite happy in their dove cote and I think I will put the French hens with them.

My dear little partridge looks even more unhappy and I cannot think what to do.

Gratefully yours,

Katherine Huntington.

Huntington Hall December 28th, 1895.

Dear Lord Gilbert,

How did you know I would like four calling birds? They simply delight me with their singing, although they can be rather noisy.

They are quite friendly with my darling partridge so I cannot imagine why he looks so sad.

The French hens and the turtle doves are cooing in the dove cote. I wonder if I can introduce them to the calling birds?

Yours,
Katherine
Huntington.

Huntington Hall,
December 29th, 1895.

Dear Lord Gilbert,

Oh, I cannot express my thanks for those lovely golden rings. I cannot possibly think how you knew the sizes. They fit perfectly! They will match my new satin dress that I will wear tonight to Lady Wentwort's ball. This evening I will wear my sapphire chain to match the rings. I simply cannot stop looking at them. You are so thoughtful. My little partridge is shivering with cold. I think I'll make him a woollen suit. Thank you many times over.

Yours for ever, Katherine Huntington.

Huntington Hall
December 30th, 1895.

Dear Lord Gilbert,

Thank you for your unusual gift of six laying geese. My big problem is where to put them. They are, at the moment, ruining my new croquet lawn and hissing. Can you tell me what to do with their eggs? No one seems to want to buy them. I dare not keep them for six geese are quite enough. The partridge is now warm in his new black and yellow woollen suit.

Sincerely yours,

Katherine Huntington.

Huntington Hall
December 31st, 1895.

Dear Lord Gilbert,

We had to put the seven swans in my lily pond. They are a bit cramped there, but my lily pond is an absolute wreck. Also I do not know what to feed them on.

I think my partridge is afraid of them and that just will not do.

Lady Katherine Huntington.

Huntington Hall
January 1st, 1896.

Lord Gilbert,

Eight cows give so much milk that soon we shall have to put the swans to swim in it. The cows made such a noise last night that I could hardly sleep. I also now have to pay eight milking maids. My partridge has a cold from drinking so much milk.

Lady Huntington.

Huntington Hall
January 2nd, 1896.

Lord Gilbert,

One of the nine fiddlers seems to be out of tune. What with their scraping, the cows mooing, pails clanking, honking, hissing and cooing, I have a slight headache. My partridge does not like it at all.

Lady Huntington.

Huntington Hall Jan. 3rd, 1896

Lord G. Faraday,

Your gift of ~~a~~ ten drummers is quite unwelcome. They are making me mad.

Lady K. Huntington.

Huntington Hall, 4.1.96

Lord Faraday,

The eleven ladies dancing are quite outrageous. They make me quite ill

Hon. Lady Huntington

Huntington Hall
5th January 1896

Dear Lord Faraday,

Lady Katherine has retired to her London home with the partridge. She is suffering from a nervous breakdown.

She requested me to return these gifts to you:

Twelve leaping lords
Eleven dancing ladies
Ten drummers
Nine fiddlers
Eight milking maids and their cows
Seven swans
Six laying geese
Four calling birds
Three French hens
Two turtle doves and a pear tree

She wishes to keep the partridge and rings.

Margaret A. E. Bowes

Margaret A. E. Bowes
Secretary to Lady Huntington

PERSUASION AND PROPAGANDA

In "Letters Make Things Happen," you learned about writing letters to get information or to give opinions. The authors of the selections you have read in this book wrote to inform or to entertain. These are just a few of the reasons for writing. Another reason for writing is to persuade. *To persuade* means "to convince or to cause (someone) to do or believe something by argument." Materials purposely written to persuade are called **propaganda**.

Do you remember the advertisement Katrin read for "Writing Secrets" in "The Writing Lessons"?

> **DO YOU WANT TO BECOME A WRITER?**
> **"WRITING SECRETS"**
> **This complete Course in Motion Picture, Novel, Short Story, Poetry, Drama, Pageantry, and Newspaper Techniques yours for only $7.00!**
> **USED BY ALL FAMOUS AUTHORS.**

The underlined sentence is an example of a technique, or method, used in propaganda. The sentence tries to convince the reader that all famous authors use "Writing Secrets," and that anyone who buys and uses it can become a famous author, too. Do you think all famous authors use "Writing Secrets"? Do you think anyone can become a famous author by using it?

It is important to learn to recognize the techniques of propaganda. If you are aware of how a writer is trying to convince you of something, you can make up your own mind about whether you want to be convinced.

Some of the commonly used propaganda techniques have special names. The ad below is an example of a **glittering generality**.

Come to Funorama and have a day to remember! We have the most exciting rides and the best entertainment of any amusement park in the country.

Will you really have a day to remember if you go to Funorama? Are their rides and entertainment the most exciting and best? When you read the ad, you probably recognized that the generalities, or general statements, made are opinions, not facts. We call them *glittering* because they are used to give the reader a highly favorable impression of Funorama.

A **testimonial** is a favorable statement that someone, often a famous person, makes about something.

> **"What soap do I use? Why, *Dream*, of course! *Dream* makes my skin feel fresh and clean, and I love that delicate scent."**
>
> **Didi Arturo**
> **famous film star**

Dream may be good soap, but the fact that Didi Arturo uses it and likes it doesn't mean that you should use it or that you will like it.

Name-calling is another propaganda technique. In **name-calling**, the writer says something bad about someone or something in hopes of turning the reader against that person or thing.

> **To the Editor:**
>
> **I am surprised and dismayed at the favorable coverage this paper has been giving to Jim Conway, candidate for mayor in the up-coming election. Why don't you print the other side of the story? Why don't you tell the public about the shameful way Mr. Conway has used public funds, about his secret deals with big business interests? In my mind, Mr. Conway is a crook. As a representative of the people, he would better be called a "misrepresentative."**
>
> **Sincerely,**
> **Martha Babcock**

By referring to Mr. Conway as a "crook" and a "misrepresentative," Martha Babcock is trying to turn the voters away from him. Mr. Conway may or may not be a crook or a "misrepresentative," but associating Mr. Conway with these terms may cause some readers to have a bad opinion of him.

ACTIVITY Read the passage below. Then write the answers to the questions on your paper.

> Wild quails were once found in abundance in Fremont County. They nested in protected places along our many streams and were a common sight to farmers and hikers. Today the story is different. According to reports of the State Fish and Game Commission, there are only a few dozen left. Still, the state has made no changes in the

hunting laws in regard to these birds. If we want to save the quails from extinction, we must act quickly. No one wants to see them disappear forever from our county. As Senator Burton has said, "The preservation of all native species is an important concern to lawmakers." You can help by writing to your representative in Congress and by sending donations to "Save the Quails Fund."

1. Which sentence or sentences use a propaganda technique?
   a. Wild quails were once found in abundance in Fremont County.
   b. According to reports of the State Fish and Game Commission, there are only a few dozen quails left.
   c. As Senator Burton has said, "The preservation of all native species is an important concern to lawmakers."
   d. No one wants to see quail disappear forever from our county.

2. Which sentence or sentences try to persuade readers that action is necessary and that they can help?
   a. If we want to save the quail from extinction, we must act quickly.
   b. Quails nested in protected places along our many streams and were a common sight to farmers and hikers.
   c. According to reports of the State Fish and Game Commission, there are only a few dozen quails left.
   d. You can help by writing to your representative in Congress and by sending donations to "Save the Quails Fund."

DEAR MR. HENSHAW

BEVERLY CLEARY

Sixth grader Leigh Botts has been writing to Mr. Henshaw, his favorite author, since second grade. At Mr. Henshaw's suggestion, Leigh has been keeping a diary. Between the diary and the letters, Leigh has written quite a bit. He describes how, when his parents were divorced, his dad took Leigh's dog, Bandit, along for company on his truck, and then lost him. He also tells about someone who keeps stealing the best things from his lunchbox. In his latest letter, Leigh talks about having trouble writing a story for a contest.

February 15

Dear Mr. Henshaw,

I haven't written to you for a long time, because I know you are busy, but I need help with the story I am trying to write for the Young Writers' Yearbook. I got started, but I don't know how to finish it.

My story is about a man ten feet tall who drives a big truck, the kind my Dad drives. The man is made of wax, and every time he crosses the desert, he melts a little. He makes so many trips and melts so much he finally can't handle the gears or reach the brakes. That is as far as I can get. What should I do now?

The boys in my class who are writing about monsters just bring in a new monster on the last page to finish off the villains with a laser. That kind of ending doesn't seem right to me. I don't know why.

Please help. Just a postcard will do.

Hopefully,
Leigh Botts
Leigh Botts

P.S. Until I started trying to write a story, I wrote in my diary almost every day.

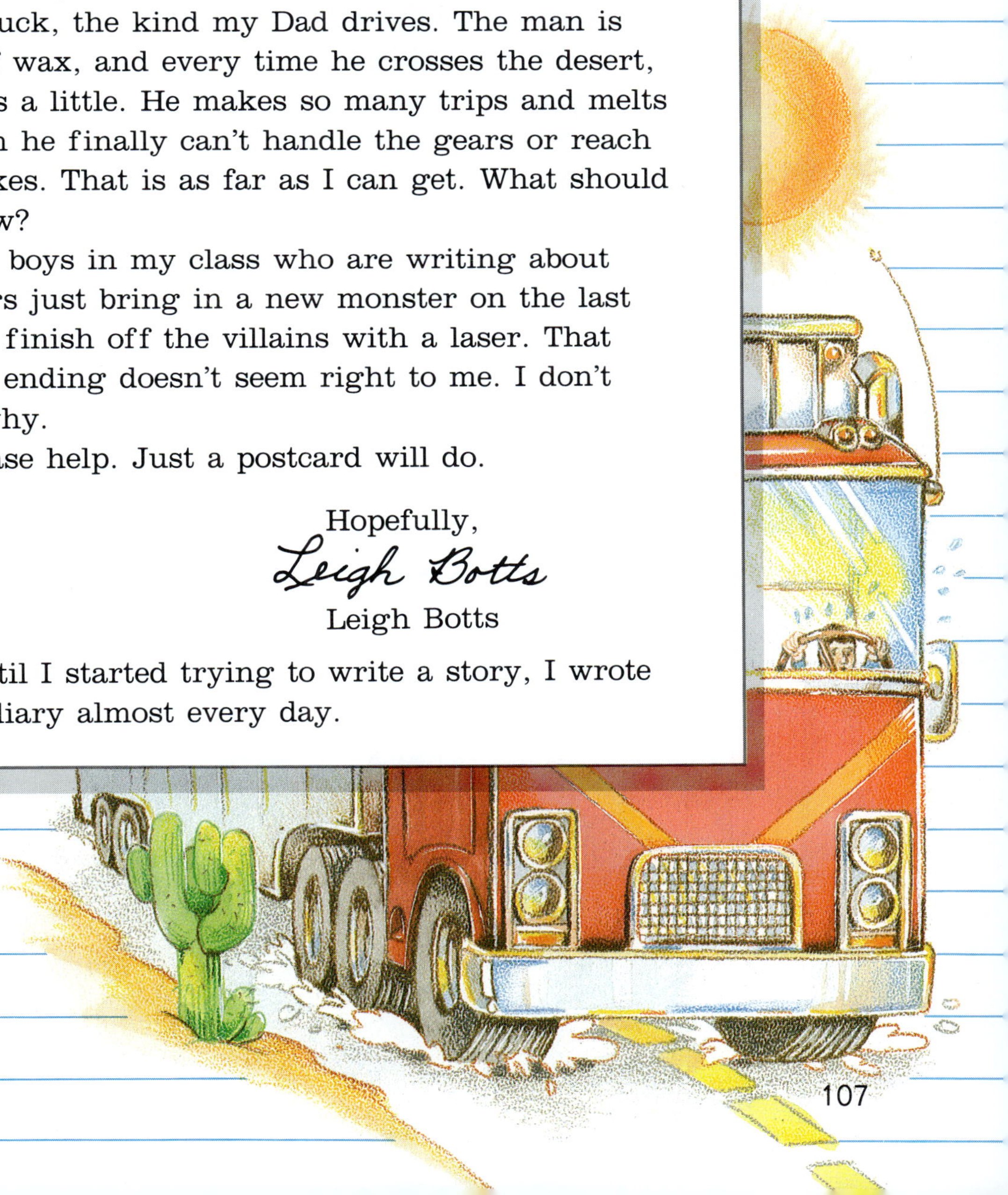

February 28

Dear Mr. Henshaw,

Thank you for answering my letter. I was surprised that you had trouble writing stories when you were my age. I think you are right. Maybe I am not ready to write a story. I understand what you mean. A character in a story should solve a problem or change in some way. I can see that a wax man who melts until he's a puddle wouldn't be there to solve anything and melting isn't the sort of change you mean. I suppose somebody could run up on the last page and make candles out of him. That would change him all right, but that is not the ending I want.

I asked Miss Martinez if I had to write a story for Young Writers, and she said I could write a poem or a description.

Your grateful friend,

Leigh Botts

Leigh

P.S. I bought a copy of *Ways to Amuse a Dog* at a garage sale. I hope you don't mind.

FROM THE DIARY OF LEIGH BOTTS
VOL. 2

Thursday, March 1

I am getting behind in this diary for several reasons, including working on my story and writing to Mr. Henshaw (really, not just pretend). I also had to buy a new notebook because I had filled up the first one.

The same day, I bought a beat-up black lunchbox in the thrift shop down the street and started carrying my lunch in it. The kids were surprised, but nobody made fun of me, because a black lunchbox isn't the same as one of those square boxes covered with cartoon characters that first and second graders carry. A couple of boys asked if it was my dad's. I just grinned and said, "Where do you think I got it?" The next day my little slices of salami rolled around cream cheese were gone, but I expected that. But I'll get that thief yet. I'll make him really sorry he ate all the best things out of my lunch.

Next I went to the library for books on batteries. I took out a couple of easy books on electricity, really easy, because I have never given much thought to batteries. About all I know is that when you want to use a flashlight, the battery is usually dead.

I finally gave up on my story about the ten-foot wax man, which was really pretty dumb. I thought I would write a poem about butterflies for Young Writers because a poem can be short, but it is hard to think about butterflies and burglar alarms at the same time, so I studied electricity books instead. The books didn't have directions for an alarm in a lunch-box, but I learned enough about batteries and switches and insulated wires, so I think I can figure it out myself.

Friday, March 2

Back to the poem tonight. The only rhyme I can think of for "butterfly" is "flutter by." I can think up rhymes like "trees" and "breeze" which are pretty boring, and then I think of "wheeze" and "sneeze." A poem about butterflies wheezing and sneezing seems silly, and anyway a couple of girls are already writing poems about monarch butterflies that flutter by.

Sometimes I start a letter to Dad thanking him for the twenty dollars he sent me to make up for losing Bandit, but I can't finish that either. I don't know why.

Saturday, March 3

Today I took my lunchbox and Dad's twenty dollars to the hardware store and looked around. I found an ordinary light switch, a little battery and a cheap doorbell. While I was looking around for the right kind of insulated wire, a man who had been watching me (boys my age always get watched when they go into stores) asked if he could help me. He was a nice old gentleman who said, "What are you planning to make, son?" *Son*. He called me son, and my dad calls me kid. I didn't want to tell the man, but when he looked at the things I was holding, he grinned and said, "Having trouble with your lunch, aren't you?" I nodded and said, "I'm trying to make a burglar alarm."

He said, "That's what I guessed. I've had workmen in here with the same problem."

It turned out that I needed a 6-volt lantern battery instead of the battery I had picked out. He gave me a couple of tips and, after I paid for the things, a little slap on the back and said, "Good luck, son."

I tore home with all the things I bought. First I made a sign for my door that said

KEEP OUT
MOM
THAT MEANS YOU

Then I went to work fastening one wire from the battery to the switch and from the other side of the switch to the doorbell. Then I fastened a second wire from the battery to the doorbell. It took me a while to get it right. Then I taped the battery in one corner of the lunchbox and the doorbell in another. I stood the switch up at the back of the box and taped that in place, too.

Here I ran into a problem. I thought I could take the wire clamp meant to hold a thermos bottle inside the lunchbox lid and hook it under the switch if I reached in carefully as I closed the box. The clamp wasn't quite long enough. After some thinking and experimenting, I twisted a wire loop onto it. Then I closed the box just enough so I could get my hand inside and push the wire loop over the button on the switch before I took my hand out and closed the box.

Then I opened the box. My burglar alarm worked! That bell inside the box went off with a terrible racket.

Monday, March 5

Today Mom packed my lunch carefully, and we tried the alarm to see if it worked. It did, good and loud. When I got to school, Mr. Fridley said, "Nice to see you smiling, Leigh. You should try it more often."

I parked my lunchbox behind the partition and waited. I waited all morning for the alarm to go off. Miss Martinez asked if I had my mind on my work. I pretended I did, but all the time I was really waiting for my alarm to go off so I could dash back behind the partition and tackle the thief. When nothing happened, I began to worry. Maybe the loop had somehow slipped off the switch on the way to school.

Lunchtime came. The alarm still hadn't gone off. We all picked up our lunches and went off to the cafeteria. When I set my box on the table in front of me, I realized I had a problem, a big problem. If the loop hadn't slipped off the switch, my alarm was still triggered. I just sat there, staring at my lunchbox, not knowing what to do.

"How come you're not eating?" Barry asked with his mouth full. Barry's sandwiches are never cut in half, and he always takes a big bite out of one side to start.

Everybody at the table was looking at me. I thought about saying I wasn't hungry, but I was. I thought about taking my lunchbox out into the hall to open, but if the alarm was still triggered, there was no way I could open it quietly. Finally I thought, Here goes. I unsnapped the two fasteners on the box and held my breath as I opened the lid.

Wow! My alarm went off! The noise was so loud it startled everybody at the table including me and made everyone in the cafeteria look around. I looked up and saw Mr. Fridley grinning at me over by the garbage can. Then I turned off the alarm.

Suddenly everybody seemed to be noticing me. The principal, who always prowls around keeping an eye on things at lunchtime, came over to examine my lunchbox. He said, "That's quite an invention you have there."

"Thanks," I said, pleased that the principal seemed to like my alarm.

Some of the teachers came out of their lunchroom to see what the noise was all about. I had to give a demonstration. It seems I wasn't the only one who had things stolen from my lunch, and all the kids said they wanted lunchboxes with alarms, too, even those whose lunches were never good enough to have anything stolen. Barry said he would like an alarm like that on the door of his room at home. I began to feel like some sort of hero. Maybe I'm not so medium after all.

Friday, March 16

Tonight I was staring at a piece of paper trying to think of something to write for Young Writers when the phone rang. Mom told me to answer because she was washing her hair.

It was Dad. My stomach felt as if it was dropping to the floor, the way it always does when I hear his voice. "How're you doing, kid?" he asked.

His call took me so by surprise that I could feel my heart pounding, and I couldn't think of anything to say until I asked, "Have you found another dog to take Bandit's place?" I think what I really meant was, Have you found another boy to take my place?

"No, but I ask about him on my CB," Dad told me. "He may turn up yet."

"I hope so." This conversation was going no place. I really didn't know what to say to my father. It was embarrassing.

Then Dad surprised me. He asked, "Do you ever miss your old Dad?"

I had to think a minute. I missed him all right, but I couldn't seem to get the words out. My silence must have bothered him because he asked, "Are you still there?"

"Sure, Dad, I miss you," I told him. It was true, but not as true as it had been a couple of months ago. I still wanted him to pull up in front of the house in his big rig, but now I knew I couldn't count on it.

Saturday, March 17

Today is Saturday, so this morning I walked to the butterfly trees again. The grove was quiet and peaceful, and because the sun was shining, I stood there a long time, looking at the orange butterflies floating through the gray and green leaves and listening to the sound of the ocean on the rocks. There aren't as many butterflies now. Maybe they are starting to go north for the summer. I thought I might write about them in prose instead of poetry, but on the way home I got to thinking about Dad and one time when he took me along when he was hauling grapes to a winery and what a great day it had been.

Tuesday, March 20

Yesterday Miss Neely, the librarian, asked if I had written anything for the Young Writers' Yearbook, because all writing had to be turned in by tomorrow. When I told her I hadn't, she said I still had twenty-four hours and why didn't I get busy? So I did, because I really would like to meet a Famous Author. My story about the ten-foot wax man went into the wastebasket. Next I tried to start a story called *The Great Lunchbox Mystery*, but I couldn't seem to turn my lunchbox experience into a story because I don't know who the thief (thieves) was (were), and I don't want to know.

Finally I dashed off a description of the time I rode with my father when he was trucking the load of grapes down Highway 152 through Pacheco Pass to a winery. I put in things like the signs that said STEEP GRADE, TRUCKS USE LOW GEAR and how Dad down-shifted and how skillful he was handling a long, heavy load on the curves. I put in about the hawks on the telephone wires and about that high peak where Black Bart's lookout used to watch for

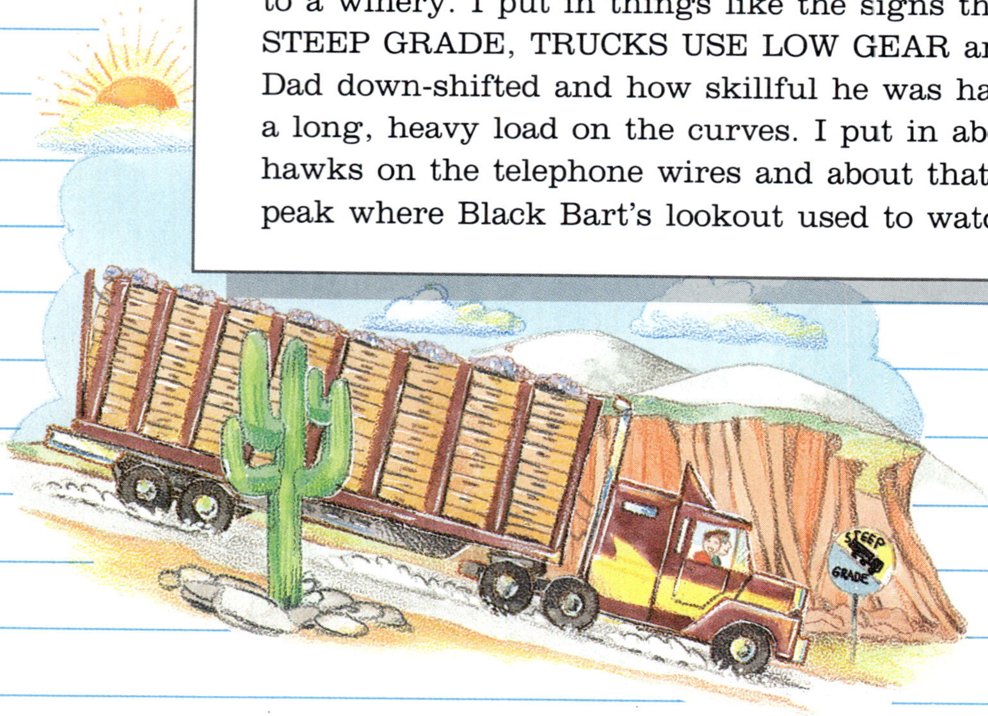

travelers coming through the pass so he could signal to Black Bart to rob them, and how the leaves on the trees along the stream at the bottom of the pass were turning yellow and how good tons of grapes smelled in the sun. I left out the part about the waitresses and the video games. Then I copied the whole thing over in case neatness counts and gave it to Miss Neely.

Monday, March 26

Today wasn't the greatest day of my life. When our class went to the library, I saw a stack of Yearbooks and could hardly wait for Miss Neely to hand them out. When I finally got mine and opened it to the first page, there was a monster story, and I saw I hadn't won first prize. I kept turning. I didn't win second prize which went to a poem, and I didn't win third or fourth prize, either. Then I turned another page and saw Honorable Mention and under it:

A DAY ON DAD'S RIG
by
LEIGH M. BOTTS

There was my title with my name under it in print, even if it was mimeographed print. I can't say I wasn't disappointed because I hadn't won a prize, I was. I was really disappointed about not getting to meet the mysterious Famous Author, but I liked seeing my name in print.

Some kids were mad because they didn't win or even get something printed. They said they wouldn't ever try to write again which I think is pretty dumb. I have heard that real authors sometimes have their books turned down. I figure you win some, you lose some.

Then Miss Neely announced that the Famous Author the winners would get to have lunch with was Angela Badger. The girls were more excited than the boys because Angela Badger writes mostly about girls with problems like big feet or pimples or something. I would still like to meet her because she is, as they say, a real live author, and I've never met a real live author. I am glad Mr. Henshaw isn't the author because then I would really be disappointed that I didn't get to meet him.

Friday, March 30

Today turned out to be exciting. In the middle of second period Miss Neely called me out of class and asked if I would like to go have lunch with Angela Badger. I said, "Sure, how come?"

Miss Neely explained that the teachers discovered that the winning poem had been copied out of a book and wasn't original so the girl who submitted it would not be allowed to go and would I like to go in her place? Would I!

Miss Neely drove us in her own car to the Holiday Inn, where some other librarians and their winners were waiting in the lobby. Then Angela Badger

arrived with Mr. Badger, and we were all led into the dining room which was pretty crowded. One of the librarians who was a sort of Super Librarian told the winners to sit at a long table with a sign that said Reserved. Angela Badger sat in the middle and some of the girls pushed to sit beside her. I sat across from her.

Mrs. Badger tried to get some of the shy people to say something without much luck, and I still couldn't think of anything to say to a lady who wrote books about girls with big feet or pimples. Finally Mrs. Badger looked straight at me and asked, "What did you write for the Yearbook?"

I felt myself turn red and answered, "Just something about a ride on a truck."

"Oh!" said Mrs. Badger. "So you're the author of *A Day on Dad's Rig*!"

Everyone was quiet. None of us had known the real live author would have read what we had written, but she had and she remembered my title.

"I just got honorable mention," I said, but I was thinking, She called me an author. *A real live author called me an author.*

"What difference does that make?" asked Mrs. Badger. "Judges never agree. I happened to like *A Day on Dad's Rig* because it was written by a boy who wrote honestly about something he knew and had strong feelings about. You made me feel what it was like to ride down a steep grade with tons of grapes behind me."

"But I couldn't make it into a story," I said, feeling a whole lot braver.

"Who cares?" said Mrs. Badger with a wave of her hand. She's the kind of person who wears rings

on her forefingers. "What do you expect? The ability to write stories comes later, when you have lived longer and have more understanding. *A Day on Dad's Rig* was splendid work for a boy your age. You wrote like *you*, and you did not try to imitate someone else. This is one mark of a good writer. Keep it up."

I noticed a couple of girls who had been saying they wanted to write books exactly like Angela Badger exchange embarrassed looks.

"Gee, thanks," was all I could say. The waitress began to plunk down dishes of ice cream. Everyone got over being shy and began to ask Mrs. Badger if she wrote in pencil or on the typewriter and did she ever have books rejected and were her characters real people and did she ever have pimples when she was a girl like the girl in her book and what did it feel like to be a famous author?

I didn't think answers to those questions were very important, but I did have one question I wanted to ask which I finally managed to get in at the last minute when Mrs. Badger was autographing some books people had brought.

"Mrs. Badger," I said, "did you ever meet Boyd Henshaw?"

"Why, yes," she said, scribbling away in someone's book. "I once met him at a meeting of librarians where we were on the same program."

"What's he like?" I asked over the head of a girl crowding up with her book.

"He's a very nice young man with a wicked twinkle in his eye," she answered. I think I have known that since the time he answered my questions when Miss Martinez made us write to an author.

On the ride home everybody was chattering about Mrs. Badger this, and Mrs. Badger that. I didn't want to talk. I just wanted to think. A real live author had called me an author. A real live author had told me to keep it up. Mom was proud of me when I told her.

The gas station stopped pinging a long time ago, but I wanted to write all this down while I remembered. I'm glad tomorrow is Saturday. If I had to go to school I would yawn. I wish Dad was here so I could tell him all about today.

March 31

Dear Mr. Henshaw,

I'll keep this short to save you time reading it. I had to tell you something. You were right. I wasn't ready to write an imaginary story. But guess what! I wrote a true story which won Honorable Mention in the Yearbook. Maybe next year I'll write something that will win first or second place. Maybe by then I will be able to write an imaginary story.

I just thought you would like to know. Thank you for your help. If it hadn't been for you, I might have handed in that dumb story about the melting wax trucker.

Your friend, the author,

Leigh Botts

Leigh Botts

P.S. I still write in the diary you started me on.

Thinking and Writing About the Selection

1. What two problems did Leigh have at the beginning of the story?
2. What did Mrs. Badger especially like about Leigh's story?
3. In his advice to Leigh, Mr. Henshaw said that a character in a story must solve a problem or change in some way. How did Leigh do both of these things?
4. Write a diary entry describing an exciting day you had.

Applying the Key Skill

Synonyms and Antonyms

The sentences below are from "Dear Mr. Henshaw." The underlined word is a synonym or antonym for a word in the story. Find the sentence in the story. Write the underlined word and the word it replaced in the sentence. Then tell if the two words are synonyms or antonyms.

1. I can think up rhymes like "trees" and "breeze" which are pretty dull, and then I think of "wheeze" and "sneeze."
2. I found an average light switch, a small battery and an inexpensive doorbell.
3. I put in things like the signs that said STEEP GRADE, TRUCKS USE LOW GEAR and how Dad down-shifted and how inexperienced he was handling a long, heavy load on the curves.
4. You wrote like you, and you did not try to copy someone else.

Dear Pencil-Pal,

SCHULZ

HAVE YOU EVER TRIED TO WRITE WITH A PEN, LINUS?
I'VE BEEN PRACTICING FOR A WEEK NOW, AND I THINK I'M GETTING BETTER...HERE, TRY IT..
11-6
DON'T BE WORRIED IF YOU DO POORLY AT FIRST....YOU'LL PROBABLY HAVE THE SAME TROUBLE THAT I....
Dear Pen-pal,
How are you?
SCHULZ

THERE GOES CHARLIE BROWN MAILING ANOTHER LETTER TO HIS PENCIL-PAL..
I KIND OF WISH I HAD A PENCIL-PAL...OF COURSE, I CAN'T WRITE ANYWAY..
ALL I COULD EVER DO IS MAKE A PAW PRINT..
THAT'S JUST WHAT I NEED...A PAW PRINT-PAL!
SCHULZ
10-18

HOW LONG DO YOU THINK IT WILL TAKE FOR YOUR LETTER TO GET TO YOUR PENCIL-PAL?
I DON'T KNOW.. A FEW DAYS I SUPPOSE..
WHAT KIND OF STAMP DID YOU PUT ON IT?
STAMP?
8-30
SCHULZ

THE BEST OF THE BOOKS

MARILYN Z. WILKES

Perhaps you've seen the silver and gold medallions on the covers of some books and wondered what they were. How could a book win a medal?

Each spring and autumn, hundreds of new books are published for young readers. In bookstores and on library shelves across the country, picture books, "easy readers" and novels appear. There are mysteries, adventure stories, folk tales, and stories about ordinary people. How can we know which of these nearly 2,000 new books are worth our time and money? How can we find the ones that deserve to become classics? How do we pick the best of the books?

More than fifty different awards and medals are given in the United States to the best author or illustrator of children's books. Probably the most important of these are the Newbery and Caldecott medals. The Newbery has been given each year since 1922 to the "most distinguished" children's book published in the United States during that year. The award was begun by Frederic Melcher, an editor and publisher. He felt the public needed to be more aware of the many fine books being written for children. He named the award, fittingly, for the man who published the first real children's books in English.

Did you think there were always books written just for children? There weren't. Before 1744, children had only two types of reading materials. One was the hornbook. This was a thin board on which a sheet of paper had been fastened. The paper contained a school lesson of some kind. It was covered with a clear sheet of horn, which protected it and also gave it its name. The only other reading materials were adult books, which were often dry and difficult. Reading in those days could hardly have been much fun. Of course, no one thought it should be.

John Newbery changed all that. In 1744 he published the first of many books for children, *A Little Pretty Pocket-Book*. It was small, cheerily illustrated, and bound in bright paper. Inside were tales, games, rhymes, and moral lessons signed by "Jack the Giant Killer." The book was a huge success and was followed by many more. Newbery also published the first English edition of *Mother Goose* illustrated by Perrault (pār ō′), which was soon reprinted in America. The

***Charlotte's Web*, a Newbery Honor Book in 1953, is still a favorite. *M.C. Higgins the Great* won the Newbery in 1975.**

world of children's literature had been created.

How is it possible to choose the "most distinguished" new book each year when there are many good ones? It isn't easy. The Newbery Committee is made up of thirteen children's librarians from across the United States. Some are appointed and the rest elected annually by members of the American Library Association. In 1981 Sara Miller, head children's librarian in White Plains, New York, was elected to the committee. In the months before the committee met, she had to read over five hundred books, not once but twice. "You cannot really discuss anything you haven't read twice," she says. "I can tell you that from experience. And every day when I came home from work, there'd be more packages of books on my doorstep." She also read reviews of all the books and discussed them with other members of the committee by phone and by letter.

Finally, the committee met to make their decision. They sat in a long room, around a long table loaded with books and

Katherine Paterson won her first Newbery in 1978 for *Bridge to Terabithia*.

Jean George's *Julie of the Wolves* won the Newbery in 1973. *My Side of the Mountain*, an earlier George novel, was a Newbery Honor Book in 1960.

pitchers of ice water. They began talking at 8:00 A.M. Each book had to be discussed individually. Discussion continued until 8:00 P.M. After a night sworn to silence, they began again at 8:00 the next morning. Sometime during that day they were ready for the first ballot. There was little agreement, but eventually the list was reduced to about twenty books, and then to ten. Every time there was a new ballot, each book had to be discussed again.

"Now you really start to fight," recalls Miss Miller. "Now you know who is voting for what and what book you really want to win. You have to choose *one*, and it drives you wild. People are standing up, practically, on chairs, reading aloud from their favorites.

At 2:00 in the morning, the balloting was finally over. The 1981 Newbery Book had been chosen. It was *Jacob Have I Loved* by Katherine Paterson. This is the story of an independent, strong-willed island girl who grows beyond her jealousy of her talented twin sister. Two Honor Books, *The Fledgling* by Jane Langton and *A Ring of Endless Light* by Madeleine L'Engle, were runners-up. Says Miss Miller, "Until I was on the Newbery, I never really understood what a group decision meant." She thinks the decision was a good one.

The Newbery Book of 1973 was *Julie of the Wolves* by Jean Craighead George. It is about a young Eskimo girl who runs away from a terrible home life and survives for a time by living with a pack of wolves.

Jean George lives in a fascinating old shingled house in Chappaqua, New York. A live bass swims in a stone pool in her front hall. An injured robin perches in a bird cage on the kitchen counter. On the walls are Eskimo ceremonial masks and the baleen of a bowhead whale, the animal featured in her latest book. Her Alaskan sled dog, Qimmiq, whines on the porch to be taken for a walk. Qimmiq was a gift from a group of Eskimo children. His name means "dog" in their native language.

Mrs. George remembers how she found out she had won the Newbery Medal.

"I was sitting at the dining room table with Luke, my youngest son," she said, "when the phone rang. He could tell it was long distance from the way I was talking. Then I said, 'Oh, no!' and his face went blank. So I said, 'I've just won the Newbery Medal.' He jumped up and down because in sixth grade, a teacher had told his class, 'If you just read all the Newbery Medal books, you'll get a good education,' and he had!

"I thought I took it very calmly," she said, laughing. "Then the next morning I came downstairs, and the book I had been reading was in the refrigerator, and the cookies that I had offered a neighbor who dropped in were dog biscuits. I had wondered why she didn't eat them."

Authors have every right to be excited when they win an award like the Newbery Medal. It means that they are considered the best by those who know children's literature. It also means money in the bank. According to an editor at one major publishing firm, awards help sell books. Publishers are delighted to promote award-winning books more because they know that schools, libraries, and bookstores will want to purchase them. Winning an award can even help boost the sales of other books by the same author.

The Caldecott Medal is awarded each year to the artist of the most distinguished picture book for children published in the United States. Like the Newbery, it was begun by Frederic Melcher. It is also awarded by the Children's Services Division of the American Library Association. The award was named in honor of the great English illustrator, Randolph Caldecott. Caldecott grew up in the English countryside in the mid-1800s and loved the country all his life. He drew and modeled animals from the age of six, but his father discouraged his artistic talent. Instead, at the age of fifteen, Caldecott was put to work in a bank. He eventually moved to London and began drawing for newspapers and magazines. Now in his twenties, he knew he wanted an art career. He traveled to Germany and drew a book of sketches about the

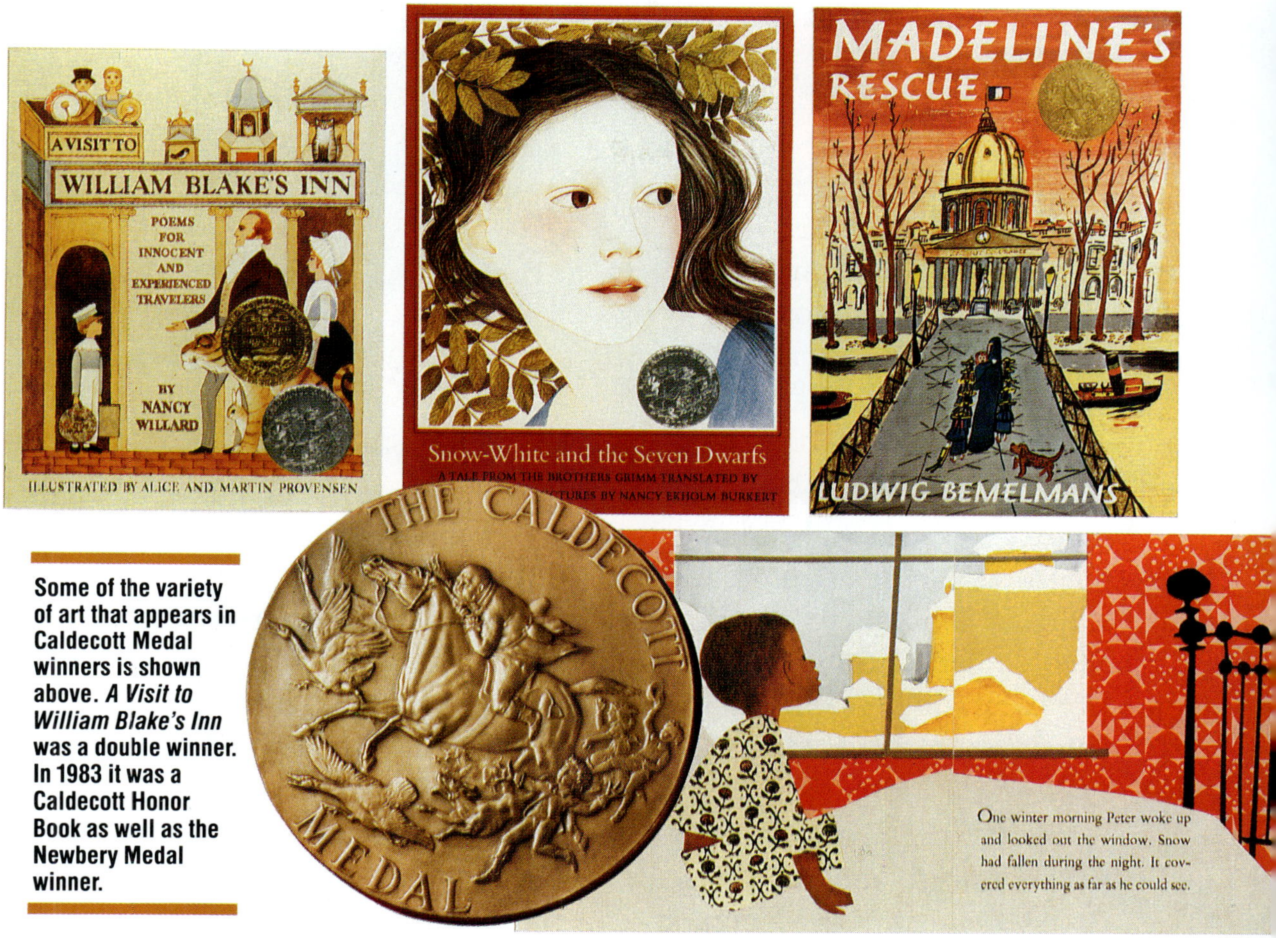

Some of the variety of art that appears in Caldecott Medal winners is shown above. *A Visit to William Blake's Inn* was a double winner. In 1983 it was a Caldecott Honor Book as well as the Newbery Medal winner.

Harz Mountains. Some of these were published in a London newspaper and others in an American magazine, *Harper's Monthly*. He was becoming famous. He drew illustrations for chapters of Washington Irving's *Sketch Book*, published under the title *Old Christmas*. Then, in 1877 he began the work for which he is best remembered, the Caldecott picture books. There were *John Gilpin's Ride* and *The House That Jack Built*, *The Queen of Hearts*, *Hey Diddle Diddle,* and many others. All of them showed his goodness, humor, and love of the outdoors. The pictures are full of children and old people, animals, birds, and huntsmen.

Many kinds of picture books have received the Caldecott

Maurice Sendak's *Where the Wild Things Are* was first published in 1963. It is still a favorite with preschoolers.

Medal. The first winner, in 1938, was called *Animals of the Bible*. In 1964 the winner was *Where the Wild Things Are* by Maurice Sendak. Other winners have included *Sam, Bangs and Moonshine* by Evaline Ness and *Sylvester and the Magic Pebble* by William Steig.

Many different kinds of prizes are given. The American Book Awards are designed to reward great authors and to interest young people in reading. The Coretta Scott King Award goes to authors and illustrators who "promote better understanding and appreciation of the culture and contribution of all peoples to the American dream." The Western Writers of America Spur Awards go to the best Western written for young people. The Laura Ingalls Wilder Award is given every five years to an author who has made a "lasting contribution to literature for children."

Many states, from California to Massachusetts, give their own awards. The winner of the Mark Twain Award is chosen by Missouri school children who read and then vote for their favorite. Many authors especially appreciate this kind of award because it comes from the children themselves. In 1978, the William Allen White Children's Book Award went to Jean Van Leeuwen for *The Great Christmas Kidnapping Caper*. This amusing tale concerns a group of clever mice and a disappearing Santa Claus in Macy's Department Store. The award is given in memory of the famous Emporia, Kansas, journalist. Kansas school children in grades four through eight vote from a master list chosen by the awards committee.

When she won, says Miss Van Leeuwen, "I was shocked, because I knew they had nominated a whole bunch of people. But it was nice, because it was from the kids. I had gotten a very funny letter from a boy, prior to finding out. He said, 'I'm going to vote for you for the award. I tell all the authors I'm going to vote for them, but this time I really mean it!'" In 1985, Jean Van Leeuwen was nominated twice for the Washington Irving Award, voted by the children of Westchester County, New York.

Why are there so many book awards? Do they serve a useful purpose? Frederic Melcher thought so. So do the librarians, publishers and others who sponsor them. These awards show us that wonderful new books are being written every day. They create excitement about books and about reading. They help us enjoy the greatest pastime of all, and that is a very good thing.

The Laura Ingalls Wilder Award, named for the author of the "Little House" books, is given to an author or illustrator for the body of his or her work. Beverly Cleary was the 1975 winner.

Thinking and Writing About the Selection

1. What is the Newbery Medal? What is the Caldecott Medal?
2. Why is it often difficult for a committee to choose which book should win an award?
3. Name an award-winning book that you have read. Do you agree that it deserved an award? Why or why not?
4. Design your own award to give to your favorite book or author. Tell what qualifications the award-winner should have, and why the book or author you chose fits the qualifications.

Applying the Key Skill
Summarize

1. Reread the third and fourth paragraphs in "The Best of the Books." What is the main idea of each paragraph? What are the most important details in each paragraph?
   Using your own words, combine the main ideas and important details into a summary of two or three sentences.
2. Reread the paragraphs that begin "Many different kinds of prizes are given." and "Many states, from California to Massachusetts, give their own awards."
   Write a summary that includes the most important information from both paragraphs.

LANGUAGE ACTIVITY

WORDS AND AWARDS FOR WINNERS

In "The Best of the Books," you learned about some of the prizes given for books for young people, such as the **Newbery Medal** and the **Caldecott Medal.** These are just two of the famous prizes or awards bestowed each year for distinguished achievement in many fields. Two other well-known prizes you have probably heard of are the Nobel prizes and the Pulitzer Prize. Like the Newbery and Caldecott medals, they are named for people.

Alfred Bernard Nobel (1833–1896), the inventor of dynamite, was a Swedish chemist and industrialist. In his will, Nobel left most of his money for a fund to reward those who do the most to benefit mankind, regardless of nationality. Winners of a **Nobel Prize** are chosen annually by the Swedish Royal Academy of Science in the fields of physics, chemistry, physiology or medicine, literature, peace, and (since 1969) economics.

A **Pulitzer Prize** is one of a group of prizes awarded each year for excellence in American journalism, literature, and music by the trustees of Columbia University. The prizes were established by the will of Joseph Pulitzer (1847–1911). Pulitzer, who was born in Hungary and emigrated to the United States when he was 17, was one of the most important newspaper publishers of his day.

In ancient times, heroes and scholars were crowned with a wreath made of laurel leaves. Although we no longer recognize winners in this simple way, the tradition is recognized symbolically by the use of laurel leaves in the design of many medals. It is also recognized in the word **laureate** ("one honored with a crown of laurel") for a winner.

OUT OF THE MAZE

ROBERT C. O'BRIEN

This story is an excerpt from the Newbery Award-winning book *Mrs. Frisby and the Rats of NIMH*. The book tells about two young rats, Nicodemus and Jenner, who lived near a market square in a large city. One evening they and dozens of other rats were in the square, feasting on a huge mound of food. Suddenly some people surrounded them and caught them in nets. They were dumped into cages and loaded into the back of a small white truck with the letters NIMH printed on its sides. As Nicodemus later found out, NIMH was a research laboratory, run by scientists who hoped to develop a strain of super-intelligent rats. The experiments proved more successful than the scientists knew.

But the rats never lost their longing to escape. It was Justin who found the way.

It was late one night that I heard Justin calling to me, speaking softly, around the wooden partition between our cages. Those partitions generally kept all of us from getting to know each other as well as we might have done, and discouraged us from talking much to one another; it was quite hard to hear around them, and of course you could never see the one you were talking to. I think Dr. Schultz had purposely had them made of some soundproof material. But you could hear, if you and your neighbor got in the corners of these cages nearest each other and spoke out through the wire front.

"Nicodemus?"

"Yes?" I went over to the corner.

"How long have we been here?"

"You mean since the beginning? Since we were caught?"

"Yes."

"I don't know. Several months—I think, but I have no way to keep track."

"I know. I don't either. Do you suppose it's winter outside now?"

"Probably. Or late fall."

"It will be cold."

"But not in here."

"No. But I'm going to try to get out."

"Get out? But how? Your cage is shut."

"Tomorrow we get injections, so they'll open it. When they do, I'm going to run."

"Run where?"

"I don't know. At least I'll get a look around. There might be some way out. What can I lose?"

"You might get hurt."

"I don't think so. Anyway *they* won't hurt me."

By *they* he meant Dr. Schultz and the other two. He added confidently, "All those shots, all the time they've spent—we're too valuable to them now. They'll be careful."

That idea had not occurred to me before, but when I thought about it, I decided he was right. Dr. Schultz, Julie, and George had spent most of their working hours with us for months; they could not afford to let any harm come to us. On the other hand, neither could they afford to allow any of us to escape.

Justin made his attempt the next morning. And it did cause a certain amount of excitement, but not at all what we expected. It was Julie who opened Justin's cage with a hypodermic in her hand. Justin was out with a mighty leap, hit the floor (about four feet down) with a thump, shook himself, and ran, disappearing from my view, heading toward the end of the room.

Julie seemed not at all alarmed. She calmly placed the needle on a shelf, then walked to the door of the laboratory and pushed a button on the wall near it. A red light came on over the door. She picked up a notebook and pencil from a desk near the door and followed Justin out of my sight.

A few minutes later Dr. Schultz and George entered. They opened the door cautiously and closed it behind them. "The outer door is shut, too," said Dr. Schultz. "Where is it?"

"Down here," said Julie, "inspecting the air ducts."

"Really? Which one is it?"

"It's one of the A group, just as you expected. Number nine. I'm keeping notes on it."

Obviously the red light was some kind of a warning signal, both outside the door and in—"laboratory animal at large." And not only had Dr. Schultz known one of us was out, but he had expected it to happen.

". . . a few days sooner than I thought," he was saying, "but so much the better. Do you realize . . ."

"Look," said Julie. "He's doing the whole baseboard—but he's studying the windows, too. See how he steps back to look up?"

"Of course," said Dr. Schultz. "And at the same time he's watching us, too. Can't you see?"

"He's pretty cool about it," said George.

"Can you imagine one of the lab rats doing that? Or even one of the controls? We've got to try to grasp what we have on our hands. The A group is now three hundred percent ahead of the control group in learning, and getting smarter all the time. B group is only twenty percent ahead. It's the new DNA that's doing it. We have a real breakthrough, and since it is DNA, we may very well have a true mutation, a brand new species of rat. But we've got to be careful with it. I think we should go ahead now with the next injection series."

"The steroids?"

(Whatever that meant.)

"Yes. It may slow them up a little—though I doubt it. But even if it does, it will be worth it, because I'm betting it will increase their life span by double at least. Maybe more. Maybe much more."

"Look," said Julie, "A-9 has found the mice."

George said, "See how he's studying them."

"Probably," said Dr. Schultz wryly, "he's wondering if they're ready for their steroid injections, too. As a matter of fact, I think the G group is. They're doing almost as well as the A group."

"Should I get the net and put him back?" George asked.

"I doubt that you'll need it," Dr. Schultz said, "now that he's learned he can't get out."

But they were underestimating Justin. He had learned no such thing.

Of course, Justin did not escape that day, nor even that year. When they—Julie—put on a glove and went to pick him up, he submitted meekly enough, and in a short time he was back in his cage.

Yet he had learned some things. He had, as Julie noticed, examined the air ducts—the openings along the wall through which warm air flowed in winter, cool air in summer—and he had studied the windows. Mainly he had learned that he could, occasionally at least, jump from his cage and wander around without incurring any anger or injury. All of this, eventually, was important. For it was Justin, along with Jenner, who finally figured out how to get away. I had a part in it, too. But all that came later.

I won't go into details about the rest of our training except for one part of it that was the most useful of all. But in general, during the months that followed, two things were happening:

First, we were learning more than any rats ever had before, and were becoming more intelligent than any rats had ever been.

The second thing could be considered, from some points of view, even more important—and certainly more astonishing—than the first. Dr. Schultz (you will recall) had said that the new series of injections might increase our life span by double or more. Yet even he was not prepared for what happened. Perhaps it was the odd combination of both types of injections—I don't know, and neither did he. But the result was that, as far as he could detect, in the A group the aging process seemed to stop almost completely.

For example—during the years we were in the laboratory, most of the rats in the control group grew old and sickly, and finally died; so did those in B group, for though they were getting injections, too, the formula was not the same as ours. But among the twenty of us in A group, no one could see any signs that we were growing older at all. Apparently (though we seldom saw them) the same thing was happening with the

G group, the mice who were getting the same injections we were.

Dr. Schultz was greatly excited about this. "The short life span has always been a prime limiting factor in education," he told George and Julie. "If we can double it, and speed up the learning process at the same time, the possibilities are enormous." Double it! Even now, years later, years after the injections, we seem scarcely any older than we were then.

We could not detect either of these things ourselves. That is, we didn't feel any different, and since we had no contact with the other groups, we had no basis for comparison. All we had to go by was what Dr. Schultz said. He and the others were preparing a research paper about us—to be published in some scientific journal—so each morning he dictated the results of the previous day's tests into a tape recorder. We heard all of it, though there was a lot of technical stuff we couldn't understand. Until the paper was published the whole experiment was to be kept secret.

The one important phase of training began one day after weeks of really hard work at the "shape recognition" that I mentioned before. But this was different. For the first time they used sounds along with the shapes, and pictures, real pictures we could recognize. For example, one of the first and simplest of these exercises was a picture, a clear photograph, of a rat. I suppose they felt sure we would know what that was. This picture was shown on a screen, with a light behind it. Then, after I had looked at the picture and recognized it, a shape flashed on the screen under it—a sort of half circle and two straight lines, not like anything I had seen before. Then the voice began:

"Are."

"Are."

"Are."

It was Julie's voice, speaking very clearly, but it had a tinny sound—it was a record. After repeating "are" a dozen times or so, that particular shape disappeared and another one came on the screen, still under the picture of the rat. It was a triangle, with legs on it. And Julie's voice began again:

"Aiee."

"Aiee."

"Aiee."

When that shape disappeared a third one came on the screen. This one was a cross. Julie's voice said:

"Tea."

"Tea."

"Tea."

Then all three shapes appeared at once, and the record said:

"Are."

"Aiee."

"Tea."

"Rat."

You will already have recognized what was going on: they were teaching us to read. The symbols under the picture were the letters R-A-T. But the idea did not become clear to any of us for quite a long time. Because, of course, we didn't know what reading *was*.

Oh, we learned to recognize the shapes easily enough, and when I saw the rat picture I knew straight away what symbols would appear beneath it. In the same way, when the picture showed a cat, I knew the same shapes would appear, except the first

CAT

one would be a half-circle, and Julie's voice would repeat: "See-see-see." I even learned that when the photograph showed not one but several rats, a fourth shape would appear under it—a snaky line—and the sound with that one was "ess-ess-ess." But as to what all this was *for*, none of us had any inkling.

It was Jenner who finally figured it out. By this time we had developed a sort of system of communication, a simple enough thing, just passing spoken messages from one cage to the next, like passing notes in school. Justin, who was still next to me, called to me one day, "Message for Nicodemus from Jenner. He says important."

"All right," I said, "what's the message?"

"Look at the shapes on the wall next to the door. He says to look carefully."

My cage, like Jenner's and those of the rest of A group, was close enough to the door so I could see what he meant. Near the doorway there was a large, square piece of white cardboard fastened to the wall—a sign. It was covered with an assortment of black markings to which I had never paid any attention (though they had been there ever since we arrived).

Now, for the first time, I looked at them carefully, and I grasped what Jenner had discovered.

The top line of black marks on the wall were instantly familiar: R-A-T-S; as soon as I saw them I thought of the picture that went with them; and as soon as I did that I was, for the first time, reading. Because, of course, that's what reading is: using symbols to suggest a picture or an idea. From that time on it gradually became clear to me what all these lessons were for, and once I understood the idea, I was eager to learn more. I could scarcely wait for the next lesson, and the next. The whole concept of reading was, to me at least, fascinating. I remember how proud I was when, months later, I was able to read and understand that whole sign. I read it hundreds of times, and I'll never forget it:

RATS MAY NOT BE REMOVED FROM THE
LABORATORY WITHOUT WRITTEN PERMISSION.

And at the bottom, in smaller letters, the word NIMH.

But then a puzzling thing came up, a thing we're still not sure about even now. Apparently Dr. Schultz, who was running the lessons, did not realize how well they were succeeding. He continued the training, with new words and new pictures every day; but the fact is, once we had grasped the idea and learned the different sounds each letter stood for, we leaped way ahead of him. I remember well, during one of the lessons, looking at a picture of a tree. Under it the letters flashed on: T-R-E-E. But in the photograph, though the tree was in the foreground, there was a building in the background, and a sign near it. I scarcely glanced at T-R-E-E, but concentrated instead on reading the sign. It said:

NIMH. PRIVATE PARKING BY PERMIT ONLY.
RESERVED FOR DOCTORS AND STAFF.
NO VISITOR PARKING.

The building behind it, tall and white, looked very much like the building we were in.

I'm sure Dr. Schultz had plans for testing our reading ability. I could even guess, from the words he was teaching us, what the tests were going to be like. For example, he taught us "left," "right," "door," "food," "open," and so on. It was not hard to imagine the test: I would be placed in one chamber, my food in another. There would be two doors, and a sign saying: "For food, open door at right." Or something like that. Then if I—if all of us—moved unerringly toward the proper door, he would know we understood the sign.

As I said, I'm sure he planned to do this, but apparently he did not think we were ready for it yet. I think maybe he was even a little afraid to try it; because if he did it too soon, or if for any other reason it did not work, his experiment would be a failure. He wanted to be sure, and his caution was his undoing.

Justin announced one evening around the partition, "I'm going to get out of my cage tonight and wander around a bit."

"How can you? It's locked."

"Yes. But did you notice, along the bottom edge there's a printed strip?"

I had not noticed it. I should perhaps explain that when Dr. Schultz and the others opened our cages we could never quite see how they did it; they manipulated something under the plastic floor, something we couldn't see.

"What does it say?"

"I've been trying to read it the last three times they brought me back from training. It's very small print. But I think I've finally made it out. It says: To release door, pull knob forward and slide right."

"Knob?"

"Under the floor, about an inch back, there's a metal thing just in front of the shelf. I think that's the knob, and I think I can reach it through the wire. Anyway, I'm going to try."

"Now?"

"Not until they close up."

"Closing up" was a ritual Dr. Schultz, George, and Julie went through each night. For about an hour they sat at their desks, wrote notes in books, filed papers in cabinets, and finally locked the cabinets. Then they checked all the cages, dimmed the lights, locked the doors and went home, leaving us alone in the laboratory.

About half an hour after they left that night, Justin said, "I'm going to try now." I heard a scuffling noise, a click and scrape of metal, and in a matter of seconds I saw his door swing open. It was as simple as that—when you could read.

"Wait," I said.

"What's the matter?"

"If you jump down, you won't be able to get back in. Then they'll know."

"I thought of that. I'm not going to jump down. I'm going to climb up the outside of the cage. It's easy. I've climbed up the inside a thousand times. Above these cages there's another shelf, and it's empty. I'm going to walk along there and see what I can see. I think there's a way to climb to the floor and up again."

"Why don't I go with you?" My door would open the same way as his.

"Better not this time, don't you think? If something goes wrong and I can't get back, they'll say: It's just A-9 again. But if two of us are found outside, they'll take it seriously. They might put new locks on the cages."

He was right, and you can see that already we both had the same idea in mind: that this might be the first step toward escape for all of us.

And so it was. By teaching us how to read, they had taught us how to get away.

Justin climbed easily up the open door of his cage and vanished over the top with a flick of his tail. He came back an hour later, greatly excited and full of information. Yet it was typical of Justin that even excited as he was, he stayed calm, he thought clearly. He climbed down the front of my cage rather than his own, and spoke softly; we both assumed that by now the other rats were asleep.

"Nicodemus? Come on out. I'll show you how." He directed me as I reached through the wire bars of the door and felt beneath it. I found the small metal knob, slid it forward and sideward, and felt the door swing loose against my shoulder. I followed him up the side of the cage to the shelf above. There we stopped. It was the first time I had met Justin face to face.

He said, "It's better talking here than around that partition."

"Yes. Did you get down?"

"Yes."

"How did you get back up?"

"At the end of this shelf there's a big cabinet—they keep the mouse cages in it. It has wire mesh doors. You can climb up and down them like a ladder."

"Of course," I said. "I remember now." I had seen that cabinet many times when my cage was carried past it. For some reason—perhaps because they were smaller—the mice were kept in the cages-within-a-cage.

Justin said, "Nicodemus, I think I've found the way to get out."

"You have! How?"

"At each end of the room there's an opening in the baseboard at the bottom of the wall. Air blows in through one of them and out the other. Each one has a metal grid covering it, and on the grid there's a sign that says: Lift to adjust air flow. I lifted one of them; it hangs on hinges, like a trapdoor. Behind it there is a thing like a metal window—when you slide it wide open, more air blows in.

"But the main thing is, it's easily big enough to walk through and get out."

"But what's on the other side? Where does it lead?"

"On the other side there's a duct, a thing like a square metal pipe built right into the wall. I walked along it, not very far, but I can figure out where it must go. There's bound to be a duct like it leading to every room in the building, and they must all branch off one main central pipe—and that one has to lead, somewhere, to the outside. Because that's where our air comes from. That's why they never open the windows. I don't think those windows can open."

He was right, of course. The building had central air conditioning; what we had to do was find the main air shaft and explore it. There would have to be an intake at one end and an outlet at the other. But that was easier said than done, and before it was done there were questions to be answered. What about the rest of the rats? There were twenty of us in the laboratory, and we had to let the others know.

So, one by one, we woke them and showed them how to open their cages. It was an odd assembly that gathered that night, under the dimmed lights in the echoing laboratory, on the shelf where Justin and I had talked. We all knew each other in a way, from the passing of messages over the preceding months; yet except for Jenner and me, none of us had ever really met. We were strangers—though, as you can imagine, it did not take long to develop a feeling of comradeship, for we twenty were alone in a strange world. Just how alone and how strange none of us really understood at first; yet in a way we sensed it from the beginning. The group looked to me as leader, probably because it was Justin and I who first set them free, and because Justin was obviously younger than I.

We did not attempt to leave that night, but went together and looked at the metal grid Justin had discovered, and made plans for exploring the air ducts. Jenner was astute at that sort of thing; he could foresee problems.

"With a vent like this leading to every room," he said, "it will be easy to get lost. When we explore, we're going to need some way of finding our way back here."

"Why should we come back?" someone asked.

"Because it may take more than one night to find the way out. If it does, whoever is doing the exploring must be back in his cage by morning. Otherwise Dr. Schultz will find out."

Jenner was right. It took us about a week. What we did, after some more discussion, was to find some equipment: first, a large spool of thread in one of the cabinets where some of us had seen Julie place it one day. Second, a screwdriver that was kept on a shelf near the electric equipment—because, as Jenner pointed out, there would probably be a screen over the end of the airshaft to keep out debris, and we might have to pry it loose. What we really needed was a light, for the ducts, at night, were completely dark. But there

was none to be had, not even a box of matches. The thread and the screwdriver we hid in the duct. We could only hope they would not be missed, or that if they were, we wouldn't be suspected.

Justin and two others (one was named Arthur) were chosen as the exploration party. They had a terrible time at first: Here was a maze to end all mazes; and in the dark they quickly lost their sense of direction. Still they kept at it, night after night, exploring the network of shafts that laced like a cubical spiderweb through the walls and ceilings of the buildings. They would tie the end of their thread to the grid in our laboratory and unroll it from the spool as they went. Time and time again they reached the end of the thread and had to come back.

"It just isn't long enough," Justin would complain. "Every time I come to the end, I think: if I could just go ten feet farther . . ."

And finally, that's what he did. On the seventh night, just as the thread ran out, he and the other two reached a shaft that was wider than any they had found before, and it seemed, as they walked along it, to be slanting gently upward. But the spool was empty.

"You wait here," Justin said to the others. "I'm going just a little way farther. Hang on to the spool, and if I call, call back." (They had tied the end of the thread around the spool so they would not lose it in the dark.)

Justin had a hunch. The air coming through the shaft had a fresher smell where they were, and seemed to be blowing harder than in the other shafts. Up ahead he thought he could hear the whir of a machine running quietly and there was a faint vibration in the metal under his feet. He went on. The shaft turned upward at a sharp angle—and then, straight ahead, he saw it: a patch of lighter-colored darkness than the pitch black around him, and in the middle of it, three stars twinkling. It was the open sky. Across the opening there was, as Jenner had predicted, a coarse screen of heavy wire.

He ran toward it for a few seconds longer, and then stopped. The sound of the machine had grown suddenly louder, changing from a whir to a roar. It had, obviously, shifted speed; an automatic switch somewhere in the building had turned it from low to high, and the air blowing past Justin came on so hard it made him gasp. He braced his feet against the metal and held on. In a minute, as suddenly as it had roared, the machine returned to a whisper. He looked around and realized he was lucky to have stopped; by the dim light from the sky he could see that he had reached a point where perhaps two dozen air shafts came together like branches into the trunk of a tree. If he had gone a few steps farther he would never have been able to distinguish which shaft was his. He turned in his tracks, and in a few minutes he rejoined his friends.

We had a meeting that night, and Justin told all of us what he had found. He had left the thread, anchored by the screwdriver, to guide us out. Some were for leaving immediately, but it was late, and Jenner and I argued against it. We did not know how long it would take us to break through the screen at the end. If it should take more than an hour or two, daylight would be upon us. We would then be unable to risk returning to the laboratory, and would have to spend the day in the shaft—or try to get away by broad daylight.

Dr. Schultz might even figure out how we had gone and trap us in the air shaft.

Finally, reluctantly, everyone agreed to spend one more day in the laboratory and leave early the next night. But it was a hard decision, with freedom so near and everyone thinking as I did: "Suppose . . ." Suppose Dr. Schultz grew suspicious and put locks on our cages? Suppose someone found our thread and pulled it out? (This was unlikely—the near end, tied to the spool, was six feet up the shaft, well hidden.) Just the same, we were uneasy.

Then, just as we were ending our meeting, a new complication arose. We had been standing in a rough circle on the floor of the laboratory, just outside the two screen doors that enclosed the mice cages. Now, from inside the cabinet, came a voice:

"Nicodemus." It was a clear but plaintive call, the voice of a mouse. We had almost forgotten the mice were there, and I was startled to hear that one of them knew my name. We all grew quiet.

"Who's calling me?" I asked.

"My name is Jonathan," said the voice. "We have been listening to your talk about going out. We would like to go, too, but we cannot open our cages."

As you can imagine, this caused a certain consternation, coming at the last minute. None of us knew much about the mice, except what we had heard Dr. Schultz dictate into his tape recorder. From that, we had learned only that they had been getting the same injections we were getting, and that the treatment had worked about as well on them as on us. They were a sort of side experiment, without a control group.

Justin was studying the cabinet.

"Why not?" he said. "If we can get the doors open."

Someone muttered, "They'll slow us down."

"No," said the mouse Jonathan. "We will not. Only open our cages when you go, and we will make our own way. We won't even stay with you, if you prefer."

"How many are you?" I asked.

"Only eight. And the cabinet doors are easy to open. There's just a simple hook, half way up."

But Justin and Arthur had already figured that out. They climbed up the screen, unhooked the hook, and the doors swung open.

"The cages open the same way as yours," said another mouse, "but we can't reach far enough to unlatch them."

"All right," I said. "Tomorrow night, as soon as Dr. Schultz and the others leave, we'll open your cages, and you can follow the thread with us to get out. After that you're on your own."

"Agreed," said Jonathan, "and thank you."

"And now," I said, "we should all get back to the cages. Justin, please hook the doors again."

The next day was terrible. I kept expecting to hear Dr. Schultz say, "Who took my screwdriver?" And then to hear Julie add, "My thread is missing, too." That could have happened and set them to thinking—but it didn't, and that night, an hour after Julie, George, and Dr. Schultz left the laboratory, we were out of our cages and gathered, the whole group of us, before the mouse cabinet. Justin opened its doors, unlatched their cages, and the mice came out. They looked very small and frightened, but one strode bravely forward.

"You are Nicodemus?" he said to me. "I'm Jonathan. Thank you for taking us out with you."

"We're not out yet," I said, "but you're welcome."

We had no time for chatting. The light coming in the windows was turning gray; in less than an hour it would be dark, and we would need light to figure out how to open the screen at the end of the shaft.

We went to the opening in the baseboard.

"Justin," I said, "take the lead. Roll up the thread as you go. I'll bring up in the rear. No noise. There's sure to be somebody awake somewhere in the building. We don't want them to hear us." I did not want to leave the thread where it might be found: the more I thought about it, the more I felt sure Dr. Schultz would try to track us down, for quite a few reasons.

Justin lifted the grid, pushed open the sliding panel, and one by one we went through. As I watched the others go ahead of me, I noticed for the first time that one of the mice was white. Then I went in myself, closing the grid behind me and pushing the panel half shut again, its normal position.

With Justin leading the way, we moved through the dark passage quickly and easily. In only fifteen or twenty minutes we had reached the end of the thread; then, as Justin had told us it would, the shaft widened; we could hear the whir of the machine ahead, and almost immediately we saw a square of gray daylight. We had reached the end of the shaft, and there a terrible thing happened.

Justin—you will recall—had told us that the machine, the pump that pulled air through the shaft, had switched from low speed to high when he had first explored through there. So we were forewarned. The trouble was, the forewarning was no use at all, not so far as the mice were concerned.

We were approaching the lighted square of the opening when the roar began. The blast of air came like a sudden whistling gale; it took my breath and flattened my ears against my head, and I closed my eyes instinctively. I was still in the rear, and when I opened my eyes again I saw one of the mice sliding past me, clawing uselessly with his small nails at the smooth metal beneath him. Another followed him, and still another, as one by one they were blown backward into the dark maze of tunnels we had just left. I braced myself in the corner of the shaft and grabbed at one as he slid by. It was the white mouse. I caught him by one leg, pulled him around behind me and held on. Another blew face-on into the rat ahead of me and stopped there—it was Jonathan, who had been near the lead. But the rest were lost, six in all. They were simply too light; they blew away like dead leaves, and we never saw them again.

In another minute the roar stopped, the rush of air slowed from a gale to a breeze, and we were able to go forward again.

I said to the white mouse, "You'd better hold on to me. That might happen again."

He looked at me in dismay. "But what about the others? Six are lost! I've got to go back and look for them."

Jonathan quickly joined him, "I'll go with you."

"No," I said. "That would be useless and foolish. You have no idea which shaft they were blown into, nor even if they all went the same way. And if you should find them—how would you find your way out again? And suppose the wind comes again? Then there would be eight lost instead of six."

The wind did come again, half a dozen times more, while we worked with the screwdriver to pry open the screen. Each time we had to stop work and hang on. The two mice clung to the screen itself; some of us braced ourselves behind them, in case they should slip. And Justin, taking the thread with him as a guideline, went back to search for the other six. He explored shaft after shaft to the end of the spool, calling softly as he went—but it was futile. To this day we don't know what became of those six mice. They may have found their way out eventually, or they may have died in there. We left an opening in the screen for them, just in case.

The screen. It was heavy wire, with holes about the size of an acorn, and it was set in a steel frame. We pried and hammered at it with the screwdriver, but we could not move it. It was fastened on the outside—we couldn't see how. Finally the white mouse had an idea.

"Push the screwdriver through the wire near the bottom," he said, "and pry up." We did, and the wire bent a fraction of an inch. We did it again, prying down, then left, then right. The hole in the wire grew slowly bigger, until the white mouse said, "I think that's enough." He climbed to the small opening and by squirming and twisting, he got through. Jonathan followed him; they both fell out of sight, but in a minute Jonathan's head came back in view on the outside.

"It's a sliding bolt," he said. "We're working on it." Inside we could hear the faint rasping as the two mice tugged on the bolt handle, working it back. Then the crack at the base of the screen widened; we pushed it open, and we were standing on the roof of NIMH, free.

CONCLUDING LEVEL 12, UNIT 1

Voices

No matter what language we speak, we can use it to voice our thoughts and feelings, to reach out to others through communication. In *Voices*, you read about people who learned to speak another language. You also learned about words that came into English from other languages. You read about people who learned to use writing of all kinds as an extension of their voices. As you develop your reading and writing skills, you will discover that you, too, have a voice to share.

Thinking and Writing About *Voices*

1. Anna and Max of "Buying Pencils" moved from Germany to France. What words discussed in "The Melting Pot" might they recognize from their native language? What words might they understand once they learn French?
2. What would Grandmother from "Grandmother's Iceberg" think of the classes Mukasa was taking and those he would take in the future? Explain your answer.
3. Which section of "Letters Make Things Happen" might have been helpful to Katrin of "The Writing Lessons"? Why?
4. What advice do you think Leigh Botts of "Dear Mr. Henshaw" might give to students who want to become writers?
5. *Dear Mr. Henshaw* won the Newbery Award in 1984. Why do you think the committee chose it? What makes it a winner?
6. Sometimes we meet a story character who seems to voice the way we ourselves feel about something. We may say, "I've felt that way before," or "That's just the way I would have said it." Write a paragraph about a character in this unit or in a book you have read that made you feel this way.

Introducing Level 12

VENTURES

Nought venture, nought have.
(Nothing ventured, nothing gained.)

John Heywood, Proverbs

UNIT

2

The stories in this unit will transport you to a time of bold adventures—the Middle Ages. You will read about the knights who ventured forth in their shining armor. You will meet some of the most famous heroes of the day, including El Cid and William the Conqueror of history, and Robin Hood and Saint George of legend. What qualities might these medieval adventurers share?

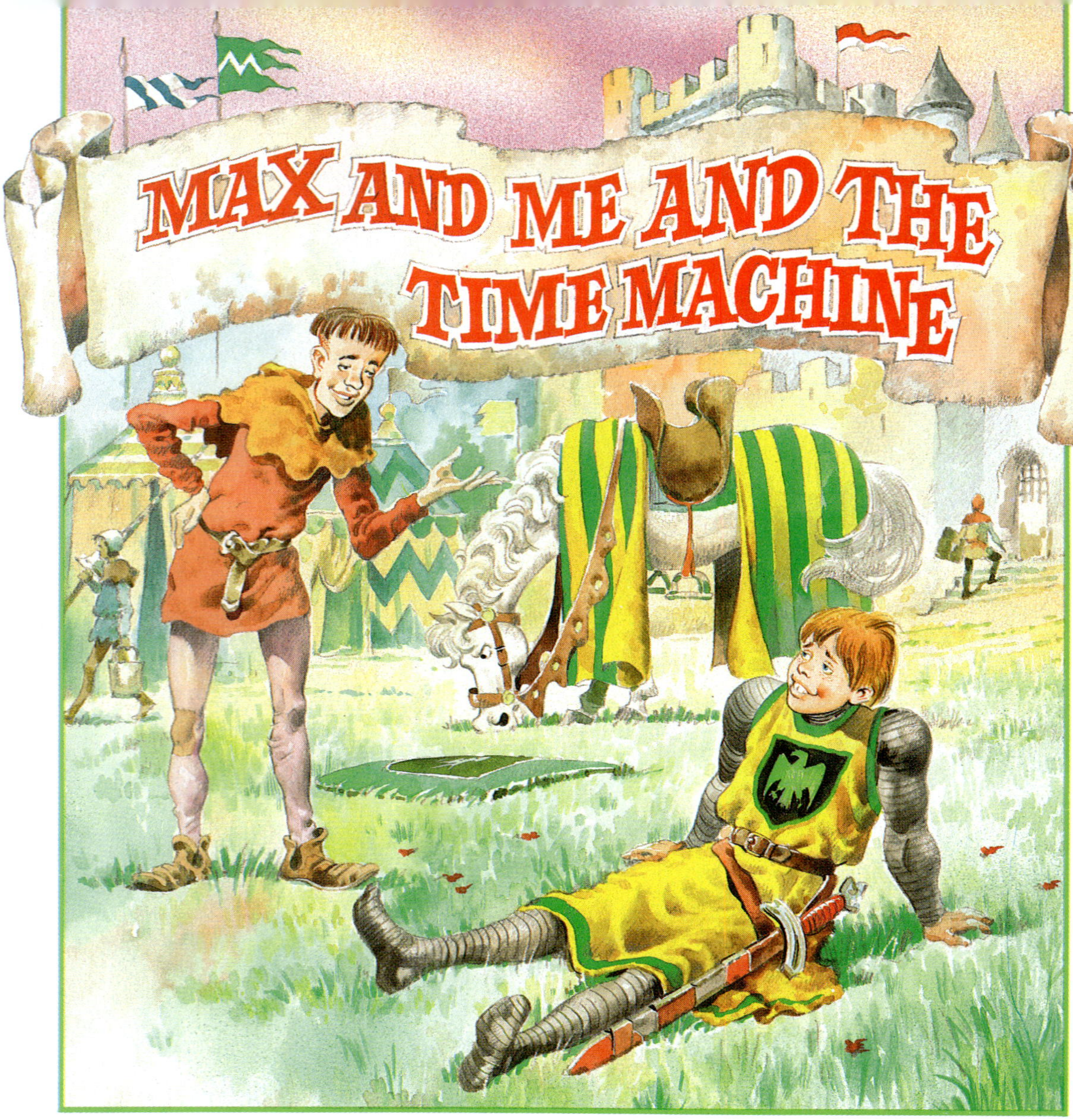

GERY GREER AND BOB RUDDICK

It took a few minutes for Steve to get his bearings and realize that the time machine he'd bought at a garage sale for $2.50 had really worked. He and his friend Max are back in the Middle Ages, but not as themselves. Steve has been transported into the body of Sir Robert Marshall, an eighteen-year-old knight. He even has a loyal squire, Niles. The problem is that while Steve occupies Sir Robert's body, he doesn't have any of the knight's skills. And where is Max?

I was on a grassy field, surrounded by a makeshift camp of large, brightly colored tents, each decorated with flags and pennants that fluttered in the breeze. Looming a short distance to the right were the gray stone walls and turrets of a medieval castle. And by my side stood a sleek white horse draped with yards and yards of green cloth trimmed in gold.

Here and there men and boys scurried, all dressed like Niles, in tunics and tights. Max could be anywhere, even miles from here.

I realized that if I were ever going to find him, I'd need a lot more information. And as Niles helped me to my feet, I thought of a plan to get it.

I shook my head as if I were still dazed. "Niles," I said, hoping I looked lost and confused, "I can't seem to get my bearings. I'm afraid that falling off my horse has made me lose my memory. Maybe if you'd tell me where we are and what we're doing here, it will all come back to me."

It worked. Niles looked up at me anxiously, with loyal devotion written all over his face. "Why, Sir Robert, we are at the Great Hampshire Tournament, where we have camped these past three days in thy tent." He gestured to the yellow-gold tent with green banners that stood behind us. "We came at the invitation of Richard Lorraine, Earl of Hampshire, who heard tales of thy great strength and skill at jousting and would try thee against his own champion. 'Tis the last day of the tourney, and thou art undefeated as usual, sire. Eighteen knights have fallen already before thy lance. There remaineth only the joust with Sir Bevis, a minor feat for someone with thy mighty talents."

I nodded cautiously. "I see. And just when is this minor jousting match supposed to take place?"

"In but a few moments, Sir Robert," he said, busily dusting off my tunic and straightening my belt. "Then the tourney will be over, and thou wilt be the champion. The people await this last joust most eagerly."

"Hmmmm. And you think I can handle Sir Bevis, do you?"

Niles laughed merrily. "Oh, Sir Robert, thou art jesting, of course. 'Twill be a sad day for English knighthood when thou, the Green Falcon, canst not best the likes of Sir Bevis."

Bingo! Jackpot! Things were looking good. Not only was I in the Middle Ages, but I was in the body of a famous knight and was actually going to be in a jousting match on the field of honor! And it was my kind of contest—me against some harmless, lily-livered, mealy-mouthed twerp.

The only problem was that it all sounded a bit beneath my talents. Why then, I wondered, were the people so eager to see this particular match? I decided to fish for a few details.

"Tell me, Niles," I said, cracking my knuckles and flexing my muscles, "who is this Bevis turkey anyway?"

"Why, Sir Bevis Thorkell," replied Niles cheerfully, "the Earl's champion and a knight known throughout all England as the Hampshire Mauler."

"The Hampshire Mauler?" I didn't like the sound of that.

"Aye, Sir Robert, and a black-hearted varlet he is. Canst thou truly remember nothing? Dost thou not recall his vow to smash thy skull and feed thy guts to the castle dogs, the saucy fellow?"

Saucy fellow? This was his idea of a saucy fellow? Something began to tell me I might not be cut out for the field of honor after all.

Niles continued gleefully. "Ho, ho! But I did put Sir Bevis in his place. Not two hours ago I met the knave within the castle walls. 'Is thy master ready to meet his doom?' he did ask me. 'Best thou lookest to thine own health,' I replied. 'Sir Robert will this very afternoon whack thee from thy horse, pommel and pound thee, and smite thee to smithereens.'"

"Gee," I said, laughing nervously. "I hope he didn't take that the wrong way."

Niles nodded happily. "That blow to thy head hath not robbed thee of thy sense of humor, Sir Robert." He chuckled contentedly to himself.

I found myself wondering if Sir Bevis and I could talk this thing over. I mean, I didn't want to be a spoil-sport or anything, but let's face it, I don't perform well under pressure.

"Niles," I said, looking for an out, "give it to me straight. What has Sir Bevis got against me?"

"'Tis no secret, sire. Sir Bevis is sore jealous that thou art a knight and are but eighteen years of age. He himself was not knighted until his twenty-first year, as is the common custom. And 'tis well known that the Earl hath taken a liking to thee during the tournament. Mayhap Sir Bevis feareth that thou wilt replace him as the Earl's champion."

Niles blushed slightly. "And, of course, there is the matter of Lady Elizabeth."

"Oh?" I asked suspiciously. "And what would that be?"

Niles's blush deepened and he looked away, embarrassed. "Ah, well, since thou has lost thy memory, Sir

Robert, I suppose I must admit that even I have noticed the glances that have passed between thyself and the Earl's fair daughter. And since Sir Bevis hopeth to make the Lady his wife, this hath only angered him the more."

"Okay," I said, shifting my weight uneasily. "Let me get this straight. Sir Bevis is a little upset because he thinks I'm trying to steal his reputation, his job, and his girl. Right?"

"Aye. And thou art just the man to do it."

Suddenly, there was a loud blast of trumpets from somewhere nearby.

"Make haste, sire!" gasped Niles. "'Tis time!"

Before I could say another word, he clapped the iron helmet back onto my head. A page ran out of a nearby tent, carrying some portable stairs which he plunked down next to the white stallion. I was still confused and stunned as Niles hustled me up the stairs and onto the horse, thrusting a shield into my left hand and a ten-foot-long lance into my right.

With a hearty "Go to, Sir Robert!" he slapped the horse's backside, and off we trotted in the direction of the trumpets.

"Where is Max now that I need him?" I groaned.

"Right here," said a deep voice from under me. "And you have my full support!"

It was Max! He was my horse!

"I heard everything Niles said," he continued with a whinny, "and I think it's safe to say that we're about to experience a little Action, Adventure, and Excitement."

With that, Max snorted noisily and pranced out onto the field of honor, proudly tossing his mane and humming the Notre Dame fight song, while I struggled wildly to hold my lance upright and stay in the saddle.

Lining one side of the large open field were long wooden bleachers crowded with cheering spectators. Women waved their scarves and handkerchiefs. Men stood and shouted. From the tops of tall poles, colored banners streamed and flapped in the breeze. On a raised platform behind the bleachers, twenty heralds snapped to attention, pressed golden trumpets to their lips, and blared out a rousing call to arms.

Little League was never like this.

Max tossed his head toward a lone figure mounted on a black steed at the opposite end of the field. "That must be Sir Bevis," he neighed.

It was the Hampshire Mauler, all right, and he looked ready to maul anything that got in his way. His chain mail, shield, sword, and helmet were coal black; and a blood-red tunic dripped from his massive shoulders. Even from a distance, he looked like a killer. I swallowed hard.

"Uh, look, Max," I stammered, "don't you think we should make a break for it before somebody around here gets hurt?"

"Relax," said Max, pawing the dirt eagerly. "I happen to know for a fact that jousting is more or less the safest of all the deadly dangerous sports in medieval England."

"Terrific," I said. "How silly of me to worry. I mean, what do I care about a ten-foot-long lance in the gut?"

Before Max could answer, the heralds blasted forth with another jarring fanfare. A hush fell over the crowd, and almost as a single body, they leaned forward in their seats. My heart took a nose dive down into where my tennis shoes should have been.

"Now what?" I hissed.

"No problem," whispered Max. "All you have to do is watch Sir Bevis and do whatever he does."

"Oh, sure," I said. "That's just great. And what if he runs me through with his lance?"

"In that case," said Max, "try not to land on your head. It'll only make matters worse."

I would have let him have it with my spurs, but I didn't have time. I caught some movement out of the corner of my eye, and I looked down the long field through the slits in my helmet. In the center were two narrow lanes separated by a low fence. And at the far end was Sir Bevis—evil, threatening, poised for the kill.

He lowered his lance until it was level and aimed steadily across the field straight at my heart.

What else could I do? I lowered my lance. It wobbled around like crazy.

Abruptly, the trumpets stopped, leaving the shock of silence. In that same instant, Sir Bevis spurred his black stallion and charged forward, his red tunic flapping and the tip of his lance glinting in the sun.

Without a word, Max too leaped forward. We were on a collision course with the Hampshire Mauler.

The muffled thunder of hoofbeats filled the air. Hypnotized, I locked my eyes on the black figure bearing down on us. A cold fear gripped my spine, and I tried desperately to steady my lance.

He was almost upon us—so close that I thought I glimpsed his wild eyes gleaming evilly behind the slits in his black helmet. I braced myself for a terrible blow.

Suddenly, just before I was due to swallow the tip of Sir Bevis's lance, Max opened his mouth, curled back his lips, and at the top of his lungs bellowed: "GERONIMO-O-O-O-O-O-O-O-O-O-O-O-O-O-O!!!!!

Sir Bevis's horse dug all four hooves into the ground and skidded to an abrupt halt.

Sir Bevis catapulted out of the saddle, sailed through the air, and fell with a noisy CLANK! onto the field. He was knocked out cold.

Child's play, I thought to myself as Max slowed to a stop and turned around. *This jousting business is mere child's play*.

The crowd went wild. And so they should. It was a brilliant performance.

Of course, from the bleachers, no one heard Max yell or saw that I had never laid a lance on Sir Bevis. All they knew was that on the very first pass, the Hampshire Mauler had been easily unhorsed and lay in a dazed heap on the field. And I was not about to spoil their fun by setting the record straight.

After all, it was the least I could do for Sir Robert while I was occupying his body. Being a hero, I mean. Keeping up the old boy's image in his absence. I'd do the same for anyone.

Max must have felt the same way, because he took plenty of time prancing past the stands, swishing his tail all over the place and snorting fiercely like some kind of wild Arabian stallion.

In the center of the stands was a special section covered with a fringed canopy. As we got closer, I could make out a stern-looking man with a rugged, sun-weathered face sitting under the canopy in a thronelike chair. Beside him was a strikingly pretty girl of about sixteen. She was blushing up a storm and had her eyes cast down at her lap, where she was twisting a long white scarf.

Max whispered up at me out of the corner of his mouth. "That man is probably our host, the Earl of Hampshire. And you're in luck, Steve. That girl must be Lady Elizabeth."

"What do you mean, I'm in luck?" I hissed back.

Max didn't answer. Instead, he pulled up in front of the fringed box and, without any warning, bent his front legs and *bowed* before the Earl! The spectators gasped and applauded even more loudly. From everywhere came cries of "Sir Robert! Sir Robert! The Green Falcon!" Flowers flew through the air and fell at our feet. I guess they'd never seen a kneeling horse before.

Unfortunately, I had never been on a kneeling horse before. I was caught by surprise and was almost pitched out of the saddle. My lance swung down into the box, nearly nicking the Earl on the nose. He sat back cross-eyed with a startled grunt.

While I struggled to recover, Lady Elizabeth sprang forward and, with lightning speed, tied her white scarf onto the tip of my lance before I could regain my balance and pull it away. Then she fell back into her seat, smiling at me shyly and fluttering her eyelashes. I was glad I was still inside my helmet.

As Max stood up again, Niles suddenly appeared at our side, leading Sir Bevis's black stallion and carrying his black sword. I had read enough about the Middle Ages to know that when a knight wins a jousting match, he wins the other knight's armor and horse, although the loser usually buys back the loot. I guessed that Niles had taken Sir Bevis's sword and horse as a sort of token, since it wouldn't have been polite to strip him of his full armor while he was out cold on the field.

Niles put the sword down and untied Lady Elizabeth's scarf from my lance.

"Ahhhh," he exclaimed in a low voice, "'twas a gesture of true love." Then, while my hands were full and I couldn't defend myself, he reached up and tucked the scarf inside my tunic—next to my heart. Lady Elizabeth giggled.

I was beginning to wish that Sir Bevis *had* run me through with his lance.

The Earl stood up to make a speech. He threw off his fur-lined cloak and stepped forward, holding up his hand for silence. The cheers died slowly away.

"Sir Robert Marshall," he boomed for all to hear, "never before have we seen such skill at arms as thou hast shown these past three days. Henceforth, let it be known throughout the land that thou wert the undefeated champion of the Hampshire Tournament in the year of our Lord, twelve hundred and fifty!"

Then, stroking his mustache, he added, "I would count it an honor, Sir Robert, if thou wouldst tarry a while as a guest here at Hampshire Castle. What sayest thou?"

Figuring that Sir Robert would want to accept, I cleared my throat and said, "I'd be happy to, your Earlship."

"Good, good," said the Earl. "Then thou wilt surely join us on the morrow for the hunt."

Without waiting for a reply, he eased himself back into his chair, and the crowd immediately broke into a new storm of cheers and applause. So, while Niles led Sir Bevis's horse back to our tent, Max and I finished parading in front of the stands.

Even when we finally turned and headed back across the field, the thunder of applause followed us. It was great, but I felt a little sad when I realized that within a few short hours we'd be leaving the Middle Ages and winging our way back to our own time. We'd be trading tournaments for a TV. It'd be good-bye to glory and hello to hanging around. I heaved a long sigh.

Max, on the other hand, was in high spirits.

"Hey, how about that Geronimo Gimmick?" he whinnied cheerfully. "Pretty terrific, don't you think? And I thought of it *joust* in time."

"Yeah," I sighed. "Terrific."

"But the best part was that Sir Bevis fell for it. Get it? *Fell* for it!"

"Oh, brother," I muttered, as Max gave a horsy guffaw and trotted briskly across the field toward Sir Robert's tent.

Steve's troubles are not yet over, for Sir Bevis wants revenge. You can read the rest of Max and Steve's adventures and find out how they escape to the twentieth century in *Max and Me and the Time Machine* by Gery Greer and Bob Ruddick.

Thinking and Writing About the Selection

1. Why had the Earl of Hampshire decided to hold the Great Hampshire Tournament?
2. How did Steve's feelings about fighting Sir Bevis differ from Max's feelings?
3. What problems do you think Steve might encounter when he goes on the hunt with the Earl?
4. Imagine that while Steve is in Sir Robert's body, Sir Robert is in Steve's body in the twentieth century. Write about an incident that might take place involving Sir Robert.

Applying the Key Skill
Draw Conclusions

Use complete sentences to answer the following questions about "Max and Me and the Time Machine."

1. At the beginning of the story, Steve wasn't sure where he was or even who he was, and he didn't know where Max was. What information did Niles provide to help Steve? Based on that information, what did Steve conclude?
2. What information from Niles led Steve to make the following conclusion?

   Sir Bevis is a little upset because he thinks I'm trying to steal his reputation, his job, and his girl.
3. Why did the spectators at the tourney conclude that Steve/Sir Robert had unhorsed Sir Bevis in the usual way?
4. How was Max able to correctly conclude who the Earl of Hampshire was?

TRAVEL BROCHURE

Prewrite

EXPERIENCE ACTION, ADVENTURE, AND EXCITEMENT!
TRAVEL TO THE MIDDLE AGES! BECOME A DARING KNIGHT!

A travel brochure for Steve and Max's trip in "Max and Me and the Time Machine" might start like that.

Writers of travel brochures have two main purposes.

1. To describe trips to specific places
2. To persuade people to take such trips

Write a brochure for a trip in Steve's time machine. Before you write, you need to do some thinking.

1. Create a history map of possible settings for your trip.

American History

COLONIAL TIMES
1607: Jamestown colony
1620: Plymouth colony

EXPLORATION
1540: Southwest
1682: Mississippi River

REVOLUTION
1773: Boston Tea Party
1781: Surrender at Yorktown

WORLD WAR II
1941: Pearl Harbor
1945: V-E Day: Europe

2. Now choose one setting from your map and do some research. What historical persons could travelers meet? What events might they witness? What sights and sounds might they see and hear?
3. List some words and phrases you might use to persuade people to take the trip.
4. Plan some art to illustrate your brochure.

Write

A travel brochure should be attractive and short but still explain important facts.

1. Plan four sections for your brochure.
   Section 1: Give the setting of your trip and write some catchy sentences to persuade people to go.
   Section 2: Discuss the events, sights, and sounds people may experience on the trip. Describe some historical persons they might meet.
   Section 3: Give information about the time and place to board the time machine, the cost, and the length of the trip.
   Section 4: Give the name and address of your travel company. Make up an advertisement or slogan for the company.
2. Try to use Vocabulary Treasures in your brochure.
3. Now write the first draft of your brochure.

VOCABULARY TREASURES

exotic	token
promote	traditional

Revise

Read your brochure. Have a friend read it, too. Think about this checklist as you revise.

1. Did you clearly describe people, events, sights, and sounds? Check your historical facts.
2. Do your sentences attract your readers' attention? Could you choose more persuasive adjectives and adverbs? Did you use long run-on sentences?
3. Check your spelling and capitalization.
4. Now rewrite your brochure to share.

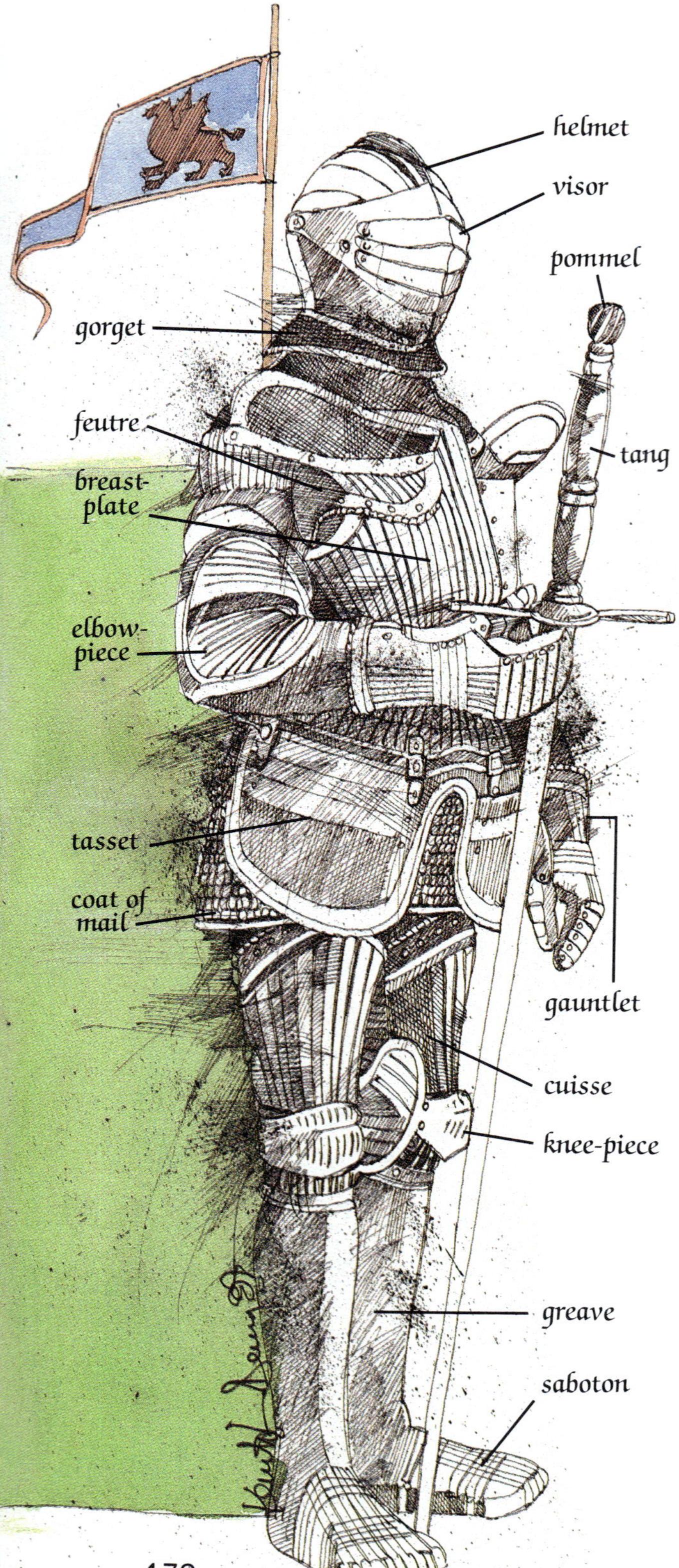

Throughout the Middle Ages, bold knights in their shining armor triumphed at tournaments and on the field of battle. They were the heroes of the day. But was the life of a knight as exciting and glamorous as it seems?

THE TRAINING OF A KNIGHT

ERNEST E. TUCKER

In medieval England if a boy wanted to be a knight—and what boy didn't—he had to begin at about the age of seven. Usually he was taken from his home and sent to school at the castle of one of the great barons, perhaps that of his father's overlord. At first he was given over to the women who taught him table manners and how to behave in the house.

These young boys were called *pages* and as they grew older they had an increasing list of duties to perform. They waited on the ladies. They ran errands. They began to learn the endless list of terms applied to hunting, to falconry, to serving at table. They might be taught to read and write by a priest, who also taught them religion. And always, they had the idea drilled into them that some day they would be knights.

When the boys could find time, they loved to loiter about the stables or the armory, caring for the horses, or listening wide-eyed to the esquires or squires who were apprentice knights. When the pages reached the age of fourteen, they could hope to pass over to this high position themselves. From the time a boy graduated from pagehood until he won his golden spurs, he was an *esquire* and spent most of his time practicing with weapons. *Esquire* means "shield bearer," and when he grew older—sixteen or so—that's exactly what he was. He was assigned to the personal service of his lord, or of some other knight. He carried the knight's heavy shield for him on journeys. He attended to the knight and armed him for

a tournament or battle. He kept his weapons in good condition, and got him out of danger if he were wounded. And all the time, of course, he was supposed to be learning the principles of chivalry from his master—courage, honor, faith, devotion to duty—and the use of arms.

Esquires also had to learn how to sing, to dance, to play a musical instrument, and to compose songs and poems. They were supposed to learn how to behave with women, too: to treat them with gentleness and courtesy, and to protect them.

On the whole, though, the esquire had a rugged life. He spent hour after hour in the practice yard under the stern eyes of an old professional, learning how to handle weapons. He swung a heavy, blunt sword at a post, or staged mock fights with other esquires. He spent hour after hour in the saddle, learning how to manage a horse with one hand and his knees, or with no hands at all. Hour after hour he wore his heavy armor until he became so accustomed to it that he was scarcely aware of having it on. Sometimes he wore the armor for days without taking it off.

He learned to shrug off bruises and cuts which would send a modern boy to the hospital. Wounds, after all, would be commonplace in his life. The squire-master might order him to go for a day or two days, without food, just to get him used to the idea of going hungry. He might have to spend a whole winter night running up and down the castle yard; or sleep without blankets in a driving rain; or carry a hundred-pound pack on his back from dawn to dusk. All this was intended to toughen him up. It did, too.

Night after night, year after year, a squire would drag himself from the tilting yard dog-tired, aching, bruised, hungry. And the next day he had nothing to look forward to but more of the same. A hard life, indeed. But if the squire stuck out the course of training until he reached manhood, he discovered it had been worthwhile. He grew up strong and tough, able to laugh at a wound or a bruise. He could handle lance or sword with the skill of a professional,

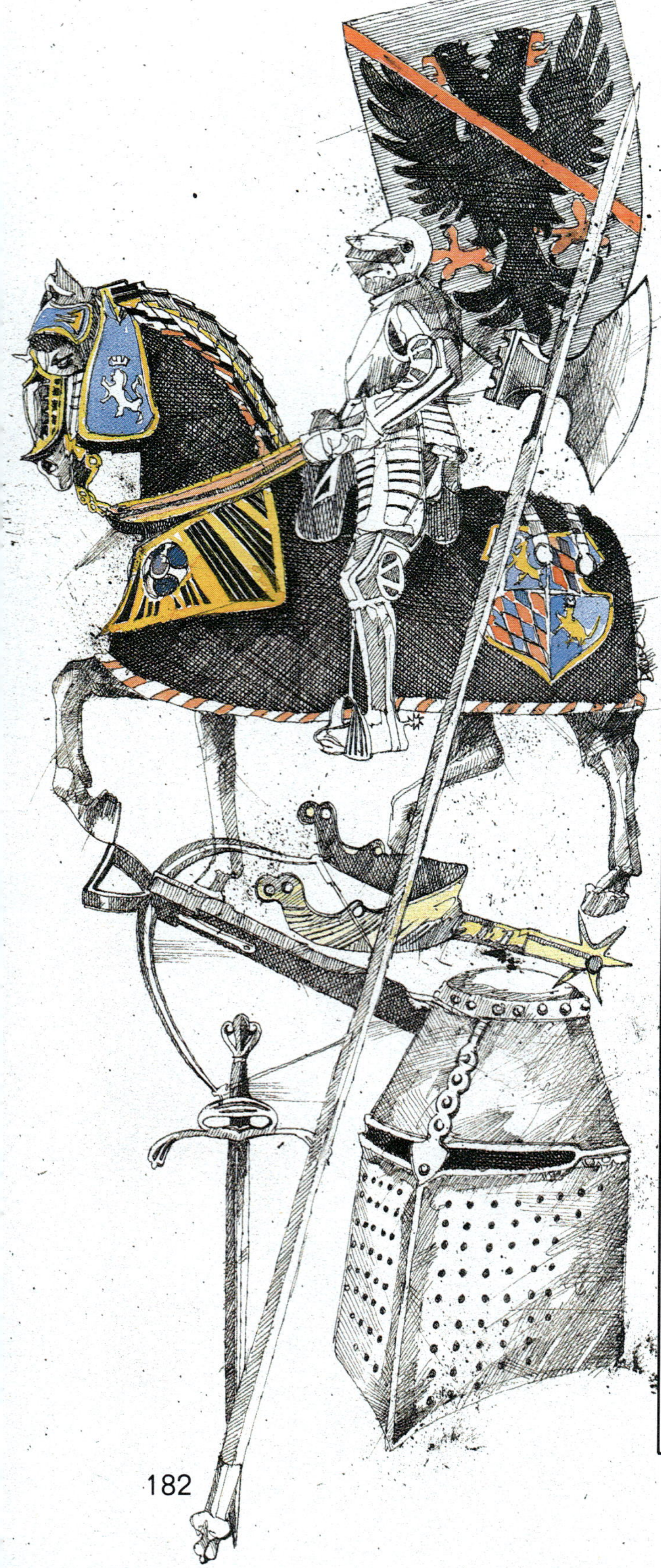

stand in the hot sun for hours swinging an ax and never breathe hard. He was ready for his life's work—fighting.

Some, of course, did not stick it through. Some decided that the life was not for them, and got out, probably to enter holy orders. And of course, a good many simply did not survive.

Many squires never became knights. They lived out their lives in service to wealthier or more able men who had won their golden spurs, or they became part of the household of a lord. It cost a good deal to be knighted, and many a boy without money stayed a simple squire. There were many responsibilities that went with knighthood, and some boys preferred not to accept them, so they too, chose to remain squires.

But if the squire was finally judged worthy and admitted into knighthood—ah, there was a proud young man! Remember that nobody ever was *born* a knight, no matter how exalted his family. He might be born a baron or an earl or even a king, but he achieved knighthood on his own merits. (Some unworthy ones sneaked in the back door, to be sure. Powerful, wealthy fathers might see to it that their sons were granted golden spurs even though they didn't deserve them, but these cases were comparatively rare, and even such candidates had to go through a form of training and acceptance.)

There was almost always a ceremony connected with the "adubment," the making of a knight. The ceremony varied widely from country to country and from century to century. It might be a simple, hurried phrase spoken on a battlefield, or a week-long festivity with feasting and pageantry. The high point was usually the words, "I dub thee knight," accompanied by a tap on the candidate's shoulder with a fist or the flat of a sword. The tap varied from a gentle touch to a lusty knock that sometimes sent the candidate sprawling.

Gradually, more and more elements were added to the ceremony. At its best, the knighting of a young man was an occasion of both joy and solemnity, of deep spiritual significance. The candidate was dressed in white,

to signify purity. He held a night-long vigil over his armor and weapons which rested before an altar, while he prayed for strength, courage, and steadfastness. He was bathed and clothed in festive garments while his sponsors, older knights, spoke of the duties and responsibilities of knighthood.

Finally, before a glittering company assembled in the Great Hall of the castle, the candidate came forth. His sword was girded on, usually with some admonition like, "Draw this only in defense of the right, in protection of the weak, in redress of wrong." His golden spurs were buckled on, and at last, as he knelt humbly, the king or a great nobleman dealt him the blow on the shoulder which admitted him to knighthood.

Then the feasting began, with the new knight, of course, the center of attention. Everybody congratulated him, wished him well and foretold great feats of daring and bravery. Girls flattered him with attention.

Then all the long, arduous years were forgotten. He was a man—and a knight.

Thinking and Writing About the Selection

1. What were the important principles of chivalry?
2. How did the squire-master try to "toughen up" a squire?
3. Why didn't all squires go on to become knights?
4. In what ways is the training of a soldier today similar to the training of a knight in the Middle Ages?

Applying the Key Skill
Main Idea and Supporting Details

Use complete sentences to answer the following questions about "The Training of a Knight."

1. What details support the main idea statement below?
   As pages grew older, they had an increasing list of duties to perform.
2. What details support the main idea statement below?
   On the whole, the esquire had a rugged life.
3. Use your own words to state the main idea of the paragraph that begins:
   "Night after night, year after year, a squire would drag himself from the tilting yard. . . ."
4. Use your own words to state the main idea of the paragraph that begins:
   "Gradually, more and more elements were added to the ceremony."

Pangur Ban

I and Pangur Ban my cat,
'Tis a like task we are at:
Hunting mice is his delight,
Hunting words I sit all night.

Better far than praise of men
'Tis to sit with book and pen;
Pangur bears me no ill will,
He too plies his simple skill.

'Tis a merry thing to see
At our tasks how glad are we,
When at home we sit and find
Entertainment to our mind.

Oftentimes a mouse will stray
In the hero Pangur's way;
Oftentimes my keen thought set
Takes a meaning in its net.

'Gainst the wall he sets his eye
Full and fierce and sharp and sly;
'Gainst the wall of knowledge I
All my little wisdom try.

When a mouse darts from its den
O how glad is Pangur then!
O what gladness do I prove
When I solve the doubts I love!

So in peace our tasks we ply,
Pangur Ban, my cat, and I;
In our arts we find our bliss,
I have mine and he has his.

Practice every day has made
Pangur perfect in his trade;
I get wisdom day and night
Turning darkness into light.

anonymous 9th century
translated by Robin Flower

David McCall Johnston

SKILLS ACTIVITY

MAIN IDEA AND SUPPORTING DETAILS

The writer of a paragraph usually has a point to make. This point, the most important information in the paragraph, is called the **main idea**. Sometimes writers state the main idea directly in a sentence that may come at the beginning, in the middle, or at the end of the paragraph. Read the paragraph below.

> During the Middle Ages, a system of living called feudalism (fū′ də liz′ əm) developed. Feudalism was based on cooperation between two classes of people, the nobles and the commoners. Nobles provided land and protection to the commoners. In return, the commoners pledged military and other services to the nobles.

Which sentence below best states the main idea?

a. Feudalism was a system of living that developed during the Middle Ages.
b. Both nobles and commoners cooperated in the feudalistic system.
c. Nobles provided land and protection to commoners.
d. Commoners promised military and other services to the nobles.

Sentence **a** above, which is also a rewording of the first sentence of the paragraph, states the main idea of the paragraph. The other sentences provide **details** that support, or tell more about, the main idea. In a well-written paragraph, the main idea is supported by details that tell more about it.

ACTIVITY Read the paragraphs below. Decide which sentence in each states the main idea and which sentences give details. Write the main idea on your paper.

1. In England, the large estates of the nobles, or lords, were called manors. The tenants on the manor produced food, clothing, tools, and other goods. They ground grain into flour at the lord's mill. They wove cloth, tanned leather, and made tools. Soap, candles, and other household goods were produced on the manor. The manor was an independent community able to provide all the necessities of life.

2. The feudal system disappeared gradually when kings grew strong enough to control the lands and maintain order. People felt safe and were willing to leave the protection of the manor. They moved to towns. Cities grew up, trade increased, and people were paid in money instead of services.

3. As towns grew and trade became important, the merchants of some towns joined together to form guilds (gildz). A guild was a group of merchants or skilled workers who organized to maintain standards of work and to protect their interests. These guilds elected officers and drew up rules which they enforced. Sometimes a merchant guild took part in the government of the town.

AWARD
CLASSICS
WINNERS
EL CID
CAMPEADOR
EDUARDO LURASCHI

One thousand years ago, Spain was a collection of small and independent kingdoms often at war with each other. Many of these kingdoms were ruled by Moorish kings whose ancestors had come to Spain from North Africa centuries earlier. Over the years, the Moors had established their system of government, customs, and art in the central provinces of Spain and along the Mediterranean Sea. There they cultivated rich farmlands and built many thriving communities.

The Spaniards had been forced to yield more and more territory to the Moors. They were pushed back to poorer lands. At that time, Fernando I, King of Castille and Leon, was the most powerful Spanish king. His ambition was to rid Spain from all trace of Moorish influence. To do this, he surrounded himself with trusted aides and men of war.

One of these was Rodrigo Díaz de Vivar. Rodrigo, the son of a distinguished scholar, had been knighted at the age of seventeen. He was agile and well trained in the martial arts. He excelled in archery, swordplay, and riding. Yet, he also had a profound sense of honor and duty.

He himself had chosen his purpose in life, something he had always dreamt of doing. He would fight for his King. He would right and avenge wrongs. Upon receiving his knighthood, he had solemnly declared to Fernando I: "I shall go forth to do battle with the Moors!" The King had embraced him as a brother.

His followers were eager and well-armed young men, boyhood friends of his from the town of Vivar. As children, they had played and fought with him in youthful games. Now they joined him to cross swords with the Moors, in quest of adventure and glory.

One afternoon in the desert, Rodrigo observed an unusual convoy. Far away, several mules laden with heavy trunks advanced slowly. Alongside them rode an escort of a dozen men, three of whom were armed. The harnesses and attire of these travelers revealed that they were Moors, accompanying a special consignment.

In seconds, Rodrigo and his swift followers descended on the advancing group. The Moorish guards were taken totally by surprise and seeing they were outnumbered, panicked and galloped away without offering the slightest resistance.

The mules of the convoy halted. The Moorish tenders who had not fled immediately fell face down in a gesture of submission. Rodrigo and his men remained silent, looking intently about them. The Moorish guards might regroup in the distance and return to fight.

When this did not happen, Rodrigo addressed the eldest of the Moors. "What convoy is this, and where are you headed?" he asked.

An old man with a white beard rose to his knees. He spoke beseechingly to Rodrigo, saying, "We have heard of thine exploits almost daily, Rodrigo Díaz de Vivar, and now meet face to face! Have pity on us! We are merchants on our way to Zaragoza and seek no harm." The old man kept his eyes downcast, his head bowed in fear and respect. "We have been given the task of delivering this most precious convoy, and now our fate lies in thine hands! Allow us to proceed safely, lest we be punished by the Emir!"[1] he pleaded.

Rodrigo's suspicions were now confirmed. This was no ordinary supply caravan. Rather, it was a special cargo intended for an important dignitary, perhaps the Emir of Zaragoza himself.

"And just what carry you toward Zaragoza?" Rodrigo demanded.

1. **Emir** (ə mir′): a high official in some Arab or Muslim areas.

The old merchant jumped up and stepped quickly to a mule towards the center of the caravan. Fastened to the mule with ropes was a square tower-like structure. Its openings were covered with blinds of very fine silk. The merchant drew aside the silken cloths. Inside the structure sat a beautiful young princess, her face covered with a thin veil. She sat with eyes downcast, her cheeks wet with tears, for she was badly frightened, and was crying silently.

"Princess Esmat is to be wed next week to the Emir of Zaragoza," the merchant said. He then pointed to the other mules. "My Lord, these bolted chests carry Princess Esmat's dowry and valuable gifts for the Emir," he said. Letting the curtains fall closed, he drew away from the structure with his head bowed and came before Rodrigo. Once more, he dropped to his knees to show respect.

Rodrigo's men, at the prospect of dividing such a large booty among themselves, raised their lances and cheered loudly. This convoy was a stroke of luck! They would hold Esmat and her retinue as captives and exchange them for a huge ransom! They would share the Emir's payment and live like princes from this day on!

Rodrigo, however, quickly ended their speculation. "Though they be Moorish, not a hair of these travelers must be touched" he declared. "Nor must we take anything from those princely coffers. We are men of honor, and shall not stand in the way of a wedding party, only days before the celebration."

Raising his hand in a farewell motion to the elder merchant, Rodrigo said, "Continue thy journey safely, my friend, and convey our salutations and congratulations to the Emir."

The merchant scrambled to his feet. "May Allah[2] reward you for your mercy, Rodrigo de Vivar," he cried.

As he was still speaking, suddenly all turned in the direction of a tall cloud of dust, as a group of horsemen bore down on them. A band of nearly twenty horses and riders pulled up and halted some yards away from Rodrigo.

Rodrigo and his men turned their horses to meet the newcomers. The tallest of them, a huge Spaniard with a thick reddish beard, separated from the group and rode forward to meet Rodrigo. Rodrigo drew his sword, *Tizona*, and waited.

"Good day, Rodrigo Díaz de Vivar!" the tall man said.

Rodrigo recognized the rider for Gonzalo de las Sierras, the boldest and most notorious of all Spain's highway bandit leaders.

2. **Allah** (al′ ə): the Muslim name for God.

"How fortunate that we arrive just in time to share the contents of these trunks with you," declared the bandit, grinning.

Rodrigo sat motionless. "These Moors are under my protection," he said. "Allow them to go on their way unhindered."

"Since my men outnumber yours three to one," said Gonzalo, "your protection will be of little help to these infidels.[3] Come now," he said. "Let us spare each other time and trouble and divide this booty fairly."

Rodrigo could see that his men, though they would be willing to die for him, were badly outnumbered, and would certainly lose a battle against the bandits. Yet he had no intention of handing over the Moorish party to Gonzalo.

"'Tis I who made them the promise. Could we not settle this matter in single combat?" he suggested.

Gonzalo laughed heartily. "Know Rodrigo, that lads like you I smash like flies." Raising his weapon, he boasted, "This sword has felled knights by the dozens, all mightier than you. Every single one is dead."

Gonzalo's teeth flashed white as he grinned. He looked back at his men, who stirred impatiently. "Why should I fight you?" he asked. "You are no match for me. Besides, at my command, my men will simply take these coffers. I do you a great favor by offering to divide this booty with you."

As Gonzalo was talking, Rodrigo was edging his horse, Babieca, closer to the bandit's horse. Both men were now only a few steps apart, Gonzalo leaning confidently forward on his Arabian charger.

Suddenly, Rodrigo leaned forward. Before Gonzalo could react, he reached out and seized a couple of hairs from Gonzalo's beard and, raising them into the air,

3. **infidels** (in′ fi dəlz′): persons who do not accept a particular faith.

shouted, "Gonzalo de las Sierras is the greatest coward ever to have crossed paths with Rodrigo de Vivar!"

Plucking a hair from a man's beard was a grave insult, and Gonzalo's face turned purple with anger. Drawing his sword he turned on Rodrigo, giving him a blow that knocked *Tizona* from his hand. But Rodrigo wheeled Babieca quickly behind Gonzalo and leaped from the saddle, pulling the bandit leader to the ground. Over and over they rolled, Rodrigo trying desperately to wrestle Gonzalo's sword from him. Then with a sudden burst of strength, Rodrigo managed to send the bandit's sword flying through the air. It landed near *Tizona*, but before Rodrigo could reach it, Gonzalo was on him with a dagger. Rodrigo twisted to escape the blow, and leaped to his feet. Both men raced for their swords, but Rodrigo was more agile, and reached *Tizona* first.

"I have no sword, Rodrigo de Vivar. Would you kill me like a dog?" panted Gonzalo.

"You are a dog and deserve no better," cried Rodrigo. "But take your sword and fight me fairly." Saying this he threw Gonzalo his sword.

Now the two men circled each other, waiting for an opportunity to attack. Suddenly Rodrigo feinted a move to Gonzalo's right. The bandit sidestepped Rodrigo's thrust, slashing at his enemy's chest, throwing himself off balance. In an instant, Rodrigo had whirled around, catching Gonzalo off guard. With all his strength he brought the flat of his sword down against the back of Gonzalo's head, knocking him out. Rodrigo's men drew their swords ready to fight, but the thieves, seeing their leader fallen, fled across the desert.

The Moorish merchants cheered Rodrigo, saying "Surely Allah sent you to us today." They swarmed around him excitedly, praising his courage, and calling him *El Mio Cid, Campeador* (el mē′ ō sēd kam pē ə dôr′), which means, "My Lord the Champion."

From that day, the fame of Rodrigo Díaz de Vivar spread quickly throughout Spain and among the Moors. He became known everywhere as *El Cid Campeador*.

Thinking and Writing About the Selection

1. What had Rodrigo de Vivar promised to do with his life?
2. Why did Rodrigo decide to let the Princess Esmat's caravan continue on its way undisturbed?
3. How did Rodrigo prove his loyalty to the principles of chivalry?
4. Rodrigo became known as El Cid Campeador. What other examples of special names or titles for people do you know? How did the people get their names?

Applying the Key Skill
Sequence of Events

Choose or provide the best answer to the following questions about the events in "El Cid Campeador."

1. What was the most important event that took place after Rodrigo and his men rode up to the Moorish convoy in the desert?
   a. The Moorish guards rode off without offering any resistance.
   b. The merchant explained what the purpose of the convoy was.
   c. Rodrigo assured the merchant that no one would be harmed.
2. What had been going on while Rodrigo was speaking to the merchant?
3. What event led directly to the fight between Rodrigo and Gonzalo?
4. What event best showed Rodrigo's true character?
   a. Rodrigo pulled Gonzalo to the ground.
   b. Rodrigo reached his sword before Gonzalo reached his.
   c. Rodrigo threw Gonzalo his sword.

THE BAYEUX TAPESTRY

A 900-year-old work of art gives us a vivid account of one of the most famous ventures of history.

NORMAN DENNY AND JOSEPHINE FILMER-SANKEY

The Bayeux (bī-yü) Tapestry is a very old version of what we usually think of as a modern thing. It is a cartoon strip, and it depicts one of the most famous historical events of all times: the Norman invasion of England in 1066 by William the Conqueror. It was made to the order of Bishop Odo, William's half-brother, and was originally meant to be displayed in Odo's cathedral at Bayeux, a little town in Normandy, in northern France.

The Bayeux Tapestry, although it is always referred to as such, is not really a tapestry at all. A tapestry is a cloth made on a loom, with its pattern or design woven into it. The Bayeux Tapestry is a piece of embroidery. The pictures are stitched in woolen threads of eight different colors on a long strip of bleached linen. The designer drew his pictures on the linen strip itself, then handed them over to the craftsmen or women who did the embroidering.

It is an immense work. The strip of linen is about two hundred and thirty feet long and twenty inches wide. It was made in eight sections, probably embroidered by separate teams of craftsmen and afterwards stitched together.

After its completion the tapestry was taken to Bayeux Cathedral, where it was hung on feast days and other special occasions. There it remained for seven centuries, well-cared for. It narrowly escaped destruction in the early days of the French Revolution and later was taken to Paris to be exhibited there by order of Napoleon. Today it hangs for all to see in a special frame in the former Palace of the Bishops of Bayeux.

Unlike modern cartoons, the tapestry has no conversation and does not make use of speech balloons. The Latin inscriptions give us some indication of what is going on, but for the most part the pictures speak for themselves. There are many gaps, and many of the details are so puzzling that scholars still cannot agree on them.

If you are to understand the story you must carry your imagination back to the medieval world. The working of the medieval mind is illustrated in the way the tapestry depicts King Harold. He is the villain of the drama, as the Normans saw it, but he is treated with respect. He is a noble figure, and it is this feeling for the nobility and dignity of humanity which makes the Bayeux Tapestry the great work of art it is.

Only part of the tapestry can be shown here. We will begin with Harold, Earl of Wessex, accepting the crown of England. Some years before, King Edward the Confessor had promised William of Normandy that he would succeed to the throne of England after Edward's death. Harold had sworn an oath of loyalty to William of Normandy.

Below, at left, Harold is offered the crown of England in succession to Edward the Confessor. He stands, axe in hand, looking at the crown and perhaps wondering if he should accept. He does accept, and in so doing breaks his solemn oath to William of Normandy. We see him seated on the throne, crowned and holding the orb and scepter which were, as they still are in England, the symbols of monarchy.

On the right, a strange star appears in the sky, a comet with a fiery tail, and the people gaze at it in terror. An astrologer tells Harold that this is an omen of misfortune. In the border below this scene we see the ghostly outlines of ships stealing across the sea. Perhaps this was Harold's dream as he lay troubled by the thought of the oath he had broken and the doom that might follow the breaking of his oath.

The comet was Halley's comet, which can be seen from the Earth in intervals of about 75 years. It would have been clearly visible in the English sky in February of that year, 1066.

In the scene above, a boat sails from England with messengers bringing William news of Harold's coronation. When William hears the news he holds a council of war. He feels he has been robbed of the English crown by Harold, and he resolves to seize it by force of arms and to get revenge for Harold's betrayal. He gives orders for a fleet of ships to

be built to carry his army to England.

Below, September 1066, the invasion fleet crosses the English Channel, the ships tight-packed with men and horses. William's ship is toward the front, with a signal lantern at its masthead and on its sternpost a carving of William's son Robert, blowing a horn and waving a spear with a *gonfanon*, or banner.

William sailed at the end of September. The wind played a great part in these events, frustrating both commanders. Harold had assembled a powerful fleet of his own. He planned to attack William from the sea while his ships were still being completed, but the wind failed him. William fretted and fumed waiting for a favorable wind to take him to England: As it turned out, the delay was greatly to his advantage, for in the meantime Harold had been forced to send his ships to London to be refitted. This was one of the reasons the Norman army was able to land unopposed.

William's armada lands without opposition. Harold has been

in the north, fighting off an invasion by the King of Norway. When he learns of the invasion by the Normans, he hurries his exhausted troops to Hastings and sets up his battle formation on top of a hill.

The date is October 14, 1066, and here, above, two scenes are separated by a clump of trees. On the left, a messenger named Vital rides up to William. He has come from one of the parties of mounted men sent ahead

to watch Harold's movements from the hilltops. William can be recognized by the mace he carries. The armies are now approaching one another. On the right we see Harold, mounted on a black horse, receiving a report from one of his own scouts. Harold's scout goes on foot. He had no horsemen to spare.

The battle has been joined. In the center of the picture below, on the ridge of high ground, we see Harold's men grouped tightly together in a "shield-wall" to resist the onslaught of the Norman cavalry. The fighting went on throughout the day, and the makers of the tapestry have handed down to us a terrible and wonderful picture of the savagery and confusion of war.

The death of Harold is shown here. There is some uncertainty about whether he is the one being struck by a rider with a sword (the Latin inscription immediately above him says, "Harold the king is killed"), or the figure to the left, who seems to be plucking an arrow from his eye. Many history books say that Harold was killed not by a blow with a sword but by an arrow that pierced his eye. This story, whether true or not, is among the most widely believed in English history.

At the right we see the last stages of the battle. The Normans are riding on in triumph. The Latin inscription following the death of Harold simply says, ". . . and the English turned and fled." There is no more to say. The Norman invasion had succeeded, and Duke William was master of the English realm.

There is reason to suppose that the original tapestry did not end quite so abruptly and that its concluding scenes may have been lost. It seems likely, indeed, that it would have been

concluded in a more solemn and splendid manner, perhaps with the crowning of William at Westminster. And perhaps also something would have been done to point out the moral of the story as the Normans tell it: the tragic doom that befell a great and gallant warrior who broke his sacred oath.

Another thing that may strike us, surveying the story as a whole, is the part that chance played in the business—above all the chance of weather. If the wind had favored William as soon as his force was assembled, he would undoubtedly have taken advantage of it to set sail perhaps six weeks earlier than he did. If he had, he would have encountered Harold's full force both by sea and by land. Most likely, he would have been defeated. There would have been no Norman conquest of England, and the history of the English people would have been profoundly changed, whether for better or for worse no one can say.

Thinking and Writing About the Selection

1. Why is the Bayeux Tapestry described as an *immense* work?
2. Why is there doubt about the meaning of certain details in some of the scenes shown in the tapestry?
3. Do you think the tapestry would have been different if someone in Harold's family rather than in William's family had ordered it to be made? Support your answer with information from the selection.
4. How do people today commemorate important events? Give examples.

Applying the Key Skill
Main Idea and Supporting Details

Use complete sentences to answer the following questions about "The Bayeux Tapestry."

1. What details support the following main idea statement?

   The Bayeux Tapestry is not really a tapestry at all.
2. What details support the following main idea statement?

   The wind played a great part in the events that allowed the Norman army to land unopposed.
3. How would you state the main idea of the next to the last paragraph? What details support the main idea?
4. How would you state the main idea of the last paragraph in the selection? What are the most important details supporting the main idea?

LANGUAGE ACTIVITY

STORIES IN STITCHES

Almost as soon as early people learned to weave, sew, and knit, they became concerned with the decoration and design of the things they made. In this way, many of the textiles and handwork that have come down to us have stories to tell. The items may be garments, household furnishings, or purely decorative pieces—such as the Bayeux Tapestry.

A **tapestry,** you learned, is a fabric with a varicolored design woven into it. The word has a long history and can be traced back to the Greek *tapes*, meaning "carpet." And in fact, the early heavy tapestries that began to appear in Europe in the ninth century were very much like carpets. They were used mainly as wall hangings in medieval castles to relieve the dark, cold stone walls and to make the rooms more comfortable. The bright colors and designs added cheer and interest.

Embroidery is the art of working a design into cloth with a needle and yarn. *Embroider* comes from the Norman French *embrouder,* "to embroider" (Old French *en-*, "in," + *brouder,* "to embroider") and may have its origin in the much older root *bhar,* meaning "point."

Crewelwork is embroidery done with a variety of worsted called "crewel." It is not known how the word *crewel* came into existence, but the word *worsted* for a "tightly twisted woolen yarn" takes its name from the town of Worstead in England, which was one of the main places it was made.

Robin Hood and Maid Marian

The story of Robin Hood, the outlaw-hero who robbed from the rich and gave to the poor, has captured the imagination of people for centuries. Through the years the legend has been made into plays, movies, and even a television program.

Was Robin Hood a real person? It is difficult to know. The stories can be traced to ballads sung as early as the 1200s, but it is thought that the legend is older than that. In most modern versions, Robin Hood is presented as a nobleman who was deprived of his lands and wealth. But in earlier versions he was a yeoman.

During the 13th and 14th centuries, the peasants were at the mercy of their overlords, with few rights and little chance for justice. Robin Hood was the peasant's ideal of someone who could give them justice.

You will read three versions of the same story. The most recent is a play. Next is a prose version, and finally a ballad, the oldest of the three, on which the newer versions were based.

Marvelous MAID MARIAN

A play by Susan Nanus

CHARACTERS

NARRATORS
MAID MARIAN
ROSALYN
CATHERINE
SIR RICHARD
ROBIN HOOD
LITTLE JOHN
SHERIFF OF NOTTINGHAM
FIRST SHERIFF'S MAN
SECOND SHERIFF'S MAN
ROBIN HOOD'S MERRY MEN
OTHER SOLDIERS

TIME: *In the olden, golden days of merry old England*

PLACE: *Maid Marian's castle and Sherwood Forest*

(NARRATORS *come out in front of the curtain.*)

NARRATOR **1**: Of Robin Hood, you've heard, I'm sure.
He robbed the rich and helped the poor.
Of course, his Merry Men, you know,
All masters of the sword and bow.

NARRATOR **2**: But have you heard of the Marvelous Maid?
Who roamed the forests unafraid.
Who learned to shoot and learned to ride,
And fought with Robin side by side?

NARRATOR 1:
Our story starts in a castle old,
Where Marian sits, depressed
and cold.
The man she loves—called
Robin Hood
Has been forced to flee to a
distant wood.

(*As the curtain opens,* MARIAN *is pacing back and forth, very upset.* CATHERINE *and* ROSALYN *sit on stools, watching her.*)

MARIAN: I shall not do it, I tell you. I shall not!

ROSALYN: But Lady Marian, your father has arranged it!

MARIAN: I do not care! I am promised to another man and I shall not marry anyone else.

CATHERINE: Lady Marian, a woman must marry the man her father chooses for her.

MARIAN: Not this woman.

ROSALYN: What choice have you? The wedding is tomorrow.

MARIAN: Oh, if only I could reach Robin Hood.

SIR RICHARD: (*entering the room*) Robin Hood? You had better forget him, my daughter.

ROSALYN AND CATHERINE: (*curtsying*) Sir Richard!

MARIAN: Father, please do not force me to marry Sir Cedric.

SIR RICHARD: Sir Cedric is a highly respected knight and a great nobleman.

MARIAN: But Father, I do not love him.

SIR RICHARD: Marian, I must see you married safely.

I will not always be here,
and you must have a husband.

MARIAN: But Sir Cedric is nearly as old as you.

SIR RICHARD: He is a good man, Marian, and can provide richly for you.

MARIAN: What do I care for his wealth? It is Robin I love.

SIR RICHARD: You must face the truth, Marian. You have had no word from Robin in nearly two years. He is an outlaw with a price on his head. You can have no future with him. (*putting his hand on* MARIAN*'s shoulder*) I want only what is best for you, Marian. You will soon be with Sir Cedric in Normandy. You will have a new life there.

MARIAN: Normandy!

SIR RICHARD: Sir Cedric must return to his land there. You will have much to do running his household.

MARIAN: Oh, Father, how can you do this to me?

SIR RICHARD: It is for the best, Marian. (*He exits.*)

MARIAN: Normandy! I will never go there!

ROSALYN: It is so terrible. Robin Hood is so far away. Why has he never contacted you?

MARIAN: He has, Rosalyn. But it has been many months since I have had word. It is very dangerous for Robin to try to contact me now. If a message were intercepted, I would be thrown into jail immediately. We agreed that he would contact me only when it is safe again.

CATHERINE: By the time it's safe, it will be too late. You will be married and far away in Normandy.

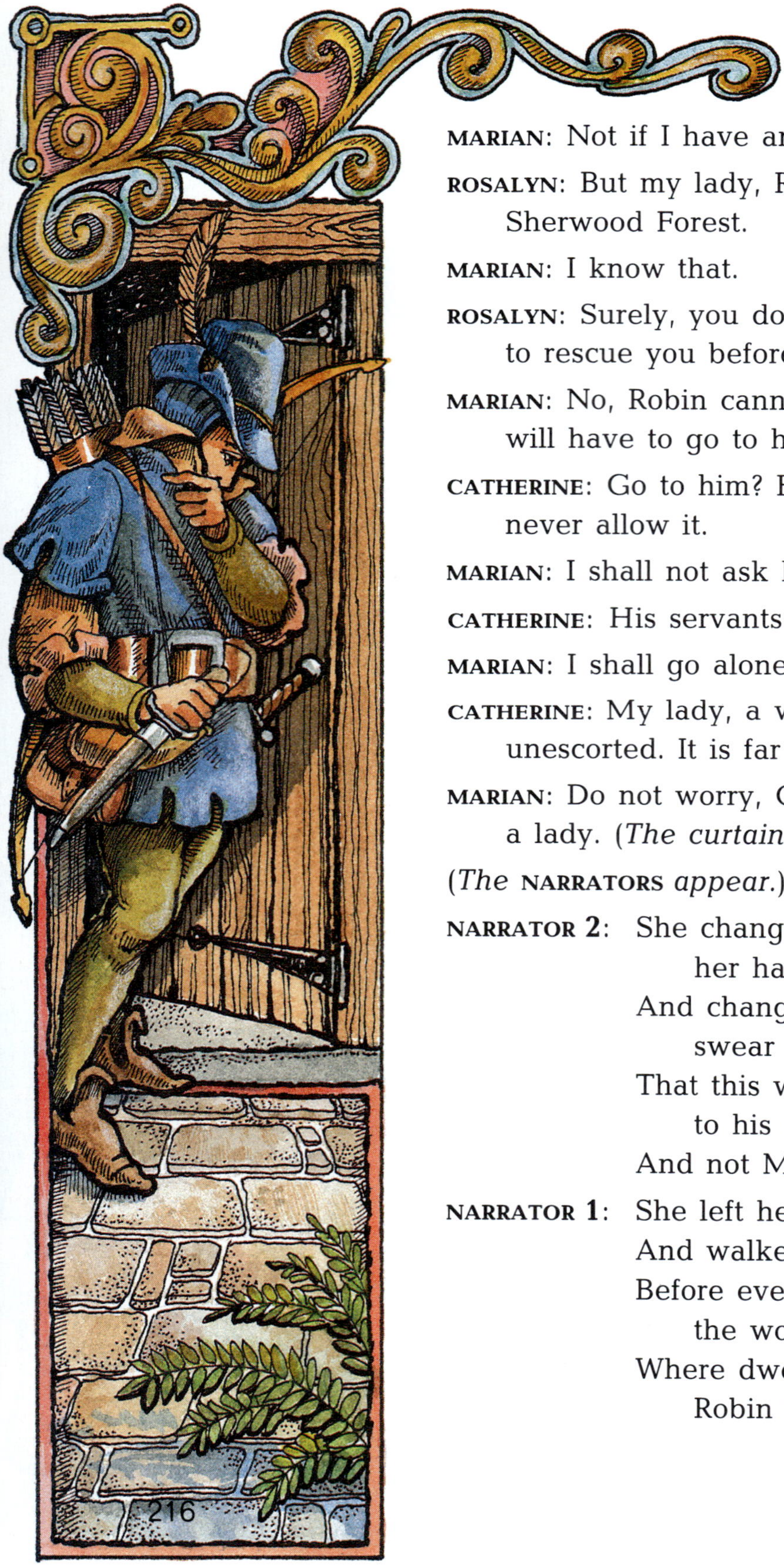

MARIAN: Not if I have anything to say about it.

ROSALYN: But my lady, Robin Hood is in distant Sherwood Forest.

MARIAN: I know that.

ROSALYN: Surely, you do not think he will be able to rescue you before the wedding?

MARIAN: No, Robin cannot come to me. Therefore, I will have to go to him.

CATHERINE: Go to him? How? Your father will never allow it.

MARIAN: I shall not ask him.

CATHERINE: His servants will inform him.

MARIAN: I shall go alone.

CATHERINE: My lady, a woman cannot travel unescorted. It is far too dangerous.

MARIAN: Do not worry, Catherine. I shall not go as a lady. (*The curtains close.*)

(*The* NARRATORS *appear.*)

NARRATOR 2: She changed her clothes, put up her hair,
And changed herself 'til you would swear
That this was a lad from his feet to his eyes,
And not Maid Marian in a disguise.

NARRATOR 1: She left her home long before day,
And walked many miles on her way.
Before eventide she'd reached the wood
Where dwelled her dear friend Robin Hood.

(*The curtain opens. The stage is now a forest with stand-up cutouts of trees and bushes scattered around the stage.* MARIAN *enters. She is now dressed as a page, wearing a sword and carrying a bow and a quiver of arrows.*)

MARIAN: Oh, I am so tired. I feel as if I have been walking for weeks. Oh, my feet! (*She sits down and takes off her boots.*) Ahh, that feels good. (*Suddenly, she hears voices.*) Oh, oh, I hear someone. I'd better hide until I see who it is. (*She picks up her boots and hides behind a tree.* LITTLE JOHN *and three other* MERRY MEN *enter, laughing and carrying sacks.*)

LITTLE JOHN: Oh, that was a good one! Did you see that fat miller's face?

FIRST MERRY MAN: When we took his purse of gold, he turned paler than flour.

SECOND MERRY MAN: He is served rightly, Will. He has cheated too many.

THIRD MERRY MAN: He'll think twice before he travels through Sherwood Forest again. How much did we get, Little John?

LITTLE JOHN: We will count it later. But the peasants he overcharged will be glad to have it back.

FIRST MERRY MAN: We'd best return to camp. The Sheriff's men are still looking for us from yesterday's exploit!

LITTLE JOHN: He can search all Sherwood before he finds us.

(*They all laugh and walk off.* MARIAN *comes out from behind the tree.*)

MARIAN: So this is Sherwood Forest. And it seems full of thieves. How shall I find Robin? I don't know whom I can trust. (*She puts on her boots and begins walking. Suddenly a man steps out from behind a tree with drawn sword. He is wearing a tattered cloak and hood and has a patch over one eye. It is Robin, but Marian does not recognize him.*)

ROBIN: Hold, stranger. What is your business in Sherwood?

MARIAN: (*drawing her own sword*) Don't move another step!

ROBIN: Take care, my friend. I am not dangerous unless provoked. But then, you better beware.

MARIAN: I always beware of strangers. State your name, if you please.

ROBIN: What business is my name to you?

(*They circle each other.*)

MARIAN: By that, I can tell if you are a friend or a foe.

ROBIN: You are a saucy lad, but no match for this. (*He lunges, but she parries, and they begin a sword fight.*)

MARIAN: As I suspected, you are no friend.

ROBIN: Yet I see you are friendly with a sword.

MARIAN: It is the only way to keep off my enemies.

ROBIN: You are but a lad, but fight well. (*They continue fighting, but neither one can beat the other.*)

MARIAN: I had a good teacher.

ROBIN: I would like to meet him.

MARIAN: If you surrender, I will take you to him. He lives in this forest.

ROBIN: Lives in Sherwood? Maybe I know him.

MARIAN: I doubt that very much. (*They fight some more and suddenly find they are pointing their swords at each other's throats.*)

ROBIN: It looks like a stalemate.

MARIAN: Does that mean you're ready to lose?

ROBIN: (*laughing*) I like your spirit, lad. Stay your hand and let us call a truce. I have a little band of men here that could use a lad like you.

MARIAN: No truce until you tell me your name.

ROBIN: Gladly. My name is . . . .

(SHERIFF OF NOTTINGHAM *and four soldiers enter.*)

SHERIFF: His name is Robin Hood.

MARIAN: Robin Hood!

SHERIFF: And you, good lad, have captured him for me. (*to the* SOLDIERS) Seize him!

(*The* SOLDIERS *grab* ROBIN.)

MARIAN: My lord Sheriff, one moment.

SHERIFF: What is it, lad?

MARIAN: My Lord, I ask a favor. I sought Robin Hood to avenge my father, whom he has wronged. Since I captured him, he is really my prisoner.

SHERIFF: What of it?

MARIAN: (*thinking quickly*) I request the right to kill him myself.

ROBIN: I never wronged you, lad.

SHERIFF: (*smiling*) The great outlaw Robin Hood put to death by a stripling? It is fair, indeed!

MARIAN: But I wish to kill him by a special method. A very slow and painful method, which he surely deserves after all the trouble he has given you.

SHERIFF: All right. Proceed, young man.

MARIAN: Well, first I need all your swords.

SHERIFF: All of them?

MARIAN: Oh, yes. (*She points her sword at* ROBIN.) Don't worry, I won't let him escape.

SHERIFF: Very well. Do as he says.

(*They all put their swords under the tree.*)

MARIAN: (*to* ROBIN) Now, give me your belt.

ROBIN: My belt?

SHERIFF: You heard him.

(ROBIN *hands* MARIAN *his belt. She gives it to the* FIRST SHERIFF'S MAN.)

MARIAN: Tie all the swords together.

FIRST SHERIFF'S MAN: Tie all the—?

SHERIFF: You heard him, you fool. Don't you see what he's doing? Making one sword with a half dozen points. (*The* FIRST SHERIFF'S MAN *ties all swords together with the belt and hands them to* MARIAN.)

MARIAN: Perfect! Now everyone move back. Move way back. (*They all move back.*) A little further. (*They move a little further.* MARIAN *turns to* ROBIN *and throws him her sword. She tosses the tied swords to one side.*) Come on, Robin! Let's go!

(*They run offstage.*)

SHERIFF: What! Stop them! Guards! After them! (*The* SHERIFF'S MEN *run after them.*) Wait! You fools! Take your swords! (*They rush back and try to untangle their swords.*) You idiots! They're escaping! (*The curtain closes.* NARRATOR *comes out.*)

NARRATOR 2: They ran to safety through the trees,
Escaped the soldiers with perfect ease,
Back to Robin's secret den
Where they told their tale to his
Merry Men.

(*The curtains open. The* MEN *are toasting* MARIAN.)

LITTLE JOHN: To you, lad!

(*The* MEN *cheer.*)

ROBIN: I thought for a moment you were an enemy after all. But you are a quick-witted lad! And a brave one. Yet still I do not know your name.

MARIAN: Robin, do you not know me? Has it been so long that you have forgotten me? (*She removes her hat and lets down her hair.*)

ROBIN: Marian? But how—

LITTLE JOHN: It's a woman!

MARIAN: I told you I had a good teacher.

LITTLE JOHN: A braver woman than many men!

ROBIN: But how . . . ? You traveled all that way alone?

MARIAN: I will tell you all about it, Robin. It is a long story.

(*The curtain closes.* NARRATOR 1 *comes out.*)

NARRATOR 1: There never was a stronger,
braver maid
Who bravely came to her true
love's aid.
She used her wits to save his life,
And spent the next years as his wife.

ROBIN HOOD AND THE STRANGER

George C. Harvey

Now, while Robin Hood was leading his men in Sherwood Forest and living the life of a bold outlaw, his thoughts were often full of someone whom he had left behind in his old home. This was Maid Marian, the beautiful daughter of a great man whose house had stood near Robin's home. Robin Hood and Maid Marian had been close friends since childhood. They had played together, hunting for birds' nests, fishing in the brook, climbing trees or running races over the meadow grass, and when Robin was forced to go out into the world he bore a sore heart with him after parting with Marian.

Since Robin's departure things had gone very hardly with Marian also. Her parents died, her friends proved unkind, and her heart often dwelt on the friend of her youth—bold, brave Robin. For a long time she did not know where he was, but at last his name began to ring through the North Countree, and she knew that her old friend had become the renowned outlaw of whose daring deeds minstrels sang, and of whom men talked as they sat about the evening fire. At last, lonely and friendless as she was, Maid Marian resolved to seek Robin in Sherwood Forest and see if he still remembered the old happy days of their childhood. But she knew how unsafe it was for a woman to travel about the country alone, so she put on the dress of a page and took quiver and bow, sword and buckler, and thus armed and disguised she set out to seek Robin. At last she reached the skirts of the great forest, and as soon as she entered the dark shades of the mighty oaks she looked eagerly forward to watch for the first sign of a forest dweller who could direct her to the haunts of her old friend.

As it happened, that very morning Robin had set out alone to make an expedition in search of news. He had taken great care to disguise himself, for his fate would be certain if he fell into the hands of the Foresters. The Sheriff had given orders that every outlaw should be put to death upon capture, and no mercy whatsoever should be shown.

So Robin went out in a ragged suit of hodden-gray,[1] with a big hat down over his face, a huge patch over his left eye, and a tattered cloak huddled over his shoulders. He had been walking an hour or more when he saw the figure of a handsomely dressed stripling coming along the way towards him. Robin at once stepped out of sight behind a bush until he could be sure that the youth was alone. In these days it behooved him to be wary, so many and so fierce were his enemies. He suspected some trap or stratagem at the sight of every stranger. But the youth came on with a quick, even step and seemed to be entirely alone. Just as he was passing the bush behind which Robin stood, the outlaw sprang out and commanded him to stand.

"Who art thou, and what dost thou want in Sherwood?" demanded Robin Hood.

The stranger was Maid Marian, and she looked at Robin and never dreamed that her old friend stood before her in the person of this wild, ragged man of the woods. She thought it was some savage freebooter who would belike plunder her, and she sprang back and laid her hand on her sword.

"This is not one of Robin's men," thought Maid Marian. "This is some footpad whom I must meet boldly or I am undone." So she said, "Stand aside, fellow, and let me go on my way. I have nought to do with thee."

1. **hodden-gray:** a coarse gray cloth

"Ay, but I may have something to do with thee," replied the tattered stranger. "Tell me whither and why thou goest through the forest or I must turn thee back."

"Turn me back," said the page. "That wilt thou never do, rude man. Put me not to the need of drawing sword in my defense or thou mayst rue the day."

"Why, this is a brave springald!"[2] laughed Robin Hood. "And what wouldst thou do with that pretty little bodkin of thine, youngster?"

"'Tis a bodkin that thou mayst find over sharp," said the page, and drew the glittering blade from its sheath and waved it on high. "Give way, for I seek the heart of the forest and none shall check me."

When Robin heard that the newcomer was bound for the depths of Sherwood, his suspicions grew fast. It seemed to him that a bold, smart lad such as this was just the person the Sheriff might send as a spy, and he became resolved to turn the page back. "Nay," said Robin, "I bid you return. Seek your own safety and leave the forest glades in peace or I shall be compelled to draw weapon also."

"Draw as thou wilt!" cried the other, "but go back I will not."

"The sight of my blade will frighten a mere lad like this," thought Robin, and he drew out his sword and sprang forward and made a lunge as if in fierce attack. But, to his surprise, the lunge was deftly turned aside, and the page met him as boldly with sword and buckler as ever Robin had been met in his life.

Clash-clash! went their swords as the keen blades grated together, but Robin did not put out the whole of his strength and skill against a mere lad like this, and so the combat lasted much longer than it would

2. **springald** (spring′ əld): youngster

otherwise have done. Nor was the page at all unskilled in sword play, for on one occasion Robin's guard was passed and he received a small wound in the face. The outlaw became full of admiration for this brave young opponent and tried to make a peaceful ending to their fray.

"Hold thy hand," said Robin Hood, "and thou shalt range the forest with bold Robin Hood and hear the sweet song of the nightingale."

"What!" screamed the page. "Robin Hood! And are you indeed Robin Hood? And oh, Robin, I have hurt you! I knew you not, Robin."

The outlaw started in surprise.

"Why, who art thou?" he said. "And why should it trouble thee that I am hurt?"

"I came hither to seek you, Robin!" cried the page, "but never dreamed that I should meet you in this guise. And Robin, don't you know me?"

Robin Hood stood for a few moments in greater wonder still at the fair blushing face, then memory rose like a flood.

"I know you!" he cried. "I know you now! You are Maid Marian. Dearest Marian, how came you here?"

"I came to seek you, Robin," she replied, "for I have no friend in the world but you. And I knew you not and have wounded you."

"Tush! that is nothing," said Robin. "We get many shrewder cuts and knocks in the greenwood. And as for not knowing me, that is no wonder, for I am disguised, lest my enemy, the Sheriff of Nottingham should seize me."

The two friends now sat down on a mossy bank near at hand and fell into talk, telling each other how their lives had passed since their separation.

"And have you room for me in the greenwood, Robin?" asked Maid Marian.

"Ay, and proud to see you there, Marian," cried the outlaw. "Come, we will seek the wife of Alan-a-Dale; she will gladly take you under her care."

So they set off together and sought the hidden glade where the band formed their camp. And right welcome did the wife of Alan-a-Dale make Maid Marian, and right merry was the feast which was held that evening. For Little John and Will Scarlet went off at once with their bows and killed a brace of fat bucks, and a joyous feast was held in honor of Maid Marian's coming to the greenwood. The yeomen formed a jovial ring around a vast fire of great oaken billets, and ate their fill of the sweet venison, and washed it down with flagons of wine and brimming bowls of nut-brown ale. And so Maid Marian came to Sherwood and reigned as queen of the forest revels.

Robin Hood and Maid Marian

The Earl of Huntington, nobly born,
That came of noble blood,
To Marian went, with good intent,
By the name of Robin Hood.

But fortune bore these lovers a spite,
And soon they were forced to part.
To merry greenwood went Robin Hood
With a sad and sorrowful heart.

And Marian, poor soul, was troubled in mind
For the absence of her friend.
With finger to eye, she'd often cry
And his person much commend.

Perplexed and vexed and troubled in mind,
She dressed herself like a page,
And searched the wood for Robin Hood,
The bravest of men in that age.

With quiver and bow, sword, buckler, and all,
Thus armed was Marian most bold,
Still wandering about to find Robin out,
Whose presence was better than gold.

But Robin Hood himself disguised,
And Marian was strangely attired.
So they proved foes and fell to blows.
Her valor bold Robin admired.

They drew their swords and to cutting they went,
For at least an hour or more,
Till blood ran apace from Robin's face,
And Marian was wounded sore.

"O hold thy hand," said Robin Hood,
"And thou shalt be one of my string,
To range in the wood with bold Robin Hood,
To hear the sweet nightingale sing."

When Marian heard her lover's voice,
Her name she did confess.
With kisses sweet she did him greet,
Like a most loyal lass.

When Robin Hood his Marian saw,
O, what a hugging was there!
With kind embraces and kissing of faces,
Providing of gallant cheer.

Then Little John took his bow in his hand
And wandered in the wood
To kill the deer and make good cheer
For Marian and Robin Hood.

Thinking and Writing About the Selection

1. According to the play, why did Maid Marian go to Sherwood Forest? Why did she go according to the version told in prose?
2. Why did Maid Marian disguise herself as a lad?
3. Why do you think stories about Robin Hood were popular among peasants in the Middle Ages? How do you think the nobles reacted to the stories?
4. Which of the three versions of the Robin Hood and Maid Marian story did you enjoy the most? Which version was the easiest to understand? Give reasons for your answers.

Applying the Key Skill
Sequence of Events

Choose or provide the best answer to the following questions about the events in "Robin Hood and Maid Marian."

1. When were stories about Robin Hood first told?
   a. during the 13th and 14th centuries
   b. in the 1200s
   c. probably before the year 1200
   d. throughout the Middle Ages
2. List the following events in order to show the correct sequence.
   Movies about Robin Hood were made.
   Minstrels sang ballads about Robin Hood.
   Stories about Robin Hood were written.
   The legend of a man called Robin Hood who took from the rich and gave to the poor developed.
3. What event in the fight between Robin and Marian described in the ballad "Robin Hood and Maid Marian" is not included in the play version or the prose version?

SKILLS ACTIVITY

MAPS

A **map** is a drawing that shows the earth's surface. It may show all or only part of the earth's surface. Simple maps usually show at least the major water and land divisions of the earth. More complex maps may show other things as well, such as cities, rivers, mountains, and roads.

There are many special kinds of maps. One special kind is called a **historical map**. A historical map shows how the earth or part of it looked at sometime in the past.

Most maps have a great deal of information, but the information is shown in a special way. In order to understand the information, you must know how to "read" the map; that is, you must be able to interpret the signs and symbols used on the map.

Directions are easy to find on a map. Most maps are printed so that north is toward the top. In any case, and to help you know for sure, maps usually have a **north arrow** indicating which way north is. If you know which way north is, you can easily find the other directions. When facing north, south is behind you, east is to your right, and west is to your left.

Much of the information on a map is shown by symbols. A **symbol** is anything that stands for something else. Commonly used map symbols are dots, lines of different kinds, shapes, and numbers. Color is a special map symbol. Colors are often used to set off political divisions from one another and to show where there is land and where there is water.

The meanings of the symbols used on a map are explained in the **key**, or legend. When reading a map, you should always check the key. A symbol used for one thing on one map may be used for an entirely different thing on another map.

No map is as large as the area it represents. How much smaller the map is than the actual area is indicated by the scale. Scale is relative size. Many maps use a scale bar to show scale. A **scale bar** is a bar or line showing how many feet, miles, meters, or kilometers on the earth are represented on the map by the length of the bar or line. Scale bars are often marked into divisions to help you measure distances less than the total length of the bar.

Maps that show the entire earth or large parts of it are called **small-scale maps**. They usually do not show things in much detail. **Large-scale maps** show small areas of the earth in great detail. Sometimes a main map will have an **inset map** in one of its corners. An inset map may show an area larger than that of the main map. In this case, the inset map includes the area of the main map and helps you place the area of the main map in relation to its surroundings. Such an inset map always has a smaller scale than that of the main map. An inset map may also show a small part of the main map in greater detail. In this case, the inset map has a larger scale than that of the main map.

The historical map on the next page may help you better understand some of the things you read about in this unit.

ACTIVITY Use the main map and the inset map above to answer the questions on the next page. Write the answers on your paper.

1. What does the main map show? What does the inset map show?
2. Which map, the main map or the inset map, has the larger scale?
3. Where did William meet to make plans for the invasion of England? When did he meet?
4. From what town did William set out for England? In what town did he land?
5. What body of water did William cross? About how far did he sail?
6. In what direction did William travel in going from Pevensey to Hastings? Did he travel by land or sea?
7. How long did it take Harold to reach the battle site from London?
8. Who traveled farther to reach the battle site, William or Harold?
9. The battle that took place between the English and Normans on October 14, 1066, is usually referred to as the Battle of Hastings. Where did the battle really take place? In what direction was the battle site from Hastings?
10. In what direction did the English and Norman battle line stretch? About how long was the battle line?
11. What general direction did the English army face?
12. What kind of Norman soldiers were on the front of the battle line?
13. In what earldom of England did the Battle of Hastings take place?
14. Why do you think William sailed for England from the place he did rather than from Bayeux? In what direction is Bayeux from Hastings? How far is it?

donjon
inner bailey
forebuilding
outer bailey
moat
drawbridge
gatehouse
curtain wall

LIVING IN A CASTLE

R.J. UNSTEAD

By the middle of the thirteenth century, there were at least 300 castles in England. A traveler would seldom ride all day without seeing one of these great fortresses which dominated the countryside. Some of the castles belonged to the king, but most were held by the great barons of the realm. A castle was the proof of a baron's power and rank. It housed his followers and served as a warning to his enemies. It was also his home, where he and his family lived, worked, and enjoyed themselves.

Let us see what life was like in a typical castle about the year 1250 by visiting Wenworth Castle, home of Earl Richard and his family.

Wenworth was a castle of average size and strength. It consisted of a massive stone tower or *donjon*, standing in a walled courtyard which contained some lean-to sheds with thatched roofs. Attached to this inner courtyard was a much bigger one, the *outer bailey*, surrounded by a *curtain wall* which the Earl had recently strengthened with some round towers. A *moat*, fed by a small stream, encircled the entire castle.

The great tower, seventy feet high (21 m) with walls eight feet thick (2.4 m), was the strongest point of defense. Its plan was very simple, for there were only two floors above a basement-storeroom. At the top there were *battlements*, with a *wall-walk* for the soldiers who could see across country for miles. There was no entrance at ground level.

If you were a visitor—or an enemy—you could only get into the tower by going up a flight of steps to the door. These steps were in the *forebuilding*, which also contained the chapel above and a prison cell below. At the top of the steps, you passed through the porter's[1] lodge into the Great Hall, the largest and most important room in the castle.

When you came in from the open air, the Hall seemed bare and gloomy, for it was lit by only two windows set in deep recesses. There was no chimney, only a hearth in the middle of the floor. The smoke had to find its way out of the door and windows. That was why the walls were freshly whitewashed every spring after the winter's grime had been cleaned away.

---

1. **porter:** the gatekeeper.

There was very little furniture. Two high-backed chairs stood on a low platform against one wall. There were several wooden benches and an iron-hinged cupboard for salt vessels, dishes, pickles, and spices. Tables were stacked to one side because each table top could be lifted off its trestles which were shaped like a carpenter's sawing-bench.

The Hall was the center of life indoors. The lord met his tenants there, listened to their grievances, collected rents, and punished wrongdoers in the *Barony Court*. The people of the household ate their meals and gathered there for merrymaking and ceremonies. Most of the men slept there on benches, or wrapped in cloaks on the floor amid the rushes. The ordinary man owned nothing except his clothes and the knife at his belt. He looked to his lord for food and shelter, but he did not expect privacy or comfort.

The Great Hall was the center of castle life.

The solar was warmer and less uncomfortable than any other room in the castle.

The *solar*, next to the Hall, was the lord's private room. Here were two windows with wide ledges for seats and a great hooded fireplace. The lower part of the walls was painted in a crisscross pattern of green and gold, and the countess had hung up a large tapestry which her sister had sent her from France.

Behind a partition, the lord's sleeping chamber contained a great double bed whose frame was laced with ropes to support a feather mattress and its linen sheets, quilt, and fur coverlet. Colored hangings surrounded the bed but these were pulled back during the day when the bed provided a comfortable seat. A couple of *truckle beds*, low frames with a mattress, could be pulled out from under the bed and on them slept the lady's maid and perhaps a nurse or a daughter.

The second floor of the tower contained a number of sleeping chambers for guests, knights, and the household officials. There was also a large dormitory for the maidservants, which served as the sewing room by day.

* * *

At daybreak, the household begins to stir. In the lord's bedchamber, the nurse rises from her pallet, puts on her gown, and goes to attend to her ladyship's youngest child in her cradle. While the nurse is feeding her, a maidservant brings a basin of warm water up from the kitchen for the baby's bath.

Meanwhile, the lady's maid, who also sleeps in the same room, has awakened. She has washed and dressed herself and has pushed her truckle bed under the big bed.

Earl Richard wakes and comes out in his undershirt to wash at a basin on a stand. He is very particular about cleanliness and will bathe in a tub at the end of the week. He uses soap made from wood ash mixed in scented mutton fat. Instead of shaving, he rubs his chin with a piece of pumice stone.

He dresses in linen drawers, hose that stretch above the knee, a loose tunic pulled over his head and a fur-lined surcoat with wide sleeves. When he has put on his *coif*, or cap, he goes into the solar where the steward[2] is already waiting.

While they talk business, the countess dresses with the help of her maid. Her clothes are very similar to those of her husband—linen shift, knee-length stockings kept up by embroidered garters, tunic fastened by a brooch, over-tunic, and a warm mantle, or cloak. She is warmly dressed, for the hour is early and the castle is always cold. Her maid braids her hair and

---

2. **steward:** the person who managed the lord's property and was responsible for the everyday running of the castle. He appointed other officials, such as the reeve, and fixed rents on farms and other lands.

hides it under a *wimple*, a linen band that goes under her chin and is covered by a white cap of stiffened linen.

After dressing, the Earl and his lady, accompanied by the chief members of the household, go to Mass[3] in the chapel. The service is said by Abbot[4] Hugh of Farley, a guest who is staying at the castle.

After a quick breakfast of bread, the lord and his steward deal with affairs of the manor. Will Bird wishes to pay a rent for his land instead of working three days a week on the lord's land but the steward is not keen on the idea of making him a freeman. Let him ask again in a year's time. The Earl agrees to have the watermill mended but the reeve[5] must find men to clean out the castle moat.

While this everyday business is being settled, an air of excitement runs through the castle. Everyone knows that the lord is going hunting with the abbot. The horses are ready in the yard with the grooms, while the knights stand about waiting.

At last, the Earl appears with the abbot. A horn sounds and the gaily dressed party canters across the drawbridge towards the forest, watched enviously by all who have to stay behind. Hunting is a passion. The poorest peasant loves to snare rabbits, and many nobles care for little else in life but the chase. The king has

---

3. **Mass:** the main religious service of the Roman Catholic Church. It was the custom for the people in the castle to go to Mass every day. Most noble households had a private chaplain.
4. **abbot:** a man who is head of a religious community.
5. **reeve:** the village foreman.

granted Earl Richard the precious right of *vert and venison* which means that he may hunt the deer and wild boar on his own land.

As the hunting party disappears from view, the people of the castle return to their tasks. Since breakfast was so early, dinner will be at ten or eleven o'clock in the morning, and preparations have been going on since sunrise. In the kitchen yard, the cook bawls orders. A servant comes in, bent under a load of firewood. Another carries a side of beef. Water is fetched from the well, spices from the wardrobe, fish, flour, and eggs from the store. A maid goes down to the herb garden, while another girl begins the tedious job of pounding sugar. Presently, they will start plucking chickens, pigeons, and various other small birds.

In the armoury, the armourer checks his stocks of lances, bows, swords, and mail. One of his problems is to keep chain mail in good order because its metal scales soon become rusty. This morning, he puts several suits in a barrel, sprinkles them with sand and vinegar, turns the barrel on its side, and tells his boy to roll it up and down. When the mail is taken out, all the rust has disappeared. Shields and helmets are polished and put back in their racks.

Down at the gatehouse, two soldiers are engaged in greasing the winding gear of the *portcullis*, as well as the hinges of the great double doors and the runners of the drawbridge. In peaceful times, the drawbridge is left in position for people and carts to cross the moat, but the doors are shut and the portcullis lowered every day at sunset.

The Countess Margaret has a dozen things to see to. First, she speaks to the nurse about the baby's health, but she does not stay for more than a few minutes. Bringing up children is not the business of a great lady. The nurse will feed and wash the child, teach her to talk, dose her with medicine, and take complete charge of her early years. Her mother expects her to grow into an obedient, well-mannered girl and, when she is about fifteen, her parents will arrange her marriage to a nobleman.

Next, she goes upstairs to the big chamber where her damsels and the sewing women are at work. Every Christmas, all members of the household are given clothes as part of their wages, but the work of making them goes on all year. Lady Margaret chooses the cloth for each garment and the proper amount of decoration and trimming. She sends her tailor to London twice a year to buy cloth.

After she has written a number of letters and has made arrangements for a supply of candles for the chapel, the countess and her maid take a walk in the open air with her little pet dog.

They go down into the outer bailey to stroll in the sunshine to the walled garden which the Earl had made for her. She loves its lilies, marigolds, roses, and gillyflowers, its neat gravelled paths, mulberry trees, and climbing vines. She has a row of beehives but the mason has not finished the great new dovecot which he has promised to build.

As dinnertime draws near, tables are put up in the Great Hall and are spread with clean linen. Servants set the top table with salts, drinking cups, and spoons made of silver. On the lower tables, earthenware cups, and wooden or horn spoons are set for the lower ranks but the household officials have *mazers*, wooden cups with silver rims, to drink from.

Each place is set with a thick slice of day-old bread called a *trencher*. This serves as a plate and, after dinner, the gravy-soaked trenchers will be thrown to the dogs or gathered up and sent to the poor.

The shrill note of a horn announces the return of the hunters, and the servants run to see how they have fared. Two men can be seen coming through the main gate carrying a fine buck slung on a pole. Someone calls out that they have killed two others and everyone grins with pleasure because, later in the week, when the venison is roasted, there may be some morsels for the lower tables.

The right of* vert *allowed nobles to cut wood on their lands. The right of* venison *allowed them to hunt animals.

Dinner commences with the ceremony of hand-washing. When the Earl, his lady, the abbot, and their other guests have taken their places, pages bring bowls of water to each person who dips his fingers and wipes them on a towel laid across the page's arm.

Meanwhile, the rest of the household wash their hands at washstands as they enter the Hall. Then they sit down in order of rank, the humblest folk farthest away from the top table.

The first course is announced by trumpet and the *hall marshal* brings in the principal dish on a silver platter, followed by servants bearing lesser dishes. These are set down, one dish between two persons. It is good manners to serve your neighbor first and to pick out the nicest morsels for a guest.

Table manners are very important and these are some of the rules of polite behavior which children learn from their nurse: Don't bite your bread but break it; don't talk with your mouth full; don't wipe your knife on the tablecloth; eat quietly and don't blow on your food if it is hot; wipe your mouth on your napkin before drinking; don't let your dog be a nuisance at table.

The meal consists of three courses. Some of the dishes the head table will be served include boiled mutton served with a pudding and spiced sauce, a pike stuffed with almonds, pheasants, venison cooked in a stew of spiced corn, eels cooked in a pie, chicken in saffron with egg yolks, a fruit pie, and "little lost eggs"—eggs and mincemeat in pastry.

At the lower tables, the food is not so rich. Bowls of thick meat soup are followed by boiled beef, eel pie, and dishes of chopped chicken and pork in a hot ginger sauce.

The lord sometimes sends the remains of a tasty dish down to the lower tables. Today he tells his page to take a piece of venison to Robert the huntsman. Robert, a well-known joker, dares to send back a lump of fat pork. This is received with loud laughter.

Someone calls for a song. Ralph the carter[6] is made to stand up and sing one of his songs, half made up as he goes along, about the marvelous adventures of the miller's boy who rode his old horse to London town.

After dinner has ended with a second washing of hands, the people go back to continue their work. It is June, when the days are longest and everyone will be out of doors until the sun has disappeared.

Supper is taken in the evening, a lighter meal with egg dishes and cheese. Then, while the steward and the wardrober[7] pore over their accounts, some of the others play chess or checkers while the ladies in the solar take up their embroidery.

No one wastes candles in summertime, and when the light has faded everyone goes to bed—everyone, that is, except the watchman up on the tower and the guards in the gatehouse.

On the morrow, the round of work and play will begin again.

---

6. **carter:** person who drove a cart or wagon.
7. **wardrober:** The word *wardrobe* meant a storage place. The wardrober had charge of the supplies and gave the steward a daily account.

Thinking and Writing About the Selection

1. What were the two main functions of a castle?
2. Why was there no entrance to the castle at ground level?
3. Do you think that a castle was a comfortable place to live? Who would be most comfortable? Who would be least comfortable? Why?
4. What would you miss most from your own home if you lived in a castle like the one described in the selection? What would come closest to replacing it?

Applying the Key Skill
Context Clues

Use context clues to choose the meaning of each underlined word in the sentences below.

1. The lord was not always a sympathetic listener when his tenants brought their grievances and problems for his consideration.
   a. griefs　　b. lawsuits
   c. payments of rent　　d. complaints
2. The hunting party, mounted on spirited horses, cantered across the drawbridge toward the forest.
   a. set out
   c. led (horses) by means of a halter
   b. rode at a slow gallop
   d. jumped
3. The serving tray was heaped high with tasty morsels of fruit, cheese, and sweets.
   a. rounded bowls　　b. meals
   c. small portions　　d. pastries

LANGUAGE ACTIVITY

MEDIEVAL TO MODERN

After reading "Living in a Castle," you may have concluded that life in the Middle Ages was a far cry from life today. You would be right. But in one important way, the Middle Ages are still with us. They survive in the words and expressions that have their origins in medieval times.

In early medieval times, a *villain* or *villein* was a serf. The word really meant no more than "villager" (from Latin *villa*, "country house"). Mobs of villeins armed with scythes, other farm implements, and homemade spears often served in armies. Later in the Middle Ages, villeins were freed and allowed to leave if they could pay their taxes and debts. Many who could not, fled to the cities to hide. Can you see how our word **villain,** meaning "a wicked, evil, or criminal person" is related to the medieval **villein**?

Medieval villagers lived in fear of attack by enemies and destruction by fire. At night the city gates were closed, and the inhabitants put up shutters and chained their doors. When the *curfeu,* or *coeverfu,* was sounded, they put out their fires. *Coeverfu* literally means "a covering of the fire" (French *couvrir,* "to cover" + *feu,* "fire"). Today a **curfew** is an order or rule requiring people to observe certain regulations, such as staying indoors during certain hours of the night.

SKILLS ACTIVITY

CONTEXT CLUES

When you read "Living in a Castle," you probably came across a lot of unfamiliar words and terms. Some of these were explained for you, but others were not.

What do you do to find out the meaning of an unknown word? Of course, you can always look it up in the dictionary. Sometimes, however, you can figure out its meaning by using other words in the sentence in which it appears. Sentences that come before and after the sentence can help, too. Other words and sentences that are used to figure out the meaning of an unknown word are called **context clues**.

Let's see how it works. Read the passage below and pay attention to the underlined word.

> The second floor of the tower contained a number of sleeping chambers for guests, knights, and the household officials. There was also a large dormitory for the maid-servants, which served as the sewing room by day.

Suppose that you don't know the meaning of *dormitory*. You know that the first sentence discusses the sleeping chambers for various people. The second sentence tells you that the dormitory was for the maidservants and that it served as the sewing room by day. The words *sleeping chambers*, *maid-servants*, and *served as the sewing room by day* should help you figure out that a dormitory is a room for several people to sleep in.

You may still want to check the definition you come up with against that in a dictionary. But using context clues as you go along allows you to continue reading without interruption.

ACTIVITY A Choose the correct meaning of each underlined word. Write the word and its meaning on your paper.

1. Among other perquisites of a lord were the rights to draw revenue from the property of underage heirs and to arrange marriages, for which he received a sum of money.

   a. duties b. special privileges c. oaths

2. Other buildings grew up around the palace of the king to accommodate what later became government offices.

   a. to make room for b. to approve c. to account for

ACTIVITY B Write a meaning for each underlined word on your paper. Check your definition in a dictionary. Then write a sentence of your own using the word.

1. The palace at Gloucester is mentioned in a contemporary account of the life of King Edward, written by his chief steward.
2. The king often gave fair justice where lesser matters were concerned, but often he perverted justice to his own ends where personal or political interests were at stake.
3. The court was itinerant; wherever the king was as he moved about the kingdom, there was the king's court.
4. The work of cutting and laying the stone for buildings was the work of masons. The sculpture and carving used to decorate the building were also part of their work.

Saint George and the Dragon

a legend retold by Margaret Hodges
and illustrated by Trina Schart Hyman

Each country has its legends about heroes and heroines. The stories of brave individuals who venture forth to fight a terrible enemy or restore justice and harmony are told and retold. The English legend of Saint George is one such story.

In the days when monsters and giants and fairy folk lived in England, a noble knight was riding across a plain. He wore heavy armor and carried an ancient silver shield marked with a red cross. It was dented with the blows of many battles fought long ago by other brave knights.

The Red Cross Knight had never yet faced a foe, and did not even know his name or where he had been born. But now he was bound on a great adventure, sent by the Queen of the Fairies to try his young strength against a deadly enemy, a dragon grim and horrible.

Beside him, on a little white donkey, rode a princess leading a white lamb, and behind her came a dwarf carrying a small bundle of food. The lady's lovely face was veiled and her shoulders were covered with a black cloak, as if she had a hidden sorrow in her heart. Her name was Una.

The dreadful dragon was the cause of her sorrow. He was laying waste to her land so that many frightened people had left their homes and run away. Others had shut themselves inside the walls of a castle with Una's father and mother, the king and queen of the country. But Una had set out alone from the safety of the castle walls to look for a champion who would face the terrible dragon. She had traveled a long, long way before she found the Red Cross Knight.

Like a sailor long at sea, under stormy winds and fierce sun, who begins to whistle merrily when he sees land, so Una was thankful.

Now the travelers rode together, through wild woods and wilderness, towards Una's kingdom. The path they had to follow was straight and narrow, but not easy to see. Sometimes the Red Cross Knight rode too far ahead of Una and lost his way. Then she had to find him and guide him back to the path. So they journeyed on. With Una by his side, fair and faithful, no monster or giant could stand before the knight's bright sword.

After many days the path became thorny and led up a steep hillside, where a good old hermit lived in a little house by himself. While Una rested, the Red Cross Knight climbed with the hermit to the top of the hill and looked out across the valley. There against the evening sky they saw a mountaintop that touched the highest heavens. It was crowned with a glorious palace, sparkling like stars and circled with walls and towers of pearls and precious stones. Joyful angels were coming and going between heaven and the High City.

Then the Red Cross Knight saw that a little path led up the distant mountain to that city, and he said, "I thought that the fairest palace in the world was the crystal tower in the city of the Fairy Queen. Now I see a palace far more lovely. Una and I should go there at once."

But the old hermit said, "The Fairy Queen has sent you to do brave deeds in this world. That High City that you see is in another world. Before you climb the path to it and hang your shield on its wall, go down into the valley and fight the dragon that you were sent to fight.

"It is time for me to tell you that you were not born of fairy folk, but of English earth. The fairies stole you away as a baby while you slept in your cradle. They hid you in a farmer's field, where a plowman found you. He called you George, which means 'Plow the Earth' and 'Fight the Good Fight.' For you were born to be England's friend and patron saint, Saint George of Merry England."

Then George, the Red Cross Knight, returned to Una, and when morning came, they went together down into the valley. They rode through farmlands where men and women working in their fields looked up and cheered because a champion had come to fight the dragon, and children clapped their hands to see the brave knight and the lovely lady ride by.

"Now we have come to my own country," said Una. "Be on your guard. See, there is the city and the great brass tower that my parents built strong enough to stand against the brassy-scaled dragon. There are my father and mother looking out from the walls, and the watchman stands at the top, waiting to call out the good news if help is coming."

Then they heard a hideous roaring that filled the air with terror and seemed to shake the ground. The dreadful dragon lay stretched on the sunny side of a great hill, like a great hill himself, and when he saw the knight's armor glistening in the sunlight, he came eagerly to do battle. The knight bade his lady stand apart, out of danger, to watch the fight, while the beast drew near, half flying, half running. His great size made a wide shadow under his huge body as a mountain casts a shadow on a valley. He reared high, monstrous, horrible, and vast, armed all over with scales of brass fitted so closely that no sword or spear could pierce them. They clashed with every movement. The dragon's wings stretched out like two sails when the wind fills them. The clouds fled before him. His huge, long tail, speckled red and black, wound in a hundred folds over his scaly back and swept the land behind him for almost half a mile. In his tail's end, two sharp stings were fixed. But sharper still were his cruel claws. Whatever he touched or drew within those claws was in deadly danger. His head was more hideous than tongue can tell, for his deep jaws gaped wide, showing three rows of iron teeth ready to devour his prey. A cloud of smothering smoke and burning sulfur poured from his throat, filling the air with its stench. His blazing eyes, flaming with rage, glared out from deep in his head. So he came toward the knight, raising his speckled breast, clashing his scales, as he leaped to greet his newest victim.

The knight on horseback fiercely rode at the dragon with all his might and couched his spear, but as they passed, the pointed steel glanced off the dragon's hard hide. The wrathful beast, surprised at the strength of the blow, turned quickly, and, passing the knight again, brushed him with his long tail so that horse and man fell to the ground.

Once more the Red Cross Knight mounted and attacked the dragon. Once more in vain. Yet the beast had never before felt such a mighty stroke from the hand of any man, and he was furious for revenge. With his waving wings spread wide, he lifted himself high from the ground, then, stooping low, snatched up both horse and man to carry them away. High above the plain he bore them as far as a bow can shoot an arrow, but even then the knight still struggled until the monster was forced to lower his paws so that both horse and rider fought free. With the strength of three men, again the knight struck. The spear glanced off the scaly neck, but it pierced the dragon's left wing, spread broad above him, and the beast roared like a raging sea in a winter storm. Furious, he snatched the spear in his claws and broke it off, throwing forth flames of fire from his nostrils. Then he hurled his hideous tail about and wrapped it around the legs of the horse, until, striving to loose the knot, the horse threw its rider to the ground.

Quickly the knight rose. He drew his sharp sword and struck the dragon's head so fiercely that it seemed nothing could withstand the blow. The dragon's crest was too hard to take a cut, but he wanted no more such blows. He tried to fly away and could not because of his wounded wing.

Loudly he bellowed—the like was never heard before—and from his body, like a wide devouring oven, sent a flame of fire that scorched the knight's face and heated his armor red-hot. Faint, weary, sore, burning with heat and wounds, the knight fell to the ground, ready to die, and the dragon clapped his iron wings in victory, while the lady, watching from afar, fell to her knees. She thought that her champion had lost the battle.

But it happened that where the knight fell, an ancient spring of silvery water bubbled from the ground. In that cool water the knight lay resting until the sun rose. Then he, too, rose to do battle again. And when the dragon saw him, he could hardly believe his eyes. Could this be the same knight, he wondered, or another who had come to take his place?

The knight brandished his bright blade, and it seemed sharper than ever, his hands even stronger. He smote the crested head with a blow so mighty that the

dragon reared up like a hundred raging lions. His long, stinging tail threw down high trees and tore rocks to pieces. Lashing forward, it pierced the knight's shield and its point stuck fast in his shoulder. He tried to free himself from that barbed sting, but when he saw that his struggles were in vain, he raised his fighting sword and struck a blow that cut off the end of the dragon's tail.

Heart cannot think what outrage and what cries, with black smoke and flashing fire, the beast threw forth, turning the whole world to darkness. Gathering himself up, wild for revenge, he fiercely fell upon the sunbright shield and gripped it fast with his paws. Three times the knight tried and failed to pull the shield free. Then, laying about him with his trusty sword, he struck so many blows that fire flew from the dragon's coat like sparks from an anvil, and the beast raised one paw to defend himself. Striking with might and main, the knight severed the other paw, which still clung to the shield.

Now from the furnace inside himself, the dragon threw huge flames that covered all the heavens with smoke and brimstone so that the knight was forced to retreat to save his body from the scorching fire. Again, weary and wounded with his long fight, he fell. When gentle Una saw him lying motionless, she trembled with fear and prayed for his safety.

But he had fallen beneath a fair apple tree, its spreading branches covered with red fruit, and from that tree dropped a healing dew that the deadly dragon did not dare to come near. Once more the daylight faded and night spread over the earth. Under the apple tree the knight slept.

Then dawn chased away the dark, a lark mounted up to heaven, and up rose the brave knight with all his hurts and wounds healed, ready to fight again. When the dragon saw him, he began to be afraid. Still he rushed

upon the knight, mouth gaping wide to swallow him whole. And the knight's bright weapon, taking advantage of that open jaw, ran it through with such strength that the dragon fell dead, breathing his last in smoke and cloud. Like a mountain he fell, and lay still. The knight himself trembled to see that fall, and his dear lady did not think to come near to thank her faithful knight until she saw that the dragon would stir no more.

Now our ship comes into port. Furl the sails and drop anchor. Safe from storm, Una is at her journey's end.

The watchman on the castle wall called out to the king and queen that the dragon was dead, and when the old king saw that it was true, he ordered the castle's great brass gates to be opened so that the tidings of peace and joy might spread through all the land. Trumpets sounded the news that the great beast had fallen. Then the king and queen came out of the city with all their nobles to meet the Red Cross Knight. Tall young men led the way, carrying laurel branches to lay at the hero's feet. Pretty girls wore wreaths of flowers and made music on tambourines. The children came dancing, laughing and singing, with a crown of flowers for Una. They gazed in wonder at the victorious knight.

But when the people saw where the dead dragon lay, they dared not come near to touch him. Some ran away, some pretended not to be afraid. One said the dragon might still be alive; one said he saw fire in the eyes. Another said the eyes were moving. When a foolish child ran forward to touch the dragon's claws, his mother scolded. "How can I tell?" she said. "Those claws might scratch my son, or tear his tender hand." At last some of the bolder men began to measure the dragon to prove how many acres his body covered.

The old king embraced and kissed his daughter. He gave gifts of gold and ivory and a thousand thanks to the

dragonslayer. But the knight told the king never to forget the poor people, and gave the rich gifts to them. Then back to the palace all the people went, still singing, to feast and to hear the story of the knight's adventures with Una.

When the tale ended, the king said, "Never did living man sail through such a sea of deadly dangers. Since you are now safely come to shore, stay here and live happily ever after. You have earned your rest."

But the brave knight answered, "No, my lord, I have sworn to give knight's service to the Fairy Queen for six years. Until then, I cannot rest."

The king said, "I have promised that the dragonslayer should have Una for his wife, and be king after me. If you love each other, my daughter is yours now. My kingdom shall be yours when you have done your service for the Fairy Queen and returned to us."

Then he called Una, who came no longer wearing her black cloak and her veil, but dressed in a lily-white gown that shimmered like silver. Never had the knight seen her so beautiful. Whenever he looked at the brightness of her sunshiny face, his heart melted with pleasure.

So Una and the Red Cross Knight were married and lived together joyfully. But the knight did not forget his promise to serve the Fairy Queen, and when she called him into service, off he rode on brave adventures, until at last he earned his name, Saint George of Merry England.

That is how it is when jolly sailors come into a quiet harbor. They unload their cargo, mend ship, and take on fresh supplies. Then away they sail on another long voyage, while we are left on shore, waving good-bye and wishing them Godspeed.

Thinking and Writing About the Selection

1. Why had Una sought the Red Cross Knight?
2. What did the hermit reveal to the Red Cross Knight about his future?
3. Do you think the Red Cross Knight would have defeated the dragon without the help he received from the spring and the apple tree? Explain your answer.
4. The dragon was described in great detail by the writer of the selection. The artist used those details to paint vivid pictures. Think of an imaginary creature. Describe it in such detail that an artist could paint it just as you imagine it to be.

Applying the Key Skill

Context Clues

1. Find the following words in "Saint George and the Dragon." List the words, phrases, or other context clues that helped you to figure out the meaning of each word. Then write a definition of the word.
   a. hermit b. gaped
   c. stench d. dragonslayer
2. Use context clues to choose the meaning of each underlined word in the sentences below.
   a. Una was filled with trepidation when she saw the flames pour out of the dragon.
      confidence relief fearful anticipation
   b. After the Red Cross Knight killed the dragon, harmony was restored throughout the kingdom.
      peace celebration government
   c. The legend of Saint George and the dragon has been recounted by storytellers and writers for centuries.
      enjoyed narrated computed

MARGARET HODGES

"I expect to end my days happily surrounded by books."

Margaret Hodges first got the idea of retelling the story of Saint George and the dragon when her professor happened to mention that he had read the poem "Faerie Queen," a similar story, to his four-year-old granddaughter. Most of Margaret Hodges' previous books had been stories of present-day boys and girls, including the popular Joshua Cobb series. Historical subjects have also been among her favorite writing topics, enlivened by details based on her own travels to the places about which she writes.

By her own account, Hodges was "born into a book-loving family.…As early as seventh grade I wrote a paragraph for the school magazine called 'Miss Matty's Library.' The description clearly shows that I thought it was bliss to be in a library. I still do."

After she was married, she continued to write dramatizations of children's stories for a radio program that later became a TV series.

In her stories, Margaret Hodges uses "things that I remember from my own childhood or from that of our three sons." But she is also always looking for new subjects. And her readers eagerly await new stories from this wide-ranging author.

More to Read *Lady Queen Anne, The Making of Joshua Cobb*

SKILLS ACTIVITY

PARTS OF A BOOK: INDEX, BIBLIOGRAPHY, FOOTNOTES

Many books have special features designed to aid you in reading. These features can help you to locate information quickly.

An **index** is a list of subjects discussed in a book, found at the back of the book. Each subject listed in an index is called a heading, or entry. Main entries are general subjects printed in heavy, or boldface, type. Subentries are specific topics indented and listed under main entries. The word *See* tells you what main entry to look under to find information for that subject. The words *See also* tell you what other main entry to look under for further information.

ACTIVITY A Use the sample index below to answer the questions. Write the answers on your paper.

Cannon, 86-88, 91-95
    ***See also* Weapons**
Castle, 21-23, 31-35,
    73-74, 98-99
Catapult, 83-84
    ***See also* Weapons**
Crusades, 39-45
    Children's Crusade, 45
    First Crusade, 39-40
    Fourth Crusade, 43-44
    Second Crusade, 41
    Third Crusade, 42-43
Defense, 74-88
Donjon, 32
Drawbridge, 14
    ***See also* Defense**
Escalading
    ***See* Attack**
Feudal system, 27-33
Fief-holding
    ***See* Feudal system**
Fortifications
    ***See* Defense**

1. On what page or pages would you look for information about castles?
2. Under what heading would you look to find information about fief-holding?
3. Where would you look to find information about the Fourth Crusade? About crusades in general?
4. Under what heading would you look to find more information about drawbridges?
5. On what page or pages would you look to find out about catapults? Under what heading would you look to find where to look for more information about catapults?

A **bibliography** is a list of books and articles found at the back of a book or at the end of an article. The list may include books and articles used by the author in writing the book or article. It may also include the titles of books and articles related to the author's subject that the author feels you might enjoy for further reading.

Books and articles in a bibliography are listed in alphabetical order by the last name of the author. In the case of a book, the author's name is followed by the title, the place of publication, the publisher, and the date of publication. In an entry for an article, the author's name is followed by the title, the name of the periodical, the volume and page numbers, and the month and year of publication.

Coulton, G.G. *Life in the Middle Ages*. New York: Macmillan Publishing Company, 1930.	**BOOK ENTRY**
Mangus, Marlyn. "Medieval Manuscripts." *Medieval Studies*, 127: 430-441, May, 1987.	**ARTICLE ENTRY**

ACTIVITY B Use the sample bibliography to answer the questions below. Write the answers on your paper.

Barton, M.F. *In the Days of King Arthur*. New York: Random House, 1981.

Kraft, Robert Martin. "The Castles of England." *National Geographic*, 141: 479-500, April, 1983.

Knudsen, Ronald. *The Story of the Crusades*. New York: E.P. Dutton & Co., 1985.

Lorrington, Marcia. "Medieval Sports and Pastimes." 82: 34-67, August, 1985.

1. Who is the author of *The Story of the Crusades*?
2. Which two entries are listed in the incorrect order? In what order should they be listed?
3. Is "The Castles of England" a book or an article?
4. What information is missing from the fourth entry?
5. What does the number 141 in the second entry refer to? What do the numbers 479-500 refer to?

A **footnote** is an explanatory note, comment, or reference. It may be found at the foot, or bottom, of a page, or at the end of a chapter, book, or article. It is indicated in the text by a numeral or symbol referring to it.

Some footnotes give pronunciations and definitions. Some give fuller explanations of a term or phrase. Others tell where the author found the facts or ideas that he or she used. In all cases, a footnote adds information without breaking into the text.

A reference footnote for the following sentence is given below.

A balista was a huge crossbow that could fire a bolt weighing five or six pounds.[1]

1. Everton, Charles. *Medieval Warfare.* (New York: Vertigo Press, 1985), p. 67.

This footnote tells you the name of the book from which the information was taken. In the footnote, the author's name is given first, followed by the title of the book. The words in parentheses tell you where and by whom the book was published, and the date of publication. The page number tells you where to look to find more information about a balista.

ACTIVITY C Read the sample paragraph. Use the footnotes below to answer the questions. Write the answers on your paper.

> Estimates of the number of English and Norman soldiers that took part in the Battle of Hastings vary greatly. One author gives the figure of 5,000 for each side.[1] In any case, the battle that took place at Senlac[2] on October 14, 1066, was one of the most decisive events in English history. When Harold's huscarls[3] failed to protect the life of their king, a turning point in Anglo-Saxon history was reached.

1. Henderson, J.E. *The Battle of Hastings.* (Boston: Prescott Press, 1984), p. 43.
2. **Senlac:** the name of the hill where the Battle of Hastings actually took place, about eight miles northwest of Hastings.
3. **huscarls:** bodyguards.

1. What author gave the estimate of 5,000 troops each on the English and Norman sides at the Battle of Hastings?
2. What does (Boston: Prescott Press, 1984) mean in footnote 1?
3. What and where is Senlac?
4. What does the word *huscarls* mean?

THE PRACTICAL PRINCESS

Barbara Eriksen

In the old tales, handsome princes were always venturing forth to perform some feat that would win them the hand of a beautiful princess. The princess in this modern fairy tale demands a different sort of prince.

In a rather small kingdom, in a castle no bigger than a very large house, there lived a princess who was not particularly beautiful. Her father, King Authbert the Average, was seldom bothered with princes beating on the door and demanding his daughter's hand in marriage. When a prince did drop in to meet Princess Gillian, she usually showed him to the door after a short visit.

"It's been nice to meet you," she would say. "Do have a pleasant journey."

This worried the king, for he wanted his daughter to find her prince as princesses had always done.

Queen Elisand was less concerned. "If the right prince comes along—fine. If not . . ." and she shrugged. "I'm sure Gillian will keep busy."

Princess Gillian herself did not seem bothered by the shortage of suitors. She was happy as a lark working in the gardens, a smudgy smock covering her plain dress. Old Abel, the gardener, was teaching her all about pruning and planting and composting, and about tending the wild trillium and columbine that grew beneath the oak tree in the corner of the garden.

Things were quite different in the neighboring kingdom. There King Griswolf the Great was besieged by a constant stream of princes pleading for the hand of Princess Dorabella, who was known far and wide for her ravishing beauty. To pick the most suitable prince, King Griswolf had devised four terrifying tests. So far, no one had passed more than three. Most of the princes could slay six dragons or swim the moat in their armor. Several even managed to carry their horses across the drawbridge to the castle. But no one could climb (barefoot and without armor) to the top of a tall thorn tree to retrieve a jeweled golden bird.

"This is no test, this is torture!" they would cry and gallop off without a backward glance. Then King Griswolf would sneer an ugly sneer, and Princess Dorabella would laugh a haughty laugh.

One day a prince, all bandaged and bloody, knocked at the door of King Authbert the Average.

"Have you a princess here?" he asked, hobbling into the throne room and clumsily attempting a bow.

"Why yes, as a matter of fact we do," answered King Authbert. "Elisand, my dear, call Gillian."

Queen Elisand went to the window that looked over the garden and called, "Gillian, come up here for a minute, dear."

A few minutes later, Princess Gillian appeared in the throne room in her usual smudgy smock, with her hair pulled straight back and tied with a piece of gardener's string. Her hands were muddy, and there was some dirt on the tip of her freckled nose.

She looked at the bandaged prince and asked, "My goodness, sir, whatever happened to you?"

"I fell from Princess Dorabella's thorn tree," he answered. "But what, may I ask, happened to you?"

Princess Gillian glanced down at her dirty smock. "I've been helping Abel the gardener plant marigolds. Would you like to see them?"

"Why, er, yes . . . why not?" answered the prince, rather surprised. This was certainly a different kind of princess!

Gillian led the bandaged prince to a garden bench in the shade of the spreading oak tree. She told him of the beauty of the trillium and columbine in the springtime. She talked about composting to make the soil rich for the tiny marigolds, so that they would grow to mounds of glorious color.

In turn, Prince Aldano told story after story of his mighty deeds of dragon-slaying and maiden-rescuing. Finally he told Princess Gillian about his quest for Princess Dorabella's hand. "And when I fell out of the thorn tree," he concluded sadly, "she laughed at me."

Princess Gillian shook her head. "I think you were very foolish to go through all those terrifying tests to win the hand of someone you didn't even know," she said.

The prince frowned. "What do you mean?" he asked.

"Well," she replied, "what if you *had* gotten the bird down? There you'd be—stuck with marrying a princess who is mean enough to laugh when someone is quite badly hurt. You should be more careful about such things in the future."

The prince frowned again. "You may have something there," he said, "but that's the way it's usually done. Anyway, you seem like a much nicer princess. Perhaps I may have your hand in marriage?"

"My goodness no," said Gillian. "Why would I wish to marry someone who just fell from Princess Dorabella's thorn tree? I can't marry you simply to make you feel better. But do stop in for tea if you come by this way again. You'll have to excuse me now; my cooking lesson is about to begin." And Princess Gillian went skipping off to the kitchen.

Prince Aldano was quite astonished. "Is your daughter always like this?" he asked.

"I'm afraid so," said King Authbert.

"She's a very practical girl," said Queen Elisand.

"I don't think I made a very good impression," said Prince Aldano.

"Better luck next time," said the king hopefully.

A few weeks later Prince Aldano knocked again on the door of King Authbert the Average. His bandages were gone, and he strode briskly up to the throne and bowed gracefully to the king and queen.

"Good afternoon, your Highnesses," he said. "I hear you have had some battles in your neighborhood lately. Did you do well?"

"Not really," sighed Queen Elisand.

"Not well at all," said King Authbert.

"Aha! What you need is someone like me to lead your troops into battle. Since I last saw you, I have slain at least a dozen dragons, rescued fifteen fair maidens, and stopped the charge of a herd of fifty fierce unicorns. And all so I could suitably ask for the hand of Princess Gillian. What do you say?" Prince Aldano smiled expectantly.

"I think you had better ask her yourself," said the king.

"I'll ring the kitchen," said Queen Elisand.

Princess Gillian entered the throne room wearing a spattered apron over her plain dress. "Prince Aldano," she smiled. "How nice to see you again." She put her flour-covered hand on his velvet sleeve. "Do come have some tea cakes. I just made them." And she led the surprised prince down the stairs to the palace kitchen.

"So this is what a kitchen looks like," Aldano muttered to himself. Then, in a loud voice, he announced, "Princess Gillian, since I last saw you I have slain a dozen dragons, rescued fifteen fair maidens, and stopped the charge of a herd of fifty fierce unicorns, just so I could ask for your hand in marriage."

"Have a tea cake," said Gillian, popping one into his mouth. "I don't recall asking you to do such things. Why did you do them?"

"To properly impress you," mumbled Prince Aldano through his tea cake.

Princess Gillian sighed and shook her head. "I'm surprised you didn't get stuck in another thorn tree," she said. "Can't you do anything useful?"

"Whatever do you mean?" asked the prince, looking puzzled.

"Can you plant a garden, construct a building, survey a road, butcher a steer, or sail a ship? I understand there is little demand for dragon-slayers and maiden-rescuers these days."

The prince frowned. "You may have something there," he said. "But your father needs a strong, old-fashioned prince to lead his army."

"If you wish to lead my father's army you'd better talk to him," said Princess Gillian. "I can't marry you just to get you the job. You must excuse me now; I am learning to sew." And Princess Gillian dashed up the stairs to the tower room to begin her lesson.

Prince Aldano was flabbergasted. "What must I do to please this princess?" he demanded of no one in particular, and rode off with a fierce frown on his handsome brow.

King Authbert scratched his head. "There he goes again," he said a little sadly. "I was rather beginning to like him. Sometimes I just don't understand Gillian."

"If only he would stop and think," sighed Queen Elisand, who understood her daughter very well.

Many months later, Prince Aldano knocked on the door of King Authbert. His velvet tunic was gone. Instead he wore serviceable leather breeches and a woolen jacket. He quickly approached the king and queen and dropped down on one knee.

"I have traveled far and have much to tell your daughter Gillian," said Prince Aldano. "Do you think she will see me?"

"I don't see why not," said King Authbert.

"I'm sure she will," smiled Queen Elisand. "I'll see if she's in her room."

While he waited, Prince Aldano paced nervously back and forth. He stopped, startled and delighted, when Princess Gillian entered the hall. She wore a lovely green dress that exactly matched the color of her eyes. A sunbeam lighted her hair and danced across her cheeks.

"How lovely you look," said the prince.

Princess Gillian smiled. "Thank you," she said. "I'm glad you like the dress; I made it myself. But you have been away for a very long time—what have you been doing?"

"I have traveled far and learned a great deal," said Prince Aldano, and he told her of his journeys. He talked excitedly of learning to sail a fishing vessel and rigging the nets, of shoeing horses and herding cattle, of weaving cloth and mending shoes.

"How wonderful," murmured Princess Gillian.

"Perhaps now I may have your hand in marriage. For I have learned another, a most important thing: You are a very special princess." Prince Aldano held his breath and waited for her answer.

Princess Gillian smiled. "I will gladly marry you," she said, "for now I know that you are a very special prince."

Some time after their simple but happy wedding, Gillian said to Aldano, "I wonder if Princess Dorabella ever found anyone to climb that thorn tree."

"I understand a prince from the north chopped the tree down and plucked the bird from the top without getting a single scratch," said Aldano.

"What a clever idea! Now why didn't you think of that?" teased Gillian.

"How lucky for me that I didn't," Aldano smiled.

"For me, too," said Gillian.

Thinking and Writing About the Selection

1. What things did Princess Gillian enjoy doing?
2. How did King Authbert feel about his daughter's chances for marriage? How did Queen Elisand feel?
3. How is "The Practical Princess" like other fairy tales you know? How is it different?
4. Do you think that Aldano and Gillian will live happily ever after? Why or why not?

Applying the Key Skill

Draw Conclusions

Use complete sentences to answer the following questions about "The Practical Princess."

1. What did Princess Gillian conclude after Prince Aldano described his quest for Princess Dorabella's hand? What information did she give to support her conclusion?
2. Why did Prince Aldano conclude that he hadn't made a very good impression on Princess Gillian after their first meeting?
3. What did Prince Aldano decide or conclude would impress Princess Gillian? How did he reach that conclusion?
4. With which of the following conclusions do you think the author of "The Practical Princess" would probably agree?
   a. Beauty is more important than intelligence.
   b. Parents should choose the person their daughter will marry.
   c. Practical intelligence is something to admire and value.
   d. What most people accept as worthwhile is not always what is truly worthy.

SERENDIPITY

If you are knightly on your daily way
to slay a dragon
and by that way
you spy a wagon
filled with jewels to the top-tippety,
that is serendipity.

Or if you are Adam adamantly out to do your duty,
and along your macadam route you encounter a beauty
who causes your heart to go flop-flippety,
that event is serendipity.
Sir, meet Lady Serendipity.

Wherever you search for thorns and turn up a rose,
there is that fortune you cannot importune:
there is where fair serendipity grows.

Eve Merriam

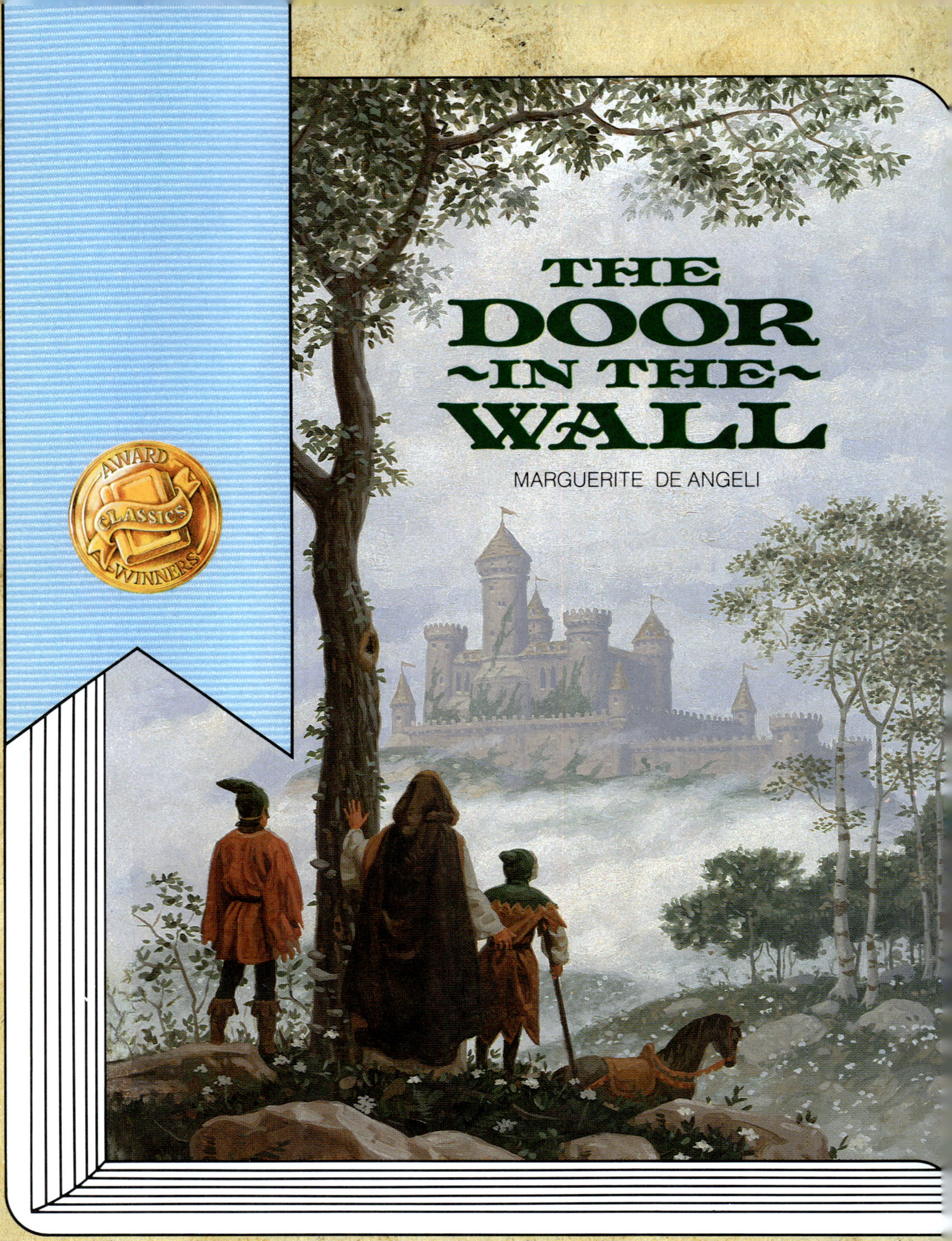
AWARD
CLASSICS
WINNERS
THE DOOR IN THE WALL
MARGUERITE DE ANGELI

The setting for this Newbery Award-winner is fourteenth-century England. While his father was with the king, fighting the Scots, and his mother was traveling with the Queen, Robin was to be sent to Sir Peter de Lindsay to begin his training for knighthood. But before he could leave, Robin fell ill. The strange illness left his legs useless. Brother Luke, a wandering friar, took Robin to St. Mark's Monastery and cared for him. There Robin learned to read and write, to whittle, and many other skills. Daily swimming lessons strengthened his arms. He learned to walk on crutches he made himself. Finally a messenger arrives—Robin is to meet his father at Castle Lindsay. After a dangerous journey, Robin, Brother Luke, and John-go-in-the-Wynd, the minstrel, reach the castle on the Welsh border. The days pass quietly until one night, under cover of dense fog, the hostile Welsh soldiers lay siege to the castle. Can Robin go for help?

The fog held for days. The Welsh could not get beyond the outer wall of the castle, and the English inside could not tell what strength the enemy possessed. They might be encamped on the surrounding hills, or they might be only a small company. Several of the guards on the wall had been injured, and sometimes the yeomen could tell that an arrow had struck home in the enemy's camp. Most of the time there was only watchful waiting on both sides.

Inside the keep, women occupied themselves with spinning, weaving, and embroidery. It helped the time to pass more quickly. The children played with toy soldiers and blocks, with hobbyhorses and with dolls. Sometimes Robin told them tales, or sang songs, but he spent most of the time in the chamber where he slept, working on the Saxon harp he was making.

Sir Peter had stood all of one night on the bastion directing and encouraging the men. They had managed to drive off a raiding party that was trying to scale the wall. Now he was in bed with a chill, and Lady Constance waited upon him.

The food in the larder dwindled, and there were many people to be fed. Besides the garrison and the household there were the yeomen from the town and those who had sought refuge when the portcullis was raised.

Usually there was a good supply of salt fish kept in barrels, but fish had not been plentiful the past summer, so now the supply was meager. There was mutton, to be sure, but it was all on four legs and scattered over the downs beyond the castle and town. The winter kill had not taken place because they waited for freezing weather. There was flour to last for a short time, but the yearly portion from the peasants' holdings was to have been brought to the castle the following week. Besides, there had been a small crop of grain because of the drought.

Then the water began to fail. As Robin came into the hall at suppertime he passed the table where the servants sat. Denis, a page, leaned to whisper in the ear of Adam the Yeoman.

"There is scarce a foot of water in the well," he whispered. "Just now as I drew it to fill this ewer the cook told me."

"How came this?" asked Adam. "'Tis known that this is a good well. Tell not her ladyship, and send the word around that the water must be used sparingly, or 'twill not last the week out, even for drinking."

He thought a moment, then said, "Someone must go for help, or we shall be forced to surrender the castle. It might be that Sir Hugh Fitzhugh would come to our aid, for he, too, is in danger from the Welsh if they break our defense. But whom shall we spare? All are needed at their posts."

"Let me go," said Robin. "I can go out the small door at the north whilst it is early morning. No one will suspect me. They think me a poor shepherd. I shall borrow a smock from William the Farrier's son, and if I am seen, I shall appear stupid."

"But thou'rt only a lad!" Adam objected, "and art cumbered with crutches as well. And how wilt thou cross the river? The bridge is well guarded at both ends."

"I shall go well, never fear," Robin assured them confidently. "I have it all in my head how it shall be done. I shall find John-go-in-the-Wynd visiting at his mother's cottage in Tripheath village. John shall set forth from there for Sir Hugh and his men.

"Now, let us plan. First, I want you, Denis, to bring me the smock, and some rags to wrap about my legs. Then, see you, find me a hood that is worn and faded. Besides, I shall need long leather thongs to tie the crutches to my back, for I shall swim the river."

"Fear you not the soldiery?" queried Denis anxiously. "Will you not fall down the steep bank? 'Tis a far distance to the bottom of the ravine, and—" He stopped suddenly, because one of the maids appeared.

"See to it," said Robin with a quick nod.

Dressed in the patched and ragged smock, his legs wound about with bits of rag to hold the ill-fitting hosen, Robin tried to sleep away the early part of the night, but excitement kept him wakeful. Even when he dozed, he was aware of what he was about to do. He counted over all the things he must remember. He must go softly with the crutches. He must remember the leather thongs. As Brother Luke had told him, he mustn't forget oil for the rusty lock of the door in the wall.

Just before dawn Brother Luke touched him.

"Come, my son," he whispered. They went down a half flight of steps and across the hall of the keep to the winding stair, making their way quietly among the sleeping servants. They went very slowly, for Robin's crutches tapped an alarm when he made haste, and the least misstep would have sent him clattering down.

There was still fog when they came into the open, but it had begun to drift and there was a gray dawn just beginning to break.

"Who goes there?" demanded the sentry at the door, but seeing Robin and the friar, he allowed them to pass.

They reached the sally port in the north wall without meeting anyone else. Brother Luke dripped oil into the lock before trying to open the door.

Robin listened.

"Hark!" he whispered. "I hear the Welsh sentry outside. We can count the paces and can tell how far away

he is. One, two, three, four . . ." They counted forty paces. "Now!"

Slowly the door opened and Robin slipped outside.

Quickly he moved away from the door and the wall. In a moment he was at the edge of the deep ravine. He could hear the river far below him, but could not see it for the fog.

Now began the dangerous descent. Carefully Robin tested each clod of earth, each bit of stone, before trusting his weight to the crutches, praying the while that the fog would hold. Sometimes he slid on his haunches, sometimes seedling trees held him till he was able to find sure footing.

"If I should start a stone rolling," he thought, "the whole Welsh army will be upon my neck."

It seemed hours to Robin that he was sliding, groping, laboring down the treacherous cliff, but it was only a few moments, for the light of morning had scarcely changed when he reached the bottom and found himself at the edge of the river.

He stopped only long enough to fasten the crutches onto his back with the leathern thong and to wind his hood into a kind of hat that perched on top of his head. Then he plunged into the icy water, not allowing himself to consider whether he had the courage to do it.

When first the water closed over him Robin thought he could not bear it. The crutches were awkward. His chest felt tightly squeezed, and as if sharp knives pierced him. He seemed unable to breathe, and his head felt ready to burst. But he struck out fiercely, and after a few strokes began to breathe more easily. Warmth crept through his body and a feeling of power, as if nothing could be too difficult for him. He swam strongly across the swift current toward the path he had seen from the top of the tower.

What if the enemy should be camped on the other side? Suppose they wouldn't believe he was the poor shepherd he pretended to be? Suppose he found it impossible to get up the bank on the other side?

"Anyone could *not* do it," he said to himself stubbornly, and thrashed his arms more fiercely.

At last he felt the stones of shallower water under his feet, the bank appeared mistily green, and he was able to hold himself steady with one hand while he untied the crutches and set them under his armpits. The bank was not very steep after all, and in a moment he was at the top, ready to go on. His teeth started to chatter in the rising wind.

His feet felt as if they had been frozen. His hands were so numb with cold he could hardly hold the crutches to steady them as he walked. He paused long enough to let down the hood into its proper shape. The warm wool felt good, although it was wet along the edges. The fog was lifting somewhat with the wind, and Robin, looking back once, caught sight of the castle he had left behind.

After passing through a patch of brush and willows Robin came out into a field. He still could not see very far ahead, but the path was straight before him, so he began to swing along as fast as he could, his crutches making great sweeping circles, his feet covering the ground in tremendous strides. There seemed to be no one about, so he made haste without regard to noise, and gradually the numbness in his hands and feet began to ease. Across the field he went, swing-step, swing-step, swing-step.

The fog wavered and lifted, swirled about in sudden drafts, floated across the path in thin layers, showed a patch of blue sky for an instant and glimpses of trees ahead.

Suddenly a voice rang out.

"Who goes there?"

Robin stopped.

"'Tis but I, Robin," he answered in a meek voice, and the chill that ran down his spine was not all from the dampness of his clothing.

"Robin who?" the voice went on.

"Robin—Robin Crookshank, some call me," answered Robin.

The fog parted, showing the fierce and scowling head of a man.

The guard drew near where he could see the boy.

"Aah," he said. "Art tha' but a shepherd boy, then?" he asked, seeing Robin's poor clothes. "And hast fallen into the river? Come, then, lad, and warm tha'self by the fire. Be not frighted. We'll not hurt thee." He took Robin's arm and tried to draw him toward the camp, which now Robin could see just at the side of the field, for now the fog was fast disappearing. But Robin held back and shook his head, trying to think what he must say and how he must speak.

"Nay," he began, trying to appear stupid, "'tis na far to the cottage." He edged away, bobbing his thanks, and went on as fast as he dared up the other side of the field

and through the hedgerow. He did not stop until he was well beyond earshot of the men in the camp, then stood only for a moment to draw long, steadying breaths.

He chuckled at the way he had fooled the Welshman.

From that point on the path led through a wood and across a shallow stream. Beyond a low-lying field and a rising slope Robin could see the wood that extended to the edge of the village where the church tower stood.

The wood behind him hid Robin from the camp in the field, for which he was thankful, because the rising ground slowed his going, and he felt as if he were a fair target for arrows. When he reached the shelter of the great trees, Robin sank down into a bed of bracken forest. He was very tired.

When breathing was easier and the pain of effort but a dull ache, Robin rose to go on. How much further had he to go? Would John be there when he arrived? Would he be able to get help in time?

In about an hour the forest began to thin, and Robin could see the blue smoke coming from the cotters' chimney pots. Which cottage belonged to John's mother? Robin remembered that John had said it was on the heath and near the church. He could see such a cottage from where he stood, so he made his way toward it hopefully. It was so exciting to be within sight of help that Robin forgot that he was tired and hungry, he forgot that he was still cold from his dousing in the river and the fright he'd had. He began to cut across the heath toward the cottage but had not gone far when John himself came out of the door.

Robin stopped.

"John!" he called at the top of his voice. "John! Oh, John-go-in-the-Wy-y-y-nd."

John heard him, looked his way, then came running.

"Master Robin!" he exclaimed. "What's amiss? How came thou here?"

Without waiting for an answer he grasped Robin's crutches and swept him up into his arms, because he could see that Robin had come as far as he was able. It was such a relief to have the weight of his body taken from his aching armpits that Robin allowed John to carry him to the cottage.

"The castle is in danger!" said Robin. "The Welsh have taken the town and are at the gates of the outer bailey. The food is giving out. The water low in the well. You must get help. You must get it soon."

"But how came thou here?" said John, amazed. "How didst escape the sentry?" John was already putting on his hood and fastening his leather jerkin.

He went on without waiting.

"I shall be gone straight away. Stay thou here for safety and to rest."

John-go-in-the-Wynd was well named, for go he did, closing the door behind him almost before he had finished speaking.

Robin sighed. It was good to be able to rest.

"Come, now," said John's mother, as she took off Robin's clothes to dry them. "Thou'lt be famished with hunger. I'll bake thee a bannock."

Robin slept after the woman fed him and didn't wake until the sun was low in the west. The sound of the door opening was what really woke him. It was John.

Robin was up on his elbow in a second.

"Did you find help then?"

"Yes, already they are well on their way from my lord Hugh Fitzhugh's castle," said John. "A large force of foot soldiers and a company of lancers go by the drovers' road, a second company by the way through wood and field, and another going around to attack from the other side of the town by way of Letham Bridge. It hath been agreed that we shall give the signal from the bell tower of the church. There are not better bowmen in England. The siege will be lifted. Thou'lt see!"

"I want to see it," declared Robin. "I want to see it all!"

"See it thou shalt," promised John.

John laid out his little harp, put bread into his pouch, and stuck a knife in his belt. After a quick meal of porridge, they made ready to start.

"I will carry thee," John said. The harp and the crutches we shall strap on so they will not cumber us." He fastened the crutches to his side and the harp around Robin's neck, so it hung down his back.

"Fare thee well, Mother," said John, embracing her. "Up, now, young master," he said to Robin, and with that they left the cottage and went on their way.

"How shall we go?" asked Robin, as John strode down the path on the way out of the village. "Shall we go by the way I came here? Or by way of Letham Bridge?"

"Neither," answered John-go-in-the-Wynd. "I know still another way. I know a path leading through the forest to the southeast. It goeth past the priory where we shall ford the river. We can come at the town easily from there. Then we can wait for nightfall, and indeed it will be nightfall ere we arrive, but there will be a moon.

"We shall creep along the river, under cover of the reeds and willows, and enter the town through the shoemaker's house, which is on the wall. He is known to me, and we have a signal between us. He knoweth the sound of my harp, and the certain tune I play will tell him we have need of him. From there it is quite simple to get into the graveyard of the church, thence into the church itself, and into the tower. There we shall see all and hear all if we are not deafened by the bells."

Although he carried Robin, John trotted along at a good speed, for he knew every curve in the path. It was only a short way to the ford of the river, near the priory, and from there across fields covered with grazing sheep to the forest. There they rested.

By the time they reached the place where the drovers' road led, John halted before crossing the road to observe the sentry. They waited for the sound of his footsteps to die away around the town. The moon was high, and by keeping well in the shadow of a tree they were able to cross the road without being seen.

"Ah," said John with a sigh of relief. "So far we have come safely. Soon Sir Hugh's men will encircle the town. By then we shall be in the church tower to give the signal for attack."

"Hark!" whispered Robin again. "All is still. The sentry is at the far end of his walk. Shall we go then?"

"Aye, 'tis time," said John. "Hast the little harp safe?"

"'Tis safe," said Robin, grasping John about the neck and getting himself settled on his back.

They crept forward again, shielded by the darkness, and made their way along a narrow path that followed the wall until the rising ground told John they were near to the shoemaker's cottage. There again they halted, to make sure no sentry was about. John, letting Robin slip to the ground, fitted the crutches under his arms and took the harp from about his neck.

The tune he played was mournful and slow, but it must have reached the ears of the shoemaker. John was just beginning to play it for the third time when there was an answer to it in the form of a bagpipe jig. Robin could see John bobbing his head up and down happily because his playing had brought forth the right response. There followed another period of waiting while the sentry passed again on the wall. They scarcely breathed until he had turned again and was going the other way. By counting his steps they knew when he was far enough away for them to act.

Then, without warning, a sort of chair was let down from a window high in the wall. John fastened Robin into it and gave the rope a jerk. Robin was hauled aloft so quickly that he had no time to think what he should do or what he should say. He found himself being lifted inside the upper room of a small house and the window drawn to. He faced a little man, who cautioned him to silence while again they waited for the sentry to come and to go.

He heard the "tramp, tramp" of the sentry and the thudding of the pikestaff as it struck the stone when the sentry turned at the wall of the house. The sound lessened, and once more the rope was lowered.

This time it was for John. Robin could see the iron wheel under the window which turned like a windlass to let out the rope.

In a moment John stood in the room with him. The rope and iron wheel were stored in an innocent-looking chest. The shoemaker quickly lifted the wheel out of the strong wooden block which held it covered with a flat board and cloth. The shoemaker motioned for Robin and John to follow him down the steep stair leading to the house below.

They did not linger in the house, but with a few words to the shoemaker, left by way of the garden. There was a door in the wall leading into the graveyard of the church, where John and Robin slipped quietly from one great tombstone to another. They entered the church by the sanctuary door, startling the sacristan who slept and ate in a small room off the entrance porch.

"Who are thou?" he called, hearing the creak of the door. "Art friend or foe?"

"Hist!" warned John, stepping quickly toward the light of the lantern held by the sacristan. "We are friends. I am John-go-in-the-Wynd, minstrel. This lad is young Master Robin, friend and ward of Sir Peter. He hath this day saved us all." The sacristan held the lantern up where he could see John's face.

"Now I mind thee," he said, nodding his head. "I knew thy father."

John told the sacristan how Robin had come to warn him and to get help, and described the plan he had made with Sir Hugh to sound the bells giving the signal for the attack.

"Come with me, then," said the sacristan, leading the way.

They went down the long, dark aisle of the church to the door of the tower.

"Give me thy crutches here, young master," said John. "Canst thou climb the ladder or wilt go pickaback? 'Tis a great height, but there are resting places."

"I can do it," said Robin shortly. Had he not climbed to the towers and turrets of the castle many times?

"We shall go to the top first," said John, "for it is yet too soon to give the signal, and from there we shall see somewhat."

From the belfry to the top of the tower it was another thirty feet of climbing. When they reached the top Robin fell in a heap onto the platform with every bit of strength gone from his legs and arms. It slowly returned. In a little while he was able to rise and stand beside John, looking out over the town.

"We agreed that I should wait an hour after curfew, when the moon will be nearly overhead," said John. "That allows time for all companies to be in place, and with the sounding of the bell to move in about the town and castle wall at once."

"How can you tell when it has been an hour?" asked Robin.

"By the feel of it," said John. "Besides, I shall play 'Love a Garland Is' and 'Lament of a Lass.' That will be half of the hour." He unslung the harp from Robin's back and began the music.

While they waited for the rest of the hour to pass, John pointed out the familiar turrets of the castle, the north tower where they had climbed once, and the tower of the keep where the household waited for deliverance. He strummed on the harp between times.

They tried to see into the hills about the town, but saw only the quiet countryside bathed in moonlight. In the town, supper fires sent up blue smoke, and here and there was the red glare of torchlight and campfire. Glints of moonlight on helmet or shield shone from the walls where sentries walked, but very little sound could be heard at that height.

The hour was up.

"Now," said John, "it is time for the alarm. Stay thou here, and I shall return. Cover thy ears well, but watch to see what happens." He was gone through the hatch into the darkness below. Robin waited, his skin prickling with excitement. Would the signal be at the right time? Would the arrows find their mark and lift the siege?

BONGGG! BONGGG! BONGGG! BONGGG!

The great bell rang, sending waves of sound that went out over the hills and came echoing back into the stone of the bell tower, which trembled with vibration.

At first Robin could see nothing different from what he had seen before. Then, it was as if a part of the landscape itself moved off there toward the south, just below the edge of the town. Gathering from the slopes were tiny moving figures, now in the open, now lost in shadow. Robin searched for another sign, this time in the direction of Letham Bridge. The sign was there where he could see more clearly.

John came up, breathing hard.

"What's to be seen?" he asked. "Are they moving? Hast seen any arrows fly?" He looked to the Letham Bridge.

Then it came.

A hail of arrows that were like dark rain sped from oncoming yeomen, dropping the sentries on the bridge and picking off men of the guard manning the wall of the town. From where they stood Robin could see it all as plainly as if it had been a toy village set in a toy landscape, and the soldiers, toy soldiers. He saw pikemen strike down sentries of the enemy at the town gate and take prisoner the Welsh guards. He saw the company of Sir Hugh's men enter and take the town.

It had been a complete surprise.

When John-go-in-the-Wynd saw what was happening and realized that the plan had been successful, he tossed his hat into the air and clasped Robin in his arms.

"We've won!" he shouted. "The Welsh are routed! Lindsay is saved once more!"

Then, setting Robin on his feet again, he said,

"Stay thou here, and watch how the Welsh are marched out of the town whilst I go below. Thou'lt hear such a peal of bells as shall nigh wake the dead lying below." Down he went again through the hatch to the belfry.

With the pealing of the bells, flares went up from castle and town, windows and doors opened. The peal of bells stopped. John came back and together they watched the lifting of the siege. They could see people running about through the streets embracing one another, tossing caps and hats into the air, and in other ways showing their joy at being freed of the Welsh invaders. In a short while they saw the enemy marched out of town.

Tears streamed down Robin's cheeks.

"I must not cry," he thought, wiping them away. "Not even for joy."

"Now," said John, lifting Robin aloft, "thou'lt be carried on my shoulder—so. For thou'rt the hero of this victory." Together they went down the long stretches of ladder and stair to the ground.

"Make haste," said Robin. "Let us go to the keep at once, so Sir Peter and Lady Constance shall know that I am safe and well. Brother Luke will be sure of it, for his prayers have followed me this day. That I know."

All the way through the town square John made his way with Robin on his shoulder high above the villagers dancing in the dawn of returning day.

They were greeted with cheers at the castle gate and followed across the courtyard to the inner gate and to the keep by the cheering crowd.

Alan-at-Gate saw them from the gatehouse. The drawbridge was lowered and the portcullis raised, and just inside the whole company of the household stood to receive them. Sir Peter was in the center with his sons and the two pages. Near him was Lady Constance with her women and little Alison and Brother Luke.

Sir Peter held out his arms and helped Robin to the ground, placing the crutches to support him. Then, placing his hand upon Robin's head, he spoke solemnly.

"Now, before God and this company," he said, "I do hail thee Conqueror and true son of thy noble father."

CONCLUDING LEVEL 12, UNIT 2

Ventures

The period of history known as the Middle Ages has captured the imagination of writers and artists. With the characters in the selections in *Ventures*, you traveled to a time of high adventure. You discovered fantasy and legend, as well as informational articles about a way of life that no longer exists. You examined an artistic record of a venture that changed the course of history. You read a basic story told in three different ways, as well as a fairy tale with a new twist. Perhaps you will venture into the Middle Ages again and into other historical periods in your quest for reading adventure.

Thinking and Writing About *Ventures*

1. What part of a knight's training as described in "The Training of a Knight" would have been helpful to Steve of "Max and Me and the Time Machine"?
2. Why wouldn't a dragon such as the one described in "Saint George and the Dragon" attack a medieval castle? What defenses would the dragon have to destroy or break through in order to reach the interior of the castle?
3. Do you think that Maid Marian of "Robin Hood and Maid Marian" and Princess Gillian of "The Practical Princess" would become friends if they met? What qualities do they share?
4. During the Middle Ages, honor and chivalry were high ideals. How were El Cid of "El Cid Campeador," William of Normandy of "The Bayeux Tapestry," and the Red Cross Knight of "Saint George and the Dragon" faithful to these ideals?
5. What characteristics are shared by the heroes of the three legends in this unit: El Cid, Robin Hood, and Saint George?
6. The Bayeux Tapestry has been compared to a comic strip. Choose one of the selections in *Ventures* and use it as the basis of your own comic strip story. Concentrate only on the major events. Use speech balloons for the dialogue.

Introducing Level 12

VOYAGES

Afoot and light-hearted I take to the open road,
Healthy, free, the world before me,
The long brown path before me leading
wherever I choose.

Walt Whitman

UNIT 3

The excitement of voyages has inspired many great writers throughout the ages. The stories in this unit will take you on voyages with a hero of ancient Greece, an Antarctic explorer, and a slave leading the way to freedom. You will also cross the Pacific by canoe, sail in a balloon, and take an adventurous road trip with some imaginary friends. If you could make any voyage, where would you go?

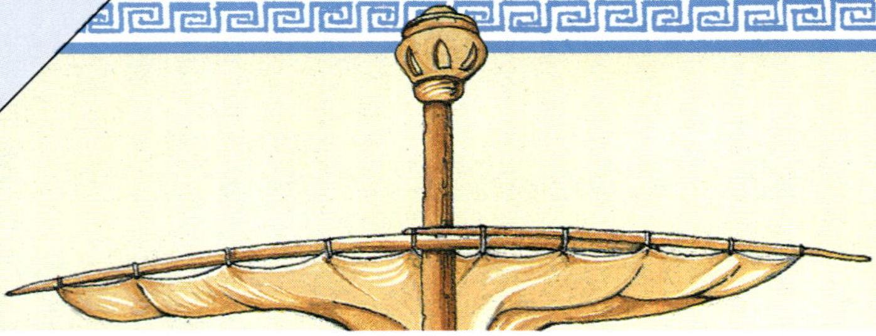

THE VOYAGE OF ODYSSEUS

based on Homer's Odyssey, *and retold by Margaret H. Lippert*

The story of Odysseus (ō dis' ē əs) is one of the oldest stories in the world. It was composed three thousand years ago by a Greek poet named Homer. He wrote **The Iliad**, *which is about the Trojan War, and* **The Odyssey**, *which is about the voyage of Odysseus from Troy back to Greece. Parts of these long poems were written down, and parts of them were learned by storytellers and told from memory.*

Odysseus was the son of the king of Ithaca. Odysseus had not wanted to leave his home, a beautiful island off the coast of Greece. He loved his wife Penelope and their infant son Telemachus (tə lem' ə kəs). But King Menelaus (men' ə lā' əs) of Sparta had needed his help. So Odysseus set sail with other princes and kings of ancient Greece. They went to Asia Minor to help King Menelaus recapture his wife, Helen, who had been abducted by Paris, a young prince of Troy. This was the beginning of the Trojan War.

For twenty long years Telemachus and his mother have waited for Odysseus to return. The Trojan War has been over for ten years, but still Odysseus has not come home. Now Telemachus has decided to embark on his own voyage, to seek news of his father.

Telemachus stood before King Menelaus, the ruler of Sparta. He wanted, more than he had ever wanted anything, to hear that his father was still alive. But he was afraid that he would be told that his father was dead. He suddenly realized that King Menelaus had addressed him, and he tried to reconstruct what he had heard. The king was speaking again. "Telemachus, son of Odysseus, what brings you here?"

"Your Majesty," Telemachus began, "I seek news of my father. He has not yet returned home from the Trojan War, and I am afraid that he may be dead. The kingdom of Ithaca is in turmoil. My grandfather, Laertes (lā ār′ tēz), is too old to rule, and wicked men are trying to seize power." His words were tumbling out rapidly now, as he explained the tragedy that had befallen his home. "My mother is besieged by suitors, who in my father's absence have moved into our palace. Each one wants to marry her, and to take for himself what rightfully belongs to us. For years she has put them off, but now they are becoming more impatient and she may soon be forced to choose one of them."

King Menelaus nodded. He understood the disorder of a kingdom without its king.

Telemachus continued. He spoke more slowly now, and his eyes never left the king's gentle face. "Your Majesty, I want my father to come home. I need him, my mother needs him, the kingdom of Ithaca needs him. We wait for him, though we do not know whether he is alive or dead. If you know, tell me. Do not spare me."

"Telemachus, you are truly your father's son. He would be proud of you because you are not afraid to seek the truth. My news is mixed. Your father is alive, but he is being held captive by a nymph named Calypso. Seven years ago she rescued him from a storm; since then she has kept him on her island against his will. All of his companions have perished, his ship was destroyed, and he has no means by which to escape and return home."

In spite of the news that his father was a captive, Telemachus was overjoyed. "If Odysseus is alive there is still hope that he will come home," he said. "I must return to Ithaca to tell my mother." Telemachus left the palace at once. He sprang into his chariot and was off. It would be a long journey, first two days along rocky roads to the coast where his ship was anchored, then a full day of sailing from there to Ithaca, and Telemachus did not want to waste time.

As Telemachus journeyed, the gods gathered for a meeting on Mount Olympus. It was their custom to discuss the events of men, and to interfere when they wished. Each god and goddess had mortal friends and enemies, depending on who had pleased or angered them. Athena had befriended Odysseus, while her uncle Poseidon (pə sī′ dən) wanted to destroy him. Athena took advantage of the fact that Poseidon was traveling in Ethiopia. She could discuss Odysseus with Zeus, without Poseidon's interference.

"Father Zeus," said Athena, "Odysseus has suffered long enough. For ten years he fought the Trojan War, in which the Greeks were victorious because he devised the trick of the huge wooden horse.* For the next three years he voyaged home, confronting and overcoming numerous hardships. For the past seven years he has remained captive on the island of Calypso. During the long years he was away, Telemachus grew into manhood, a brave son who recently ventured forth to seek news of the father he knew only through stories. I ask you now," pleaded Athena, "to assist Odysseus in returning home."

In Poseidon's absence, Zeus was able to take action for Athena to help Odysseus. He sent Hermes to Calypso with a message that she was to release Odysseus and allow him to return to Ithaca.

Calypso had to obey. Although she would miss Odysseus, she did not want any harm to come to him. Thus she decided to assist him in building a seaworthy raft for his voyage home. Odysseus was overjoyed. Thoughts of his family and of the land he loved flooded over him as he set to work on the boat that would carry him home.

First Calypso showed Odysseus a place on the island where tall, straight trees grew. With an ax that she loaned him, he cut down twenty trees, smoothed them, and fastened them tightly together with wooden pegs. At the stern he built a rudder to guide his craft. Around the perimeter he made a low wall

---

* **Trojan horse:** The Greek soldiers hid inside a huge wooden horse, which was presented as a gift to Troy, and wheeled inside the city gates. Once inside, the Greeks attacked and defeated the Trojans.

of tightly woven rushes. He set a tall mast in the boat and fashioned a yard-arm for the sail. Calypso presented Odysseus with a sail and with provisions for the voyage: a large skin filled with fresh water, a heavy sack of corn, and some special delicacies that she had made for him so that he might enjoy the voyage and remember her friendship. When all was ready, as a parting gift she called forth a warm gentle wind. He set sail then and turned toward home.

For seventeen days and nights Odysseus sailed, navigating by the sun during the day and by the stars at night. On the morning of the eighteenth day he sighted the shore of Phaeacia (fē ā′ shə), which was only a day's sail from Ithaca. Joyfully he looked up to adjust his sails, but was surprised and dismayed to see dark storm clouds gathering overhead. Before long the clouds had thickened and blocked out the light of the sun. The wind freshened, and the waves began rolling over the gunwales. As lightning flashed and thunder roared over the sea, the waves mounted higher and higher.

The storm was the work of Poseidon, who was on his way back from Ethiopia to Mount Olympus when he spotted Odysseus. Furious that Zeus had arranged for Calypso to free Odysseus, Poseidon determined to prevent his arrival home. To finish off Odysseus, Poseidon sent a mountainous wave which broke over the boat. Odysseus was washed overboard and was plunged deep into the raging sea. Poseidon continued to Mount

Olympus to vent his fury against his brother.

Odysseus struggled to get his head above the water. Finally his face broke the surface of the sea, and he took huge gulps of air. He looked around for his boat, but it had been torn apart by the force of the mighty waves. The beams once proudly joined for the kingly craft now floated singly on the waves. One bobbed not far from Odysseus, and realizing it was his only hope, he swam toward it. With the little strength he had left, he managed to lock his arms around it so that he could not be dislodged. Totally exhausted from his ordeal, he lay face down on the log, thinking only of his wife and son.

Athena, who had been watching and waiting for the departure of Poseidon, now calmed the storm winds and sent a strong onshore breeze to carry Odysseus toward Phaeacia. For two days he floated steadily toward land. On the morning of the third day Athena guided him between the jagged rocks that dominated the coast to a safe landing on a sandy beach at the mouth of a river. Odysseus lay on the shore, wet and cold, and realized at once that he must find a warmer place to rest if he still hoped to survive. He staggered up the beach to the woods that came down to the sand, and crawled through the undergrowth until he came to a clearing carpeted with a thick layer of leaves. There he lay down, covered himself with leaves, and fell into a deep sleep.

Odysseus was awakened by the sound of voices and peeked through the trees to see a group of young women playing ball by the river. Seeking information that would help him get home, he approached them. One seemed to be the leader, and she told him that her name was Nausicaä (nô sik′ ē ə). She was the daughter of King Alcinous (al sin′ ō əs) of Phaeacia. Although she did not know who the stranger was, she realized that he needed help. She gave him some food they had brought with them, then took him back to the palace with her.

At the palace, King Alcinous was told of the arrival of the shipwrecked traveler. He ordered a feast prepared in honor of the visitor, and Odysseus was led to the seat next to the king.

"What good fortune that you have landed on our shore," said the king. "You must have marvelous adventures of your travels to relate. But first, tell us your name, where you come from, and whither you are bound."

"You are most gracious, Your Majesty," responded Odysseus, "to welcome a stranger so warmly to your palace. Your kindness is matched by that of your daughter, who assisted me when I was near death, and so saved my life. I hope that I will be as proud of my own son, when I return home, as you must be of your resourceful daughter. But here I am, thinking of my home, when I still have not told you my name. I am Odysseus."

The King was astonished to be seated beside the legendary Odysseus, hero of the Trojan War, and long-lost wayfarer. "You are Odysseus, son of Laertes?" he asked.

"Yes," replied Odysseus, "I am."

"Then you are the rightful King of Ithaca. Your father is too old to rule, and your wife and son bravely await your return. Tomorrow morning you will go in one of my ships to Ithaca. My sailors will see you safely home."

"Thank you. I appreciate both the generous loan of your ship, and the haste with which I may set sail."

"But now," King Alcinous continued, "we have a whole evening before us. Tell us about your journey, your adventures and misfortunes. Why has the voyage from Troy to Ithaca, which can be made in five days, taken you years?"

"Telling you the story of my journey is the least I can do to repay your kindness," Odysseus said. "It is a story that begins with twelve proud ships and ends with one survivor. It begins ten long

THE VOYAGE OF ODYSSEUS
THE UNDERWORLD
AEAEA
ITALY
ADRIATIC SEA
LAND OF THE LAESTRYGONIANS
GREECE
LAND OF THE CICONES
TROY
CALYPSO
AEOLUS
SICILY
ITHACA
CRETE
LAND OF THE LOTUS EATERS
MEDITERRANEAN SEA

years ago and ends this morning, on your shore; it covers many lands and many people.

"Ten years ago twelve ships, each carrying fifty sailors, left Troy with me. The wind bore us northward to the land of the Cicones (si kō′ nēz), who were allies of the Trojans. We plundered their town so that we might return home with treasure. Then I ordered the men back to the ships so that we could depart before the Cicones had time to retaliate. My men did not heed me. Rather, they lingered to drink wine and make merry. The townspeople then gathered men from the neighboring countryside to join them in attacking us, and before we could get away they had killed six men from each ship.

"We mourned our lost comrades, but gave thanks that we ourselves had been spared. We had not sailed far when a bitter north wind began to roar over the ocean. I ordered the men to lower the sails so they would not be ripped to shreds. For two days we rowed, then on the morning of the third day the storm subsided so that we could raise the sails and be carried again by the wind. With luck we would have rounded Malea and returned home in a day or two, but the wind and current conspired against us and pushed us far off our course.

"For nine days we fought the elements, and on the tenth we came to a strange land. We drew fresh water from a spring, and after

our midday meal I sent three men to explore. The men never returned, so I went with several others to seek them. We found them bewitched. They had been given lotus plants to eat, which made them forget who they were. I had to have them carried back to the ship.

"Then we sailed on and came to the land of the Cyclopes (sī klō′ pēz), a giant people. They do not cooperate with one another as we do. Each family lives in a separate cave and tends a herd of sheep and goats. I decided to go ashore to seek provisions for our voyage. Ordering the other boats to wait for us at sea, I sailed on into the harbor.

"As soon as we had anchored, I selected twelve of my strongest companions to accompany me. Wishing to take a gift for our hosts, I filled a wineskin with very strong wine.

"Above us on the hillside we could see a yawning cavern. We climbed upwards and, seeing no one, entered the cave. At the back of the cave were pens filled with kids and lambs. Bowls and containers of every description lined one side of the cave, and great cheeses were stored on shelves above them. In the center of the floor was a smoldering fire.

"My companions begged me to take some cheeses and leave immediately, but unfortunately I did not heed their advice. I wanted to address the occupant and request gifts that we might take with us.

"At twilight we felt the ground begin to shake, and we looked up

to see a monstrous giant at the entrance. He was in the form of a man but had only one eye, which was right in the center of his forehead. We shrank back in fear and watched him guide his flocks of sheep and goats into the cave. After rolling a massive stone into the opening of the cave, he sat down to milk the ewes and nanny goats. Then he set half of the milk aside for his supper and curdled the rest to make cheese. When he was finished, he stirred the fire. We had been watching in frozen horror. Then one of us moved. The movement caught his eye, and his voice came thundering toward us: 'Who are you, who dare to come uninvited into my home?'

"My men were speechless, but I answered, 'We are voyagers, who have come to ask you for gifts to take back home with us.'

"The giant roared with laughter. 'You ask for gifts of Polyphemus (pol' i fē' məs), son of Poseidon? What have you to give to me?'

"I brought forth the wine and offered it to him. He took it and greedily drank his fill. 'This gift is good,' he said. 'Tell me your name, and I will give you a gift after all.'

"I answered craftily, 'My name is Nobody.'

"'Nobody, my gift to you is that I will eat you last,' he laughed and at once he picked up two of my men. Before we could rescue them, he swallowed them whole, washed down by the milk he had saved.

"The rest of us would soon be dead unless I could devise a plan by which we could escape. I encouraged Polyphemus to have more wine so that he would fall into a deep sleep, and when he was snoring, we set to work.

"There was a huge wooden log in the cave, from which we cut off a piece about a fathom long. This we smoothed and sharpened to a point, then we heated it in the fire. When it was ready to burst into flame, we thrust this red-hot poker into his eye, blinding him instantly. He leaped up in agony, and cried out for help. His neighbors came running.

"'Move the rock away,' Polyphemus called, 'and let me out. Nobody has blinded me.' When the other Cyclopes heard that, they went away, calling that if nobody had injured him, then surely the gods must be punishing him.

"Now Polyphemus was angry. He determined to catch us as we tried to escape from the cave. He moved the rock aside a little, and

blocked the opening with his huge hands so that he could grab us and eat us as we ran out. I then thought of a trick whereby we could leave safely. I bound each of my men under a sheep, and tied the sheep together in groups of three. As the sheep began to leave the cave to go to pasture, Polyphemus felt along the backs and sides of each group to see if we might be riding them to safety. But he never thought to check underneath them. I myself was the last one out, and because there was no one to tie me on, I clung to the wool on the belly of the largest sheep and so escaped with my men.

"We rushed back to our ship and weighed anchor, meeting the other ships at sea. I was thrilled that my ruses had worked so well and could not resist a parting taunt. Thus I called back over the water, 'Polyphemus, son of Poseidon, it was not Nobody who blinded you, but Odysseus himself.' In a rage, he broke off the top of the cliff and heaved it in the direction of my voice. It just missed our steering oar, and so we were able to sail out of danger.

"Our next stop was the Aeolian (ē ō′ lē ən) islands, where we spent a month entertaining Aeolus, the king of the winds, with tales of the Trojan War and of our adventures. On our departure he gave me a parcel containing the storm winds, which he directed me not to open. We sailed for nine days and were in sight of our homeland when my sailors became impatient and opened the package containing the fierce winds. They escaped and blew us back the way we had come, all the way to the Aeolian islands, and beyond to the land of Laestrygones (les′ tri gō′ nəs).

"There we saw a lovely harbor, so enticing that all the other ships entered it. I alone was suspicious and anchored my ship outside. Several unfortunate sailors went up to the town and were shown to the palace of the king. There they were attacked and killed by the king and his family, even as the king was giving orders for our ships to be destroyed. The Laestrygonians (les′ tri gō′ nē ənz) stormed down the cliffs and hurled rocks onto the helpless sailors. All eleven ships, and every man aboard, were lost, and we were only saved because we had not entered that awful place. Swiftly I cut the anchor rope that we might escape, and we sailed off, grieving for our lost comrades.

"Before long we came to the island of Aeaea (e′ ē ə), home of the enchantress Circe (sėr′ sē), where she offered us rest and rich food. Here we stayed for a year, recovering from our ordeals and preparing for our return home. At the end of the year, I decided to visit the land of the dead and speak with the spirit of the seer Tiresias (tī rē′ sē əs), so that I might ask him to foresee the future and tell me what I must do to return home.

"We set sail for the ocean at the end of the world. There lies the land of the Cimmerians, wrapped in mist, where I went ashore and entered the underworld. I found the spirit of Tiresias and received a reassuring prophecy indicating that I would survive many tribulations and return home to die an old man, in peace.

"I returned to my ship and sailed back to Circe. She warned me of dangers we would encounter on our homeward voyage, and told me how I might best overcome them. Then we departed.

"The first peril was the song of the Sirens, which was said to be so sweet that unsuspecting sailors were lured to their deaths on the rocks. Circe had advised me to have myself bound to the mast so that I might listen to the song without endangering the lives of my men. I was to fill their ears with beeswax so that they could not hear the bewitching song. I did as she advised me, and all went well. When hearing the lovely song, I struggled to get free and sail to my death, but the sailors bound me more tightly. Not until we were safely by did they remove the wax from their ears and free me from my bonds.

"The next hazards were the threats of Scylla (sil′ ə) and Charybdis (kə rib′ dis), who dwelt on opposite sides of a strait so narrow that an arrow could be shot from one side to the other. Charybdis was a whirlpool who swallowed everything nearby three times a day. Scylla was a six-headed monster who plucked six sailors, one for each head, from every boat that passed. Circe advised me to sail as far from Charybdis as possible,

even though by doing this I would come close enough to Scylla to lose six men, because otherwise I might lose my entire ship and every one of my men. I did as she advised, but was still surprised and shocked when Scylla reached forth and grasped six of my best and strongest sailors to satisfy her hunger. I could only be thankful that most of us had been spared.

"The last danger was the one that proved to be the downfall of the rest of my men. Circe warned that we should not hunt the cattle of Helios (hē′ lē os′), the sun god, on his island. When we arrived there, all went well at first. My men feasted on food given to us by Circe, and they did not disturb the cattle. Then the wind shifted so that we could not sail. We were forced to stay there a month, our food ran out, and my men grew restless. At last one day they did kill some of the fattest cows. When we finally set sail, Zeus sent a thunderbolt to strike our ship in retribution. The mast crashed to the deck, the ship was destroyed, and all of my companions were drowned. I alone was spared. I rode for ten days on a piece of the mast and finally was carried to Ogygia (ō jij′ ē ə), the island of Calypso, where I was held captive for seven years, and from which I have now come."

King Alcinous sighed. "The gods favor you, Odysseus. Come, it is time to rest, for you have the end of your journey before you tomorrow."

In the morning, King Alcinous bade Odysseus farewell and showered him with gifts. After loading the ship, they were off. Now relieved of having to captain and navigate the ship himself, Odysseus fell asleep. When the ship arrived, the sailors gently carried Odysseus to shore and laid him on the soft grass with his rich gifts around him.

Upon waking Odysseus hid his gifts in a nearby cave, then went to look for assistance. Athena appeared to him and advised him to disguise himself as a beggar, and to enter the palace incognito, so that he might gain an advantage over the traitors living there. He could then overpower them one by one, and claim his wife and land for his own. First, however, Athena arranged a special welcome for Odysseus. She led him to a nearby hut, then brought a handsome young man to greet him. Odysseus took one look at the man and recognized himself standing there. For a moment he was confused, then realized it was not himself he was facing but his own dear son. He took Telemachus in his arms and wept for joy.

"Father," gasped Telemachus, "it really is you. I knew you would come back to us. When I heard you were still alive after all these years, I returned home to wait for you. I cannot believe my waiting is over."

"Telemachus, my son, I never stopped thinking of you. I never stopped dreaming of you. But I never knew how much I loved you until this very moment. Now, sit down and I will tell you the plan for defeating those who have betrayed our trust." Father and son talked together long into the night. As the moon rose, Odysseus said, "Now it is time for you to return to the palace. Remember, tell no one I have returned. We must surprise our enemies. Soon they will be destroyed, and peace will return to our land."

Telemachus rose and walked to the door of the hut. He embraced his father, then stepped out into the moonlight. Odysseus watched his son until his shadow blended with the night and he could see him no longer. Then he turned and entered the hut. His voyage was over, but the next day a new struggle would begin. Love for his brave son and for his faithful wife filled him with joy, and he looked forward to the new day.

Thinking and Writing About the Selection

1. Why had Odysseus left his home?
2. What events had taken place during Odysseus's absence?
3. How did Athena assist Odysseus? How did Poseidon try to defeat him?
4. Imagine that you are working for a company that is making a movie about Odysseus. Whom would you suggest as the actor to play the leading role? What qualities and abilities does the actor have that make him like Odysseus?

Applying the Key Skill
Plot, Setting, Mood, Theme, Narrative Point of View

Use complete sentences to answer the following questions about "The Voyage of Odysseus."

1. What is the setting?
2. Which of the following best describes the narrative point of view?
   a. first person, Odysseus's point of view
   b. first person, Telemachus's point of view
   c. third person, narrator's point of view
   d. third person, Odysseus's point of view
3. What were the major plot events between Odysseus's departure from Troy and his arrival in Phaecia? (Refer to the map for help.)
4. What is the mood at the end of the story?
5. Which of the following best describes the theme?
   a. Long voyages are dangerous.
   b. Those who do not heed warnings will suffer punishment.
   c. After many trials and hardships, a brave and honorable wanderer may find the way home again.
   d. Those who give up hope are not true to themselves.

▪ LANGUAGE ACTIVITY ▪

OUT OF THE MYTHS

Many words and expressions we use today have their origins in the myths and legends of ancient Greece. Knowing the stories behind them may help you appreciate them and remember their meanings.

The selection you have just read, "The Voyage of Odysseus," is based on Homer's story *The Odyssey.* The story takes its name from its hero, Odysseus. It tells of the long wanderings and many adventures of Odysseus after the fall of Troy and his eventual return home. Today we use the word **odyssey** to apply to an extended adventurous wandering or series of travels.

The gods and goddesses who took a hand in Odysseus's fate from time to time were super-human beings who lived on Mt. Olympus. From their abode, we have the word **olympian,** meaning "majestic in manner" or "superior to ordinary affairs."

Odysseus also faced the hazards of Scylla and Charybdis. Scylla was a six-headed monster who seized sailors from passing vessels. She dwelt across a narrow strait from the whirlpool Charybdis. A boat seeking to avoid the one came in danger of the other. Thus we have the expression **"between Scylla and Charybdis,"** meaning a choice between two equally great dangers.

PLOT, SETTING, MOOD, THEME, NARRATIVE POINT OF VIEW

Have you ever told a friend about a story you read and liked, in the hopes that he or she, too, might want to read it? How did you begin? You probably began by describing the people in the story, the characters. Characters are, of course, very important to a story. Readers may become involved with the characters and identify with them.

Your friend would probably want to know what happened to the characters. You might then go on to describe the action that occurred. You also might tell where and when the story took place, describe how the story made you feel, and explain what general truth about life the author expressed through the story. When you talk about a story in this way, you are describing four important literary elements: plot, setting, mood, and theme.

Plot refers to the action of a story. Everything that takes place in the story, everything that happens to the characters, is part of the plot. The events of the plot are arranged in a certain order. Story plots usually follow a pattern.

In the beginning of a story, the main characters are introduced and the time and place of the story are established or indicated. Then as the action begins, a problem, or conflict, arises for one or more character. As the action continues, the conflict becomes greater—we sometimes say "the plot thickens"—and the reader becomes more curious. Finally it becomes clear how the conflict will come out. The conflict is then actually resolved, and the story soon ends.

The **setting** is the time and place in which the story action occurs. The time may be the past, the present, or the future. The place may be real or imaginary.

The **mood** of the story is the general feeling that the story produces in the reader. Different stories may produce moods of suspense, happiness, horror, or sorrow. The mood of a story may change from one part to another, but there is usually an overall mood that prevails.

The **theme** of a story is the idea or message that is conveyed through the experiences of the characters. It is often a general truth about life that the author wants to express. In most stories, the theme is not directly stated. To figure it out, you can ask yourself these questions: What were the characters like? What did the characters learn about themselves and others? How is the title of the story related to the story?

Point of view refers to the teller of the story, that is, the person through whose eyes the story is narrated. Most stories are narrated in the third person. In such stories, the author, as an outside observer, reports all the action. Sometimes the author is "all-knowing," that is, he or she knows everything about everyone in the story and can tell how each character thinks, talks, and acts. Sometimes the third person point of view is limited to what a single character can observe. The author reveals the thoughts and feelings of only one character.

In a story written in the first person, events are described from a personal point of view by someone called "I." The "I" can be a character in the story or an outside observer. In either case, the "I" can tell only what he or she observes.

ACTIVITY Read the story below. Then, on your paper, write the best answer choice to each question.

All the gods and goddesses of Greece, with the exception of Eris, the goddess of discord, had been invited to an important wedding. Furious, Eris appeared at the festivities and threw a golden apple among the guests. On it was inscribed, "For the fairest." Juno, Venus, and Minerva each claimed the apple. Jupiter, not wanting to make a decision, sent the goddesses to Paris, the son of the king of Troy.

Paris had been reared in obscurity because it had been foretold that he would bring ruin to the state. He lived as a shepherd-prince on Mt. Ida, in Troy. There he had wedded a nymph, and until the arrival of the goddessess, he had been quite happy.

Now he had to make a judgment. Each goddess appealed to him. Juno promised power and great wealth, Minerva glory and victory in war, Venus the fairest woman in the kingdom. Paris, forgetting his wife, decided in favor of Venus. His decision made Juno and Minerva his enemies. Under the protection of Venus, Paris sailed to Greece, where he became the guest of King Menelaus. Helen, the beautiful wife of Menelaus, was the prize Venus had in mind for Paris. Helen had been sought by many suitors. They had all agreed to uphold her choice and avenge her cause if necessary. With the aid of Venus, Paris persuaded Helen to elope with him, and he carried her off to Troy. This was the cause of the famous Trojan War. Menelaus called on the great chieftains of Greece to come to his aid in getting back his wife.

The defenders of Helen sided with Troy. The gods and goddesses, too, took sides. The war lasted nine years and resulted in the defeat of Troy and the death of many famous Greeks and Trojans.

1. Which sentence best describes the plot of the story?
   a. It is difficult to judge beauty.
   b. By throwing the apple of discord, Eris set off a series of events that resulted in the Trojan War.
   c. Paris had lived a contented life on Mt. Ida until the goddesses arrived and demanded that he make a judgment.

2. What is the setting of the story?
   a. Greece and Troy in the past
   b. Greece in the present
   c. an imaginary land in the past

3. Which word best describes the mood of the story?
   a. joy b. horror c. doom

4. Which sentence best states the theme of the story?
   a. People should not make decisions without careful consideration.
   b. Things done in the name of love are always justified.
   c. Human events often seem to be beyond the control of human beings.

5. From which point of view is the story told?
   a. first person, Paris's point of view
   b. third person, Paris's point of view
   c. third person, "all-knowing" point of view

ATLANTIC OCEAN
South Georgia
Falkland Islands
Elephant Island
Weddell Sea
South America
ANTARCTICA
South Pole
INDIAN OCEAN
PACIFIC OCEAN
Ross Sea

SHACKLETON'S EPIC VOYAGE

MICHAEL BROWN

In the early years of this century, Antarctica was one of the few unexplored regions of the world. Beginning in 1901, scientists made several expeditions to Antarctica to study the earth's magnetism and to find out about the creatures that lived in the southern seas. A great public interest developed in the area, and people began to wonder which nation would be the first to reach the South Pole. In 1911, Roald Amundsen of Norway and Robert Scott of Great Britain led rival expeditions. Amundsen won, reaching the South Pole on December 14, 1911, beating Scott by a month. The trip ended in tragedy for Scott—the party died of starvation and cold on the return trip.

Ernest Shackleton, an Irish explorer, had accompanied Scott in 1902 on an earlier polar expedition. He led an expedition of his own in 1908, coming within 112 miles (180 km) of the Pole, a record at the time. Then in 1914, Shackleton organized another expedition—to cross Antarctica on foot. But his ship, the Endurance, *became trapped in the Weddell Sea and was crushed by the ice. Using lifeboats, the expedition was able to reach tiny Elephant Island. From there Shackleton and five companions went on for help—a seemingly impossible voyage across 800 miles (1,290 km) of ocean to South Georgia in the Falkland Islands.*

"Stand by to abandon ship!"

The command rang out over the Antarctic seas, and it meant the end of all Ernest Shackleton's plans. He was the leader of an expedition which had set out to cross the unknown continent of Antarctica. It was a journey no one before him had ever attempted.

For months his ship, the *Endurance*, had been trapped in ice. It drifted helplessly in the Weddell Sea, over 400 miles (645 km) east of the Antarctic mainland and 1,200 miles (1,935 km) south of the southernmost tip of South America. The pressure on the hull of the *Endurance* was extreme, and the ship's timbers groaned under the strain.

Now Shackleton's first goal was to lead his men to safety. They would try to cross the polar sea on foot, head for the nearest tiny island, 250 miles (403 km) to the west.

Slowly they climbed overboard with the ship's stores.

Shackleton, a gaunt bearded figure, gave the order "Hoist out the boats!" There were three, and they would be needed if the ice thawed.

Two days later, on October 30, 1915, the *Endurance* broke up and sank beneath the ice. In the bitter cold, the chances of survival seemed small. But spurred on by Shackleton the twenty-seven men set off, dragging their stores and the boats on sledges across the uneven ice.

For five months the crew of the *Endurance* pushed their way slowly northwest across the frozen seas. Sometimes they dragged the sledges painfully behind them. Sometimes they drifted on large ice floes that slowly split into smaller and smaller pieces until they had to be abandoned. At times they took to the boats and sailed or rowed through melting ice. At last, in April 1916, they reached Elephant Island—a tiny, barren, rocky outcrop 540 miles (870 km) from the nearest inhabited land, Port Stanley in the Falkland Islands.

By now the situation was grim. Food and other supplies were low. Still worse, five months of constant cold and hardship had weakened all of the men. They were in poor condition to face the coming winter.

Seeing this, Shackleton knew that he and his crew could not last much longer. He decided on a desperate attempt to find help before winter set in. He turned to the men. "We will make our camp here. Six of us will take the *James Caird* and try to reach Stromness. It's our only chance." Stromness was a whaling base on the island of South Georgia, 800 miles (1,290 km) northeast of Elephant Island. To reach it they must cross some of the stormiest seas in the world.

The *James Caird* was the biggest of the ship's boats. Even so she looked pitifully small to face the great gray seas of the southern ocean. Shackleton had the keel strengthened and added make-shift decking to give more shelter.

By April 24th all was ready, and the *James Caird* was launched from the beach. Some of the crew were soaked to the skin as they worked; this could be deadly in the bitter cold and wind so they changed clothes with those who were to stay behind. Shackleton shook hands with the men he was leaving, and then amidst cheers the *James Caird* set sail for South Georgia.

The little knot of men left behind was dwarfed by the high peaks of Elephant Island and was soon lost from sight.

The *James Caird* was alone on the vast heaving seas. With one arm gripping the mast, Shackleton guided the boat through the ice floes that threatened to hole the sides. At last they were in clear water and, with a fair wind, set their course for South Georgia.

STORES TAKEN IN THE *JAMES CAIRD*

			FOOD
30	boxes matches	3	cases sledging rations
6	1/2 gallons primus[1] fuel	30	packets powdered milk
1	tin methylated spirit[2]	1	case lump sugar
1	box blue lights[3]	2	cases nut food
2	primus stoves	2	cases biscuits
1	Nansen cooker	1	tin salt
	a few spare socks	36	gallons water
	candles and blubber oil	112	lb. ice

1. **primus** (prī′ məs): kind of portable, oil-burning stove.
2. **methylated** (meth′ ə lā′ tid) **spirit:** alcohol compound burned as fuel.
3. **blue lights:** signals or flares.

Now began a fierce ordeal for the crew of the *James Caird*. The boat was small and crowded. It was almost impossible for the men to find space among the stores and the rocks carried for ballast. All cooking must be done over a single primus stove that needed three men to handle it. One held a lamp, the other two lifted the cooking pot off whenever the violent pitching of the boat threatened to upset it. A fine spray of water constantly soaked its way through the flimsy decking.

There were storms, and seas so big that in the trough of a wave the boat seemed surrounded by mountains of water. The waves towering above cut off the wind so that the sails flapped uselessly.

Four days passed. A gale sprang up that threatened to swamp the *James Caird* and hurl her crew into the icy seas. "Lower the sails," shouted Shackleton, above the roar of the wind. "We'll heave-to under bare poles and lie to the sea anchor." The sea anchor was a triangular canvas bag at the end of a long line which held the bow of the boat into the wind. If the seas hit them sideways on, they would capsize.

No man aboard had faced such waves before. Sometimes looking out abeam they could see a great tunnel formed as the crest of a towering wave hung toppling over its base, then broke. Time after time it seemed they *must* be overwhelmed, but they survived.

The spray shot at them like burning arrows. It froze thick on the canvas decks and the bare mats, and would soon make the boat top-heavy. Shackleton saw the danger. "We must get the ice off, or we'll capsize," he warned.

Some of the men struggled on to the heaving deck and chipped ice away with axes to free the boat of the deadly weight. Others hurled things overboard—spare oars and sleeping bags—anything they could do without that would lighten the load.

At last on the morning of the seventh day, the wind dropped. The sea calmed, the skies cleared, and for the first time the sun shone. Thankfully, the men dragged out sleeping bags and sodden clothes and hung them in the rigging to dry. Cape pigeons flew overhead and porpoises played in the sea alongside. Shackleton and his men lay on deck soaking up the warmth. Hope surged in them; life was not so miserable after all.

For three days they sailed steadily on, and then a gale hit them like a blast from a great gun. Sun, pigeons, and porpoises disappeared. Snow squalls and huge waves hid everything from sight. At midnight Shackleton was at the helm when he thought he saw a break in the sky. Was the weather clearing? Then, to his horror, he realized that he was looking at the foam-capped top of the most gigantic wave he had ever seen!

"Hold on! It's got us!" he shouted from the helm. The breaking wave seized the boat and flung it forward, out of control, with the sea surging and foaming around it. Water poured in. "Bail for your lives!" cried Shackleton.

The men bailed frantically. At last they had flung enough water over the side to be safe, but conditions aboard were now much worse. Everything was drenched, there was not a dry place in the boat. For three hours they struggled to light the stove and boil up some milk to warm themselves against the biting cold.

The next day the weather was better, but now there was a new danger. The water supply was running out. Unless the *James Caird* reached South Georgia soon, her crew would die of thirst.

Shackleton and his men were weary and down-hearted. Tortured by thirst, they sailed listlessly on, believing that the end was near, yet hoping to sight land. Then on the morning of the fourteenth day, they saw two shags perched on a mass of seaweed. These birds never flew far from shore. Surely, surely land was near.

At noon, through a break in the clouds, Shackleton glimpsed the dark cliffs of South Georgia. It was a glad moment.

He steered the boat inshore, looking for a landing place, but everywhere rocky reefs or sheer cliffs barred the way. Night was closing in and there was no hope of getting ashore until next morning. It was a bitter disappointment to spend another night at sea.

But the same night another storm blew up. As hours passed it swelled in strength until the wind was hurricane force. Nothing could be seen through the driving spray. The *James Caird*, tough as she was, strained to the utmost so that her seams cracked open and water poured in. To add to this nightmare, the wind swung round and drove the boat slowly backwards, toward the dangerous coast they had seen the day before.

When all seemed lost, a miracle happened. The wind dropped and shifted to blow them offshore. They were saved from the reefs! But not from the torment of thirst.

Shackleton knew they must land soon and find water. After one more night at sea, the boat neared the shore again. They could see a wide bay. The wind was rising and Shackleton decided he must run for that bay and take his chance. But as the *James Caird* neared the entrance, the crew saw that the way was blocked once more by a line of rocks like broken teeth. The sea thundered over them sending up fountains of white spume.

The men braced themselves. They were sure that the *James Caird* would be dashed against the rocks.

Suddenly Shackleton shouted to the helmsman. He had seen a narrow gap. The next wave carried them forward and through this opening, so narrow that they could almost touch the rocks on either side. Then, at last, they

were safe in calm water. In the gathering darkness they beached the boat and Shackleton leaped ashore. At his feet ran a stream of fresh water, and in a minute he and his crew were on their knees slaking their thirst. The worst was over.

Now Shackleton and his men began to explore the cove where they had landed. They found a small cave in which they lit a fire, and for the first time in two weeks they spent a night ashore. But a long and perilous journey was still ahead.

The whaling station at Stromness lay beyond high mountains which had never yet been scaled. Shackleton set off with the two strongest members of his party, leaving the others with enough food for a few days.

The mountains rose 4,000 feet (1,219 m) and the three men were often forced to turn back. They had no tent and kept going through the night, resting now and then, but not for long. They were exhausted but knew that if they stopped they would freeze to death.

Early the next morning they heard a strange sound. It was shrill and high pitched, eerie, spine tingling.

But it did not, after all, signal their death. It was a man-made sound—a steam whistle calling the men of the Stromness whaling station to work.

Shackleton and his men topped a final ridge. Below them were huts and distant figures.

In astonished silence the workers watched as Shackleton and his men staggered towards them, like creatures from some earlier savage time. Two little boys took one look and ran, terrified by the sight of the ravaged, bearded faces and tattered clothes.

But the epic journey was over. Rescue of the entire crew was now certain. By his courage, Captain Shackleton had led his men through the perils of ice, thirst, wind, and storm. They had challenged the sea and won.

Thinking and Writing About the Selection

1. What was the goal of Shackleton's expedition?
2. What prevented Shackleton from reaching his goal?
3. What do you think was the most dangerous threat faced by the men on the *James Caird*?
4. Ernest Shackleton was an able leader who inspired his men. What qualities did he have? What made him a competent leader?

Applying the Key Skill
Judgments

Use complete sentences to answer the following questions about "Shackleton's Epic Voyage."

1. Why did Shackleton decide to abandon the *Endurance*?
2. What facts and circumstances did Shackleton evaluate before he made the decision to take the *James Caird* and try to reach Stromness? What information was probably the most discouraging?
3. What judgments did Shackleton make during the gale the *James Caird* faced after only four days at sea?
4. Why was the sight of the shags an encouraging sign?

Pole-Star

I am the star of mariners
On the sea.
Nelson and Drake and Shackleton
Sailed by me.

I am the guide of adventurers
Through the dark.
Marco Polo my namesake
Knew my mark.

All who travelled the Northern
Hemisphere,
Powder monkey and admiral,
Privateer,

Scott, Paul Jones and Frobisher,
Captain Cook,
Sinbad and Long John Silver
And James Hook,

Nansen, Raleigh, Columbus,
Were my friends.
I beheld their beginnings
And their ends.

I am the heaven-set steersman
Of the deep,
All ships and all sea-farers
In my keep.

Eleanor Farjeon

SKILLS ACTIVITY

FIGURATIVE LANGUAGE

Sometimes when we write or speak, we mean exactly what we say. We are using language in a literal way. At other times, we use language in a figurative way. What we write or say has a meaning different from that given to it by the individual words we use.

An **idiom** is an expression whose meaning cannot be understood from the individual words that make it up. We use idioms all the time. Many are so common that we don't even think about them: "throw a party," "turn down," "run into," and "keep your word." Others are more colorful: "by the skin of your teeth," "straight from the horse's mouth."

Hyperbole is intentional exaggeration. When we make statements such as "he carries the weight of the world on his shoulders," and "a million thoughts flashed through my mind," we are using hyperbole.

Personification is a figure of speech in which human feelings, motives, or actions are given to nonhuman things or objects. A writer using personification gives personalities to things, ideas, or qualities. Here is an example.

The waves beckoned me.

ACTIVITY A Read each sentence below. Write **I** for idiom, **H** for hyperbole, or **P** for personification. If the sentence includes none of these, write **N**.

1. Mother put everything in the kitchen into the stew.
2. We're not going to let this defeat make us roll over and play dead.

3. The spray shot at them like burning arrows.
4. Tina finished her homework in no time.
5. Day is dead; Dark Night hath slain her in her bed.
6. The tide turned at the end of the fifth inning.

ACTIVITY B Identify the figurative language used in each sentence as **idiom**, **hyperbole**, or **personification**. Then write the letter of the sentence that gives the literal meaning of the sentence.

1. The sharp wind bit at his face.
   a. The sharp wind was very strong.
   b. The sharp wind was extremely cold.
   c. The sharp wind hurt his face.

2. Ted and Eric hit it off right away.
   a. Ted and Eric fought with each other.
   b. Ted and Eric quickly became friends.
   c. Ted and Eric played ball together.
3. The counselor advised Jane not to bite off more than she could chew.
   a. The counselor advised Jane not to undertake more than she could accomplish.
   b. The counselor advised Jane not to eat so much.
   c. The counselor advised Jane to be more calm.
4. The thirsty boy drank gallons of water.
   a. The thirsty boy drank a large amount of water.
   b. The thirsty boy couldn't get enough water.
   c. The thirsty boy drank too much water.

Island of the Blue Dolphins

Scott O'Dell

In the Pacific, off the coast of California, is an island shaped like the dolphins that live in the sea around it. Karana's people had lived on this island for centuries. Then one day hunters came and tried to cheat the Indians. A battle was fought and most of the tribe was killed. The survivors feared the hunters would return and kill the rest of them. When a group of white sailors offered to take the Indians to the mainland, Karana's people decided to leave. But Karana was left behind.

As the weeks passed, Karana waited for a ship to rescue her. While she waited she built a shelter, made weapons, and fought her enemies, the wild dogs. But Karana's worst enemy was loneliness. One night she decided to take a canoe and make the voyage eastward to the land to which her people had gone.

Summer is the best time on the Island of the Blue Dolphins. The sun is warm then and the winds blow milder out of the west, sometimes out of the south.

It was during these days that the ship might return, and now I spent most of my time on the rock, looking out from the high headland into the east, toward the country where my people had gone, across the sea that was never-ending.

Once while I watched I saw a small object which I took to be the ship, but a stream of water rose from it and I knew that it was a whale spouting. During those summer days I saw nothing else.

The first storm of winter ended my hopes. If the white men's ship was coming for me it would have come during the time of good weather. Now I would have to wait until winter was gone, maybe longer.

The thought of being alone on the island while so many suns rose from the sea and went slowly back into the sea filled my heart with loneliness. I had not felt so lonely before because I was sure that the ship would return. Now my hopes were dead. Now I was really alone. I could not eat much, nor could I sleep without dreaming terrible dreams.

The storm blew out of the north, sending big waves against the island and winds so strong that I was unable to stay on the rock. I moved my bed to the foot of the rock and for protection kept a fire going throughout the night. I slept there five times. The first night the dogs came and stood outside the ring made by the fire. I killed three of them with arrows, but not the leader, and they did not come again.

On the sixth day, when the storm had ended, I went to the place where the canoes had been hidden, and let myself down over the cliff. This part of the shore was sheltered from the wind and I found the canoes just as they had been left. The dried food was still good, but the water was stale, so I went back to the spring and filled a fresh basket.

I had decided during the days of the storm, when I had given up hope of seeing the ship, that I would take one of the canoes and go to the country that lay toward the east.

I knew that my ancestors had crossed the sea in their canoes, coming from that place that lay beyond. I was not nearly so skilled with a canoe as these men, but I must say that whatever might befall me on the endless waters did not trouble me. It meant far less than the thought of staying on the island alone, without a home or companions, pursued by wild dogs, where everything reminded me of those who were dead and those who had gone away.

Of the four canoes stored there against the cliff, I chose the smallest, which was still very heavy because it could carry six people. The task that faced me was to push it down the rocky shore and into the water, a distance four or five times its length.

This I did by first removing all the large rocks in front of the canoe. I then filled in all these holes with pebbles and along this path laid down long strips of kelp, making a slippery bed. The shore was steep and once I got the canoe to move with its own weight, it slid down the path and into the water.

The sun was in the west when I left the shore. The sea was calm behind the high cliffs. Using the two-bladed paddle I quickly skirted the south part of the island. As I reached the sandspit the wind struck. I was paddling from the back of the canoe because you can go faster kneeling there, but I could not handle it in the wind.

Kneeling in the middle of the canoe, I paddled hard and did not pause until I had gone through the tides that run fast around the sandspit. There were many small waves and I was soon wet, but as I came out from behind the spit the spray lessened and the waves grew long and rolling. Though it would have been easier to go the way they slanted, this would have taken me in the wrong direction. I therefore kept them on my left hand, as well as the island, which grew smaller and smaller, behind me.

At dusk I looked back. The Island of the Blue Dolphins had disappeared. This was the first time that I felt afraid.

There were only hills and valleys of water around me now. When I was in a valley I could see nothing and when the canoe rose out of it, only the ocean stretching away and away.

Night fell and I drank from the basket. The water cooled my throat.

The sea was black and there was no difference between it and the sky. The waves made no sound among themselves, only faint noises as they went under the canoe or struck against it. Sometimes the noises seemed angry and at other times like people laughing. I was not hungry because of my fear.

The first star made me feel less afraid. It came out low in the sky and it was in front of me, toward the east. Other stars began to appear all around, but it was this one I kept my gaze upon. It was in the figure that we call a serpent, a star which shone green and which I knew. Now and then it was hidden by mist, yet it always came out brightly again.

Without this star I would have been lost, for the waves never changed. They came always from the same direction and in a manner that kept pushing me away from the place I wanted to reach. For this reason the canoe made a path in the black water like a snake. But somehow I kept moving toward the star which shone in the east.

This star rose high and then I kept the North Star on my left hand, the one we call "the star that does not move." The wind grew quiet. Since it always died down when the night was half over, I knew how long I had been traveling and how far away the dawn was.

About this time I found that the canoe was leaking. Before dark I had emptied one of the baskets in which food was stored and used it to dip out the water that came over the sides. The water that now moved around my knees was not from the waves.

I stopped paddling and worked with the basket until the bottom of the canoe was almost dry. Then I searched around, feeling in the dark along the smooth planks, and found the place near the bow where the water was seeping through a crack as long as my hand and the width of a finger. Most of the time it was out of the sea, but it leaked whenever the canoe dipped forward in the waves.

The places between the planks were filled with black pitch which we gather along the shore. Lacking this, I tore a piece of fiber from my skirt and pressed it into the crack, which held back the water.

Dawn broke in a clear sky and as the sun came out of the waves I saw that it was far off on my left. During the night I had drifted south of the place I wished to go, so I changed my direction and paddled along the path made by the rising sun.

There was no wind on this morning and the long waves went quietly under the canoe. I therefore moved faster than during the night.

I was very tired, but more hopeful than I had been since I left the island. If the good weather did not change I would cover many leagues before dark. Another night and another day might bring me within sight of the shore toward which I was going.

Not long after dawn, while I was thinking of this strange place and what it would look like, the canoe began to leak again. This crack was between the same planks but was a larger one and close to where I was kneeling.

The fiber I tore from my skirt and pushed into the crack held back most of the water which seeped in whenever the canoe rose and fell with the waves. Yet I could see that the planks were weak from one end to the other, probably from the canoe being stored so long in the sun, and that they might open along their whole length if the waves grew rougher.

It was suddenly clear to me that it was dangerous to go on. The voyage would take two more days, perhaps longer. By turning back to the island I would not have nearly so far to travel.

Still I could not make up my mind to do so. The sea was calm and I had come far. The thought of turning back after all this labor was more than I could bear. Even greater was the thought of the deserted island I would return to, of living there alone and forgotten. For how many suns and how many moons?

The canoe drifted idly on the calm sea while these thoughts went over and over in my mind, but when I saw the water seeping through the crack again, I picked up the paddle. There was no choice except to turn back toward the island.

I knew that only by the best of fortune would I ever reach it.

The wind did not blow until the sun was overhead. Before that time I covered a good distance, pausing only when it was necessary to dip water from the canoe. With the wind I went more slowly and had to stop more often because of the water spilling over the sides, but the leak did not grow worse.

This was my first good fortune. The next was when a swarm of dolphins appeared. They came swimming out of the west, but as they saw the canoe they turned around in a great circle and began to follow me. They swam up slowly and so close that I could see their eyes, which are large and the color of the ocean. Then they swam on

ahead of the canoe, crossing back and forth in front of it, diving in and out, as if they were weaving a piece of cloth with their broad snouts.

Dolphins are animals of good omen. It made me happy to have them swimming around the canoe, and though my hands had begun to bleed from the chafing of the paddle, just watching them made me forget the pain. I was very lonely before they appeared, but now I felt that I had friends with me and did not feel the same.

The blue dolphins left me shortly before dusk. They left as quickly as they had come, going on into the west, but for a long time I could see the last of the sun shining on them. After night fell I could still see them in my thoughts and it was because of this that I kept paddling when I wanted to lie down and sleep.

More than anything, it was the blue dolphins that took me back home.

Fog came with the night, yet from time to time I could see the star that stands high in the west, the red star called Magat which is part of the figure that looks like a crawfish and is known by that name. The crack in the planks grew wider so I had to stop often to fill it with fiber and to dip out the water.

The night was very long, longer than the night before. Twice I dozed kneeling there in the canoe, though I was more afraid than I had ever been. But the morning broke clear and in front of me lay the dim line of the island like a great fish sunning itself on the sea.

I reached it before the sun was high, the sandspit and its tides that bore me into the shore. My legs were stiff from kneeling and as the canoe stuck the sand I fell when I rose to climb out. I crawled through the shallow water and up the beach. There I lay for a long time, hugging the sand in happiness.

Thinking and Writing About the Selection

1. What dangers did Karana face on the island?
2. Why did Karana choose the smallest canoe to make her voyage in?
3. How did Karana know she was going in the right direction when she set out from the island, and how did she keep track of her course during the voyage?
4. If you were trapped alone on an island, what would you need to survive? How would you go about providing for your needs?

Applying the Key Skill
Character's Motives and Feelings

Choose the best answer or answers to each of the following questions about "Island of the Blue Dolphins."

1. Why did Karana spend most of her time in the summer looking out to sea from the high headland?
   a. She was sure that a ship would come to rescue her.
   b. She hoped to see a ship returning to the island.
   c. She had little else to do.
   d. She knew the headland was the safest place on the island.
2. How did Karana feel after the first storm of winter?
   a. afraid b. lonely c. hopeful d. disappointed
3. Why did Karana decide to take a canoe and leave the island?
   a. She knew no ship would come to the island during the winter.
   b. She was frightened of the wild dogs.
   c. She believed her skill was equal to the skill of her ancestors.
   d. She knew it was her only hope.
4. How did Karana feel when she returned to the island?
   a. grateful b. unafraid c. hopeful d. glad

MEET THE AUTHOR

Scott O'Dell

"Writing for children is more fun than writing for adults, and more rewarding. Children have the ability, which most adults have lost, the knack to be someone else, of living through stories the lives of other people."

Unlike most children's writers, Scott O'Dell came to his true calling rather late in life. After attending several colleges, he worked in the film industry as a cameraman, then as a newspaper reporter, book reviewer, and magazine writer. The highlight of his career in the movies was using the first Technicolor camera to film *Ben Hur* (the early version) on location in Italy. *Island of the Blue Dolphins,* O'Dell's first children's book, was not published until the author was fifty-eight years old.

Scott O'Dell grew up in southern California when Los Angeles was still a small town. As a child his family once lived in a house on stilts on Rattlesnake Island near Los Angeles, surrounded by the ocean and sailing ships. With other boys, he often "sailed" the waters around the island on rough logs. These memories all went into his first children's book.

"Writing is hard work," says O'Dell. "The only part of it I really enjoy is the research, which takes three or four months. The story itself as a rule takes about six months." His routine when writing a book is to write from 7 A.M. to noon every day. He uses an electric typewriter "because when you turn it on, it has a little purr that invites you to start writing instead of looking out the window. I sometimes use a pen and work very slowly." Whichever method he uses, Scott O'Dell continues to create memorable stories.

More to Read *The Black Pearl, Sing Down the Moon, Zia*

VOYAGE TO
★ FREEDOM ★

DOROTHY STERLING

It was 1862. The nation was at war, North against South. Robert Smalls, a black slave, was pilot of the Confederate flagship* Planter*, harbored in Charleston, South Carolina. The Union fleet lay only seven miles away across Charleston Bay.

Then Robert learned that slavery had been abolished in Washington, D.C. Night after night Robert and his wife, Hannah, discussed plans. Could they find a way to reach freedom, and, at the same time, strike a blow that would help the Union win the war?

When they finally arrived at a solution it was so simple that Robert wondered why he hadn't thought of it before. It started with Captain Relyea's hat, the broad-brimmed straw hat that he wore to protect his eyes from the glare of the sun on the water. The officers had gone ashore for the night and the crew were talking together in the pilot-house.

"Just fooling around," Robert explained to Hannah. "Alfred Gridiron—he's the fireman—put Relyea's hat on my head. I walked around with my arms folded across my chest the way he does. They laughed because I looked so much like the captain."

It was true, Hannah thought. Both men were short and strongly built. Except for their skin color, they did look alike. But what difference did it make?

"All the difference in the world," Robert assured her. "The difference between slavery and freedom. One night when the officers are on shore, we're going to take the boat. Put you and the children aboard and sail it out to the bar. With me wearing Relyea's hat, the sentries'll think it's him and let us pass. It's very simple."

It was daringly simple, dangerously simple.

On a Sunday afternoon in April the crew of the *Planter* met in the Smallses' rooms on East Bay Street. Swearing them to secrecy, Robert explained his plan. The women and children—there would be five women and three youngsters—

would be hidden on a merchant ship in the Cooper River. Under cover of darkness the *Planter* would sail up the river and take them aboard. Then Robert would head for the Union blockading fleet beyond the bar.

One by one he answered their objections until his confidence won them over. There was still one matter left to be settled. Suppose they were caught? Suppose a sentry gave the alarm? Suppose they were stopped at Fort Johnson or at Sumter?

All eyes turned to Robert. "Then we scuttle the ship to keep it from the Rebels. If it doesn't sink fast enough to keep us from being captured, we take hold of each other's hands and jump overboard."

The silence was heavy in the little room as they thought over the meaning of his words. A chair squeaked and someone coughed nervously. Then there was a slow nodding of heads.

"It's good weather for swimming. Water in the harbor's getting warm," Jebel Turner cheerfully announced, and the tension in the room turned to laughter.

The next weeks were anxious ones. The decision about the date of departure had been left up to Robert. He refused to be hurried.

"No use going empty-handed," he explained. "There's some new plan they're talking about at headquarters. I aim to find out what it is before we start."

Daily he eavesdropped on the captain's conversations. General Ripley was shortening his defense lines. General Ripley expected a Union attack through the main ship channel. General Ripley was stripping his defenses along the inland waterways and placing all available guns and men in the harbor forts.

Then came the day when the *Planter* was ordered to Cole's Island at the mouth of the Stono River, to move guns from there to Fort Ripley.

"Removing the batteries on Cole's Island?" Smith, the mate,

questioned the order. "With those batteries gone, the river's wide open for an enemy attack. And the Stono River's the back door to Charleston."

Robert stared straight ahead, pretending not to hear the conversation. Everyone in Charleston knew that the British had taken the city during the Revolution by sailing their fleet up the Stono River and bypassing the forts in the harbor.

When Smith pointed this out, Captain Relyea only shrugged his shoulders. "The General orders us to Cole's Island to remove the guns," he repeated.

"Yes, sir." As Smith saluted and left the pilot-house Robert's heart skipped a beat. This was the information he had been waiting for. The *Planter* would help to open the back door to Charleston—and then the *Planter* would invite the Union to come in.

For the next two days the *Planter* anchored off Cole's Island while her crew dismantled the batteries and moved the guns to the dock. On Sunday when she returned to Charleston, Robert asked for a few hours' leave.

"My little boy's been sick," he explained, "and I'm anxious after him."

"You know the orders, Bob," the captain reminded him. "Officers and crew to remain on board day and night, even in the harbor."

Robert knew the orders. He also knew that the officers often disregarded them and were, in fact, planning to attend a party ashore the following evening. But all that he replied was, "Yes, sir."

Relyea considered the problem further. Robert was a good pilot, a steady man. "All right," he agreed. "But be sure to report back by five o'clock."

"Aye, aye, sir. Thank you, sir." Robert's voice betrayed nothing of the excitement that was bubbling inside him.

Taking his leave of the crew, he walked along the Battery toward his home, pausing at Atlantic Wharf to see which merchant vessels were tied up there. When he turned in at the stable on East Bay Street, his footsteps quickened and he took the stairs two at a time. A glance at his face told Hannah the news.

"Tomorrow."

Briefly he outlined the plan. Tomorrow evening she was to take the children and board the *Etowan* at Atlantic Wharf. Members of the crew would hide them until the *Planter* pulled up alongside.

"Tomorrow." He traveled through the city bringing the message to the other women, making arrangements with the steward of the *Etowan*.

"Tomorrow." Even Elizabeth, catching the mood of her parents, repeated the word when he returned home. He held her on his lap, rumpling her hair, as he went over last-minute details with Hannah. Nothing must be forgotten.

The bells of St. Michael's were striking five when Robert entered the crew's quarters of the *Planter* with a laundry bag slung over his shoulder—a bag containing a surprising number of children's shirts and dresses and Hannah's best white sheet, which was to serve as a flag of truce.

Early the next morning the *Planter* headed down the Stono for her last trip to Cole's Island. "All guns to be aboard by noon and delivered to Fort Ripley before dark," the captain commanded.

The captain commanded, but the crew decided otherwise. Perhaps it was because the weather was unseasonably warm for May. Perhaps the men had eaten something that disagreed with them. Whatever the reason, Captain Relyea had never seen them work so slowly or so carelessly.

Ropes that should have been fastened came untied. Lines slipped through fumbling hands. Twice the block and tackle crashed to the deck and a cannon almost fell into the river. When John dropped a board on Abram's foot all hands left their tasks to see the damage and to give advice to the limping man.

By noon, only one gun had been moved aboard. The captain

was purple with rage, the men polite and regretful. Robert could hardly keep a straight face as he listened to the cheerful chorus of "Aye, aye," that greeted Relyea's bellowed orders.

It was not until four in the afternoon, too late for the trip to Fort Ripley that day, that the remainder of the arms were made fast on deck of the *Planter*. There were a 7-inch rifle and four cannons, one of them a cannon belonging to Fort Sumter that had been damaged during the Rebel attack and recently repaired. Robert checked its moorings carefully. Now there must be no slack lines or slipping knots. He intended to return this cannon to its rightful owner.

As soon as the *Planter* tied up at Southern Wharf, Relyea and his officers went ashore. There was a party that night at Fort Sumter, a ball given by the ladies of Charleston for their city's gallant defenders. There would be dancing on the moonlit parade ground and a round of toasts to President Davis.[1]

"Mind you take on fuel for an early start in the morning," the captain ordered. "And mind you work properly tomorrow or I'll send the lot of you to Ryan's for a whipping."

"Aye aye, sir," Robert answered for the crew. "We'll be ready for an early start in the morning."

* * *

There were twenty cords of wood stacked in the engine room when the sentry guarding General Ripley's headquarters fifty yards away from Southern Wharf singsonged:

"Ten o'clock and all's well."

The tides were checked, the signals studied and for the tenth time Robert rehearsed the plan with the crew.

"Eleven o'clock and all's well."

Faint sounds drifted across the harbor from Fort Sumter. The regimental band of the First South Carolina Artillery was playing "Dixie," "Nellie Gray," "In the Gloaming." Then came the strains

1. **President Davis:** Jefferson Davis, president of the Confederacy.

of "Auld Lang Syne." It was midnight and the ball was over. Soon the *Marion*, the *Planter*'s sister ship, tied up at the dock to discharge a boatload of merrymakers. Once more the waterfront was quiet.

"One o'clock and all's well."

By the light of the moon, Robert and Alfred broke into the captain's cabin. When they returned to the crew's quarters they had revolvers in their pockets and muskets under their arms. Robert, wearing Relyea's gold-trimmed jacket, imitated the captain's walk as he distributed the guns. The men laughed nervously.

"This waiting sure is hard," William Morrison murmured. "When do we start?"

"Soon. You can write, can't you, Will?" Robert asked. Morrison nodded.

"Here's the ship's log. Keep it just like the mate does. Put down our names, when we start and all, like on a regular trip."

Will leafed through the logbook, glad of something to occupy his mind. Alfred and John left to light the fires while Jebel and Sam stood on deck, ready to cast off.

It was three o'clock on the morning of May 13, 1862, when Alfred reported a full head of steam in the boilers. In the bow, Jebel quietly cut the moorings of the boat, using strings to lower the cables into the water so that no splash would arouse the sentry. At the stern, Sam hoisted the palmetto flag[2] and the Stars and Bars[3] to the top of the flagstaff.

Robert backed the *Planter* out of her berth alongside the *Marion* and headed upriver. On shore the sentry sleepily reported:

"All's well."

Dropping anchor close to the *Etowan*, Robert sent a small boat for the women. The muffled oars scarcely rippled the dark waters of the river. In a quarter hour, the boat headed back with its precious human cargo. Soon they were aboard—five women, three children, and the steward of the

2. **palmetto flag:** the South Carolina state flag.
3. **Stars and Bars:** the first Confederate flag. It had three bars (red, white, and red), and a blue field with white stars in a circle.

Etowan, who had decided to cast his lot with the Union, too.

There was no time for greetings. As Jebel led them to the hold, Robert swung the wheel around, turning the ship until her bow pointed toward the sea.

"We leave Charleston at one-half past 3 o'clock on Tuesday morning," Will wrote in the log.

Slowly the ship glided through the waters of the harbor, past Castle Pinckney, abreast of Fort Johnson. Robert leaned forward, pulling the cord of the steam whistle to give the salute. The sentry at the fort wondered what the *Planter* was about so early in the morning. But there was nothing unusual in her movements and he waved his cap as she went by.

They had passed Fort Johnson, passed Fort Moultrie, when Alfred appeared at Robert's side, grimy and worried.

"Sumter's next. Let's put on steam and sail by fast, without stopping," he suggested.

"And have every gun at the fort trained on us, ready to blow us out of the water?" Robert had thought this through many times before. "No, we'll take it nice and easy, like always."

Alfred sighed. Robert was right, but the suspense was almost more than a man could bear. As he returned to the engine room, Robert peered through the captain's field glasses. There was Fort Sumter, enormous, forbidding, and almost dead ahead.

Three miles beyond, just visible in the first rays of the morning sun, were the ships of the Union fleet. A flag was slowly traveling to the top of a mast and Robert thought he could hear a bugle playing reveille.

Now the *Planter* was within hailing distance of Fort Sumter. The engines throbbed, the paddle wheels cut through the water, but a dead silence blanketed the men on the ship. Even the children below decks were quiet. Suppose the sentry insisted on speaking to one of the officers? Suppose there was a new order to be given, a question asked?

Turning the wheel over to Sam, Robert leaned on the window sill of the pilot-house with his arms folded across his chest and Captain Relyea's broad-brimmed straw hat shadowing his face. He stared into the muzzles of Sumter's guns as he raised his hand for the signal cord.

One, two, three short blasts on the steam whistle, then a long hissing sound.

He could hear Sam's breathing and the screeching of the gulls overhead. After a moment that seemed like an hour there was a shout from the sentinel on the parapet:

"Corporal of the guard, the *Planter*, flagship for General Ripley, giving the prescribed signal with her whistle."

"Pass the *Planter*, flagship for General Ripley," the guard replied.

Pass the *Planter!* Never had ordinary words sounded so sweet. The early morning sun shone with a special brightness and in the hold Hannah began to croon a song to her baby.

In the crew's quarters Will leaned on a sea chest to scrawl, "We pass Fort Sumter one-quarter past 4 o'clock." Three more miles to go.

The *Planter* continued with a leisurely pace until she was outside the range of Sumter's guns. Then Robert signaled for more steam and the ship leaped ahead, ploughing through the water. Puzzled by her burst of speed, the look-out on Sumter's high wall followed her course through his glasses. He watched her pass Morris Island and continue out to sea.

Something was wrong. Calling to the corporal of the guard, he gave the alarm. Signals flashed—from Sumter to Morris Island, from Sumter to Charleston—but it was too late to stop the *Planter*.

The ship was now in no man's land, between the two opposing forces. As they neared the bar, Robert ordered the Rebel flags to be lowered and the white bedsheet flag of truce run up to the top of the foremast.

He steered for the *Onward*,

the forward ship of the Union fleet. They were near enough now to hear the beating of drums! Robert's heart sank. The drums were a signal for all hands to make ready for the enemy.

The *Onward* was turning, her cannon trained on the *Planter* and her open portholes bristling with guns. In the morning mist her officers had failed to see the white flag of truce.

Robert's hands tightened on the spokes of the wheel. Had he brought the ship this far, only to be fired on by Union men? Leaning hard on the wheel, he swung the *Planter* around, hoping to pass the *Onward*'s bow, and continued his seaward course.

As the *Planter* turned, heading into the wind, the limp bedsheet on her mast caught the ocean breeze and billowed outward. Staring at the flapping sheet, the Union commander ordered his men to hold their fire.

"Ahoy there, what steamer is that?" he shouted. "State your business."

"The *Planter*, out of Charleston," Robert bellowed. "Come to join the Union fleet."

There was a moment of stunned silence. Then a command floated across the water. "Pull alongside. But keep your men away from the guns or I'll blow you to bits."

Five minutes later, the *Planter* had dropped anchor next to the *Onward* and an astonished Union officer was climbing aboard the Confederate ship. Robert left the pilot-house to salute him.

"I have the honor, sir, to present the *Planter*, formerly the flagship of General Ripley. In addition to her own armament, she carries four cannon which were to have been delivered to Fort Ripley this morning. I thought they might be of some service to Uncle Abe."

As the *Planter*'s crew stood at attention, the white flag was lowered and the Stars and Stripes raised in its place. In the log Will noted, "We arrive at blockading squadron at Charleston Bar at a quarter to 6. We give three cheers for the Union flag once more."

Thinking and Writing About the Selection

1. Why did Robert Smalls put off the date of departure?
2. Why did the crew of the *Planter* work carelessly and slowly while they loaded the guns from the fort on Cole's Island?
3. What do you think would have happened to Robert Smalls if he and the *Planter* had been caught?
4. If you had been on board the *Planter*, when would you have felt the most nervous or afraid? When would you have felt the most hopeful?

Applying the Key Skill
Judgments

Use complete sentences to answer the following questions about "Voyage to Freedom."

1. Why did Robert Smalls believe that the sentries would mistake him for Captain Relyea?
2. What were the possible risks involved in the plan Robert Smalls had developed? What were the possible rewards?
3. Why did Smalls pick the day he did for the escape attempt? What information did he use to make his decision?
4. Smalls rejected Alfred's suggestion that they sail by Fort Sumter without stopping. Why?
5. Why were the officers on the *U.S.S. Onward* ready to fire on the *Planter*? Why didn't they do so?

SKILLS ACTIVITY

LIBRARY RESOURCES: CARD CATALOG, REFERENCE SOURCES

After reading "Voyage to Freedom," you might want to find out more about the Civil War. Where should you begin to look? The card catalog and the reference section of your library are good places to begin. These are important library resources.

The **card catalog** is a list of books in the library, kept on small, separate cards in a cabinet.* It usually includes three cards for each nonfiction book in the library—an author card, a title card, and a subject card. Except for the top line, all three cards are the same. They are filed in alphabetical order in the drawers of the cabinet. Here are examples of the three cards for a single book.

917.58 Myers, Robert My Manson (ed.) The children of pride. New Haven: Yale University Press, 1972.	The Children of Pride 917.58 Myers, Robert My Manson (ed.) The children of pride. New Haven: Yale University Press, 1972.	CIVIL WAR 917.58 Myers, Robert My Manson (ed.) The children of pride. New Haven: Yale University Press, 1972.
author card	**title card**	**subject card**

Each card gives the author (or editor) the title, the place and date of publication, and the name of the publisher. It also has

*Many libraries arrange the entries that appear in a card catalog in bound books instead of on cards. Some libraries also include the information in a computer.

a call number in the upper left-hand corner. This number tells you where in the library to look for the book.

If you know the name of the author of a book you want, you should look for the author card. (An author card lists the last name of the author first.) If you know the title, you should look for the title card. If you are looking for a book on a particular subject, for example the Civil War, you should look through the cards filed under the subject heading, in this case, CIVIL WAR.

ACTIVITY A Write the best answer to each question below on your paper.

1. If you wanted to find a book about the origin and practice of slavery in the United States, what key word would you use to check in the card catalog?

   a. origin b. practice c. slavery d. United States

2. The number in the upper left-hand corner of a catalog card tells you which of the following?

   a. when the book was published
   b. where to look for the book in the library
   c. how many pages there are in the book

3. A card for a book by Douglas Southall Freeman would be filed under what word?

   a. Douglas b. Southall c. Freeman

4. If you wanted to find out if your library had the book *Glory Road*, you would look for which kind of card?

   a. author card b. title card c. subject card

The reference section is a special part of the library where there are books with important information on all kinds of subjects. Some of the most useful reference books you will find in the library are encyclopedias, almanacs, and atlases.

An **encyclopedia** is a book or a set of books with articles on a great variety of subjects—people, places, events, ideas, and general topics. It is important to decide on a **key word** when looking for information in an encyclopedia. For example, if you wanted to find out the names of the important battles fought in the South during the Civil War, you would use the key words *Civil War*.

An **almanac** is a single reference volume that is usually published every year. It includes information on current events, and gives facts, figures, and brief information on a great variety of subjects. It may have charts and tables. It is a good place to look for winners of sports events, names of current government officials, current population figures, and winners of important prizes or awards. To find information in an almanac, you must use the index or table of contents, which lists the pages where particular information can be found.

An **atlas** is a book of maps. The title of the atlas tells you for what parts of the world maps are included. A **world atlas** has maps of all parts of the world. A **United States atlas** would include only maps of the United States. An index at the back of the book lists particular features found on the maps—cities, states, lakes, rivers, and mountain ranges, for example. The index tells you the page number of the map on which to look for each feature. The location is indicated by giving latitude and longitude or by giving the coordinates of the map.

In addition to general atlases, there are many kinds of special atlases. A **road atlas**, for example, shows major roads that link different places and gives their names or numbers. A **historical atlas** includes maps with political and physical information about places at times in the past. A historical atlas of the United States would probably include maps showing what states belonged to the Confederacy and maps that show important battle sites of the Civil War.

ACTIVITY B Number your paper from 1 to 12. Next to each number write the name of the reference book—**encyclopedia**, **almanac**, or **atlas**—that would be the best place to look for the information listed.

1. when the Emancipation Proclamation was issued
2. how far it is between Washington, D.C., and Charleston, South Carolina
3. the name of the current governor of South Carolina
4. where Abraham Lincoln was born
5. the most recent population figures for Richmond, Virginia
6. the zip codes and area codes of United States cities with a population of more than 5,000
7. the names of different categories of boats and the differences among them
8. the best and most direct car route from Chicago to Denver
9. the winners of last year's NCAA basketball championships
10. what states belonged to the Confederacy
11. what Francis Scott Key is noted for
12. in what direction Charleston International Airport is from downtown Charleston

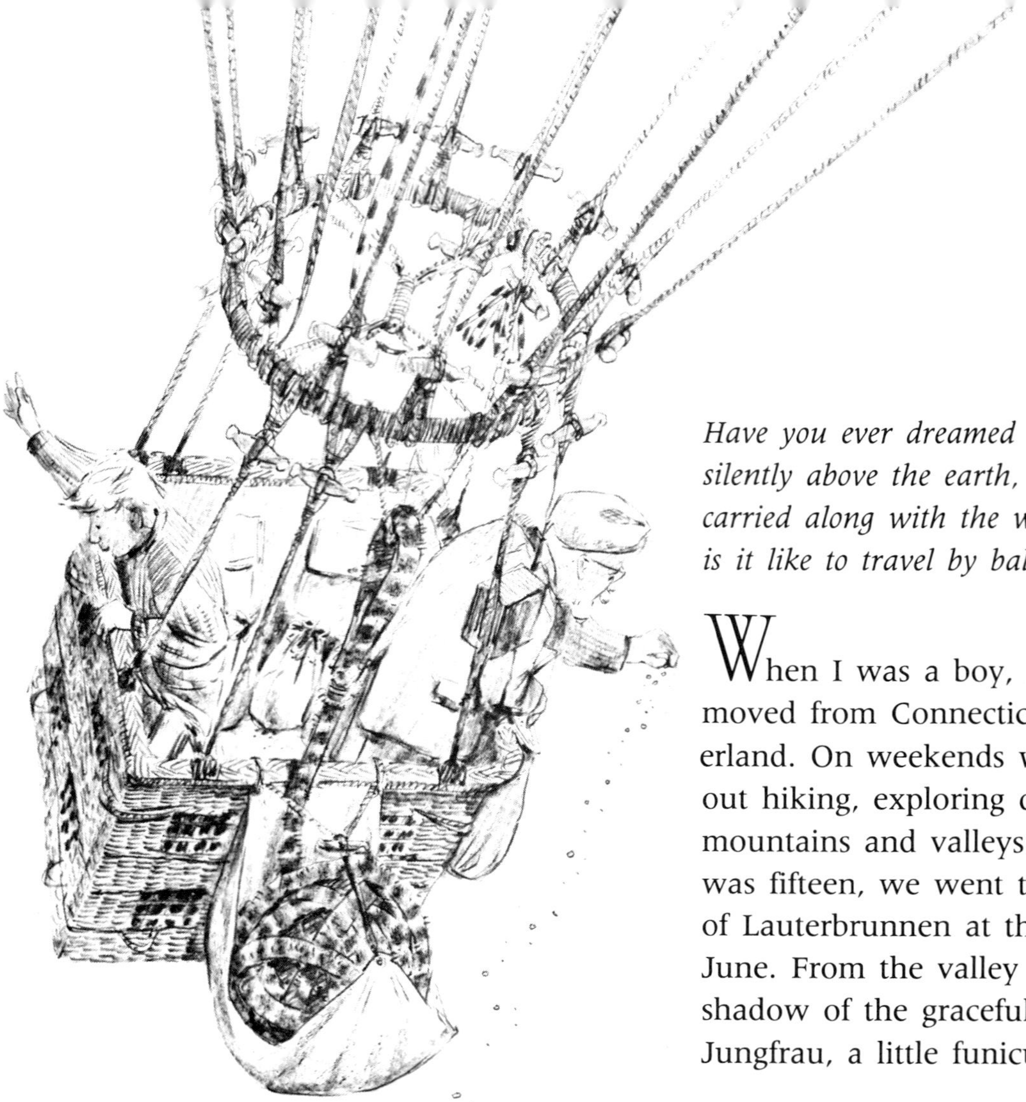

Have you ever dreamed of sailing silently above the earth, being carried along with the wind? What is it like to travel by balloon?

When I was a boy, my family moved from Connecticut to Switzerland. On weekends we went out hiking, exploring different mountains and valleys. When I was fifteen, we went to the valley of Lauterbrunnen at the end of June. From the valley floor in the shadow of the graceful white Jungfrau, a little funicular railway

BALLOON TRIP

A SKETCHBOOK BY HUCK SCARRY

took us up and up, past fields of cows and lacy waterfalls, to the tiny village of Murren.

What a surprise we found there! Peeking over the roofs of the sunburnt chalets were huge, glistening, brightly colored balls. I ran ahead to see what was going on and saw a wide field full of balloons! It would have been an extraordinary sight anywhere, and it was all the more so when seen against the mighty snow-clad Alps.

We had arrived during the International Alpine Ballooning Week, when balloonists go aloft together on an adventurous trip over the Alps, to land wherever the winds have taken them. Perhaps in Italy, Austria, or France! We cancelled our hike and spent the morning admiring these marvelous ships of the sky and watching their preparation for flying. I even helped arrange sandbags around a balloon's netting.

When all was ready, the pilots climbed into their creaking baskets. They took out some of the sandbags. Then, without a sound, they moved off the planet and quickly grew very small in the great blue sky above us.

Although the balloons were gone, my enthusiasm wasn't, and for several years I cherished the thought of one day taking off in a balloon myself. Recently, that opportunity arose. I was invited on a short trip, starting near the Rhine River in northern Switzerland. I'll admit I was just a bit scared, but mostly excited!

Here is how it went . . .

"DRINNGG!" went the alarm clock. I bounced up from under the thick comforter on the bed. It was cold and dark. I switched on the bedside lamp—only 5:00 A.M.! Hurriedly I got dressed, laced my boots, and crept quietly down the corridor of the old Swiss hotel.

The front door was locked. Thank goodness for the window! Rucksack out first, then me—flop! Into a flower bed. (Luckily, I had paid my bill the night before.) I hopped into my car, turned the key, and was off.

Where to so early? Why, to my first balloon flight! And I was already late, for the ground crew started work at 6:00, and I didn't want to miss a single detail.

The "airfield" was next to a soda factory in the town of Zurzach on the Rhine. When I arrived, the ground crew, all dressed in snappy red overalls, were rolling a small trailer out of a hanger. On it was a big wicker basket. "*Gruetzi*!" I called (which in Swiss-German means "Hello!"). But before we see how these men prepared the balloon, let's take a look at the finished product.

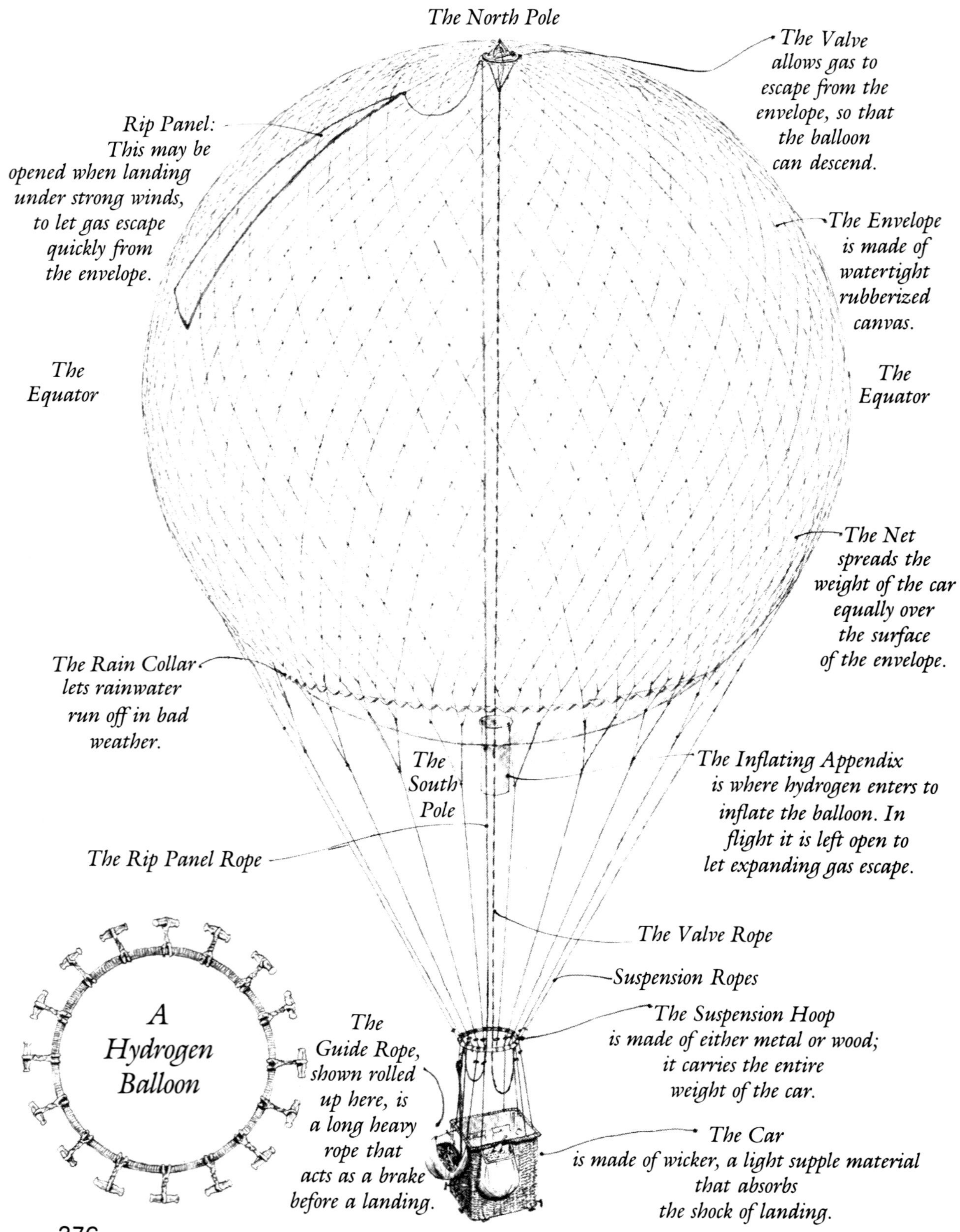
The North Pole
The Valve allows gas to escape from the envelope, so that the balloon can descend.
Rip Panel: This may be opened when landing under strong winds, to let gas escape quickly from the envelope.
The Envelope is made of watertight rubberized canvas.
The Equator
The Equator
The Net spreads the weight of the car equally over the surface of the envelope.
The Rain Collar lets rainwater run off in bad weather.
The South Pole
The Inflating Appendix is where hydrogen enters to inflate the balloon. In flight it is left open to let expanding gas escape.
The Rip Panel Rope
The Valve Rope
Suspension Ropes
A Hydrogen Balloon
The Guide Rope, shown rolled up here, is a long heavy rope that acts as a brake before a landing.
The Suspension Hoop is made of either metal or wood; it carries the entire weight of the car.
The Car is made of wicker, a light supple material that absorbs the shock of landing.

The ground crew worked as swift as lightning. They unpacked and arranged all the cumbersome equipment with the grace and precision of a ballet troupe! First, the envelope that holds the gas was unfolded and laid flat on the ground. One man hopped into a hole in the envelope and walked it to the center. The "North Pole" valve would be fitted in this hole. The ropes that control this valve and the rip panel were then threaded through this hold and out of the inflation appendix, at the "South Pole." Once the valve itself was in place, the net could be laid over the envelope and heavy sand canisters attached around it.

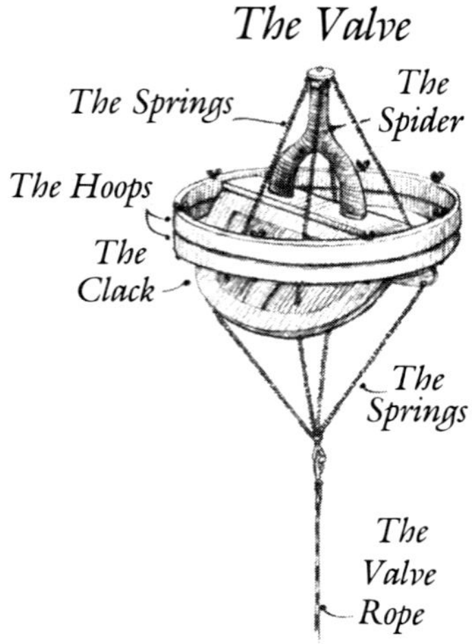

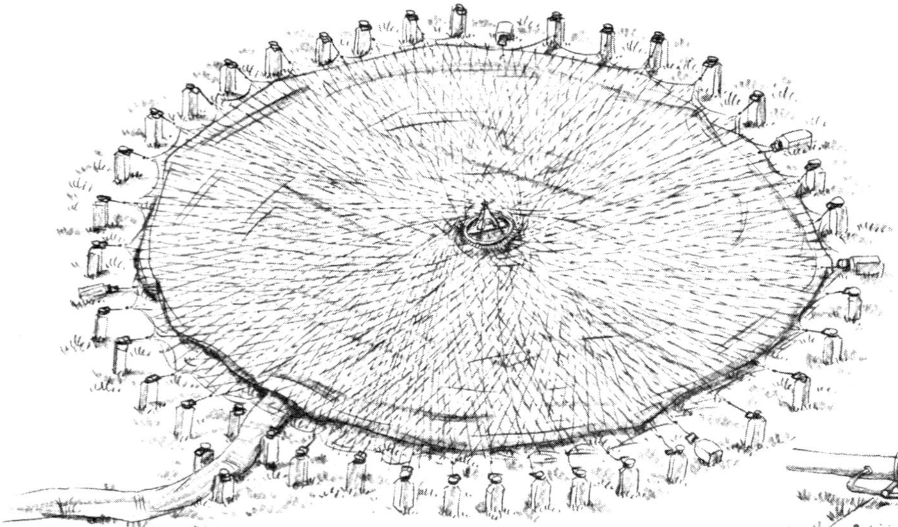

The appendix was attached to the gas main (coming from the soda factory), and when this was opened, gas began to fill the envelope.

As the envelope filled with gas, it rose like a soufflé restrained by the net laid over it and weighted down by the ring of sand canisters.

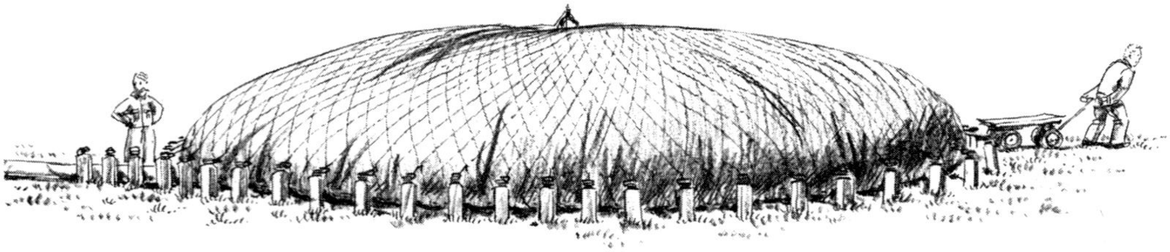

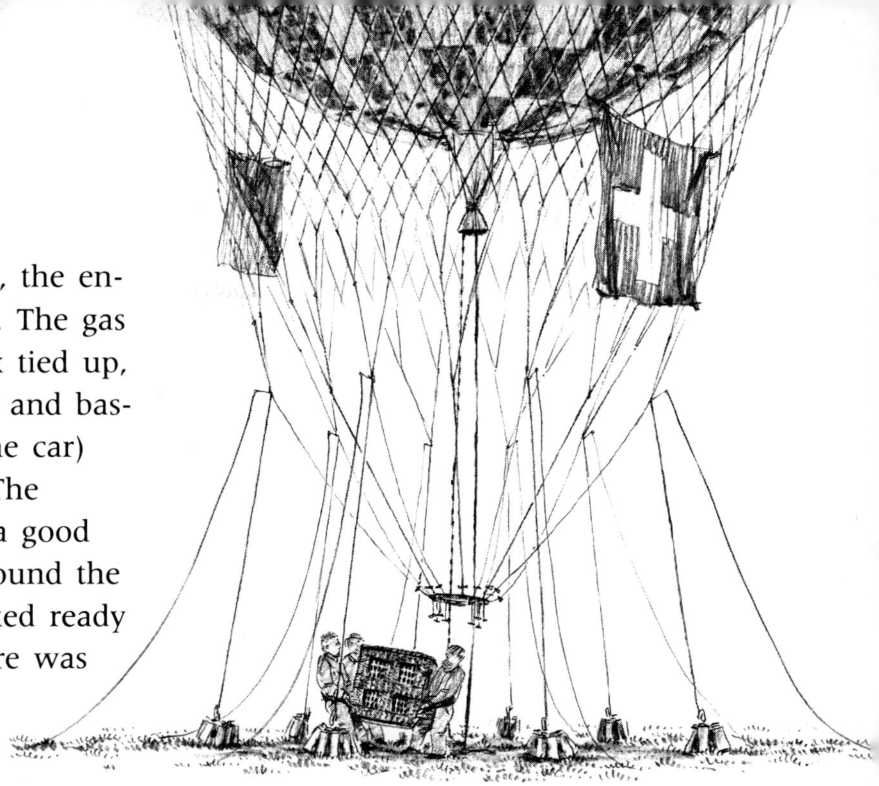

When completely filled, the envelope hovered overhead. The gas was cut off, the appendix tied up, and the suspension hoop and basket (or more correctly, the car) were attached below it. The ground crew then hung a good number of accessories around the car, and the balloon looked ready for the winds! Now where was my pilot?

Punctual as a Swiss clock, across the field came a bespectacled gentleman with white hair, white goatee, and a broad white smile. It was my pilot, Mr. Fred Dolder. He greeted the ground crew, checked out the balloon, and frequently looked at the sky. "Get your gear together, and let's climb aboard!" he said. But when I looked in the car, it seemed there was no room for *anyone*! It was filled with sandbags, food, a horn, instruments, and a two-way radio. It looked more like a housewife's shopping basket than a ship to sail the sky!

Once we were aboard, the crew gingerly picked up the great balloon, and we were "walked up" to our starting point, a little way down a country lane leading to the river bank.

There was scarcely a wind to be felt, so a small "pilot balloon" about one meter around was sent aloft to check the direction we too would take.

Then came the "weighing in." Mr. Dolder passed sandbags out of the balloon to lighten it until it rested on the ground as gently as a kitten. The balloon just balanced between earth and heaven. Mr. Dolder gave the famous sharp cry, "Hands off!" and although I felt no movement at all, I noticed that the ground crew was moving away below us. And so was everything else. We had silently and carefully *detached* ourselves from the surface of the earth. It was incredible!

Alone, like pioneers, we had left our friends on the bottom of the great atmospheric ocean, and now we glided like tiny sea plankton, buoyed in the currents of the winds!

In the car, we sensed no movement at all, be it right, left, up, or down. The earth, however, was moving from *us*, and when it seemed to slow down, Mr. Dolder dipped his hand into the sand-pouch and sprinkled some grains overboard as carefully as a pastry chef dusting sugar on a cake. The little difference in weight was enough to push the earth away again!

A balloon pilot has about as much control of his destiny as a tumbling autumn leaf. Balloons have no motor but the winds of nature, including rising and descending thermal currents. All the pilot can do is influence the vertical movements of his craft. To do this, he has two tools: ballast and gas.

Simply put, to go up, he throws out some ballast. This lightens the balloon and it rises. To go down, he pulls on the valve cord, letting some gas escape from the envelope. Robbed of its lifting force, the balloon descends. Although it sounds easy, piloting a balloon properly demands tremendous skill and patience.

So many factors—wind, sunlight, clouds, temperature—constantly change the lifting force, and therefore the balloon's direction. The balloonist constantly weighs his ship against its element as delicately as a goldsmith measures his gold.

A filled hydrogen balloon will not rise up through the air indefinitely. As you go up, the atmosphere thins out, and so exerts less pressure on the balloon. As the difference in weight between the contained gas and the outer atmosphere decreases, so does the lifting force of the hydrogen.

The weighted balloon will finally balance out with the atmosphere and will have reached its "point of equilibrium." From here it will begin a long descent back to earth, unless more ballast is jettisoned; if it is, the balloon will rise to a new, higher point of equilibrium.

As less and less pressure is exerted against the envelope of the rising balloon, the gas inside expands. The appendix is left open during the flight to allow the expanding gas to escape. (If the envelope were closed, it would simply explode!)

Balloons which are to rise to high altitudes are only partially filled at takeoff. The expanding gas fills the envelope as it rises, without any loss of precious gas.

Our balloon, however, was fully inflated at takeoff, for Mr. Dolder did not plan to take us too high. I soon understood why. The sky above us was filled with birds—the species Swissair, Alitalia, and TWA! These great birds were on their way to the Zurich-Kloten International Nest, and we were naturally an obstacle to their entry flight. Mr. Dolder remained in two-way radio contact with the airport air controllers to tell them where we were.

The airline passengers must have had a lovely first image of Switzerland: a country of chocolate, watches, and balloons!

Our flying ceiling was so limited that at one point we were able to clear a wooded hill only by riding upon the treetops.

Below us the countryside rolled slowly by as if placed on a silent conveyor belt. We saw cows, hens, handkerchief-waving villagers, and an OOMPAH tuba band. We even crossed frontier posts without showing our passports!

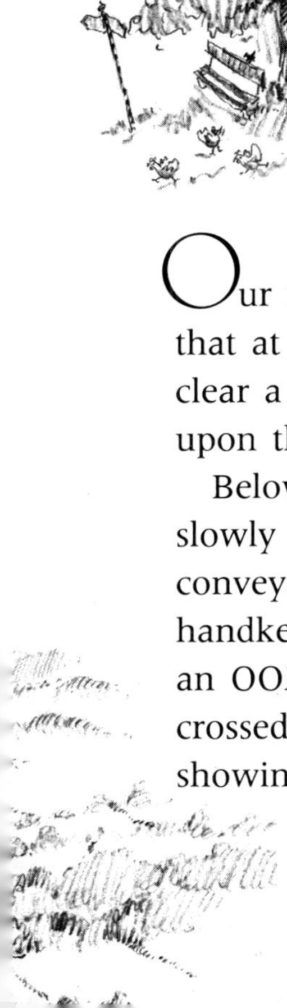

Maintaining a limited ceiling tested Mr. Dolder's skills. He was constantly checking our altitude with small throws of ballast and brief tugs on the valve cord. Soon he decided that it was time to land. This is very difficult, for you can't choose your landing site! As we descended, everything loose was securely tied up in the car.

Then Mr. Dolder let go of the guide rope. It tumbled earthwards and its tail snapped like a whip. The guide rope brakes the descent, and the movement of the balloon, by means of its friction against the earth. It also is an automatic height regulator. As the balloon descends, more rope lies on the ground, less on the balloon. Lightened in this way, the balloon rises again. As it rises, less rope lies on the ground, more on the balloon. This weights the balloon, it descends again, and so on!

Before the days of telephone lines and high tension wires, "guide roping" might last much of the journey, allowing a pilot to keep a steady height while saving ballast and using the valve less often. The rope left a narrow track as it trailed along the countryside, perhaps at worst meeting a laundry line!

A small grassy field lay ahead. But just as we were to land, the balloon picked up speed, caught by a gust of wind. We were headed for a wood . . . not the soft treetops, but the hard, wide trunks!

Mr. Dolder ordered the last bags of ballast jettisoned, and we rose up the tree branches just in time. The car wound its way through pine needles and cones, and my pilot ordered, "Grab a tree!" I clutched the nearest one and it swayed as if making a gracious bow.

Mr. Dolder sounded his horn, and soon I saw faces of startled Sunday picnickers under the green canopy. We were too high to throw them a line, so Mr. Dolder let out some gas. I could hold on no more and I felt my stomach rise up to my heart. The car plummeted down. The faces which had run up to help us now ran back under the trees. The earth raced to us like a boxer's punch . . . and BOOM!! It hit us.

We took a wicked jolt, but I felt no broken bones! Then the merry faces reappeared from behind the trees. Children, farmers, housewives, all told what they'd seen and greeted us like extraterrestrial beings from outer space. "Where do you come from?" "How did you get here?"

Once recovered from our violent meeting with the "stony planet," we were able to climb out of the car. Everyone was delighted to give a hand folding up the net and envelope after all the gas had escaped from the valve. We heaved and hoed the folded balloon to a car and trailer that had been following us below. I found that a balloon isn't as light as all that! Once all was secured, we thanked our new friends and climbed into a more familiar kind of car.

We bounced along a dirt road into the village of Rüdlingen (how much harder earth travel is!), and here we popped our "balloon-mail" into a mailbox.

The next day the postman brought my daughter this card!

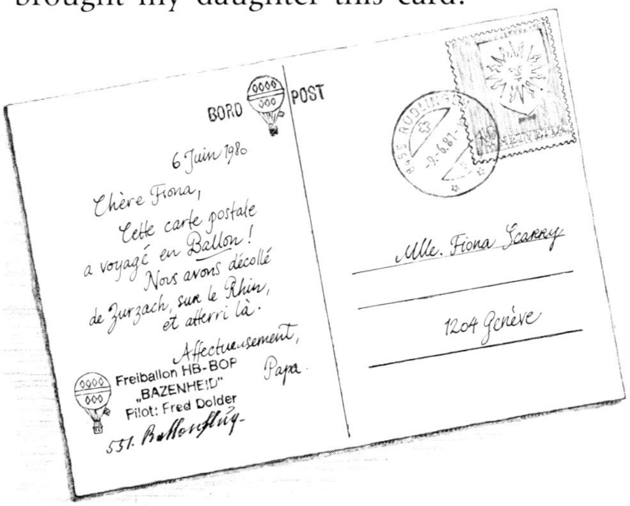

Thinking and Writing About the Selection

1. How can the pilot control the upward movement of the balloon? How can the downward movement be controlled?
2. Why won't a hydrogen-filled balloon keep rising through the air?
3. Why is it difficult to land in a balloon? Why might it take a long time to land?
4. Would you like to take a balloon trip? Why or why not?

Applying the Key Skill
Directions

Write the following directions in the correct sequence, based on what you read in "Balloon Trip."

Preparing for Take-Off

Move the hole to the center of the envelope.
Attach sand canisters around the net.
Fill the envelope with gas.
Unfold the envelope and lay it flat on the ground.
Fit the "North Pole" valve into the hole.
Lay the net over the envelope.
Attach the suspension hoop and basket below the appendix.
Thread the ropes to control the valve and the rip panel through the "North Pole" hole and out the inflation appendix at the "South Pole."
Tie up the appendix.

WRITING ACTIVITY

SHORT STORY

Prewrite

You have been reading about people who travel to distant places. Now you are going to write a short story about a real trip you have taken or a trip you have always wanted to take. Before you begin to write, think and plan these elements of your story.

Plot and Setting: Consider these questions in planning.

1. Is the trip real or imaginary? What is the destination?
2. How will I travel and what will be my route?
3. What places will I visit?
4. How long will my trip take?
5. Who will go with me?
6. What information do I have and what do I need?

You may want to draw a map of your route showing the different stops or settings. Then make notes of the events that happen or could happen at each stop.

Your plot could be organized in two ways. You could tell about all of the events in chronological, or time, order. Or you might use flashback, that is, begin the story at your destination and then go back in time and tell about the events that happened on the way.

Point of View: You may write your story in first person, as in the story "Balloon Trip." You may choose to write in third person, as in the story "Shackleton's Epic Voyage."

Mood and Theme: Is your trip mysterious, dangerous, exciting? Choose words that help your reader feel the mood of your trip. Would you like your reader to learn something more from the story than a summary of your trip? Discuss possible themes with your class.

Write

1. Review your notes and the map of your trip.
2. Your first paragraph should attract the attention of your readers. It may introduce your characters and your destination. Try to avoid a beginning sentence like this: "I had a good trip to Alaska." Perhaps use one like this: "The last American frontier was what I wanted to see, and see it I did!"
3. The remaining paragraphs should tell about the events and settings of your trip.
4. Try to use Vocabulary Treasures in your story.
5. Now write the first draft of your short story.

VOCABULARY TREASURES

cumbersome	plummeted
enticing	suspense

Revise

Read your short story. Have a friend read it, too. Think about this checklist as you revise.

1. Do your characters seem like real people? Did they do some funny or exciting things? Pep up your descriptions by using analogies or similes.
2. Did you give correct information about the settings and route of your trip?
3. Read just the subject and predicate of each sentence. Do they make sense? Have you used too many linking verbs? Do your adjectives and adverbs help the reader see a clear mental picture of places, characters, and events in the plot?
4. Check your punctuation, spelling, and capitalization.
5. Now rewrite your short story to share.

SKILLS ACTIVITY

ANALOGIES

An **analogy** is a way of comparing things. In making an analogy, we are expressing how things that are otherwise unlike are similar in some way.

One kind of analogy compares two pairs of words. The words in one pair are related in some way. The words in the other pair are related in the same way. Look at the example of this kind of analogy below.

Oak is to tree as mosquito is to insect.

The words of the first pair are *oak* and *tree*. They are related in this way: an oak is a kind of tree. The words of the second pair are *mosquito* and *insect*. They are related in the same way that *oak* and *tree* are related: a mosquito is a kind of insect.

Analogies comparing two pairs of words are often written in this way:

oak:tree::mosquito:insect

The symbol : means "is to" and the symbol :: means "as."

Analogies may show many different kinds of relationships. They may relate words with opposite meanings (antonyms), words with similar meanings (synonyms), parts to the whole, actions to objects, or users to things used.

When asked to supply the missing word to complete an analogy, you should think about the kind of relationship that exists between the words in the complete pair. Look for a word among the answer choices that has the same relationship to the remaining word. Try this:

pilot:plane::driver:____

a. ride   b. car   c. road   d. passenger

Since a *pilot* guides or steers a *plane*, the missing word must tell what a *driver* guides or steers. You probably chose the correct answer, *car*.

ACTIVITY A Number your paper from 1 to 4. Write the word that correctly completes each analogy next to the number.

1. tree: ____::sand:beach

   a. apple   b. forest   c. grow   d. ocean

2. near:close::____ :carpet

   a. rug   b. floor   c. room   d. far

3. 1:____::10:100

   a. 2   b. 10   c. 100   d. 1,000

4. ____:bank::books:library

   a. save   b. store   c. money   d. building

ACTIVITY B Write an analogy based on the stated relationship by using the four words in parentheses.

1. antonyms (cold, high, low, hot)
2. part to the whole (year, minute, month, hour)
3. purpose (write, shovel, pen, dig)
4. quality (fur, sandpaper, soft, rough)
5. action to thing (swim, bird, fly, fish)

THE BORROWERS ALOFT

MARY NORTON

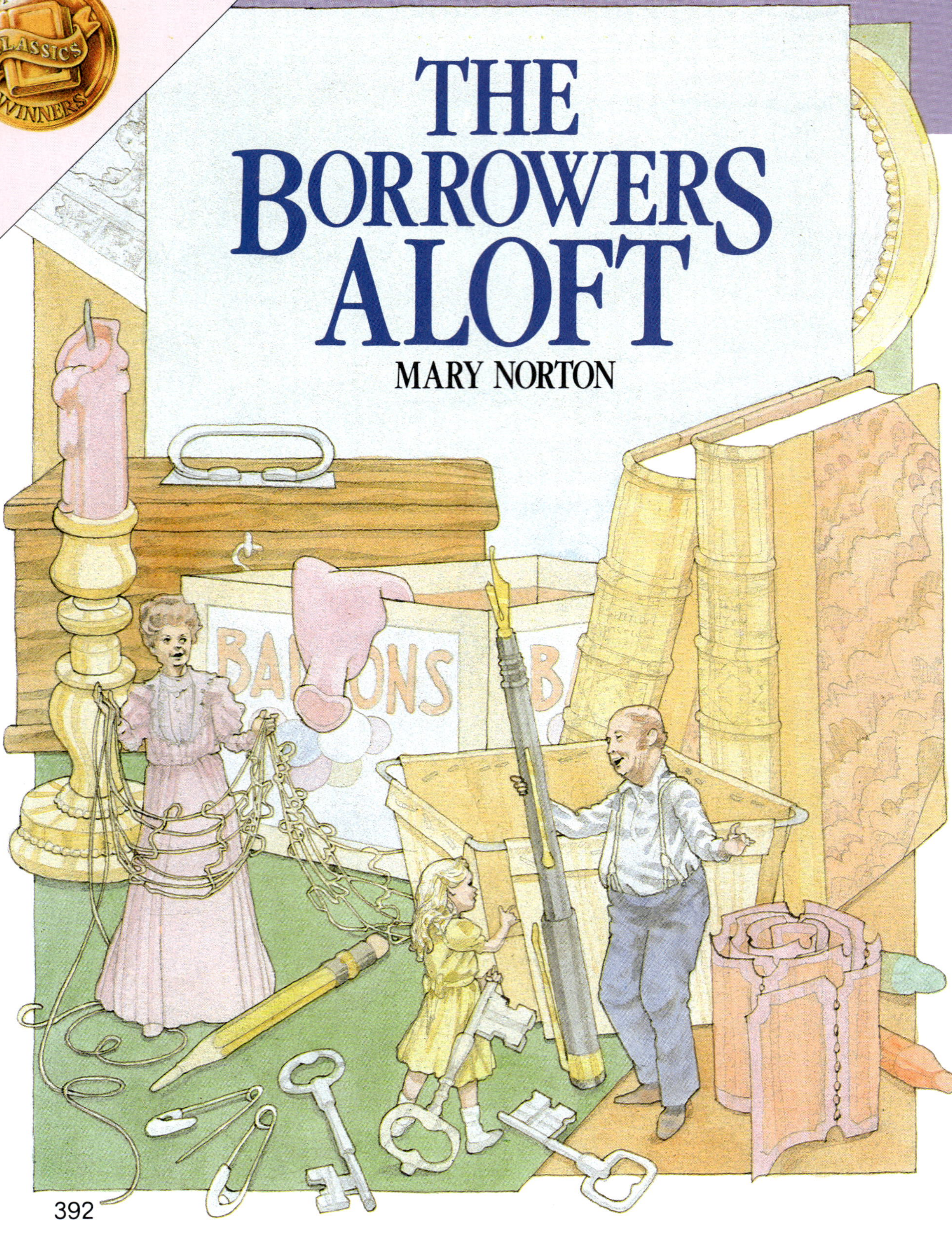

What happens to all the sewing needles, pencil stubs, safety pins, matchboxes that people lose? Where do they go? Who takes them? The Borrowers, of course.

Mary Norton created the Borrowers—the miniature people who live quite close to us in secret places, between the floors, or behind the wall paneling. They are very clever at making do with things that humans misplace.

In Mary Norton's first book about the Borrowers, the tiny family—Pod, Homily, and their daughter, Arrietty—were forced from their home in the big house at Firbank. They had many adventures, but finally settled down in the miniature village of Little Fordham where life seemed ideal.

One day, however, the three were kidnapped by Mr. and Mrs. Platter, the owners of a rival miniature village. The Platters wanted to feature the Borrowers as a live attraction the following spring. During the winter in the Platters' attic, the Borrowers planned ways to escape, but things seemed pretty hopeless until Arrietty discovered the article on ballooning in the **Illustrated London News**.

They soon found all they needed to make the balloon. The Platters had boxes of balloons they were saving for the spring opening of the miniature village; one of these would serve as the envelope. The shrimping net covered the balloon and a strawberry basket became the car. With ballast (a roll of tickets, and some keys) and a fountain pen lever to adjust gas flow, Pod could control the balloon. The gas jet in the attic would provide the gas to fill the envelope.

After several weeks of practicing and many warnings from Pod ("This isn't a joy ride . . ."), the longed-for day finally arrived.

But it did seem a joy ride to Arrietty when—on the twenty-eighth of March, having opened the window for the last time and left it open—they drifted slowly out into the pale spring sunshine.

The moment of actual departure had come with a shock of surprise, depending as it did on wind and weather. The night before they had gone to bed as usual, and this morning, before Mabel and Sidney had brought their breakfast, Pod, studying the ilex branch, had announced that this was The Day.

It had seemed quite unreal to Arrietty, and it still seemed unreal to her now. Their passage was so dreamlike and silent. At one moment they were in the room, which seemed now almost to smell of their captivity, and the next moment—free as thistledown—they sailed softly into a vast ocean of landscape—undulating into distance and brushed with the green veil of spring.

There was a smell of damp earth and for a moment the smell of something frying in Mrs. Platter's kitchen. There were a myriad of tiny sounds—a bicycle bell, the sound of a horse's hoofs and a man's voice growling "Gid-dup. . . ." Then suddenly they heard Mrs. Platter calling to Mr. Platter from a window: "Put on your coat, dear, if you're going to stay out long. . . ." And looking down at the gravel path below them, they saw Mr. Platter on his way to the island. He looked a strange shape from above—head down between his shoulders and feet twinkling in and out as he hurried toward his object.

"He's going to work on the cage-house," said Homily.

They saw with a kind of distant curiosity the whole layout of Mr. Platter's model village and the river twisting

away beyond it to the three distant poplars that marked what Pod now referred to as their L.Z.[1]

During the last few days he had taken to using abbreviations of ballooning terms, referring to the music box they took off from as the T.O.P.[2] They were now, with the gleaming slates of the roof just below them, feeling their way toward a convenient C.A.[3]

1. **L.Z.:** Landing Zone. 2. **T.O.P.:** Take-Off Point. 3. **C.A.:** Chosen Altitude.

Strangely enough, after their many trial trips up and down the ceiling, the basket felt quite homelike and familiar. Arrietty, whose job was "ballast," glanced at her father who stood looking rapt and interested—but not too preoccupied—with his hand on the lever of the cut-off fountain pen. Homily, although a little pale, was matter-of-factly adjusting the coiled line of the grapnel, one spike of which had slid below the level of the basket. "Might just catch in something," she murmured. The grapnel consisted of two large open safety pins, securely wired back to back. Pod, who for days had been studying the trend of the ilex leaves, remarked, "Wind's all right but not enough of it," as very gently, as though waltzing, they twisted above the roof. Pod, looking ahead, had his eye on the ilex.

"A couple of tickets now, Arrietty," he said. "Takes a few minutes to feel the effect."

She tore them off and dropped them overboard. They fluttered gently and ran a little on the slates of the roof and then lay still.

"Let's give her two more," said Pod. And within a few seconds, staring at the ilex tree as slowly it loomed nearer, he added, "Better make it three."

"We've had six shillings' worth already," Arrietty protested.

"All right," said Pod, as the balloon began to lift, "let's leave it at that."

"But I've done it now," she said.

They sailed over the ilex tree with plenty of height to spare, and the balloon still went on rising. Homily gazed down as the ground receded.

"Careful, Pod," she said.

"It's all right," he told them. "I'm bringing her down."

And in spite of the upturned tube, they smelled a slight smell of gas.

Even from this height the noises were quite distinct. They heard Mr. Platter hammering at the cage-house and—although the railway looked so distant—the sound of a shunting train. As they swept down rather faster than Pod had bargained for, they found themselves carried beyond the confines of Mr. Platter's garden and drifting—on a descending spiral—above the main road. A farm cart crawled slowly beneath them on the broad sunlit stretch, which, curving ribbon-like into the distance, looked frayed along one side by the shadows thrown from the hedges and from the spindly wayside woods.

"We're heading away from our L.Z.," said Pod. "Better give her three more tickets—there's less wind down here than above."

As the balloon began to lift, they passed over one of Mr. Platter's lately built villas in which someone was practicing the piano. A stream of metallic notes flowed up, and about them a dog began to bark.

They began to rise quite swiftly—on the three tickets and an extra one-and-sixpenny's worth—thrown down by Arrietty. She did it on an impulse and knew at once that it was wrong. Their very lives depended on obedience to the pilot, and how could the pilot navigate if she cheated on commands? She felt very guilty as the balloon continued to rise. They were passing over a field of cows, which, second by second, as she stared down at them, were becoming steadily smaller; all the same, a tremulous "Moo" surged up to them through the quiet air and eddied about their ears. She could hear a lark singing, and over a spreading cherry orchard she smelled the sticky scent of sun-warmed

buds and blossoms. It's more like mid-April, Arrietty thought, than the twenty-eighth of March.

Suddenly something came between them and the sun, and a chill struck the basket. The top of the envelope had melted into mist, and the earth below them disappeared from sight.

They stared at each other. Nothing else existed now except the familiar juice-stained basket, hung in a limbo of whiteness, and their three rather frightened selves.

"It's all right," said Pod. "We're in a cloud. I'll let out a little gas."

They were silent while he did so, staring intently at his steady hand on the lever—it hardly seemed to move.

"Not too much," he explained in a quiet conversational voice. "The condensation on the net will help us: there's a lot of weight in water. And I think we've found the wind!"

They were in sunshine again quite suddenly and cruising smoothly and softly on a gentle breeze toward their still distant L.Z.

"Shouldn't wonder," remarked Pod cheerfully, "if we hadn't hit on our right C.A. at last."

Homily shivered. "I didn't like that at all."

"Nor did I," agreed Arrietty. There was no sense of wind in the basket, and she turned up her face to the sun, basking gratefully in the suddenly restored warmth.

They passed over a group of cottages set about a small, squat church. Three people with baskets were grouped about a shop, and they heard a sudden peal of very hearty laughter. In a back garden they saw a woman with her back to them, hanging washing on a line; it hung quite limply.

"Not much wind down there," remarked Pod.

"Nor all that much up here," retorted Homily.

They stared down in silence for a while.

"I wonder why no one ever looks up," Arrietty exclaimed suddenly.

"Human beings don't look up much," said Pod. "Too full of their own concerns." He thought a moment. "Unless, maybe, they hear a sudden loud noise . . . or see a flash or something. They don't have to keep their eyes open like borrowers do."

"Or birds," said Arrietty, "or mice . . ."

"Or anything that's hunted," said Pod.

"Isn't there anything that hunts human beings?" Arrietty asked.

"Not that I know of," said Pod. "Might do 'em a bit of good if there were. Show 'em what it feels like, for once."

Homily stared down below at a man on a bicycle. He looked quite ordinary—almost like a borrower from here—and wobbled slightly on the lower slopes of what appeared to be a hill. She stared incredulously until the rider turned in to the lower gate of the churchyard.

There was a sudden smell of Irish stew, followed by a whiff of coffee.

"Must be getting on for midday," said Pod, and as he spoke, the church clock struck twelve.

"I don't like these eddies," said Pod some time later, as the balloon, once again on a downward spiral, curved away from the river. ". . . something to do with the ground warming up and that bit of hill over there."

"Would anybody like something to eat?" suggested Homily suddenly. There were slivers of ham, a crumbly knob of cheese, a few grains of cold rice pudding, and a long segment of orange on which to quench their thirst.

"Better wait a while," said Pod, his hand on the valve. The balloon was moving downward.

"I don't see why," said Homily. "We must all be getting hungry."

"I know," said Pod, "but it's better we hold off, if we can. We may have to jettison the rations, and you can't do that once you've eaten them."

"I don't know what you mean," complained Homily.

"Throw the food overboard," explained Arrietty who, on Pod's orders, had torn off several more tickets.

"You see," said Pod, "what with one thing and another, I've let out a good deal of gas."

Homily was silent. After a while she said, "I don't like the way we keep turning round. First the church is on our right; the next it's run round to the left. I mean, you don't know where you are, not for two minutes together."

"It'll be all right," said Pod, "once we've hit the wind. Let go another two," he added to Arrietty.

It was just enough; they rose gently, held on a steady current, and moved slowly toward the stream.

"Now," said Pod, "if we keep on like this, we're all right." He stared ahead to where, speckled by the sunshine, the poplar trees loomed nearer. "We're going nicely now."

"You mean we might hit Little Fordham?"

"Not unlikely," said Pod.

"If you ask me," exclaimed Homily, screwing up her eyes against the afternoon sun, "the whole thing's hit or miss!"

"Not altogether," said Pod, and he let out a little more gas. "We bring her down slowly, gradually losing altitude. Once we're in reach of the ground, we steady her with the trail rope. Acts like a kind of brake. And directly I give her the word, Arrietty releases the grapnel."

Homily was silent again. Impressed but still rather anxious, she stared steadily ahead. The river swam gently toward them until and at last it came directly below. The light wind seemed to follow the river's course as it curved ahead into the distance. The poplars now seemed to beckon as they swayed and stirred in the breeze, and their long shadows—even longer by now—were stretching directly toward them. They sailed as though drawn on a string.

Pod let out more gas. "Better uncoil the trail rope," he said to Arrietty.

"Already?"

"Yes," said Pod, "you got to be prepared . . ."

The ground swayed slowly up toward them. A clump of oak trees seemed to move aside, and they saw just ahead and slightly tilted a bird's-eye view of their long lost Little Fordham.

"You wouldn't credit it!" breathed Homily, as raptly they stared ahead.

They could see the railway lines glinting in the sunshine, the weathercock flashing on the church's steeple, the uneven roofs along the narrow High Street, and the crooked chimney of their own dear home. They saw the garden front of Mr. Pott's thatched cottage, and beyond the dark green of the holly hedge a stretch of sunlit lane. A tweed-clad figure strode along it in a loose-limbed, youthful way. They knew it was Miss Menzies—going home to tea. And Mr. Pott, thought Arrietty, would have gone inside for his.

The balloon was sinking fast.

"Careful, Pod!" urged Homily, "or you'll have us in the river!"

As swiftly the balloon sank down, a veil-like something suddenly appeared along the edge of the garden. As they sank down, they saw it to be a line of strong wire fencing girding the bank of the river. Mr. Pott had taken precautions, and his treasures (the village and its inhabitants) were now caged in.

"Time, too!" said Homily grimly. Then, suddenly, she shrieked and clung to the sides of the basket as the stream rushed up toward them.

"Get ready the grapnel!" shouted Pod. But even as he spoke, the basket had hit the water and tilted sideways in a flurry of spray. They were dragged along the surface. All three were thrown off balance, and knee-deep in rushing water, they clung to raffia bridles while the envelope surged on ahead. Pod just managed to close the valve as Arrietty, clinging on with one hand, tried with the other to free the grapnel. But Homily, in a panic and before anyone could stop her, threw out the knob of cheese. The balloon shot violently upward, accompanied by Homily's screams, and then—just as violently—snapped back to a sickening halt. The roll of tickets shot up between them and sailed down into the water. Except for their grips on the bridles, the occupants would have followed. They were thrown up into the air, where they hung for a moment before tumbling back in the basket: a safety pin of the grapnel had caught in the wire of the fence. The tremblings, creakings, twistings, and strainings seemed enough to uproot the fence, and Pod, looking downward as he clung to the reopened valve lever, saw the barb of the safety pin slide.

"That won't hold for long," he gasped.

The quivering basket was held at a terrifying tilt—almost pulled apart, it seemed, between the force of the upward surge and the drag of the grapnel below. The gas was escaping too slowly—it was clearly a race against time.

There was a steady stream of water from the dripping basket. Their three backs were braced against the tilted floor and their feet against one side. As white-faced they all stared downward, they could hear each other's breathing. The angle of the opened pin was slowly growing wider.

Pod took a sudden resolve. "Get hold of the trail rope," he said to Arrietty, "and pass it to me. I'm going down the grapnel line and taking the trail rope with me."

"Oh, Pod!" cried Homily miserably. "Suppose we shot up without you!"

He took no notice. "Quick!" he urged. And as Arrietty pulled up the length of dripping twine, he took one end in his hand and swung over the edge of the basket onto the line of the grapnel. He slid away below them in one swift downward run, his elbow encircling the trail rope. They watched him steady himself on the top of the fence and climb down a couple of meshes. They watched his swift one-handed movement as he passed the trail rope through the mesh and made fast with a double turn. Then his small square face turned up toward them.

"Get a hold on the bridles," he called. "There's going to be a bit of a jerk—" He shifted himself a few meshes sideways from where he could watch the pin.

It slid free with a metallic ping, even sooner than they had expected, and was flung out in a quivering arch, which—whiplike—thrashed the air. The balloon shot up in a frenzied leap but was held by the knotted twine. It seemed frustrated as it strained above them, as though striving to tear itself free. Arrietty and Homily clung together, half laughing and half crying, in a wild access of relief. He had moored them just in time.

"You'll be all right now," Pod called up cheerfully. "Nothing to do but wait."

***Pod, Homily, and Arrietty did reach their home in Little Fordham safely, but soon made an important decision. You can read about their adventures in* The Borrowers Aloft, *and* The Borrowers Avenged.**

Thinking and Writing About the Selection

1. What materials did the Borrowers use to make their balloon?
2. How did the Borrowers control their C.A.?
3. Why do you think the humans below didn't notice the Borrowers' balloon?
4. If the Borrowers came to your house, where do you think they would choose to live? Why?

Applying the Key Skill
Character's Motives and Feelings

Choose the best answer or answers to each of the following questions about "The Borrowers Aloft."

1. Why did the Borrowers decide to escape from the attic?
   a. They wanted to return to their own home.
   b. They did not want to be "put on display."
   c. They knew they could get away safely.
   d. They had the materials they needed to make an escape attempt.
2. How did the Borrowers feel when the balloon entered a cloud?
   a. relieved b. confused c. frightened d. surprised
3. Why did Pod decide to climb down the grapnel line when it became caught in the wire fence?
   a. He knew the safety pin would keep the balloon aloft.
   b. He thought the balloon might be pulled apart if he didn't act quickly.
   c. He saw the safety pin opening wider and wider.
   d. He knew Arrietty could handle the balloon without him.

LANGUAGE ACTIVITY

UP IN THE AIR

When the Borrowers were *aloft*, they were "in a place far above the ground." **Aloft** comes from the Norse words *a*, "in," and *lopt*, "air, sky." We often use the expression "up in the air" in a literal way to mean *aloft*. But the words also have a figurative meaning—"not decided, uncertain; in suspense." Can you see how the literal and figurative meanings of "up in the air" are related?

Balloons were the first successful inventions for leaving the ground and traveling in the air. **Balloon** can be traced back to the German *balle*, meaning "ball"—and that is what a balloon looks like, a very large ball.

In time, balloons assumed elongated shapes and acquired engines and propellers. They became the airships we called **dirigibles** (from Latin *dirigere*, "to guide, direct") and **blimps** (from a popular model, the *type B-limp*).

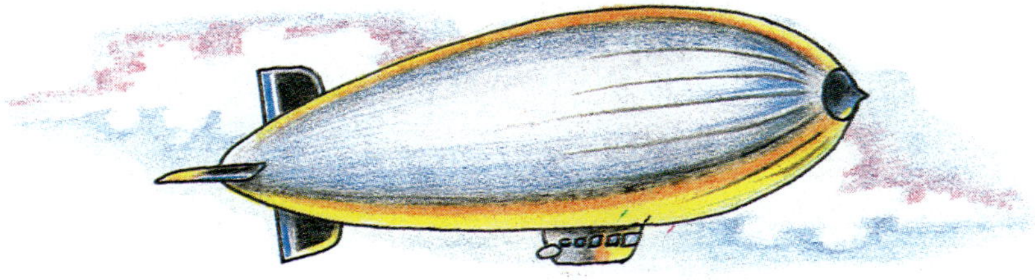

It is not surprising that the new field of ballooning borrowed many words and terms from sailing. After all, balloons and airships do "sail" through the air. And an **airship** is literally "a ship of the air."

An **aeronaut** is a person who pilots a balloon or airship. It probably doesn't surprise you that it literally means "air sailor" (Greek *aer*, "air," + Greek *nautes*, "sailor").

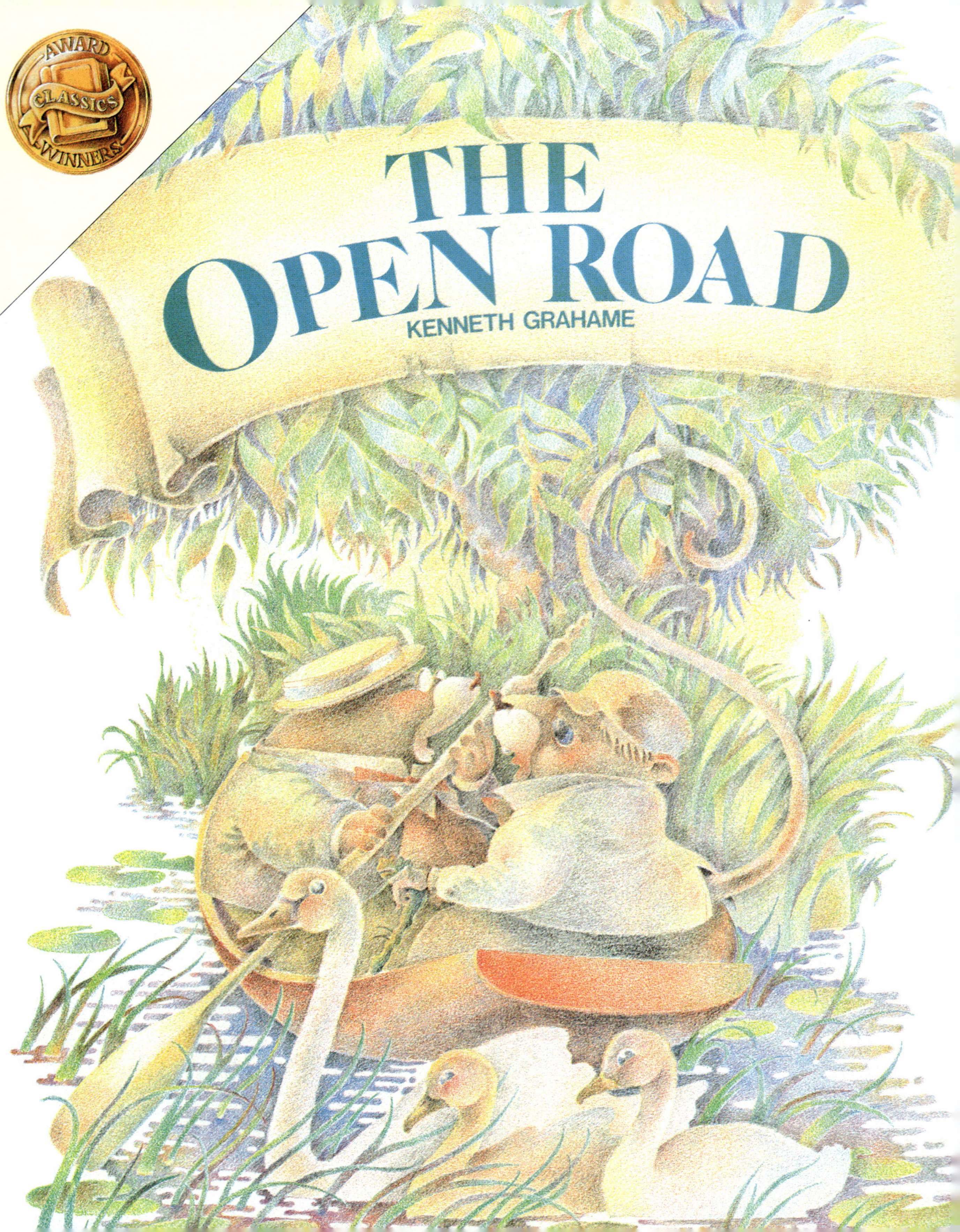
AWARD
CLASSICS
WINNERS
THE OPEN ROAD
KENNETH GRAHAME

***The Wind in the Willows**, of which "The Open Road" is a part, was published in 1908. Years before that, however, Kenneth Grahame had been thinking about the characters in the book. He first wrote about them in a series of letters to his son, Alistair.*

Mole and Rat are introduced in the first chapter. In the second chapter, "The Open Road," these two friends visit Mr. Toad. It is the beginning of an adventure they will not soon forget.

"Ratty," said the Mole suddenly, one bright summer morning, "if you please, I want to ask you a favor. What I wanted to ask you was, won't you take me to call on Mr. Toad? I've heard so much about him, and I do so want to make his acquaintance."

"Why, certainly," said the good-natured Rat, jumping to his feet. "Get the boat out, and we'll paddle up there at once. It's never the wrong time to call on Toad. Early or late he's always the same fellow. Always good-tempered, always glad to see you, always sorry when you go!"

"He must be a very nice animal," observed the Mole, as he got into the boat and took the sculls, while the Rat settled himself comfortably in the stern.

"He is indeed the best of animals," replied Rat. "So simple, so good-natured, and so affectionate. Perhaps he's not very clever—we can't all be geniuses; and it may be that he is both boastful and conceited. But he has got some great qualities, has Toady."

Rounding a bend in the river, they came in sight of a handsome, dignified old house of mellowed red brick, with well-kept lawns reaching down to the water's edge.

"There's Toad Hall," said the Rat; "and that creek on the left, where the notice board says, 'Private. No landing allowed,' leads to his boathouse, where we'll leave the boat. The stables are over there to the right. That's the banqueting hall you're looking at

now—very old, that is. Toad is rather rich, you know, and this is really one of the nicest houses in these parts, though we never admit as much to Toad.''

They glided up the creek, and the Mole shipped his sculls as they passed into the shadow of a large boathouse. Here they saw many handsome boats, slung from the crossbeams or hauled up on a slip, but none in the water; and the place had an unused and a deserted air.

The Rat looked around him. ''I understand,'' said he. ''Boating is played out. He's tired of it, and done with it. I wonder what new fad he has taken up now? Come along and let's look him up. We shall hear all about it quite soon enough.''

They disembarked, and strolled across the gay flower-decked lawns in search of Toad, whom they presently happened upon resting in a wicker garden chair, with a preoccupied expression of face, and a large map spread out on his knees.

"Hooray!" he cried, jumping up on seeing them. "This is splendid!" He shook the paws of both of them warmly, never waiting for an introduction to the Mole. "How *kind* of you!" he went on, dancing round them. "I was just going to send a boat down the river for you, Ratty, with strict orders that you were to be fetched up here at once, whatever you were doing. I want you badly—both of you. Now what will you take? Come inside and have something! You don't know how lucky it is, your turning up just now!"

"Let's sit quiet a bit, Toady," said the Rat, throwing himself into an easy chair, while the Mole took another by the side of him and made some civil remark about Toad's "delightful residence."

"Finest house on the whole river!" cried Toad boisterously. "Or anywhere else, for that matter," he could not help adding.

Here the Rat nudged the Mole. Unfortunately the Toad saw him do it and turned very red. There was a moment's painful silence. Then Toad burst out laughing. "All right, Ratty," he said. "It's only my way, you know. And it's not such a very bad house, is it? You know you rather like it yourself. Now, look here. Let's be sensible. You are the very animals I wanted. You've got to help me. It's most important!"

"It's about your rowing, I suppose," said the Rat, with an innocent air. "You're getting on fairly well, though you splash a good bit still. With a great deal of patience, and any quantity of coaching, you may—"

"O, pooh! boating!" interrupted the Toad, in great disgust. "Silly boyish amusement. I've given that up *long* ago. Sheer waste of time, that's what it is. It makes me downright sorry to see you fellows, who ought to know better, spending all your energies in that aimless manner. No, I've discovered the real thing, the only genuine occupation for a lifetime. I propose to devote the remainder of mine to it, and can only regret the wasted years, that lie behind me, squandered in trivialities. Come with me, dear Ratty, and your amiable friend also, if he will

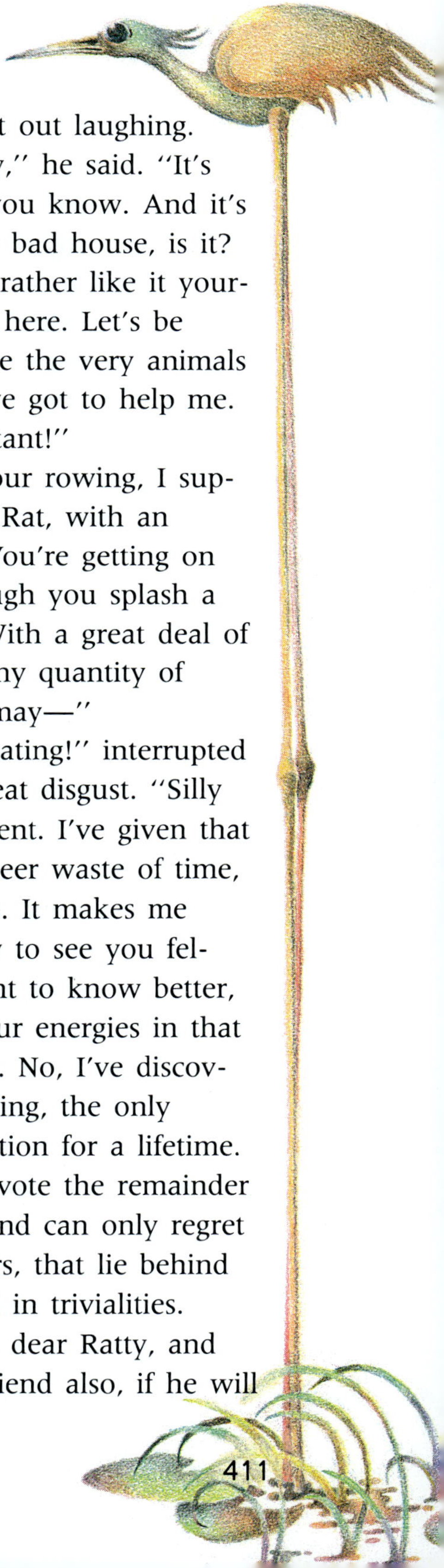

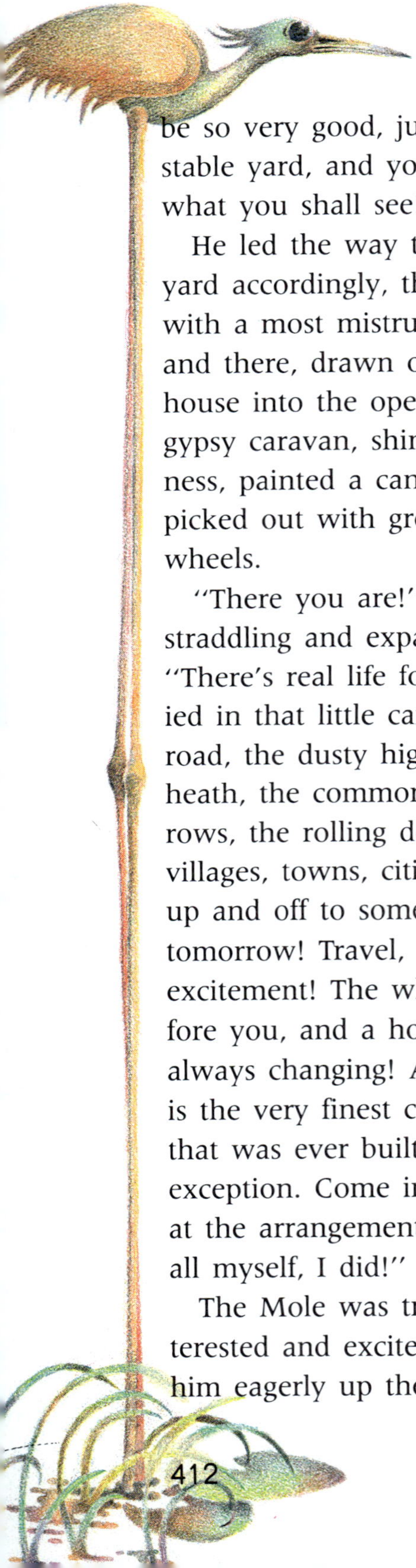

be so very good, just as far as the stable yard, and you shall see what you shall see!"

He led the way to the stable yard accordingly, the Rat following with a most mistrustful expression; and there, drawn out of the coach house into the open, they saw a gypsy caravan, shining with newness, painted a canary yellow picked out with green, and red wheels.

"There you are!" cried the Toad, straddling and expanding himself. "There's real life for you, embodied in that little cart. The open road, the dusty highway, the heath, the common, the hedgerows, the rolling downs! Camps, villages, towns, cities! Here today, up and off to somewhere else tomorrow! Travel, change, interest, excitement! The whole world before you, and a horizon that's always changing! And mind, this is the very finest cart of its sort that was ever built, without any exception. Come inside and look at the arrangements. Planned 'em all myself, I did!"

The Mole was tremendously interested and excited, and followed him eagerly up the steps and into the interior of the caravan. The Rat only snorted and thrust his hands deep into his pockets, remaining where he was.

It was indeed very compact and comfortable. Little sleeping-bunks—a little table that folded up against the wall—a cooking stove, lockers, bookshelves, a bird cage with a bird in it; pots, pans, jugs, and kettles of every size and variety.

"All complete!" said the Toad triumphantly, pulling open a locker. "You see—biscuits, potted lobster, sardines—everything you can possibly want. Soda water here—'baccy there—letter paper, bacon, jam, cards and dominoes—you'll find," he continued, as they descended the steps again. "You'll find that nothing whatever has been forgotten, when we make our start this afternoon."

"I beg your pardon," said the Rat slowly, as he chewed a straw, "but did I overhear you say something about *we* and *start* and *this afternoon*?"

"Now, you dear good old Ratty," said Toad imploringly, "don't begin talking in that stiff and sniffy sort of way, because you know you've *got* to come. I

can't possibly manage without you, so please consider it settled, and don't argue—it's the one thing I can't stand. You surely don't mean to stick to your dull fusty old river all your life, and just live in a hole in a bank, and *boat*? I want to show you the world! I'm going to make an *animal* of you, my boy!"

"I don't care," said the Rat doggedly. "I'm not coming, and that's flat. And I am going to stick to my old river, and live in a hole, and boat, as I've always done. And what's more, Mole's going to stick to me and do as I do."

"Of course I am," said the Mole loyally. "I'll always stick to you, Rat, and what you say is to be—has got to be. All the same, it sounds as if it might have been—well, rather fun, you know!" he added wistfully. Poor Mole! The Life Adventurous was so new a thing to him, and so thrilling; and this fresh aspect of it was so tempting; and he had fallen in love at first sight with the canary-colored cart and all its little fitments.

The Rat saw what was passing in his mind, and wavered. He hated disappointing people, and he was fond of the Mole, and would do almost anything to oblige him. Toad was watching both of them closely.

"Come along in and have some lunch," he said diplomatically, "and we'll talk it over. We needn't decide anything in a hurry. Of course, *I* don't really care. I only want to give pleasure to you fellows. 'Live for others!' That's my motto in life."

During luncheon—which was excellent, of course, as everything at Toad Hall always was—the Toad simply let himself go. Disregarding the Rat, he proceeded to play upon the inexperienced Mole as on a harp. Naturally a voluble animal, and always mastered by his imagination, he painted the prospects of the trip and the joys of the open life and the roadside in such glowing colors that the Mole could hardly sit in his chair for excitement. Somehow, it soon seemed taken for granted by all three of them that the trip was a settled thing; and the Rat, though still unconvinced in his mind, allowed his good nature to override his personal objections. He could not bear to disappoint his two friends, who were already deep in schemes and anticipations, planning out each day's separate occupation for several weeks ahead.

When they were quite ready, the now triumphant Toad led his companions to the paddock and set them to capture the old gray horse, who, without having been consulted, and to his own extreme annoyance, had been told off by Toad for the dustiest job in this dusty expedition. He frankly preferred the paddock, and took a deal of catching. Meantime Toad packed the lockers still tighter with necessaries, and hung nose bags, nets of onions, bundles of hay, and baskets from the bottom of the cart. At last the horse was caught and harnessed, and they set off, all talking at once, each animal either trudging by the side of the cart or sitting on the shaft, as the humor took him. It was a golden afternoon. The smell of the dust they kicked up was rich and satisfying; birds called and

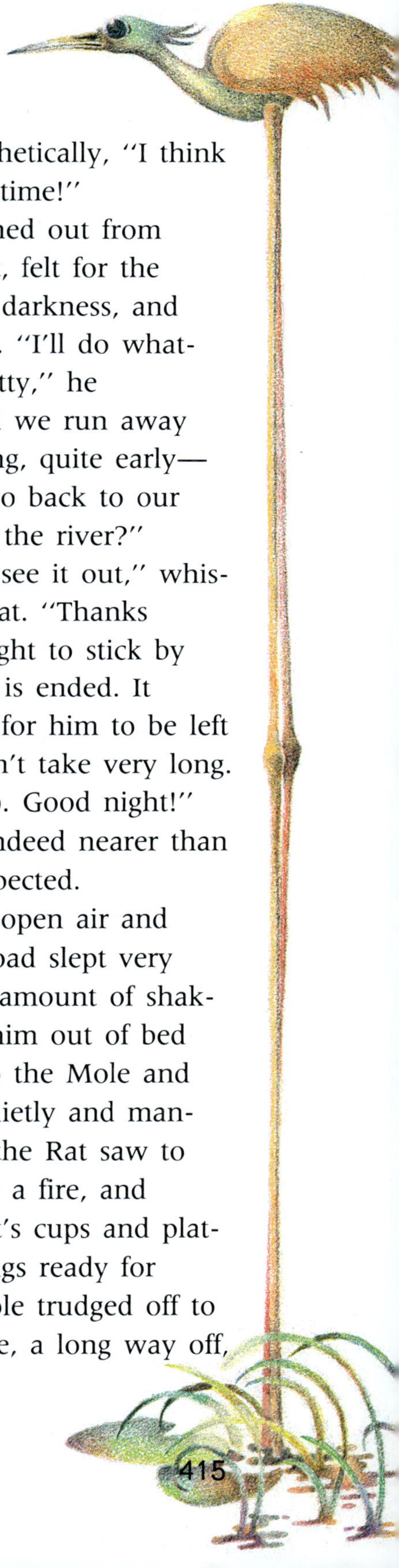

whistled to them cheerily; good-natured wayfarers, passing them, gave them "Good day," or stopped to say nice things about their beautiful cart; and rabbits, sitting at their front doors in the the hedgerows, held up their fore-paws, and said, "O my! O my!"

Late in the evening, tired and happy and miles from home, they drew up on a remote common far from habitations, turned the horse loose to graze, and ate their simple supper sitting on the grass by the side of the cart. Toad talked big about all he was going to do in the days to come, while stars grew fuller and larger all around them, and a yellow moon, appearing suddenly and silently from nowhere in particular, came to keep them company and listen to their talk. At last they turned into their little bunks in the cart; and Toad, kicking out his legs, sleepily said, "Well, good night, you fellows! This is the real life for a gentleman! Talk about your old river!"

"I *don't* talk about my river," replied the patient Rat. "You *know* I don't, Toad. But I *think* about it," he added pathetically, "I think about it—all the time!"

The Mole reached out from under his blanket, felt for the Rat's paw in the darkness, and gave it a squeeze. "I'll do whatever you like, Ratty," he whispered. "Shall we run away tomorrow morning, quite early—*very* early—and go back to our dear old hole on the river?"

"No, no, we'll see it out," whispered back the Rat. "Thanks awfully, but I ought to stick by Toad till this trip is ended. It wouldn't be safe for him to be left to himself. It won't take very long. His fads never do. Good night!"

The end was indeed nearer than even the Rat suspected.

After so much open air and excitement the Toad slept very soundly, and no amount of shaking could rouse him out of bed next morning. So the Mole and Rat turned to, quietly and manfully, and while the Rat saw to the horse, and lit a fire, and cleaned last night's cups and platters, and got things ready for breakfast, the Mole trudged off to the nearest village, a long way off,

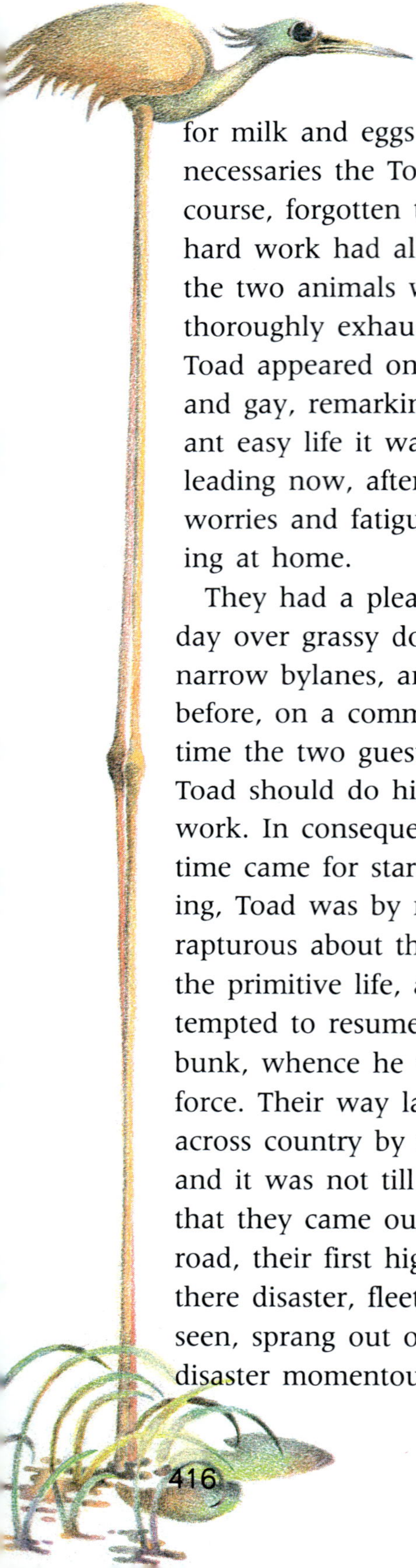

for milk and eggs and various necessaries the Toad had, of course, forgotten to provide. The hard work had all been done, and the two animals were resting, thoroughly exhausted, by the time Toad appeared on the scene, fresh and gay, remarking what a pleasant easy life it was they were all leading now, after the cares and worries and fatigues of housekeeping at home.

They had a pleasant ramble that day over grassy downs and along narrow bylanes, and camped, as before, on a common, only this time the two guests took care that Toad should do his fair share of work. In consequence, when the time came for starting next morning, Toad was by no means as rapturous about the simplicity of the primitive life, and indeed attempted to resume his place in his bunk, whence he was hauled by force. Their way lay, as before, across country by narrow lanes, and it was not till the afternoon that they came out on the high road, their first high road; and there disaster, fleet and unforeseen, sprang out on them—disaster momentous indeed to their expedition, but simply overwhelming in its effect on the after-career of Toad.

They were strolling along the high road easily, the Mole by the horse's head, talking to him, since the horse had complained that he was being frightfully left out of it, and nobody considered him in the least; the Toad and the Water Rat walking behind the cart talking together—at least Toad was talking, and Rat was saying at intervals, "Yes, precisely; and what did *you* say to *him*?"—and thinking all the time of something very different, when far behind them they heard a faint warning hum, like the drone of a distant bee. Glancing back, they saw a small cloud of dust, with a dark center of energy, advancing on them at incredible speed, while from out the dust a faint "Poop-poop!" wailed like an uneasy animal in pain. Hardly regarding it, they turned to resume their conversation, when in an instant (as it seemed) the peaceful scene was changed, and with a blast of wind and a whirl of sound that made them jump for the nearest ditch, it was on them! The "poop-poop" rang with a brazen shout in their ears, they had a moment's glimpse of an interior of glittering plate glass and rich morocco, and the magnificent motorcar, immense, breath-snatching, passionate, with its pilot tense and hugging his wheel, possessed all earth and air for the fraction of a second, flung an enveloping cloud of dust that blinded and enwrapped them utterly, and then dwindled to a speck in the far distance, changed back into a droning bee once more.

The old gray horse, dreaming, as he plodded along, of his quiet paddock, in a new raw situation such as this simply abandoned himself to his natural emotions. Rearing, plunging, backing steadily, in spite of all the Mole's efforts at his head, and all the Mole's lively language directed at his better feelings, he drove the cart backwards towards the deep ditch at the side of the road. It wavered an instant—then there was a heart-rending crash—and the canary-colored cart, their pride

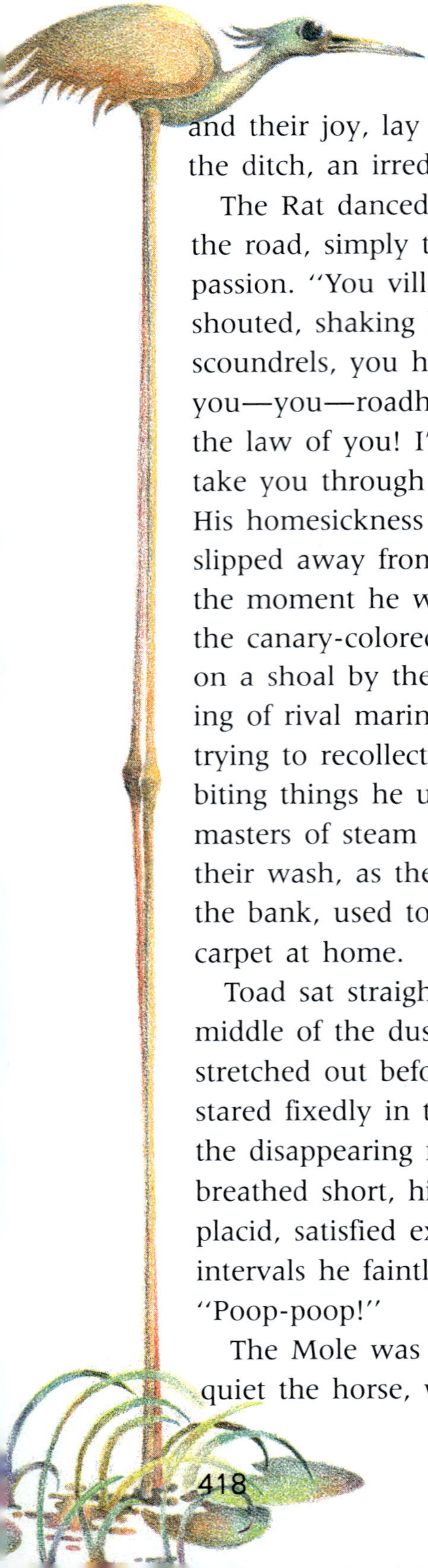

and their joy, lay on its side in the ditch, an irredeemable wreck.

The Rat danced up and down in the road, simply transported with passion. "You villains!" he shouted, shaking both fists, "You scoundrels, you highwaymen, you—you—roadhogs!—I'll have the law of you! I'll report you! I'll take you through all the Courts!" His homesickness had quite slipped away from him, and for the moment he was the skipper of the canary-colored vessel driven on a shoal by the reckless jockeying of rival mariners, and he was trying to recollect all the fine and biting things he used to say to masters of steam launches when their wash, as they drove too near the bank, used to flood his parlor carpet at home.

Toad sat straight down in the middle of the dusty road, his legs stretched out before him, and stared fixedly in the direction of the disappearing motorcar. He breathed short, his face wore a placid, satisfied expression, and at intervals he faintly murmured "Poop-poop!"

The Mole was busy trying to quiet the horse, which he succeeded in doing after a time. Then he went to look at the cart, on its side in the ditch. It was indeed a sorry sight. Panels and windows smashed, axles hopelessly bent, one wheel off, sardine tins scattered over the wide world, and the bird in the bird cage sobbing pitifully and calling to be let out.

The Rat came to help him, but their united efforts were not sufficient to right the cart. "Hi! Toad!" they cried. "Come and bear a hand, can't you!"

The Toad never answered a word, or budged from his seat in the road; so they went to see what was the matter with him. They found him in a sort of trance, a happy smile on his face, his eyes still fixed on the dusty wake of their destroyer. At intervals he was still heard to murmur "Poop-poop!"

The Rat shook him by the shoulder. "Are you coming to help us, Toad?" he demanded sternly.

"Glorious, stirring sight!" murmured Toad, never offering to move. "The poetry of motion! The *real* way to travel! The *only* way to travel! Here today—in next week tomorrow! Villages skipped, towns and cities jumped—always somebody else's horizon! O bliss! O poop-poop! O my! O my!"

"O *stop*, Toad!" cried the Mole despairingly.

"And to think I never *knew*!" went on the Toad in a dreamy monotone. "All those wasted years that lie behind me, I never knew, never even *dreamt*! But *now*—but now that I know, now that I fully realize! O what a flowery track lies spread before me, henceforth! What dust clouds shall spring up behind me as I speed on my reckless way! What carts I shall fling carelessly into the ditch in the wake of my magnificent onset! Horrid little carts—common carts—canary-colored carts!"

"What are we to do with him?" asked the Mole of the Water Rat.

"Nothing at all," replied the Rat firmly. "Because there is really nothing to be done. You see, I know him from old. He is now possessed. He has got a new craze, and it always takes him that way, in its first stage. He'll continue like that for days now, like an animal walking in a happy dream, quite useless for all practical purposes. Never mind him. Let's go and see what there is to be done about the cart."

A careful inspection showed them that, even if they succeeded in righting it by themselves, the cart would travel no longer. The axles were in a hopeless state, and the missing wheel was shattered into pieces.

The Rat knotted the horse's reins over his back and took him by the head, carrying the bird cage and its hysterical occupant in the other hand. "Come on!" he said grimly to the Mole. "It's five or six miles to the nearest town, and we shall just have to walk it. The sooner we make a start the better."

"But what about Toad?" asked the Mole anxiously, as they set off together. "We can't leave him here, sitting in the middle of the road by himself, in the distracted state he's in! It's not safe. Supposing another Thing were to come along?"

"O, *bother* Toad," said the Rat savagely. "I've done with him!"

They had not proceeded very far on their way, however, when there was a pattering of feet behind them, and Toad caught them

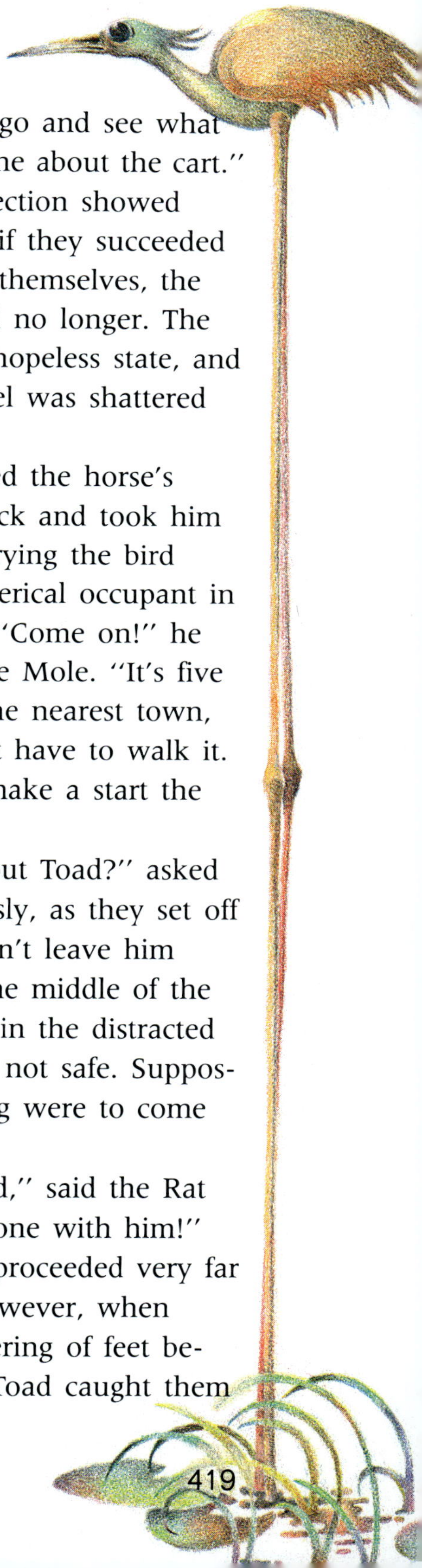

up and thrust a paw inside the elbow of each of them; still breathing short and staring into vacancy.

"Now, look here, Toad!" said the Rat sharply. "As soon as we get to the town, you'll have to go straight to the police station, and see if they know anything about that motorcar and who it belongs to, and lodge a complaint against it. And then you'll have to go to a blacksmith's or a wheelwright's and arrange for the cart to be fetched and mended and put to rights. It'll take time, but it's not quite a hopeless smash. Meanwhile, the Mole and I will go to an inn and find comfortable rooms where we can stay till the cart's ready, and till your nerves have recovered their shock."

"Police station! Complaint!" murmured Toad dreamily. "Me *complain* of that beautiful, that heavenly vision that has been vouchsafed me! *Mend* the *cart*! I've done with carts for ever. I never want to see the cart, or to hear of it, again. O, Ratty! You can't think how obliged I am to you for consenting to come on this trip! I wouldn't have gone without you, and then I might never have seen that—that swan, that sunbeam, that thunderbolt! I might never have heard that entrancing sound, or smelt that bewitching smell! I owe it all to you, my best friends!"

The Rat turned from him in despair. "You see what it is?" he said to the Mole, addressing him across Toad's head. "He's quite hopeless. I give it up—when we get to the town we'll go to the railway station, and with luck we may pick up a train there that'll get us back to River Bank tonight. And if ever you catch me going a-pleasuring with this provoking animal again!" He snorted, and during the rest of that weary trudge addressed his remarks exclusively to Mole.

On reaching the town they went straight to the station and deposited Toad in the second-class waiting room, giving a porter twopence to keep a strict eye on him. They then left the horse at an inn stable, and gave what directions they could about the cart and its contents. Eventually, a slow train having landed them at a station not very far from Toad Hall, they escorted the spellbound, sleep-walking Toad to his door, put him inside it, and instructed his housekeeper to feed him, undress him, and put him to bed. Then they got out their boat from the boathouse, sculled down the river home, and at a very late hour sat down to supper in their own cozy riverside parlor, to the Rat's great joy and contentment.

The following evening the Mole, who had risen late and taken things very easy all day, was sitting on the bank fishing, when the Rat, who had been looking up his friends and gossiping, came strolling along to find him. "Heard the news?" he said. "There's nothing else being talked about, all along the river bank. Toad went up to Town by an early train this morning. And he has ordered a large and very expensive motorcar."

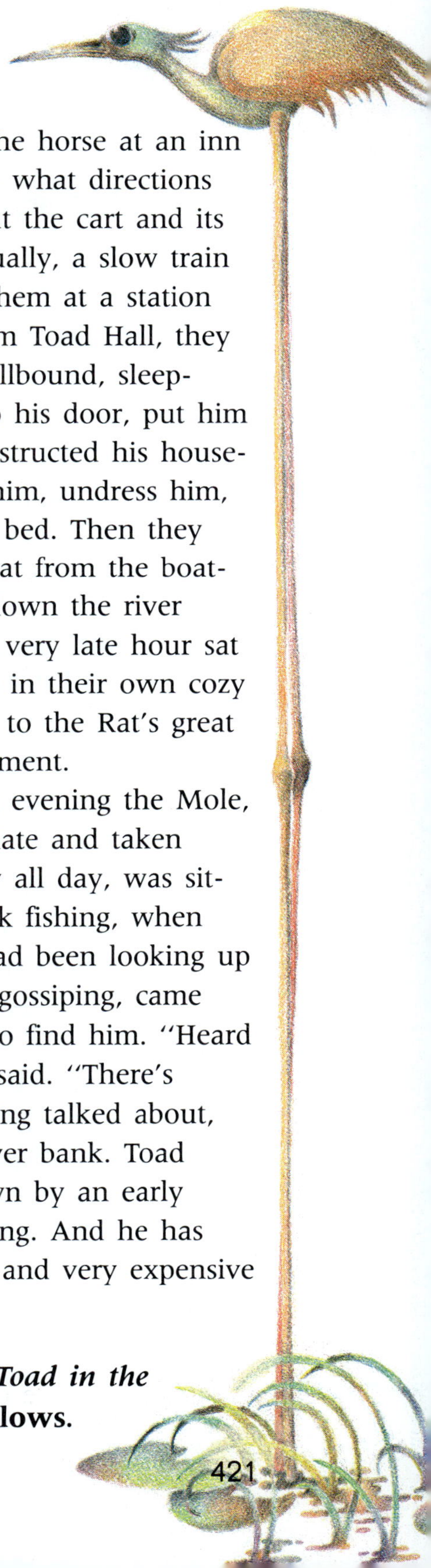

***You can read about the further adventures of Toad in the other chapters of* The Wind in the Willows.**

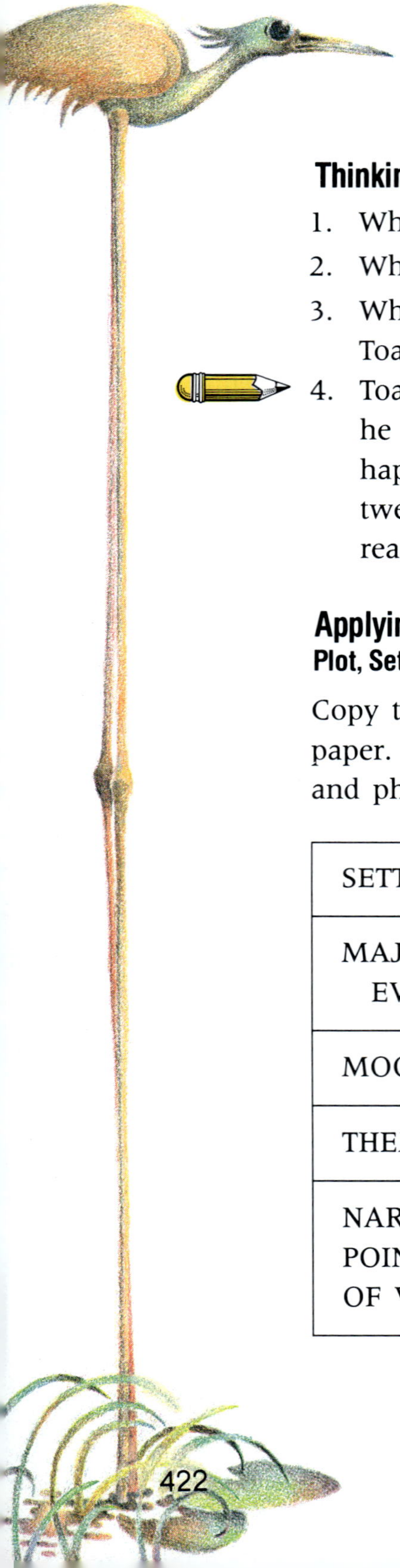

Thinking and Writing About the Selection

1. Why did Rat and Mole go to visit Mr. Toad?
2. Why was Toad so glad to see his two visitors?
3. What effect did the sight of the motor car have on Toad? Why was his reaction not surprising to Rat?
4. Toad gave up boating for the canary-colored cart. Then he gave up the cart for the motor car. What might happen if Toad saw a balloon? Write a dialogue between Toad and Rat in which Toad describes his reactions

Applying the Key Skill
Plot, Setting, Mood, Theme, Narrative Point of View

Copy the following chart about "The Open Road" on your paper. Then complete the chart by using your own words and phrases.

SETTING	
MAJOR PLOT EVENTS	
MOOD	
THEME	
NARRATIVE POINT OF VIEW	

TRAVEL

The railroad track is miles away,
    And the day is loud with voices speaking,
Yet there isn't a train goes by all day
    But I hear its whistles shrieking.

All night there isn't a train goes by,
    Though the night is still for sleep and dreaming
But I see its cinders red on the sky
    And hear its engine steaming.

My heart is warm with the friends I make,
    And better friends I'll not be knowing,
Yet there isn't a train I wouldn't take,
    No matter where it's going.

Edna St. Vincent Millay

THE HOBBIT

J.R.R. TOLKIEN

Hobbits are little people, about half our height. They have no beards and are inclined to be fat in the stomach. They wear no shoes because their feet grow natural leathery soles and thick warm brown hair. They dress in bright colors and especially like green and yellow.

Bilbo Baggins was a hobbit, a perfectly ordinary hobbit who liked a comfortable life with his meals (six a day) on time. He was not one to go on adventures. Yet it had been rumored that on Bilbo's mother's side (she was Belladonna Took) there was something unhobbitlike. The Tooks did have adventures, though the family hushed it up.

One fine morning Bilbo was visited by the wizard Gandalf who invited Bilbo to go on an adventure. Bilbo politely refused but, in a fluster, invited Gandalf to return the next day for tea.

Just before tea-time there came a tremendous ring on the front-door bell, and then he remembered! He rushed and put on the kettle, and put out another cup and saucer, and an extra cake or two, and ran to the door.

"I am so sorry to keep you waiting!" he was going to say, when he saw that it was not Gandalf at all. It was a dwarf with a blue beard tucked into a golden belt, and very bright eyes under his dark-green hood. As soon as the door was opened, he pushed inside, just as if he had been expected.

He hung his hooded cloak on the nearest peg, and "Dwalin at your service!" he said with a low bow.

"Bilbo Baggins at yours!" said the hobbit, too surprised to ask any questions for the moment. When the silence that followed had become uncomfortable, he added: "I am just about to take tea; pray come and have some with me." A little stiff perhaps, but he meant it kindly. And what would you do, if an uninvited dwarf came and hung his things up in your hall without a word of explanation?

They had not been at table long, in fact they had hardly reached the third cake, when there came another even louder ring at the bell.

"Excuse me!" said the hobbit. Off he went to the door.

"So you have got here at last!" was what he was going to say to Gandalf this time. But it was not Gandalf. Instead there was a very old-looking dwarf on the step with a white beard and a scarlet hood; and he too hopped inside as soon as the door was open, just as if he had been invited.

"I see they have begun to arrive already," he said when he caught sight of Dwalin's green hood hanging up. He hung his red one next to it, and "Balin at your service!" he said with his hand on his breast.

"Thank you!" said Bilbo with a gasp. It was not the correct thing to say, but *they have begun to arrive* had flustered him badly. He liked visitors, but he liked to know them before they arrived, and he preferred to ask them himself. He had a horrible thought that the cakes might run short, and then he—as the host: he knew his duty and stuck to it however painful—he might have to go without.

"Come along in, and have some tea!" he managed to say after taking a deep breath.

"A little beer would suit me better, if it is all the same to you, my good sir," said Balin with the white beard. "But I don't mind some cake—seed-cake, if you have any."

"Lots!" Bilbo found himself answering, to his own surprise; and he found himself scuttling off, too, to the cellar to fill a pint beer-mug, and to the pantry to fetch two beautiful round seed-cakes which he had baked that afternoon for his after-supper morsel.

When he got back Balin and Dwalin were talking at the table like old friends (as a matter of fact they were brothers). Bilbo plumped down the beer and the cake in front of them, when loud came a ring at the bell again.

"Gandalf for certain this time," he thought as he puffed along the passage. But it was not. It was two more dwarves, both with blue hoods, silver belts, and yellow beards; and each of them carried a bag of tools and a spade. In they hopped, as soon as the door began to open—Bilbo was hardly surprised at all.

"What can I do for you, my dwarves?" he said.

"Kili at your service!" said the one. "And Fili!" added the other. They both swept off their blue hoods and bowed.

"At yours and your family's!" replied Bilbo, remembering his manners this time.

"Dwalin and Balin here already, I see," said Kili. "Let us join the throng!"

"Throng!" thought Mr. Baggins. "I don't like the sound of that. I really must sit down for a minute and collect my wits, and have a drink." He had only just had a sip—in the corner, while the four dwarves sat around the table, and talked about mines and gold and troubles with the goblins, and the depredations of dragons, and lots of other things which he did not understand, and did not want to, for they sounded much too adventurous—when, *ding-dong-a-ling-dang*, his bell rang again, as if some naughty little hobbit-boy was trying to pull the handle off.

"Someone at the door!" he said, blinking.

"Some four, I should say by the sound," said Fili. "Besides, we saw them coming along behind us in the distance."

The poor little hobbit sat down in the hall and put his head in his hands, and wondered what had happened, and what was going to happen, and whether they would all stay to supper. Then the bell rang again louder than ever, and he had to run to the door. It was not four after all, it was FIVE. Another dwarf had come along while he was wondering in the hall. He had hardly turned the knob, before they were all inside, bowing and saying "at your service" one after another. Dori, Nori, Ori, Oin, and Gloin were their names; and very soon two purple hoods, a gray hood, a brown hood, and a white hood were hanging on the pegs, and off they marched with their broad hands stuck in their gold and silver belts to join the others. Already it had almost become a throng. Some called for ale, and some for porter, and one for coffee, and all of them for cakes; so the hobbit was kept very busy for a while.

A big jug of coffee had just been set in the hearth, the seed-cakes were gone, and the dwarves were starting on a round of buttered scones, when there came—a loud knock. Not a ring, but a hard rat-tat on the hobbit's beautiful green door. Somebody was banging with a stick!

Bilbo rushed along the passage, very angry, and altogether bewildered and bewuthered—this was the most awkward Wednesday he ever remembered. He pulled open the door with a jerk, and they all fell in, one on top of the other. More dwarves, four more! And there was Gandalf behind, leaning on his staff and laughing. He had made quite a dent on the beautiful door; he had also knocked out the secret mark that he had put there the morning before.

"Carefully! Carefully!" he said. "It is not like you, Bilbo, to keep friends waiting on the mat, and then open the door like a pop-gun! Let me introduce Bifur, Bofur, Bombur, and especially Thorin!"

"At your service!" said Bifur, Bofur, and Bombur standing in a row. Then they hung up two yellow hoods and a pale green one; and also a sky-blue one with a long silver tassel. This last belonged to Thorin, an enormously important dwarf, in fact no other than the great Thorin Oakenshield himself, who was not at all pleased at falling flat on Bilbo's mat with Bifur, Bofur, and Bombur on top of him. For one thing Bombur was immensely fat and heavy. Thorin indeed was very haughty, and said nothing about *service*; but poor Mr. Baggins said he was sorry so many times, that at last he grunted "pray don't mention it," and stopped frowning.

"Now we are all here!" said Gandalf, looking at the row of thirteen hoods—the best detachable party hoods—and his own hat hanging on the pegs. "Quite a merry gathering! I hope there is something left for the late-comers to eat and drink! What's that? Tea! No thank you! A little red wine, I think, for me."

"And for me," said Thorin.

"And raspberry jam and apple-tart," said Bifur.

"And mince-pies and cheese," said Bofur.

"And pork-pie and salad," said Bombur.

"And more cakes—and ale—and coffee, if you don't mind," called the other dwarves through the door.

"Put on a few eggs, there's a good fellow!" Gandalf called after him, as the hobbit stumped off to the pantries. "And just bring out the cold chicken and pickles!"

"Seems to know as much about the inside of my larders as I do myself!" thought Mr. Baggins, who was feeling positively flummoxed, and was beginning to wonder whether a most wretched adventure had not come right into his house. By the time he had got all the bottles and dishes and knives and forks and glasses and plates and spoons and things piled up on big trays, he was getting very hot, and red in the face, and annoyed.

"Confusticate and bebother these dwarves!" he said aloud. "Why don't they come and lend a hand?" Lo and behold! there stood Balin and Dwalin at the door of the kitchen, and Fili and Kili behind them, and before he could say *knife* they had whisked the trays and a couple of small tables into the parlour and set out everything afresh.

Gandalf sat at the head of the party with the thirteen dwarves all round: and Bilbo sat on a stool at the fireside, nibbling at a biscuit (his appetite was quite taken away), and trying to look as if this was all perfectly ordinary and not in the least an adventure. The dwarves ate and ate, and talked and talked, and time got on. At last they pushed their chairs back, and Bilbo made a move to collect the plates.

"I suppose you will all stay to supper?" he said in his politest unpressing tones.

"Of course!" said Thorin. "And after. We shan't get through the business till late, and we must have some music first. Now to clear up!"

Thereupon the twelve dwarves—not Thorin, he was too important, and stayed talking to Gandalf—jumped to their feet, and made tall piles of all the things. Off they went, not waiting for trays, balancing columns of plates, each with a bottle on the top, with one hand, while the hobbit ran after them almost squeaking with fright: "please be careful!" and "please, don't trouble! I can manage." But the dwarves only started to sing:

Chip the glasses and crack the plates!
Blunt the knives and bend the forks!
That's what Bilbo Baggins hates—
Smash the bottles and burn the corks!
Cut the cloth and tread on the fat!
Pour the milk on the pantry floor!
Leave the bones on the bedroom mat!
Splash the wine on every door!
Dump the crocks in a boiling bowl;
Pound them up with a thumping pole;
And when you've finished, if any are whole,
Send them down the hall to roll!
That's what Bilbo Baggins hates!
So, carefully! carefully with the plates!

And of course they did none of these dreadful things, and everything was cleaned and put away safe as quick as lightning, while the hobbit was turning round and round in the middle of the kitchen trying to see what they were doing. Then they went back, and found Thorin with his feet on the fender smoking a pipe. He was blowing the most enormous smoke-rings, and wherever he told one to go, it went—up the chimney, or behind the clock on the mantel-piece, or under the table, or round and round the ceiling; but wherever it went it was not quick enough to escape Gandalf. Pop! he sent a smaller smoke-ring from his short clay-pipe straight through each one of Thorin's. Then Gandalf's smoke-ring would go green and come back to hover over the wizard's head. He had quite a cloud of them about him already, and in the dim light it made him look strange and sorcerous. Bilbo stood still and watched—he loved smoke-rings—and then he blushed to think how proud he had been yesterday morning of the smoke-rings he had sent up the wind over The Hill.

"Now for some music!" said Thorin. "Bring out the instruments!"

Kili and Fili rushed for their bags and brought back little fiddles; Dori, Nori, and Ori brought out flutes from somewhere inside their coats; Bombur produced a drum from the hall; Bifur and Bofur went out too, and came back with clarinets that they had left among the walking-sticks. Dwalin and Balin said: "Excuse me, I left mine in the porch!" "Just bring mine in with you," said Thorin. They came back with viols as big as themselves, and with Thorin's harp wrapped in a green cloth. It was a beautiful golden harp, and when Thorin struck it the music began all at once, so sudden and sweet that Bilbo forgot everything else, and was swept away into dark lands under strange moons, far over The Water and very far from his hobbit-hole under The Hill.

The dark came into the room from the little window that opened in the side of The Hill; the firelight flickered—it was April—and still they played on, while the shadow of Gandalf's beard wagged against the wall.

The dark filled all the room, and the fire died down, and the shadows were lost, and still they played on. And suddenly first one and then another began to sing as they played, deep-throated singing of the dwarves in the deep places of their ancient homes; and this is like a fragment of their song, if it can be like their song without their music.

Far over the misty mountains cold
To dungeons deep and caverns old
We must away ere break of day
To seek the pale enchanted gold.

The dwarves of yore made mighty spells,
While hammers fell like ringing bells
In places deep, where dark things sleep,
In hollow halls beneath the fells.

For ancient king and elvish lord
There many a gleaming golden hoard
They shaped and wrought, and light they caught
To hide in gems on hilt of sword.

On silver necklaces they strung
The flowing stars, on crowns they hung
The dragon-fire, in twisted wire
They meshed the light of moon and sun.

Far over the misty mountains cold
To dungeons deep and caverns old
We must away, ere break of day,
To claim our long-forgotten gold.

Goblets they carved there for themselves
And harps of gold; where no man delves
There lay they long, and many a song
Was sung unheard by men or elves.

The pines were roaring on the height,
The winds were moaning in the night.
The fire was red, it flaming spread;
The trees like torches blazed with light.

The bells were ringing in the dale
And men looked up with faces pale;
The dragon's ire more fierce than fire
Laid low their towers and houses frail.

The mountain smoked beneath the moon;
The dwarves, they heard the tramp of doom.
They fled their hall to dying fall
Beneath his feet, beneath the moon.

Far over the misty mountains grim
To dungeons deep and caverns dim
We must away, ere break of day,
To win our harps and gold from him!

As they sang the hobbit felt the love of beautiful things made by hands and by cunning and by magic moving through him, a fierce and jealous love, the desire of the hearts of dwarves. Then something Tookish woke up inside, and he wished to go and see the great mountains, and hear the pine-trees and the waterfalls, and explore the caves, and wear a sword instead of a walking-stick. He looked out of the window. The stars were out in a dark sky above the trees. He thought of the jewels of the dwarves shining in dark caverns. Suddenly in the wood beyond The Water a flame leapt up—probably somebody lighting a wood-fire—and he thought of plundering dragons settling on his quiet Hill and kindling it all to flames. He shuddered; and very quickly he was plain Mr. Baggins of Bag-End, Under-Hill, again.

He got up trembling. He had less than half a mind to fetch the lamp, and more than half a mind to pretend to, and go and hide behind the beer barrels in the cellar, and not come out again until all the dwarves had gone away. Suddenly he found that the music and the singing had stopped, and they were all looking at him with eyes shining in the dark.

"Where are you going?" said Thorin, in a tone that seemed to show he guessed both halves of the hobbit's mind.

"What about a little light?" said Bilbo apologetically.

"We like the dark," said the dwarves. "Dark for dark business! There are many hours before dawn."

"Of course!" said Bilbo, and sat down in a hurry. He missed the stool and sat in the fender, knocking over the poker and shovel with a crash.

"Hush!" said Gandalf. "Let Thorin speak!" And this is how Thorin began.

"Gandalf, dwarves, and Mr. Baggins! We are met together in the house of our friend and fellow conspirator, this most excellent and audacious hobbit—may the hair on his toes never fall out! all praise to his wine and ale!—" He paused for breath and for a polite remark from the hobbit, but the compliments were quite lost on poor Bilbo Baggins, who was wagging his mouth in protest at being called *audacious* and worst of all *fellow conspirator*, though no noise came out, he was so flummoxed. So Thorin went on:

"We are met to discuss our plans, our ways, means, policy, and devices. We shall soon before the break of day start on our long journey, a journey from which some of us, or perhaps all of us (except our friend and counsellor, the ingenious wizard Gandalf) may never return. It is a solemn moment. Our object is, I take it, well known to us all. To the estimable Mr. Baggins, and perhaps to one or two of the younger dwarves (I think I should be right in naming Kili and Fili, for instance), the exact situation at the moment may require a little brief explanation—"

This was Thorin's style. He was an important dwarf. If he had been allowed, he would probably have gone on like this until he was out of breath, without telling any one there anything that was not known already. But he was rudely interrupted. Poor Bilbo couldn't bear it any longer. At *may never return* he began to feel a shriek coming up inside, and very soon it burst out like the whistle of an engine coming out of a tunnel. All the dwarves sprang up knocking over the table. Gandalf struck a blue light on the end of his magic staff, and in its firework glare the poor little hobbit could be seen kneeling on the hearth-rug, shaking like a jelly that was melting. Then he fell flat on the floor, and kept on calling out "struck by lightning, struck by lightning!" over and over again; and that was all they could get out of him for a long time. So they took him and laid him out of the way on the drawing-room sofa with a drink at his elbow, and they went back to their dark business.

"Excitable little fellow," said Gandalf, as they sat down again. "Gets funny queer fits, but he is one of the best, one of the best—as fierce as a dragon in a pinch."

If you have ever seen a dragon in a pinch, you will realize that this was only poetical exaggeration applied to any hobbit, even to Old Took's great-granduncle Bullroarer, who was so huge (for a hobbit) that he could ride a horse. He charged the ranks of the goblins of Mount Gram in the Battle of the Green Fields, and knocked their king Golfimbul's head clean off with a wooden club. It sailed a hundred yards through the air and went down a rabbit-hole, and in this way the battle was won and the game of Golf invented at the same moment.

In the meanwhile, however, Bullroarer's gentler descendant was reviving in the drawing-room. After a while and a drink he crept nervously to the door of the parlour. This is what he heard, Gloin speaking: "Humph!" (or some snort more or less like that). "Will he do, do you think? It is all very well for Gandalf to talk about this hobbit being fierce, but one shriek like that in a moment of excitement would be enough to wake the dragon and all his relatives, and kill the lot of us. I think it sounded more like fright than excitement! In fact, if it had not been for the sign on the door, I should have been sure we had come to the wrong house. As soon as I clapped eyes on the little fellow bobbing and puffing on the mat, I had my doubts. He looks more like a grocer than a burglar!"

Then Mr. Baggins turned the handle and went in. The Took side had won. He suddenly felt he would go without bed and breakfast to be thought fierce. As for *little fellow bobbing on the mat* it almost made him really fierce. Many a time afterwards the Baggins part regretted what he did now, and he said to himself: "Bilbo, you were a fool; you walked right in and put your foot in it."

"Pardon me," he said, "if I have overheard words that you were saying. I don't pretend to understand what you are talking about, or your reference to burglars, but I think I am right in believing" (this is what he called being on his dignity) "that you think I am no good. I will show you. I have no signs on my door—it was painted a week ago—, and I am quite sure you have come to the wrong house. As soon as I saw your funny faces on the door-step, I had my doubts. But treat it as the right one. Tell me what you want done, and I will try it, if I have to walk from here to the East of East and fight the wild Were-worms in the Last Desert. I had a great-great-great-granduncle once, Bullroarer Took, and—"

"Yes, yes, but that was long ago," said Gloin. "I was talking about *you*. And I assure you there is a mark on this door—the usual one in the trade, or used to be. *Burglar wants a good job, plenty of Excitement and reasonable Reward,* that's how it is usually read. You can say *Expert Treasure-*

hunter instead of *Burglar* if you like. Some of them do. It's all the same to us. Gandalf told us that there was a man of the sort in these parts looking for a Job at once, and that he had arranged for a meeting here this Wednesday tea-time."

"Of course there is a mark," said Gandalf. "I put it there myself. For very good reasons. You asked me to find the fourteenth man for your expedition, and I chose Mr. Baggins. Just let any one say I choose the wrong man or the wrong house, and you can stop at thirteen and have all the bad luck you like, or go back to digging coal."

He scowled so angrily at Gloin that the dwarf huddled back in his chair; and when Bilbo tried to open his mouth to ask a question, he turned and frowned at him and stuck out his bushy eyebrows, till Bilbo shut his mouth tight with a snap. "That's right," said Gandalf. "Let's have no more argument. I have chosen Mr. Baggins and that ought to be enough for all of you. If I say he is a Burglar, a Burglar he is, or will be when the time comes. There is a lot more in him than you guess, and a deal more than he has any idea of himself. You may (possibly) all live to thank me yet. Now Bilbo, my boy, fetch the lamp, and let's have a little light on this!"

On the table in the light of a big lamp with a red shade he spread a piece of parchment rather like a map.

"This was made by Thror, your grandfather, Thorin," he said in answer to the dwarves' excited questions. "It is a plan of the Mountain."

"Long ago in my grandfather Thror's time" Thorin began to explain, "our family was driven out of the far North, and came back with all their wealth and their tools to this Mountain on the map. It had been discovered by my far ancestor, Thrain the Old, but now they mined and they

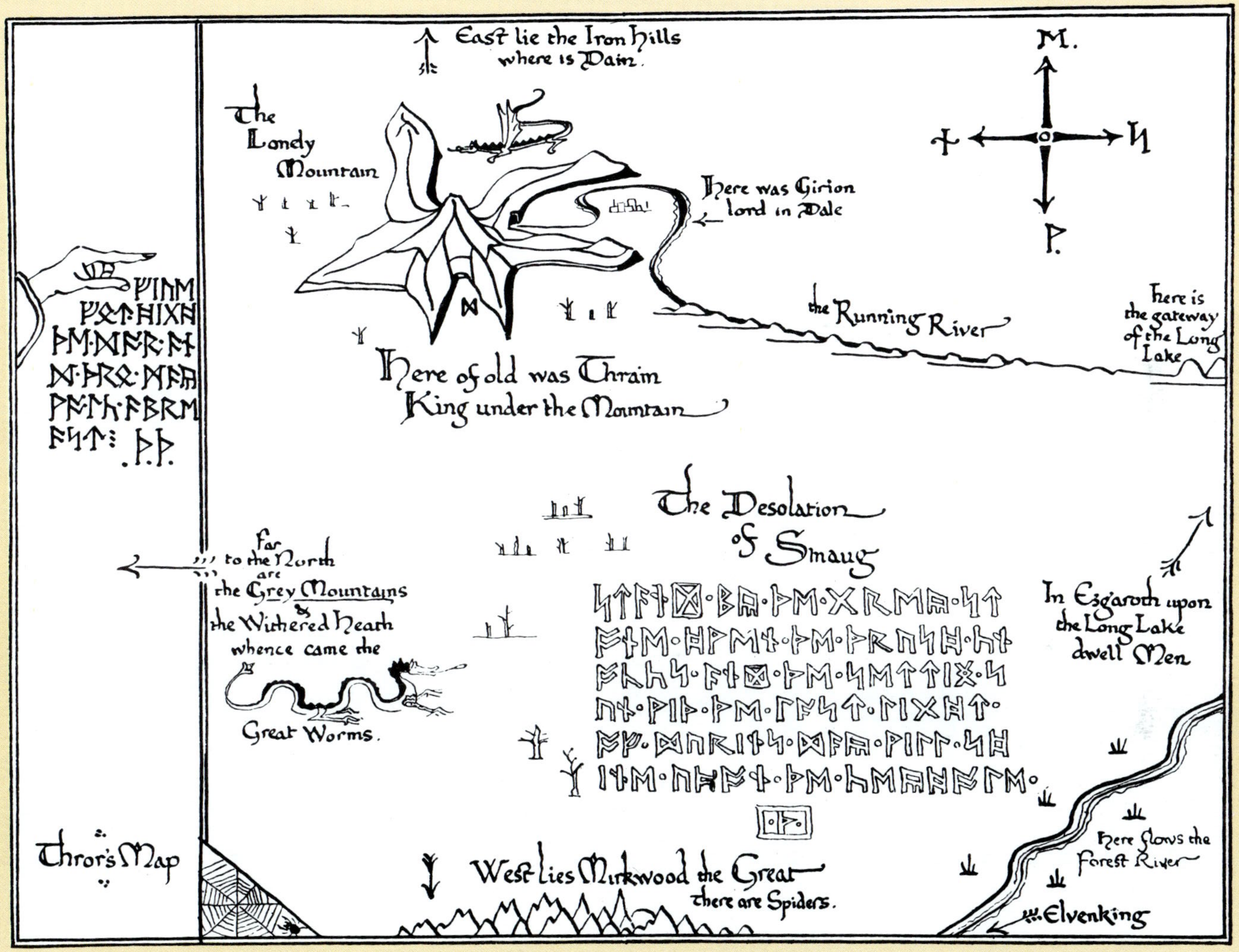
East lie the Iron Hills where is Dain.
The Lonely Mountain
Here was Girion lord in Dale
the Running River
Here is the gateway of the Long Lake
Here of old was Thrain King under the Mountain
The Desolation of Smaug
Far to the North are the Grey Mountains & the Withered Heath whence came the Great Worms.
In Esgaroth upon the Long Lake dwell Men
Thror's Map
West lies Mirkwood the Great there are Spiders.
Here flows the Forest River
Elvenking

tunnelled and they made huger halls and greater workshops—and in addition I believe they found a good deal of gold and a great many jewels too. Anyway they grew immensely rich and famous, and my grandfather was King under the Mountain again and treated with great reverence by the mortal men, who lived to the South, and were gradually spreading up the Running River as far as the valley over-shadowed by the Mountain. They built the merry town of Dale there in those days. Kings used to send for our smiths, and reward even the least skillful most richly. Fathers would beg us to take their sons as apprentices, and pay us handsomely, especially in food-supplies, which we never bothered to grow or find for ourselves. Altogether those were good days for us, and the poorest of us had money to spend and to lend, and leisure to make beautiful things just for the fun of it, not to speak of the most marvelous and magical toys, the like of which is not to be found in the world now-a-days. So my grandfather's halls became full of armour and jewels and carvings, and the toy-market of Dale was the wonder of the North.

"Undoubtedly that was what brought the dragon. Dragons steal gold and jewels, you know, from men and elves and dwarves, wherever they can find them; and they guard their plunder as long as they live (which is practically forever, unless they are killed), and never enjoy a brass ring of it. Indeed they hardly know a good bit of work for a bad, though they usually have a good notion of the current market value; and they can't make a thing for themselves, not even mend a little loose scale of their armour. There were lots of dragons in the North in those days, and gold was probably getting scarce up there, with the dwarves flying south or getting killed, and all the general waste and

destruction dragons make going from bad to worse. There was a most specially greedy, strong and wicked worm called Smaug. One day he flew up into the air and came south. The first we heard of it was a noise like a hurricane coming from the North, and the pine-trees on the Mountain creaking and cracking in the wind. Some of the dwarves who happened to be outside (I was one luckily—a fine adventurous lad in those days, always wandering about, and it saved my life that day)—well, from a good way off we saw the dragon settle on our mountain in a spout of flame. Then he came down the slopes and when he reached the woods they all went up in fire. By that time all the bells were ringing in Dale and the warriors were arming. The dwarves rushed out of their great gate; but there was the dragon waiting for them. None escaped that way. The river rushed up in steam and a fog fell on Dale, and in the fog the dragon came on them and destroyed most of the warriors—the usual unhappy story, it was only too common in those days. Then he went back and crept in through the Front Gate and routed out all the halls, and lanes, and tunnels, alleys, cellars, mansions, and passages. After that there were no dwarves left alive inside, and he took all their wealth for himself. Probably, for that is the dragons' way, he has piled it all up in a great heap far inside, and sleeps on it for a bed. Later he used to crawl out of the great gate and come by night to Dale, and carry away people, especially maidens, to eat, until Dale was ruined, and all the people dead or gone. What goes on there now I don't know for certain, but I don't suppose anyone lives nearer to the Mountain than the far edge of the Long Lake now-a-days.

"The few of us that were well outside sat and wept in hiding, and cursed Smaug; and there we were unexpectedly joined by my father and my grandfather with singed beards. They looked very grim but they said very little. When I asked how they had got away, they told me to hold my tongue, and said that one day in the proper time I should know. After that we went away, and we have had to earn our livings as best we could up and down the lands, often enough sinking as low as blacksmith-work or even coal-mining. But we have never forgotten our stolen treasure. And even now, when I will allow we have a good bit laid by and are not so badly off"—here Thorin stroked the gold chain round his neck—"we still mean to get it back, and bring our curses home to Smaug—if we can.

"I have often wondered about my father's and my grandfather's escape. I see now they must have had a private Side-door which only they knew about. But apparently they made a map, and I should like to know how Gandalf got hold of it, and why it did not come down to me, the rightful heir."

"I did not 'get hold of it,' I was given it," said the wizard. "Your grandfather Thror was killed, you remember, in the mines of Moria by Azog the Goblin."

"Curse his name, yes," said Thorin.

"And Thrain your father went away on the twenty-first of April, a hundred years ago last Thursday, and has never been seen by you since—"

"True, true," said Thorin.

"Well, your father gave me this to give to you; and if I have chosen my own time and way for handing it over, you can hardly blame me, considering the trouble I had to find you. Your father could not remember his own name when he gave me the paper, and he never told me yours; so on the whole I think I ought to be praised and thanked! Here it is," said he handing the map to Thorin.

"I don't understand," said Thorin, and Bilbo felt he would have liked to say the same. The explanation did not seem to explain.

"Your grandfather," said the wizard slowly and grimly, "gave the map to his son for safety before he went to the mines of Moria. Your father went away to try his luck with the map after your grandfather was killed; and lots of adventures of a most unpleasant sort he had, but he never got near the Mountain. How he got there I don't know, but I found him a prisoner in the dungeons of the Necromancer."

"Whatever were you doing there?" asked Thorin with a shudder, and all the dwarves shivered.

"Never you mind. I was finding things out, as usual; and a nasty dangerous business it was. Even I, Gandalf, only just escaped. I tried to save your father, but it was too late. He was witless and wandering, and had forgotten almost everything except the map and the key."

"We have long ago paid the goblins of Moria," said Thorin; "we must give a thought to the Necromancer."

"Don't be absurd! He is an enemy quite beyond the powers of all the dwarves put together, if they could all be collected again from the four corners of the world. The one thing your father wished was for his son to read the map and use the key. The dragon and the Mountain are more than big enough tasks for you!"

"Hear, hear!" said Bilbo, and accidentally said it aloud.

"Hear what?" they all said turning suddenly towards him, and he was so flustered that he answered "Hear what I have got to say!"

"What's that?" they asked.

"Well, I should say that you ought to go East and have

a look round. After all there is the Side-door, and dragons must sleep sometimes, I suppose. If you sit on the door-step long enough, I daresay you will think of something. And well, don't you know, I think we have talked long enough for one night, if you see what I mean. What about bed, and an early start, and all that? I will give you a good breakfast before you go."

"Before *we* go, I suppose you mean," said Thorin. "Aren't you the burglar? And isn't sitting on the door-step your job, not to speak of getting inside the door? But I agree about bed and breakfast. I like eggs with my ham, when starting on a journey: fried not poached, and mind you don't break 'em."

After all the others had ordered their breakfasts without so much as a please (which annoyed Bilbo very much), they all got up. The hobbit had to find room for them all, and filled all his spare-rooms and made beds on chairs and sofas, before he got them all stowed and went to his own little bed very tired and not altogether happy. One thing he did make his mind up about was not to bother to get up very early and cook everybody else's wretched breakfast. The Tookishness was wearing off, and he was not now quite so sure that he was going on any journey in the morning.

As he lay in bed he could hear Thorin still humming to himself in the best bedroom next to him:

Far over the misty mountains cold
To dungeons deep and caverns old
We must away, ere break of day,
To find our long-forgetten gold.

***You can read how Bilbo—alone and unaided—confronted the great dragon Smaug in* The Hobbit.**

CONCLUDING LEVEL 12, UNIT 3

Voyages

Writers have been using the idea of a voyage to tell their stories for hundreds of years. In *Voyages*, you read many kinds of literature and journeyed with many different characters. You met an epic hero in a story that is thousands of years old. You read of an explorer's extraordinary voyage at the beginning of this century. You have been with characters, both historical and imaginary, as they bravely sought freedom. You have journeyed by sea and by air, and perhaps you, too, heard the call of the open road. Through literature, your opportunity for voyages is unlimited.

Thinking and Writing About *Voyages*

1. The ancient Greeks believed that gods and goddesses controlled the wind and the sea. Suppose Homer, the author who first told the story of Odysseus, were to tell about Shackleton's voyage to the Falklands. How might Homer have described the hazards that Shackleton faced?
2. Karana of "Island of the Blue Dolphins" made a decision to leave the island. Later, she decided to return to the island. Which decision do you think was more difficult for her? Why?
3. Use the information in "Balloon Trip" to prepare a short glossary of ballooning terms. Who might use such a glossary?
4. The Borrowers were clever at using things they found to make the tools and other things they needed. Think of an object found in your classroom or home and describe how the Borrowers might use it.
5. It takes a powerful reason for someone to undertake a long or difficult voyage. Which character in *Voyages* do you think had the strongest motive for his or her trip? Explain your choice.
6. Choose two of the voyages described in this unit to compare and contrast. How were the voyages similar? How were they different?

Introducing Level 12

VIEWPOINTS

UNIT

4

There was a young lady named Bright
Who could travel much faster than light
She started one day
in the relative way
And came back on the previous night.

Anonymous

The stories in this unit explore all sorts of interesting possibilities. You will meet characters who have unique ways of looking at things, and you will visit some very unusual places. You will also be presented with different mathematical ideas about numbers and shapes, and about time, speed, and light. How would you explain your viewpoint of mathematics now?

THE ROAD TO DIGITOPOLIS

NORTON JUSTER

This selection is an excerpt from Norton Juster's fantasy *The Phantom Tollbooth*. In the book, a boy named Milo received a mysterious present—a cardboard tollbooth. Milo assembled it, jumped into his toy car, drove up to the tollbooth, and entered the "Lands Beyond." There he met a watchdog named Tock (he was part watch and part dog), and a large insect called the Humbug.

With Tock and the Humbug, Milo drove along the road to Digitopolis, the "number city," to meet the Mathemagician. But first, he was about to meet someone with a unique way of looking at things.

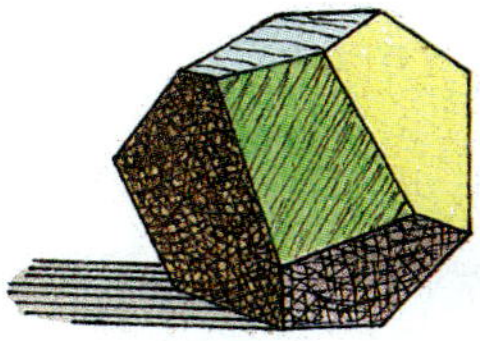

"Ah, the open road!" exclaimed the Humbug, breathing deeply, for he now seemed happily resigned to the trip. "The spirit of adventure, the lure of the unknown, the thrill of a gallant quest. How very grand indeed." Then, pleased with himself, he folded his arms, sat back, and left it at that.

In a few more minutes they had left the open countryside and driven into a dense forest.

THIS IS THE SCENIC ROUTE:
STRAIGHT AHEAD TO POINT OF VIEW

announced a rather large road sign; but, contrary to its statement, all that could be seen were more trees. As the car rushed along, the trees grew thicker and taller and leafier until, just as they'd hidden the sky completely, the forest abruptly ended and the road bent itself around a broad promontory. Stretching below, to the left, the right, and straight ahead, as far as anyone could see, lay the rich green landscape through which they had been traveling for hours.

"Remarkable view," announced the Humbug, bouncing from the car as if he were responsible for the whole thing.

"Isn't it beautiful?" gasped Milo.

"Oh, I don't know," answered a strange voice. "It's all in the way you look at things."

"I beg your pardon?" said Milo, for he didn't see who had spoken.

"I said it's all in how you look at things," repeated the voice.

Milo turned around and found himself staring at two very neatly polished brown shoes, for standing directly in front of him (if you can use the word "standing" for anyone suspended in mid-air) was another boy just about his age, whose feet were easily three feet off the ground.

"For instance," continued the boy, "if you happened to like deserts, you might not think this was beautiful at all."

"That's true," said the Humbug, who didn't like to contradict anyone whose feet were that far off the ground.

"For instance," said the boy again, "if Christmas trees were

people and people were Christmas trees, we'd all be chopped down, put up in the living room, and covered with tinsel, while the trees opened our presents."

"What does that have to do with it?" asked Milo.

"Nothing at all," he answered, "but it's an interesting possibility."

"How do you manage to stand up there?" asked Milo, for this was the subject which most interested him.

"I was about to ask you a similar question," answered the boy, "for you must be much older than you look to be standing on the ground."

"What do you mean?" Milo asked.

"Well," said the boy, "in my family everyone is born in the air, with his head at exactly the height it's going to be when he's an adult, and then we all grow toward the ground. When we're fully grown up or, as you can see, grown down, our feet finally touch. Of course, there are a few of us whose feet never reach the ground no matter how old we get, but I suppose it's the same in every family."

He hopped a few steps in the air, skipped back to where he started, and then began again.

"You certainly must be very old to have reached the ground already."

"Oh no," said Milo seriously. "In my family we all start on the ground and grow up, and we never know how far until we actually get there."

"What a silly system." The boy laughed. "Then your head keeps changing its height and you always see things in a different way? Why, when you're fifteen things won't look at all the way they did when you were ten, and at twenty everything will change again."

"I suppose so," replied Milo, for he had never really thought about the matter.

"We always see things from the same angle," the boy continued. "It's much less trouble that way. Besides, it makes more sense to grow down and not up. When you're very young, you can never hurt yourself falling down if you're in mid-air, and you can't get into trouble for scuffing up your shoes or marking the floor if there's nothing to scuff them on and the floor is three feet away."

"That's very true," thought Tock, who wondered how the dogs in the family liked the arrangement.

"But there are many other ways to look at things," remarked the boy. "For instance, you had orange juice, boiled eggs, toast and jam, and milk for breakfast," he said, turning to Milo. "And you are always worried about people wasting time," he said to Tock. "And you are almost never right about anything," he said, pointing at the Humbug, "and, when you are, it's usually an accident."

"A gross exaggeration," protested the furious bug, who didn't realize that so much was visible to the naked eye.

"Amazing," gasped Tock.

"How do you know all that?" asked Milo.

"Simple," he said proudly.

"I'm Alec Bings; I see through things. I can see whatever is inside, behind, around, covered by, or subsequent to anything else. In fact, the only thing I can't see is whatever happens to be right in front of my nose."

"Isn't that a little inconvenient?" asked Milo, whose neck was becoming stiff from looking up.

"It is a little," replied Alec, "but it is quite important to know what lies behind things, and the family helps me take care of the rest. My father sees to things, my mother looks after things, my brother sees beyond things, my uncle sees the other side of every question, and my little sister Alice sees under things."

"How can she see under things if she's all the way up there?" growled the Humbug.

"Well," added Alec, turning a neat cartwheel, "whatever she can't see under, she overlooks."

"Would it be possible for me to see something from up there?" asked Milo politely.

"You could," said Alec, "but only if you try very hard to look at things as an adult does."

Milo tried as hard as he could, and, as he did, his feet floated slowly off the ground until he was standing in the air next to Alec Bings. He looked around very quickly and, an instant later, crashed back down to earth again.

"Interesting, wasn't it?" asked Alec Bings.

"Yes, it was," agreed Milo, rubbing his head and dusting himself off, "but I think I'll continue to see things as a child. It's not so far to fall."

"A wise decision, at least for the time being," said Alec. "Everyone should have his own point of view."

"Isn't this everyone's Point of View?" asked Tock, looking around curiously.

"Of course not," replied Alec, sitting himself down on nothing. "It's only mine, and you certainly can't always look at things from someone else's Point of View. For instance, from here that looks like a bucket of water," he said, pointing to a bucket of water; "but from an ant's point of view it's a vast ocean, from an elephant's it's just a cool drink, and to a fish, of course, it's home. So, you see, the way you see things depends a great deal on where you look at them from. Now, come along and I'll show you the rest of the forest."

He ran quickly through the air, stopping occasionally to beckon Milo, Tock, and the Humbug along, and they followed as well as anyone who had to stay on the ground could.

"Does everyone here grow the way you do?" puffed Milo when he had caught up.

"Almost everyone," replied Alec, and then he stopped a moment and thought. "Now and then, though, someone does begin to grow differently. Instead of down, his feet grow up toward the sky. But we do our best to discourage awkward things like that."

"What happens to *them*?" insisted Milo.

"Oddly enough, they often grow ten times the size of everyone else," said Alec thoughtfully, "and I've heard that they walk among the stars." And with that he skipped off once again toward the woods.

Milo, Tock, and Humbug returned to the car to continue their journey.

The car was just where they'd left it, and in a moment they were on their way again as the road turned away from the sea and began its long climb into the mountains.

"I hope we reach Digitopolis soon," said Milo. "I wonder how far it is."

Up ahead, the road divided into three and, as if in reply to Milo's question, an enormous road sign, pointing in all three directions, stated clearly:

D I G I T O P O L I S

5	Miles
1,600	Rods
8,800	Yards
26,400	Feet
316,800	Inches
633,600	Half inches

AND THEN SOME

"Let's travel by miles," advised the Humbug. "It's shorter."

"Let's travel by half inches," suggested Milo. "It's quicker."

"But which road should we take?" asked Tock. "It must make a difference."

As they argued, a most peculiar little figure stepped nimbly from behind the sign and approached them, talking all the while. "Yes, indeed; indeed it does; my, yes; it does make a difference; undoubtedly."

He was constructed (for that's really the only way to describe him) of a large assortment of lines and angles connected together into one solid many-sided shape—somewhat like a cube that's had all its corners cut off and then had all its corners cut off again. Each of the edges was neatly labeled with a small letter, and each of the angles with a large one.

He wore a handsome beret on top, and peering intently from one of his several surfaces was a very serious face. Perhaps if you look at the picture you'll know what I mean.

When he reached the car, the figure doffed his cap and recited in a loud clear voice:

> "My angles are many.
> My sides are not few.
> I'm the Dodecahedron.
> Who are you?"

"What's a Dodecahedron?" inquired Milo, who was barely able to pronounce the word.

"See for yourself," he said, turning around slowly. "A Dodecahedron is a mathematical shape with twelve faces."

Just as he said it, eleven other faces appeared, one on each surface, and each one wore a different expression.

"I usually use one at a time," he confided, as all but the smiling one disappeared again. "It saves wear and tear. What are you called?"

"Milo," said Milo.

"That is an odd name," he said, changing his smiling face for a frowning one. "And you only have one face."

"Is that bad?" asked Milo, making sure it was still there.

"You'll soon wear it out using it for everything," replied the Dodecahedron. "Now I have one for smiling, one for laughing, one for crying, one for frowning, one for thinking, one for pouting, and six more besides. Is everyone with one face called a Milo?"

"Oh no," Milo replied. "Some are called Henry or George or Robert or John or lots of other things."

"How terribly confusing," he cried. "Everything here is called exactly what it is. The triangles

are called triangles, the circles are called circles, and even the same numbers have the same name. Why, can you imagine what would happen if we named all the twos Henry or George or Robert or John or lots of other things? You'd have to say Robert plus John equals four, and if the four's name were Albert, things would be hopeless."

"I never thought of it that way," Milo admitted.

"Then I suggest you begin at once," admonished the Dodecahedron from his admonishing face, "for here in Digitopolis everything is quite precise."

"Then perhaps you can help us decide which road to take," said Milo.

"By all means," he replied happily. "There's nothing to it. If a small car carrying three people at thirty miles an hour for ten minutes along a road five miles long at 11:35 in the morning starts at the same time as three people who have been traveling in a little automobile at twenty miles an hour for fifteen minutes on another road exactly twice as long as one half the distance of the other, while a dog, a bug, and a boy travel an equal distance in the same time or the same distance in an equal time along a third road in mid-October, then which one arrives first and which is the best way to go?"

"Seventeen!" shouted the Humbug, scribbling furiously on a piece of paper.

"Well, I'm not sure, but—" Milo stammered after several minutes of frantic figuring.

"You'll have to do better than that," scolded the Dodecahedron, "or you'll never know how far you've gone or whether or not you've ever gotten there."

"I'm not very good at problems," admitted Milo.

"What a shame," sighed the Dodecahedron. "They're so very useful. Why, did you know that if a beaver two feet long with a tail a foot and a half long can build a dam twelve feet high and six feet wide in two days, all you would need to build Boulder Dam is a beaver sixty-eight feet long with a fifty-one-foot tail?"

"Where would you find a beaver that big?" grumbled the Humbug as his pencil point snapped.

"I'm sure I don't know," he replied, "but if you ever did, you'd certainly know what to do with him."

"That's absurd," objected Milo, whose head was spinning from all the numbers and questions.

"That may be true," he acknowledged, "but it's completely accurate, and as long as the answer is right, who cares if the question is wrong? If you want sense, you'll have to make it yourself."

"All three roads arrive at the same place at the same time," interrupted Tock, who had patiently been doing the first problem.

"Correct!" shouted the Dodecahedron. "And I'll take you there myself. If you hadn't done this one properly, you might have gone the wrong way."

"I can't see where I made my mistake," said the Humbug, frantically rechecking his figures.

"But if all the roads arrive at the same place at the same time, then aren't they all the right way?" asked Milo.

"Certainly not!" he shouted, glaring from his most upset face. "They're all the *wrong* way. Just because you have a choice, it doesn't mean that any of them *has* to be right."

He walked to the sign and quickly spun it around three times. As he did, the three roads vanished and a new one suddenly appeared, heading in the very direction that the sign now pointed.

"Is every road five miles from Digitopolis?" asked Milo.

"I'm afraid it has to be," the Dodecahedron replied, leaping onto the back of the car. "It's the only sign we've got."

The new road was quite bumpy and full of stones, and each time they hit one, the Dodecahedron bounced into the air and landed on one of his faces, with a sulk or a smile or a laugh or a frown, depending upon which one it was.

"We'll soon be there," he announced happily, after one of his short flights. "Welcome to the land of numbers."

"It doesn't look very inviting," the bug remarked, for, as they climbed higher and higher, not a tree or a blade of grass could be seen anywhere. Only the rocks remained.

"Is this the place where numbers are made?" asked Milo as the car lurched again, and this time the Dodecahedron sailed off down the mountainside, head over heels and grunt over grimace, until he landed sad side up at what looked like the entrance to a cave.

"They're not made," he replied, as if nothing had happened. "You have to dig for them. Don't you know anything at all about numbers?"

"Well, I don't think they're very important," snapped Milo, too

embarrassed to admit the truth.

"NOT IMPORTANT!" roared the Dodecahedron, turning red with fury. "Could you have tea for two without the two—or three blind mice without the three? Would there be four corners of the earth if there weren't a four? And how would you sail the seven seas without a seven?"

"All I meant—" began Milo, but the Dodecahedron, overcome with emotion and shouting furiously, carried right on.

"If you had high hopes, how would you know how high they were? And did you know that narrow escapes come in all different widths? Would you travel the whole wide world without ever knowing how wide it was? And how could you do anything at long last," he concluded, waving his arms over his head, "without knowing how long the last was? Why, numbers are the most beautiful and valuable things in the world. Just follow me and I'll show you." He turned on his heel and stalked off into the cave.

"Come along, come along," he shouted from the dark hole. "I can't wait for you all day." And in a moment they'd followed him into the mountain.

It took several minutes for their eyes to become accustomed to the dim light, and during that time strange scratching, scraping, tapping, scuffling noises could be heard all around them.

"Put these on," instructed the Dodecahedron, handing each of them a helmet with a flashlight attached to the top.

"Where are we going?" whispered Milo, for it seemed like

the kind of place in which you whispered.

"We're here," he replied with a sweeping gesture. "This is the numbers mine."

Milo squinted into the darkness and saw for the first time that they had entered a vast cavern lit only by a soft, eerie glow from the great stalactites which hung ominously from the ceiling. Passages and corridors honeycombed the walls and wound their way from floor to ceiling, up and down the sides of the cave. And, everywhere he looked, Milo saw little men no bigger than himself busy digging and chopping, shoveling and scraping, pulling and tugging carts full of stone from one place to another.

"Right this way," instructed the Dodecahedron, "and watch where you step."

As he spoke, his voice echoed and re-echoed and re-echoed again, mixing its sound with the buzz of activity all around them. Tock trotted along next to Milo, and the Humbug, stepping daintily, followed behind.

"Whose mine is it?" asked Milo, stepping around two wagons.

"BY THE FOUR MILLION EIGHT HUNDRED AND TWENTY-SEVEN THOUSAND SIX-HUNDRED AND FIFTY-NINE HAIRS ON MY HEAD, IT'S MINE, OF COURSE!" bellowed a voice from across the cavern. And striding toward them came a figure who could only have been the Mathemagician.

He was dressed in a long, flowing robe covered entirely with complex mathematical equations and a tall pointed cap that made him look very wise. In his left hand he carried a long staff with a pencil point at one end and a large rubber eraser at the other.

"It's a lovely mine," apologized the Humbug, who was always intimidated by loud noises.

"The biggest number mine in the kingdom," said the Mathemagician proudly.

"Are there any precious stones in it?" asked Milo excitedly.

"PRECIOUS STONES!" he roared, even louder than before. And then he leaned over toward Milo and whispered softly, "By the eight million, two hundred and forty-seven thousand, three hundred and twelve threads in my robe, I'll say there are. Just look at these."

He reached into one of the carts and pulled out a small object, which he polished vigorously on his robe. When he held it up to the light, it sparkled brightly.

"But that's a five," objected Milo, for that was certainly what it was.

"Exactly," agreed the Mathemagician. "As valuable a jewel as you'll find anywhere. Look at some of the others."

He scooped up a great handful of stones and poured them into Milo's arms. They included all the numbers from one to nine, and even an assortment of zeros.

"We dig them and polish them right here," volunteered the Dodecahedron, pointing to a group of workers busily employed at the buffing wheels. "And then we send them all over the world. Marvelous, aren't they?"

"They are exceptional," said Tock, who had a special fondness for numbers.

"So that's where they come from," said Milo, looking in awe at the glittering collection of numbers. He returned them to the Dodecahedron as carefully as possible but, as he did, one dropped to the floor with a smash and broke in two. The Humbug winced and Milo looked terribly concerned.

"Oh, don't worry about that," said the Mathemagician as he scooped up the pieces. "We use the broken ones for fractions."

"Haven't you any diamonds or emeralds or rubies?" asked the bug irritably, for he was quite disappointed in what he'd seen so far.

"Yes, indeed," the Mathemagician replied, leading them to the rear of the cave. "Right this way."

There, piled into enormous mounds that reached almost to the ceiling, were not only diamonds and emeralds and rubies but also sapphires, amethysts, topazes, moonstones, and garnets. It was the most amazing mass of wealth that any of them had ever seen.

"They're such a terrible nuisance," sighed the Mathemagician, "and no one can think of what to do with them. So we just keep digging them up and throwing them out."

And for the first time in his life the astonished bug couldn't think of a thing to say.

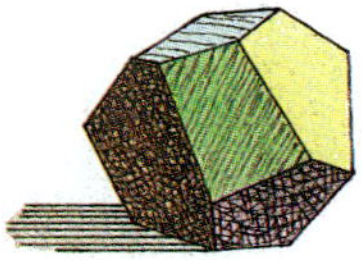

You can discover what happens to Milo and his friends in Digitopolis if you read *The Phantom Tollbooth*.

Thinking and Writing About the Selection

1. What advantages did Alec Bing say there were in growing down rather than up?
2. Why did the Dodecahedron think that *Milo* was the name given to everyone with one face?
3. Do you agree with the Dodecahedron's comment that "Just because you have a choice, it doesn't mean that any of them *has* to be right"? Give an example to support your answer.
4. What other things related to numbers do you think Milo, Tock, and the Humbug might discover in Digitopolis?

Applying the Key Skill
Generalizations

Use the information in "The Road to Digitopolis" to list three details or facts that support the generalizations below.

a. The way you look at things depends a great deal on where you look at them from.
b. Here in Digitopolis everything is quite precise.
c. Numbers are the most beautiful and valuable things in the world.

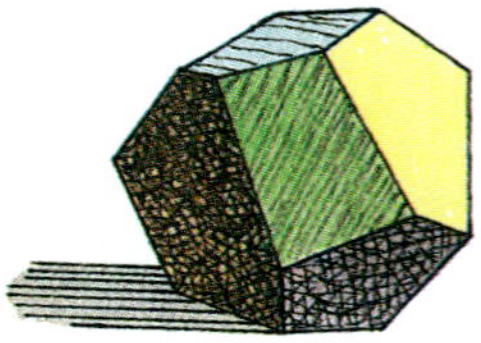

LANGUAGE ACTIVITY

NUMBER NAMES

The Dodecahedron that Milo, Tock, and the Humbug met was certainly a curious figure. His name, too, was curious, and it may have seemed difficult to you. But if we take it apart, we will see that it's not so hard as it may appear at first.

dodeca	+	**hedron**	=	**dodecahedron**
(Greek *dodeka,* "twelve")		(Greek *-edron,* from *hedra,* "seat-, base")		a geometric figure having 12 faces or surfaces

Dodeca- is one of a group of special prefixes called numerical prefixes. Although *dodeca-* may not be familiar to you, you probably already know many of the numerical prefixes listed in the chart below.

Numerical Prefix	Meaning
uni-	one
bi-	two
tri-	three
quad-, quadri-, tetra-	four
penta-	five

Numerical Prefix	Meaning
hexa-	six
sept-	seven
octa-, octo-	eight
nona-	nine
deca-, deka-	ten
poly-, multi-	many

The names for many solid geometric figures are made up of a numerical prefix and the word part *-hedron,* which indicates a figure having a certain number of faces or surfaces (as in the example *dodecahedron* above). How many faces does a **tetrahedron** have? An **octahedron**? How would you define a **polyhedron**? If a **tetrahexahedron** has 24 faces, how many faces does a **hexoctahedron** have?

SKILLS ACTIVITY

GRAPHS

In "The Road to Digitopolis," the Dodecahedron became very upset when Milo said that he didn't think numbers were very important. Whether or not you think numbers are important, you would probably agree that you are presented with a great deal of numerical information almost every day. The information may be presented in sentences or paragraphs you read, or it may be presented in a graph. Read the paragraph below and then study the graph.

The sixth-grade class decided to vote on the three proposals that had been made for a money-making project. Twenty-two students voted for a book fair, twelve voted to have a food sale, and eight wanted to have a play.

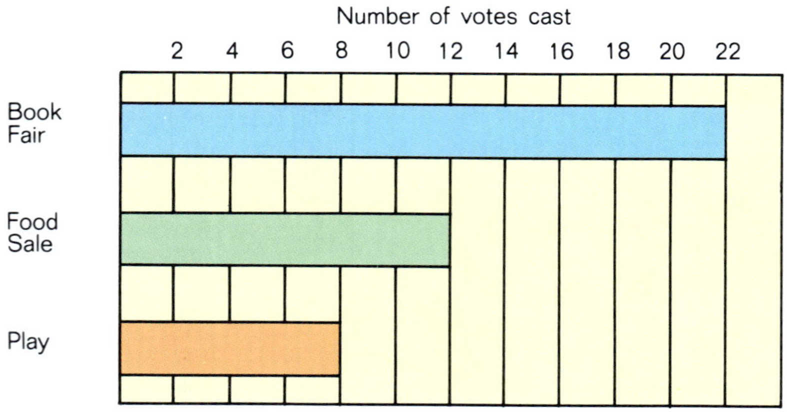

VOTES CAST FOR MONEY-MAKING PROJECTS

The paragraph and the graph both tell you the same thing. The graph, however, presents the information in a visual way that makes it easy to understand and that allows you to quickly make comparisons.

A **graph** presents similarities, differences, and relationships among numerical data visually. The three most common kinds of graphs are bar graphs, line graphs, and circle graphs.

A **bar graph** uses bars to show information. The bars are usually the same width, but their length is proportional to the number they represent. Sometimes the bars run up and down (vertical bar graph), and sometimes they run from right to left (horizontal bar graph). What kind of bar graph is the graph on the left?

The information in the bar graph about money-making projects could also have been presented in a circle graph. A **circle graph**, sometimes called a pie graph, shows how parts are related to the whole.

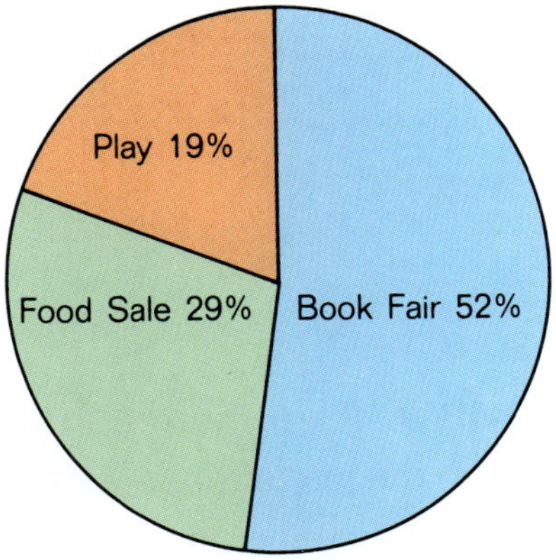

VOTES CAST FOR MONEY-MAKING PROJECTS

The entire circle represents the total number of votes cast—100 percent. The circle is divided into parts, or segments, to show what percent of the votes were cast for the book fair, the food sale, and the play. The parts are in proportion to the percent they represent. The percentage of votes for each project is given, but even if it were not, you could easily see that more than half of the total votes were cast for the book fair.

A **line graph** uses lines to connect points that give numerical information. Line graphs are used to show changes through time. The line graph below shows the number of students in the sixth grade at Grant School for the years 1981 through 1986.

To find the number of students in any given year, move your finger up from that year to the point on the graph. Then move it across to the scale on the left, where you can read the number. For example, in 1983, there were 40 students.

NUMBER OF STUDENTS IN SIXTH GRADE AT GRANT SCHOOL 1981-1986

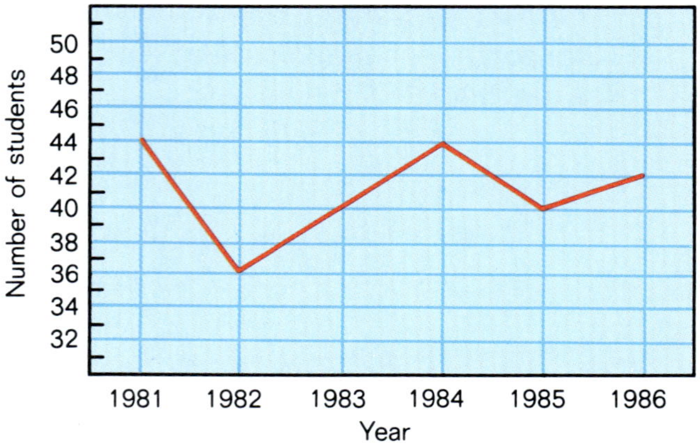

ACTIVITY A Use the graph to answer the questions. Write the answers on your paper.

1. What kind of graph, circle, bar, or line, is the graph?
2. Did Biblio Press publish more hardcover or paperback books in 1986?
3. What category of books accounted for 25% of the books published by Biblio Press in 1986?
4. What percent of all books published by Biblio Press in 1986 were accounted for by hardcover and paperback fiction?

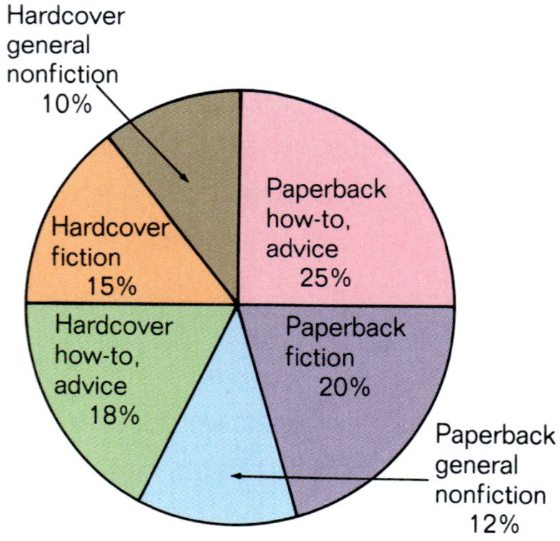

BOOKS PUBLISHED BY BIBLIO PRESS 1986

ACTIVITY B Refer to the graph at the right to answer the questions. Write the answers on your paper.

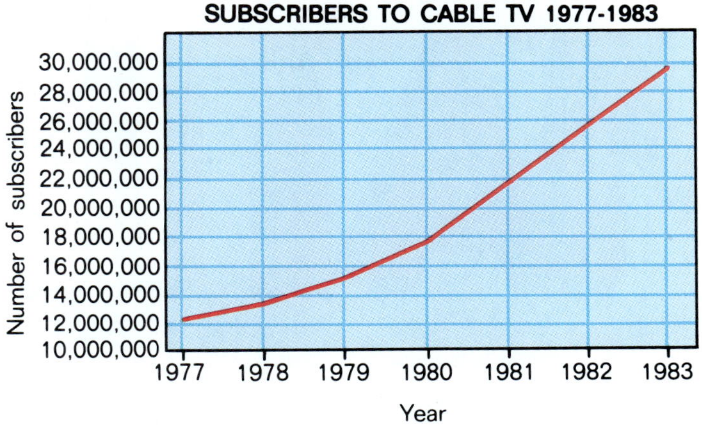

1. What kind of graph is the above graph?
   a. circle   b. line   c. bar

2. What does the graph show?
   a. the number of television sets between 1977 and 1983
   b. the number of cable TV subscribers between 1977 and 1983
   c. the number of cable TV stations between 1977 and 1983

3. How many more cable TV subscribers were there in 1983 than there were in 1977?
   a. about 13,000,000   b. about 15,000,000
   c. about 17,000,000

4. Which of the following is a valid statement based on the graph?
   a. The number of cable TV subscribers decreased steadily between 1977 and 1983.
   b. The number of cable TV subscribers increased steadily between 1977 and 1983.
   c. The number of cable TV subscribers did not noticeably change between 1977 and 1983.

THE MAGIC OF MATH

One-sided pieces of paper? Magic squares? You don't need to be a magician to do tricks with numbers.

THE MYSTERIOUS AND MAGICAL MÖBIUS STRIP!

If you have a piece of paper, that paper will have two sides, right? If you wanted to, you could color one side red and the other blue, couldn't you? And if you roll the paper into a tube, it still has two sides—an inside and an outside.

But could you have a piece of paper that has only *one* side?

Well, let's see. Get a piece of paper and cut off a long, narrow strip. With a pencil, put an A at the left end of the strip, and a B at the right end. Now turn the strip over, keeping the B on your right. Bring the two ends together. Next, twist the B end and place the B on top of the A. Tape the ends together with transparent tape. Put tape on both sides. Now you have a loop with a half twist in it.

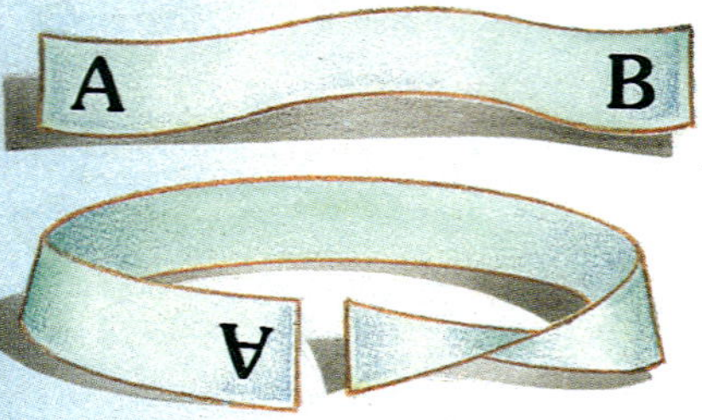

The loop looks as if it has two sides, doesn't it? If you had a giant loop, you and a friend could begin coloring each side—one side red and the other side blue. But if you did, you would be amazed to find that your colors would bump into each other! For this kind of loop actually has only one side! Start coloring your small loop red and see for yourself.

This kind of twisted loop is called a Möbius (mō′ bē əs) strip, after the man who invented it. And it's a strange and almost "magical" sort of toy that you can do some surprising things with. For example, what do you think would happen if you were to cut a Möbius strip straight down the middle? Do you think you would get two loops? No, indeed! After you finish cutting it in "half," you'll find that you still have only *one* loop—but it is twice as long as the one you started with!

A mathematician confided
That a Möbius strip is one-sided.
And you'll get quite a laugh
If you cut one in half
For it stays in one piece when divided!

What do you think would happen if you cut *that* loop down the middle? Well, try it and see!

MAGIC SQUARES

Have you ever seen a magic square? At one time, people gave all kinds of meanings to magic squares. But of course there is nothing really magic about them. They are just a special arrangement of numbers.

To the right is a magic square that someone in China figured out thousands of years ago. When you add up any three numbers across, or

down, or diagonally (slantwise), you always get the same answer! Try it and see.

Here is a different kind of magic square. To use this square, pick any number in it—say 5. Cross out, or cover up, *all* the numbers above and below it, and to the right and left of it.

Next, pick any number that is left—let's say 9. Now cover up the numbers above and below, and to the right or left of the 9.

Now you have three numbers left—1, 5, and 9. Add them up and you'll see that they total 15. No matter what number you start with, you'll always end up with three numbers that total 15! Try it a few times and see.

The magic square below is a famous one by the German artist Dürer. It is only a small part of a large picture. But this magic square is more marvelous than most. With all magic squares, you can add up the numbers across, down, or diagonally and the total is the same—in this case 34. But this is only the beginning. Look at some of the other ways you can get 34.

The numbers in the four corners total 34. The four numbers in the center add up to 34. The two middle numbers in the top row, 3 and 2, and the two middle numbers in the bottom row, 15 and 14, total 34. The two numbers in the middle of the first column (5 and 9) and the two in the middle of the last column (8 and 12) add up to 34. And the four numbers in each quarter—such as 16, 3, 5, and 10—total 34!

Why did Dürer pick the number 34 for his magic square? We can't be sure, but there is something very curious about it. He made the

engraving when he was 43 years old. This was in the year 1514. Look at the date. Take 1 from 5 and you get 4. Take 1 from 4 and you get 3. So, you get the number 43—the same as his age. Turn 43 around and you get—34!

BUILDING NUMBERS

You have probably put together models of cars and airplanes. You've probably made clay models of animals. But have you ever tried to make a model of a number?

Remember, to get a square number, you multiply any number by itself. If you multiply 2 × 2, you get the square number 4. A square is a flat shape, so you can make a model of the square number 4 very easily. All you need are four toothpicks and four tiny balls of clay. The four balls of clay stand for the four ones that make up the number four.

Make two squares like the one shown. Then, join them together with four toothpicks.

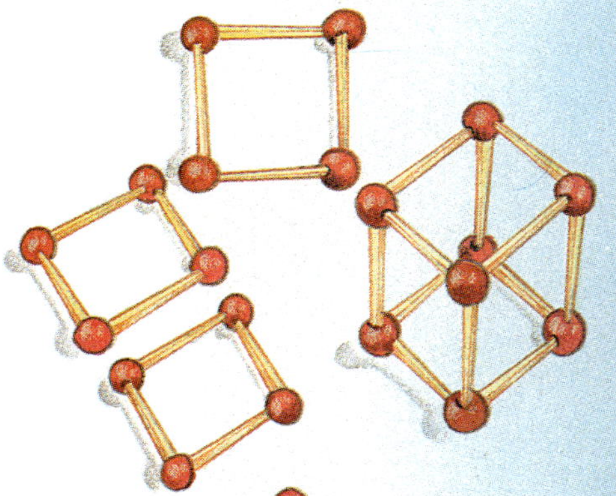

Now, you have a shape called a cube. Count the balls of clay and you'll see there are eight. You've made a model of the *cubic* number 8.

To make a cubic number, you multiply any number by itself *three* times, such as 2 × 2 × 2. Multiplying the first two numbers gives you a square number—4 and when you multiply by 2 again, you get 8, which is a cubic number. The number 4 is the square of 2, and the number 8 is the cube of 2. When you cube 3, you multiply 3 × 3 × 3. You get the cubic number 27. A model of this cubic number would look like this:

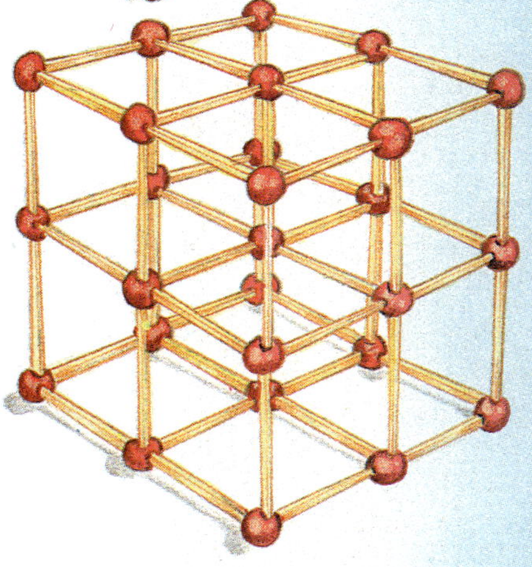

What cubic number do you get when you cube 4 ($4 \times 4 \times 4$)? Try making a model of the number.

THE STRANGE ROW OF NUMBERS

Just for fun, a mathematician once made up a puzzle about rabbits. It went like this.

Suppose that you have a boy rabbit and a girl rabbit. Each month, your pair of rabbits has a boy rabbit and a girl rabbit.

Suppose each pair of rabbits is grown in just two months. Then they have a pair of baby rabbits each month. How many rabbits will there be at the end of a year?

You can figure it out quite easily for a while. First, there are two rabbits.

By the end of one month, the two rabbits have a pair of baby rabbits. So now you have four rabbits.

By the end of the second month, the first two rabbits have another pair of babies. Now there are six rabbits altogether.

In the third month, things begin to get harder to figure out. The first pair of rabbits have another pair of babies. That makes eight rabbits. But now the baby rabbits born in the first month are old enough to have their first pair of babies. So altogether that makes ten rabbits.

It gets even more complicated during the fourth month. The first rabbits have another pair of babies, making twelve rabbits. The second pair of rabbits also has another pair of babies making fourteen rabbits. And now the pair of rabbits born in the second month are old enough to have a pair of babies. That makes a total of sixteen rabbits in the fourth month.

As you can see, things are now going to get harder and harder to figure out.

Actually, there's a way of finding out the answer without counting up any more pairs of rabbits. It's hidden in the first five numbers we got by counting up all the rabbits.

Write the five numbers—2, 4, 6, 10, 16—on a piece of paper. Can you see the secret?

If you add up any two numbers that are next to one another, the sum is the same as the following number! Add up the first two numbers 2 and 4, and you get the third number, 6. Add the second and third numbers, 4 and 6, and you get the fourth number 10. And add the third and fourth numbers, 6 and 10, and you get 16, which is the fifth number!

So you see, you can find out the answer to the rabbit problem simply by adding up two numbers at a time. Add the last two numbers in the column—10 and 16 —and then put the new number you get at the end of the column. Then add up the last two numbers you now have. Keep doing this until you have a total of thirteen numbers in the column.

The first number—2 is the number of rabbits that you started with. The next twelve numbers—one number for each month of the year—show how many rabbits you had by the end of each month. The last number is the number of rabbits at the end of the year.

A series of numbers of this sort is called a sequence, which means "a group of things that are connected together." The mathematician who worked out the rabbit puzzle discovered a number sequence that goes 0, 1, 1, 2, 3, 5, 8, 13, 21, 34 and so on.

As you can see, any two numbers that are next to each other add up to the next number. Thus 0 and 1 are 1, 1 and 1 are 2, 1 and 2 are 3, and so on. This sequence is called the Fibonacci (fē bə nä′ chē) sequence, after the man who discovered it.

Now, there's something really strange about the Fibonacci sequence. Nature uses it! The bumps upon a pineapple, the scales on a pine cone, the leaves on the stem of a rose bush, and the little bumps in the head of a daisy are all arranged in Fibonacci sequence!

For example, if you look at a daisy you'll see that all of the little yellow bumps make up winding rows called spirals. Some of the spirals go to the left and some go to the right.

If you count the spirals that go to the left, you'll see there are 21 of them. Count the spirals that go to the right and you'll see there are 34. And the numbers 21 and 34 are next to one another in Fibonacci sequence!

If you count the spirals on a pineapple, you'll find there are 8 going one way and 13 going another—and 8 and 13 are next to one another in the Fibonacci sequence. Count the spirals on a pine cone and you'll get the numbers 5 and 8. They, too, are in the Fibonacci sequence. It looks as if nature uses mathematics too!

Thinking and Writing About the Selection

1. How do you make a Möbius strip?
2. What happens when you cut a Möbius strip straight down the middle? What happens when you cut the loop you made down the middle?
3. What number would you get if you squared the number 5? What number is the cube of 5?
4. Make up a sequence of 15 or 20 numbers. Make sure the numbers in your sequence follow a pattern. Exchange your sequence with some friends. See if they can figure out the pattern.

Applying the Key Skill
Generalizations

1. Use the information in "The Magic of Math" to list details or facts that support the generalizations below.
   a. The magic square Dürer created is more marvelous than most.
   b. Nature uses the Fibonacci sequence.
2. Write a generalization that describes the magic square and the number sequences below.

a.

4	3	8
9	5	1
2	7	6

b. 1 4 8 11 15 18 22
c. 1 3 6 8 11 13 16

THE ROADS OF MATH

JEFFREY DIELLE

Take a straight line,
    And divide it into three.
Make the three lines form three angles,
    And a triangle have we.

Now take this little triangle
    And twirl it about in space.
Twirl the triangle 'round and 'round;
    A cone is what we face.

Now look at the bottom of our cone.
    We see a circle true.
Now let's examine the circle
    And what it can do for you.

Let's draw a line through the center
    Of our circle round.
We've discovered something new:
    The diameter we've found.

Let's look at the line 'round the circle.
    The circumference says, "Hi!"
Divide the circumference by the diameter,
    And we've found the number Pi.

Now take our semicircle
And take a point on the rim.
Using the diameter form a triangle.
(It doesn't take much vim.)

Look carefully at this triangle.
If you do, something different you'll see,
For the largest of its angles
Has exactly ninety degrees.

Now take two of these new right angles.
Put their vertices in the circle's
center, there.
With the diameter under one side of
each angle,
We're ready to form a square.

Mark the points on the circumference
Where the right angles do fall.
Construct triangles in both semicircles,
And that is all.

From a line, to a triangle, to a cone,
To a circle, to Pi, to a square.
We have traveled the roads of math,
Which will take you anywhere.

SKILLS ACTIVITY

DIAGRAMS

Do you flip through the pages of a story or book to look at the illustrations before you begin to read? Most of us do. Illustrations often make what we read more appealing to us. Some kinds of illustrations do more—they help us better understand what we read.

A **diagram** is a special kind of drawing that is used to help us visualize something by showing its important parts or by showing how it works. Diagrams are also used to show us how to do something. Think about the diagrams in "The Magic of Math." Would you have understood and enjoyed the selection as much without them?

Many times diagrams are used to explain what would be very difficult to put into words. Read the puzzle below and look at the diagram. Think about how you would explain in words what the diagram shows.

Arrange 12 toothpicks as shown below. Change the position of four toothpicks to make three squares, all the same size, with no toothpicks left over.

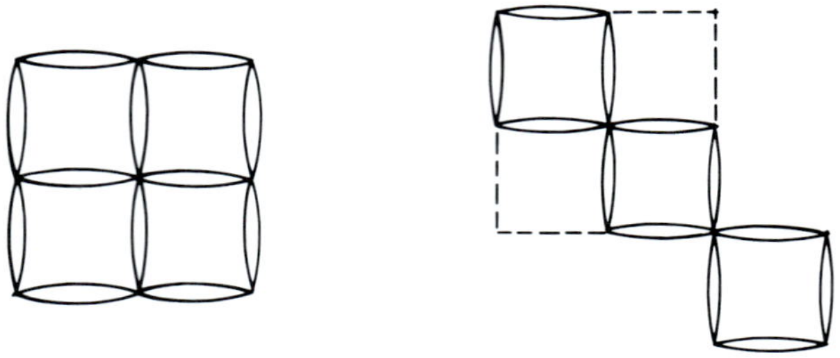

The diagram above helped us quickly visualize the problem and its solution. You have probably concluded that it would be very difficult to express in words what the diagram shows.

ACTIVITY Refer to the diagram below to answer the questions. Write the answers on your paper.

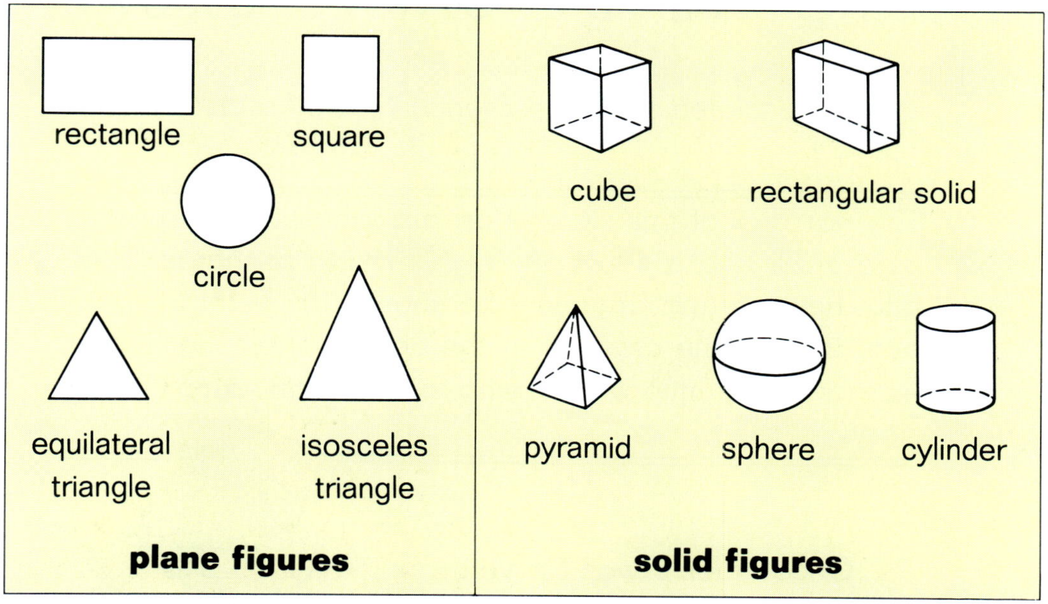

SOME COMMON PLANE (TWO-DIMENSIONAL) AND SOLID (THREE-DIMENSIONAL) FIGURES

1. Which plane figure(s) have four angles? Three sides? No angles?
2. What plane figure is related to the cube? How many sides does a cube have?
3. What plane figure is a sphere related to?
4. How many triangles make up the pyramid shown? What other plane figure is part of the pyramid?
5. Would a pyramid made up of equilateral triangles be more pointed or less pointed than one made up of isosceles triangles?
6. Which plane figure(s) shown have all their sides of equal length?

The Little Prince

ANTOINE DE SAINT-EXUPÉRY

translated from the French by Katherine Woods

The narrator of this story is an airplane pilot who even as a child had a special way of looking at things. The pilot never found anyone who shared his point of view until the day he crashed in the desert. There he met an extraordinary little prince who told him an extraordinary story.

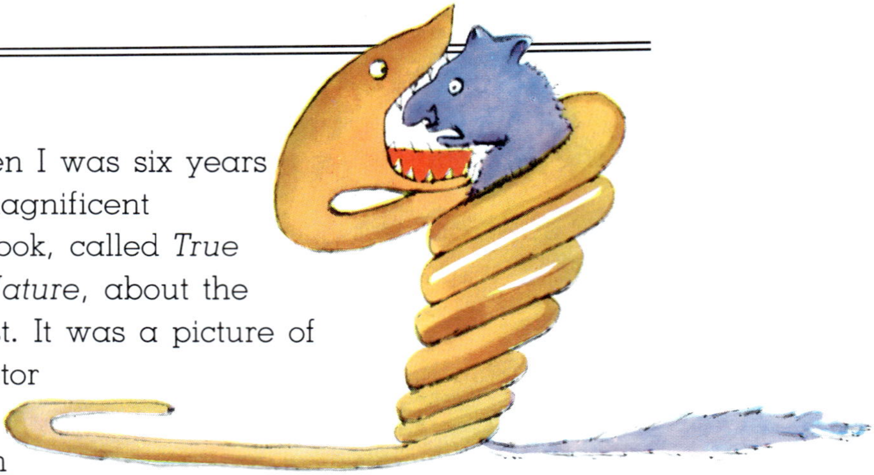

Once when I was six years old I saw a magnificent picture in a book, called *True Stories from Nature*, about the primeval forest. It was a picture of a boa constrictor in the act of swallowing an animal. Here is a copy of the drawing.

In the book it said: "Boa constrictors swallow their prey whole, without chewing it. After that they are not able to move, and they sleep through the six months that they need for digestion."

I pondered deeply, then, over the adventures of the jungle. And after some work with a colored pencil I succeeded in making my first drawing. My Drawing Number One. It looked like this:

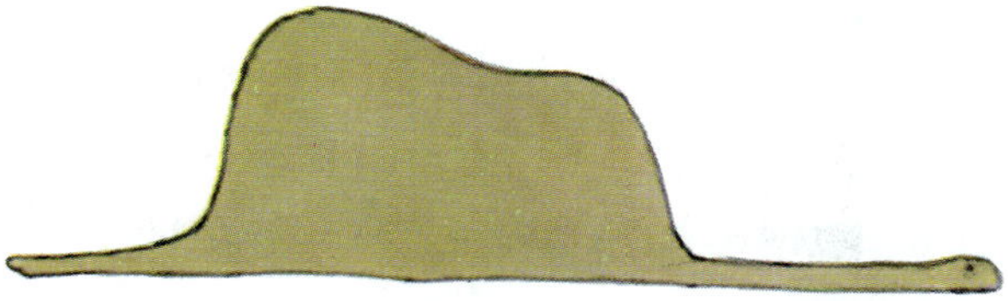

I showed my masterpiece to the grown-ups, and asked them whether the drawing frightened them.

But they answered: "Frighten? Why should any one be frightened by a hat?"

My drawing was not a picture of a hat. It was a picture of a boa constrictor digesting an elephant. But since the grown-ups were not able to understand it, I made another drawing: I drew the inside of the boa constrictor, so that the grown-ups could see it clearly. They always need to have things explained. My Drawing Number Two looked like this:

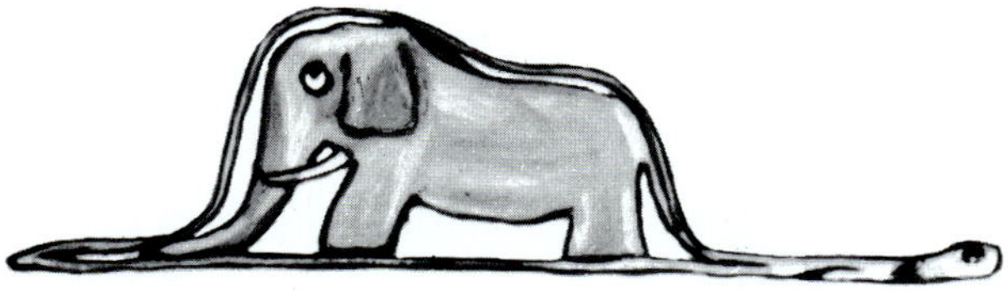

The grown-ups' response, this time, was to advise me to lay aside my drawings of boa constrictors, whether from the inside or the outside, and devote myself instead to geography, history, arithmetic, and grammar. That is why, at the age of six, I gave up what might have been a magnificent career as a painter. I had been disheartened by the failure of my Drawing Number One and my Drawing Number Two. Grown-ups never understand anything by themselves, and it is tiresome for children to be always and forever explaining things to them.

So then I chose another profession and learned to pilot airplanes. I have flown a little over all parts of the world; and it is true that geography has been very useful to me. At a glance, I can distinguish China from Arizona. If one gets lost in the night, such knowledge is valuable.

In the course of this life I have had a great many encounters with a great many people who have been concerned with matters of consequence. I have lived a great deal among grown-ups. I have seen them intimately, close at hand. And that hasn't much improved my opinion of them.

Whenever I met one of them who seemed to me at all clear-sighted, I tried the experiment of showing him my Drawing Number One, which I have always kept. I would try to find out, so, if this was a person of true understanding. But, whoever it was, he, or she, would always say:

"That is a hat."

Then I would never talk to that person about boa constrictors, or primeval forests, or stars. I would bring myself down to his level. I would talk to him about bridge, and golf, and politics, and neckties. And the grown-up would be greatly pleased to have met such a sensible man.

So I lived my life alone, without anyone that I could really talk to, until I had an accident with my plane in the Desert of Sahara, six years ago. Something was broken in my engine. And as I had with me neither a mechanic nor any passengers, I set myself to attempt the difficult repairs all alone. It was a question of life or death for me: I had scarcely enough drinking water to last a week.

The first night, then, I went to sleep on the sand, a thousand miles from any human habitation. I was more isolated than a shipwrecked sailor on a raft in the middle of the ocean. Thus you can imagine my amazement, at sunrise, when I was awakened by an odd little voice. It said:

"If you please—draw me a sheep!"

"What!"

"Draw me a sheep!"

I jumped to my feet, completely thunderstruck. I blinked my eyes hard. I looked carefully all around me. And I saw a most extraordinary small person, who stood there examining me with great seriousness. Here you may see the best portrait that, later, I was able to make of him. But my drawing is certainly very much less charming than its model.

That, however, is not my fault. The grown-ups discouraged me in my painter's career when I was six years old, and I never learned to draw anything, except boas from the outside and boas from the inside.

Now I stared at this sudden apparition with my eyes fairly starting out of my head in astonishment. Remember, I had crashed in the desert a thousand miles from any inhabited region. And yet my little man seemed neither to be straying uncertainly among the sands, nor to be fainting from fatigue or hunger or thirst or fear. Nothing about him gave any suggestion of a child lost in the middle of the desert, a thousand miles from any human habitation. When at last I was able to speak, I said to him:

"But—what are you doing here?"

And in answer he repeated, very slowly, as if he were speaking of a matter of great consequence:

"If you please—draw me a sheep."

When a mystery is too overpowering, one dare not disobey. Absurd as it might seem to me, a thousand miles from any human habitation and in danger of death, I took out of my pocket a sheet of paper and my fountain-pen. But then I remembered how my studies had been concentrated on geography, history, arithmetic, and grammar, and I told the little chap (a little crossly, too) that I did not know how to draw. He answered me:

"That doesn't matter. Draw me a sheep."

But I had never drawn a sheep. So I drew for him one of the two pictures I had drawn so often. It was that of the boa constrictor from the outside. And I was astounded to hear the little fellow greet it with,

"No, no, no! I do not want an elephant inside a boa constrictor. A boa constrictor is a very dangerous creature, and an elephant is very cumbersome. Where I live, everything is very small. What I need is a sheep. Draw me a sheep."

So then I made a drawing.

He looked at it carefully, then he said:

"No. This sheep is already very sickly. Make me another."

So I made another drawing.

My friend smiled gently and indulgently.

"You see yourself," he said, "that this is not a sheep. This is a ram. It has horns."

So then I did my drawing over once more.

But it was rejected too, just like the others.

"This one is too old. I want a sheep that will live a long time."

By this time my patience was exhausted, because I was in a hurry to start taking my engine apart. So I tossed off this drawing.

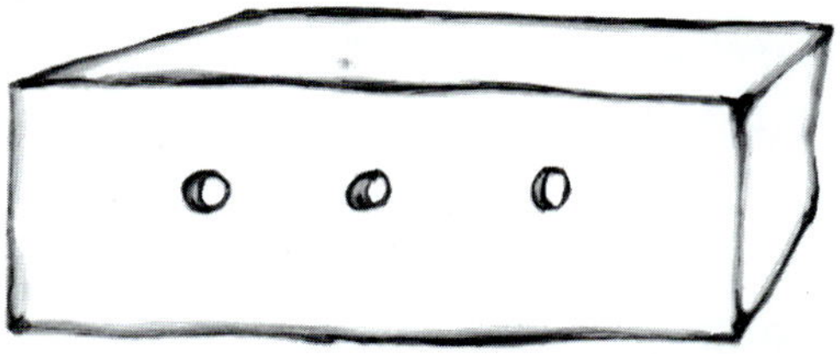

And I threw out an explanation with it.

"This is only his box. The sheep you asked for is inside."

I was very surprised to see a light break over the face of my young judge:

"That is exactly the way I wanted it! Do you think that this sheep will have to have a great deal of grass?"

"Why?"

"Because where I live everything is very small."

"There will surely be enough grass for him," I said. "It is a very small sheep that I have given you."

He bent his head over the drawing:

"Not so small that—Look! He has gone to sleep."

And that is how I made the acquaintance of the little prince.

It took me a long time to learn where he came from. The little prince, who asked me so many questions, never seemed to hear the ones I asked him. It was from words dropped by chance that, little by little, everything was revealed to me.

The first time he saw my airplane, for instance (I shall not draw my airplane; that would be much too complicated for me), he asked me:

"What is that object?"

"That is not an object. It flies. It is an airplane. It is my airplane."

And I was proud to have him learn that I could fly.

He cried out, then:

"What! You dropped down from the sky?"

"Yes," I answered, modestly.

"Oh! That is funny!"

And the little prince broke into a lovely peal of laughter, which irritated me very much. I like my misfortunes to be taken seriously.

Then he added:

"So you, too, come from the sky! Which is your planet?"

At that moment I caught a gleam of light in the impenetrable mystery of his presence; and I demanded, abruptly:

"Do you come from another planet?"

But he did not reply. He tossed his head gently, without taking his eyes from my plane:

"It is true that on that you can't have come from very far away. . . ."

And he sank into a reverie, which lasted a long time. Then, taking my sheep out of his pocket, he buried himself in the contemplation of his treasure.

You can imagine how my curiosity was aroused by this half-confidence about the "other planets." I made a great effort, therefore, to find out more on this subject.

"My little man, where do you come from? What is this 'where I live,' of which you speak? Where do you want to take your sheep?"

After a reflective silence he answered:

"The thing that is so good about the box you have given me is that at night he can use it as his house."

"That is so. And if you are good I will give you a string, too, so that you can tie him during the day, and a post to tie him to."

But the little prince seemed shocked by this offer.

"Tie him! What a queer idea!"

"But if you don't tie him," I said, "he will wander off somewhere, and get lost."

My friend broke into another peal of laughter:

"But where do you think he would go?"

"Anywhere. Straight ahead of him."

Then the little prince said, earnestly:

"That doesn't matter. Where I live, everything is so small!"

And, with perhaps a hint of sadness, he added:

"Straight ahead of him, nobody can go very far . . . ."

I had thus learned a second fact of great importance: this was that the planet the little prince came from was scarcely any larger than a house!

But that did not really surprise me much. I knew very well that in addition to the great planets—such as the Earth, Jupiter, Mars, Venus—to which we have given names, there are also hundreds of others, some of which are so small that one has a hard time seeing them through the telescope. When an astronomer discovers one of these he does not give it a name, but only a number. He might call it, for example, "Asteroid 325."

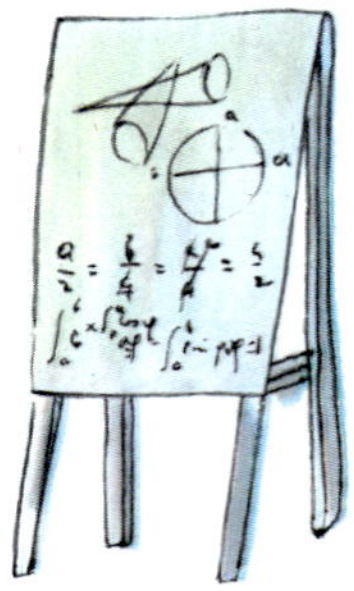

I have serious reason to believe that the planet from which the little prince came is the asteroid known as B-612.

This asteroid has only once been seen through the telescope. That was by a Turkish astronomer, in 1909.

On making his discovery, the astronomer had presented it to the International Astronomical Congress, in a great demonstration. But he was in Turkish costume, and so nobody would believe what he said.

Grown-ups are like that.

Fortunately, however, for the reputation of Asteroid B-612, a Turkish dictator made a law that his subjects, under pain of death, should change to European costume. So in 1920 the astronomer gave his demonstration all over again, dressed with impressive style and elegance. And this time everybody accepted his report.

If I have told you these details about the asteroid, and made a note of its number for you, it is on account of the grown-ups and their ways. Grown-ups love figures. When you tell them that you have made a new friend, they never ask you any questions about essential matters. They never say to you, "What does his voice sound like? What game does he love best? Does he collect butterflies?" Instead, they demand: "How old is he? How many brothers has he? How much does he weigh? How much money does his father make?" Only from these figures do they think that they have learned anything about him.

If you were to say to the grown-ups: "I saw a beautiful house made of rosy brick, with geraniums in the windows and doves on the roof," they would not be able to get any idea of that house at all.

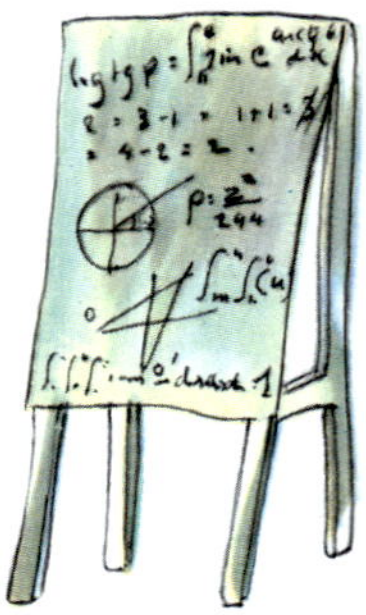

You would have to say to them: "I saw a house that cost $20,000." Then they would exclaim: "Oh, what a pretty house that is!"

Just so, you might say to them: "The proof that the little prince existed is that he was charming, that he laughed, and that he was looking for a sheep. If anybody wants a sheep, that is proof that he exists." And what good would it do to tell them that? They would shrug their shoulders, and treat you like a child. But if you said to them: "The planet he came from is Asteroid B-612," then they would be convinced, and leave you in peace from their questions.

They are like that. One must not hold it against them. Children should always show great forbearance toward grown-up people.

But certainly, for us who understand life, figures are a matter of indifference. I should have liked to begin this story in the fashion of the fairy-tales. I should have liked to say: "Once upon a time there was a little prince who lived on a planet that was scarcely any bigger than himself, and who had need of a sheep. . . ."

To those who understand life, that would have given a much greater air of truth to my story.

For I do not want any one to read my book carelessly. I have suffered too much grief in setting down these memories. Six years have already passed since my friend went away from me, with his sheep. If I try to describe him here, it is to make sure that I shall not forget him. To forget a friend is sad. Not every one has had a friend. And if I forget him, I may become like the grown-ups who are no longer interested in anything but figures.

It is for that purpose, again, that I have bought a box of paints and some pencils. It is hard to take up drawing again at my age, when I have never made any pictures except those of the boa constrictor from the outside and the boa constrictor from the inside, since I was six. I shall certainly try to make my portraits as true to life as possible. But I am not at all sure of success. One drawing goes along all right, and another has no resemblance to the subject. I make some errors, too, in the little prince's height: in one place he is too tall and in another too short. And I feel some doubts about the color of his costume. So I fumble along as best I can, now good, now bad, and I hope generally fair-to-middling.

In certain more important details I shall make mistakes, also. But that is something that will not be my fault. My friend never explained anything to me. He thought, perhaps, that I was like himself. But I, alas, do not know how to see sheep through the walls of boxes. Perhaps I am a little like the grown-ups. I have had to grow old.

As each day passed, I would learn, in our talk, something about the little prince's planet, his departure from it, his journey. The information would come very slowly, as it might chance to fall from his thoughts. It was in this way that I heard, on the third day, about the catastrophe of the baobabs.

This time, once more, I had the sheep to thank for it. For the little prince asked me abruptly—as if seized by a grave doubt—"It is true, isn't it, that sheep eat little bushes?"

"Yes, that is true."

"Ah! I am glad."

I did not understand why it was so important that sheep should eat little bushes. But the little prince added:

"Then it follows that they also eat baobabs?"

I pointed out to the little prince that baobabs were not little bushes, but on the contrary, trees as big as castles;

and that even if he took a whole herd of elephants away with him, the elephants would not eat up one single baobab.

The idea of the herd of elephants made the little prince laugh.

"We would have to put them one on top of the other," he said.

But he made a wise comment:

"Before they grow so big, the baobabs start out by being little."

"That is strictly correct," I said. "But why do you want the sheep to eat the little baobabs?"

He answered me at once. "Oh, come, come!" as if he were speaking of something that was self-evident. And I was obliged to make a great mental effort to solve this problem, without any assistance.

Indeed, as I learned, there were on the planet where the little prince lived—as on all planets—good plants and bad plants. In consequence, there were good seeds from good plants and bad seeds from bad plants. But seeds are invisible. They sleep deep in the heart of the earth's darkness, until some one among them is seized with the desire to awaken. Then this little seed will stretch itself and begin—timidly at first—to push a charming little sprig inoffensively upward toward the sun. If it is only a sprout of radish or the sprig of a rose-bush one would let it grow wherever it might wish. But when it is a bad plant, one must destroy it as soon as possible, the very first instant that one recognizes it.

Now there were some terrible seeds on the planet that was the home of the little prince; and these were the seeds of the baobab. The soil of that planet was infested with them. A baobab is something you will never, never be able to get rid of if you attend to it too late. It spreads over the entire planet. It bores clear through it with its roots. And if the planet is too small, and the baobabs are too many, they split it in pieces.

"It is a question of discipline," the little prince said to me later on. "When you've finished your own toilet in the morning, then it is time to attend to the toilet of the planet, just so, with the greatest care. You must see to it that you pull up regularly all the baobabs, at the very first moment when they can be distinguished from the rose bushes which they resemble so closely in their earliest youth. It is very tedious work," the little prince added, "but very easy."

And one day he said to me: "You ought to make a beautiful drawing, so that the children where you live can see exactly how all this is. That would be very useful to them if they were to travel some day. Sometimes," he added, "there is no harm in putting off a piece of work until another day. But when it is a matter of baobabs, that always means a catastrophe. I knew a planet that was inhabited by a lazy man. He neglected three little bushes. . . ."

So, as the little prince described it to me, I have made a drawing of that planet. I do not much like to take the tone of a moralist. But the danger of the baobabs is so little understood, and such considerable risks would be run by anyone who might get lost on an asteroid, that for once I am breaking through my reserve. "Children," I say plainly, "watch out for the baobabs!"

My friends, like myself, have been skirting this danger for a long time, without ever knowing it; and so it is for them that I have worked so hard over this drawing.

The lesson which I pass on by this means is worth all the trouble it has cost me.

Perhaps you will ask me, "Why are there no other drawings in this book as magnificent and impressive as this drawing of the baobabs?"

The reply is simple. I have tried. But with the others I have not been successful. When I made the drawing of the baobabs I was carried beyond myself by the inspiring force of urgent necessity.

Thinking and Writing About the Selection

1. How did the narrator meet the little prince?
2. What was unusual about the little prince's home?
3. Why do you think the little prince had left his planet? Do you think he will stay away for very long? Why or why not?
4. If you met the little prince, what would you ask him? What questions might he ask you? How would you answer?

Applying the Key Skill
Author's Purpose and Point of View

Choose the best answer or answers to each of the following questions about "The Little Prince."

1. The author probably wrote the story to ____.
   a. entertain
   b. inform
   c. describe
   d. explain
   e. give factual information
2. With which of the following statements do you think the author would probably agree?
   a. Children can understand some things that grown-ups may not understand.
   b. The way people dress is important.
   c. How people dress has nothing to do with the importance of what they have discovered.
   d. Figures are necessary to provide a true description of a person or place.
   e. Friendship is valuable, but not everyone discovers what true friendship is.

Antoine de Saint-Exupéry

"Before writing, one must live, one must learn to see; no literary artifice can cover the lack of these essentials."

Into his forty-four years on earth (and *above* it, for his passion was flying), Antoine de Saint-Exupéry crammed more living than most writers. His writing was rewarded. His books for adults won several major prizes, while *The Little Prince*, his only children's book, has sold millions worldwide.

"Saint Ex," as he was called by his pilot buddies, came to an early interest in both flying and writing. Born in Lyons, France, he was writing poems and drawing airplane engines at the age of six.

At the age of nine, he was sent to a boarding school. The classes were strict, but he enjoyed vacations near a large airfield, where he was given his first plane ride.

After college, Saint-Exupéry joined the French Army Air Force, received his pilot's license, and wrote: "I fly because it releases my mind from the tyranny of petty things; it gives me a sense of wider horizons."

As a commercial pilot in West Africa and South America, he began writing the essays and books that explored his ideas about life. "I admire Science, of course," he said, "but I also admire wisdom."

Saint-Exupéry was famous for his reckless disregard for danger. He had several air crashes and was injured. During a flight on July 31, 1944, he disappeared over the Mediterranean Sea. No trace of his body or aircraft has ever been found.

More to Read *Wind, Sand and Stars; Night Flight*

WHAT DO YOU MEAN BY AVERAGE?

ELIZABETH JAMES
AND CAROL BARKIN

We use the word average every day for many different things. But what does it really mean?

We take you now to the sleepy little town of Normal City, where Jill Slater and her friends are having a meeting.

"I came up with a great idea for my campaign," Jill announces. "We're going to prove that I'm the most average person in our school, so I'll be the best person to represent everyone."

"That sounds terrific!" Harriet exclaims. "With that campaign you're sure to be our next Student Council president."

"Sure," David says, "but how do we prove it?"

"And what do you mean by 'average'?" asks Steve.

Average is a word you hear every day. You may know the batting averages of your favorite ballplayers. You're sure to know that C is an average grade in school, but the average score on the last math test may have been 85.

Averages are used to give information about all kinds of everyday things (not just in school!). Averages are convenient tools, but they can be misleading if not used correctly. In our next installment, Jill's campaign committee begins to find out about averages.

As we return to the sleepy little town of Normal City, Jill's campaign is waking a few people up.

"Hey, Jill, we got the lists of heights and weights for everyone in school!" David yells.

"Now what do we do?" asks Harriet.

"Well, get some pencils and a lot of scratch paper," Jill replies. "We have to add up all the heights and all the weights, and then divide the totals by the number of kids in school."

"Oh, no!" Steve groans. "I thought this was going to be more fun than that!"

Jill's campaign committee is finding the *mean*, or average, of height and weight for students in their

school. A mean (or average) can be computed for any collection of items that have numerical values: measurements, quantities, scores, and prices are often averaged. For example, when you plan a winter ski vacation, you may want to know the average snowfall for December in Utah or Vermont. On a cross-country trip, you may need to know the average price of a hamburger at roadside restaurants as well as the average temperatures for the places you'll pass through (if it's August and the average temperature in Death Valley is 106° in the shade, plan a different route!).

Means are always found by adding up the numerical values of all the items you're averaging and then dividing this total by the number of items. Because the mean is calculated from the numerical values, it is often called the *arithmetic mean*. To find the average daily high temperature for July, you first need to know the high temperature for each day in the month. These 31 numbers are added to get a total; the total is then divided by 31 to give the mean high temperature for July. But for February, you would have only 28 temperatures to add, and you would divide the total by 28 (unless it's leap year!).

Back at campaign headquarters, Steve is knee-deep in scratch paper.

"Finally—that's finished!" he says. "Lucky for you, Jill, that I was always good at division."

"Let's see the results," says Harriet. She reads off, "Average height—151 centimeters. Average weight—38 kilograms."

"Fantastic!" David exclaims. "That's exactly your height and weight, Jill!"

"I told you, I'm totally average." Jill smiles.

"Let's do another one," says David. "You're on the basketball team, Jill—are you an average player? What was your score in the last game?"

Players	**Score**
Jill	8
Carmela	7
Diane	13
Jody	19
Arlene	10
Martha	0
Rosa	3
Cynthia	4
	$64 \div 8 = 8$

"Look at that!" says Harriet. "If everyone on the team had made the same score you did, the total score would still have been 64."

A mean represents a whole group of scores or other numbers; it is the score each person would have if the scores of the whole group were evened out. The individual scores themselves are called the *raw data*. The *spread* of the raw data is the distance from the lowest number to the highest—in this case the spread is 0 to 19.

When you look at the raw data, you can see that Jill was the only player whose score was the same as the team's average. Knowing the mean doesn't tell you how high or low any individual scores were, and it also doesn't tell you the spread of the raw data. What it does tell you is the performance of the team as a whole.

"This averaging isn't too hard—we can use it for everything," says Harriet. "I've always wondered what the average allowance is—let's do that next."

Later that day:

"The kids thought we were really nosy," says David, "but we found out how much allowance everyone in our homeroom gets."

"Good work, team," says Jill. "Let's tally up the results."

List of allowances:

1.75
2.75
2.00
2.00
2.00
2.75
2.50
2.50
1.50
1.75
2.00
2.25 (Jill's)
2.75
3.00
2.00
2.50
2.00
2.75
1.75
25.00
2.50
2.50
1.50
2.00
2.75

total = $78.75

$78.75 ÷ 25 = $3.15 *(mean)*

"Oh, Jill, this is terrible," Harriet moans. "Your allowance isn't anywhere near the average!"

David looks up from his scratch paper. "This doesn't even make sense," he says. "There isn't anyone who actually gets $3.15 for allowance. Did we do something wrong?"

David doesn't have to worry—their calculations are correct. Since an arithmetic mean is found by adding and dividing a group of numbers, it may be the same or it may *not* be the same as any of the numbers used; in fact, it can be the same as all the numbers. You can easily see this for yourself:

$$\begin{array}{r} 3 \\ 4 \\ \underline{5} \\ 12 \div 3 = 4 \end{array} \qquad \begin{array}{r} 2 \\ 3 \\ \underline{7} \\ 12 \div 3 = 4 \end{array}$$

$$\begin{array}{r} 4 \\ 4 \\ \underline{4} \\ 12 \div 3 = 4 \end{array}$$

Remember that a mean doesn't represent any individual item of the raw data; it is the number that each item would be if they were all evened out to be the same.

"Okay," says Steve, "but we have another really big problem. Only one person in the whole class gets more than a $3.00 allowance, so I don't call $3.15 average."

"You've got something there," Harriet says. "If we didn't have that rich guy Harvey in the class, the average would be much lower."

"But we do have him," David says. "We can't just leave him out of the calculations."

The campaign committee has run into a real problem here. Sometimes raw data is spread out very unevenly: in the list of allowances, most are grouped in a small range from $1.50 to $3.00, while one item is much higher than all the others. This higher figure brings the mean above the range of the other data. In any group of data, a few items that are much higher or lower than the rest will pull the mean up or down; for this situation, an arithmetic mean doesn't give the most useful information.

However, there is a different and more helpful way to look at raw data that are unevenly distributed.

As the sun sinks over the sleepy little town of Normal City, Jill snaps her fingers and shouts, "Aha! I've got the answer to our problem! We have to find a *median* instead of a mean."

"What's that?" the campaign committee asks.

"It's the middle item in a group when the group is arranged in order," answers Jill. "Let's try it and see what we get."

(1)	$1.50	(14)	$2.50
(2)	$1.50	(15)	$2.50
(3)	$1.75	(16)	$2.50
(4)	$1.75	(17)	$2.50
(5)	$1.75	(18)	$2.50
(6)	$2.00	(19)	$2.75
(7)	$2.00	(20)	$2.75
(8)	$2.00	(21)	$2.75
(9)	$2.00	(22)	$2.75
(10)	$2.00	(23)	$2.75
(11)	$2.00	(24)	$3.00
(12)	$2.00	(25)	$25.00
(13)	$2.25 median		

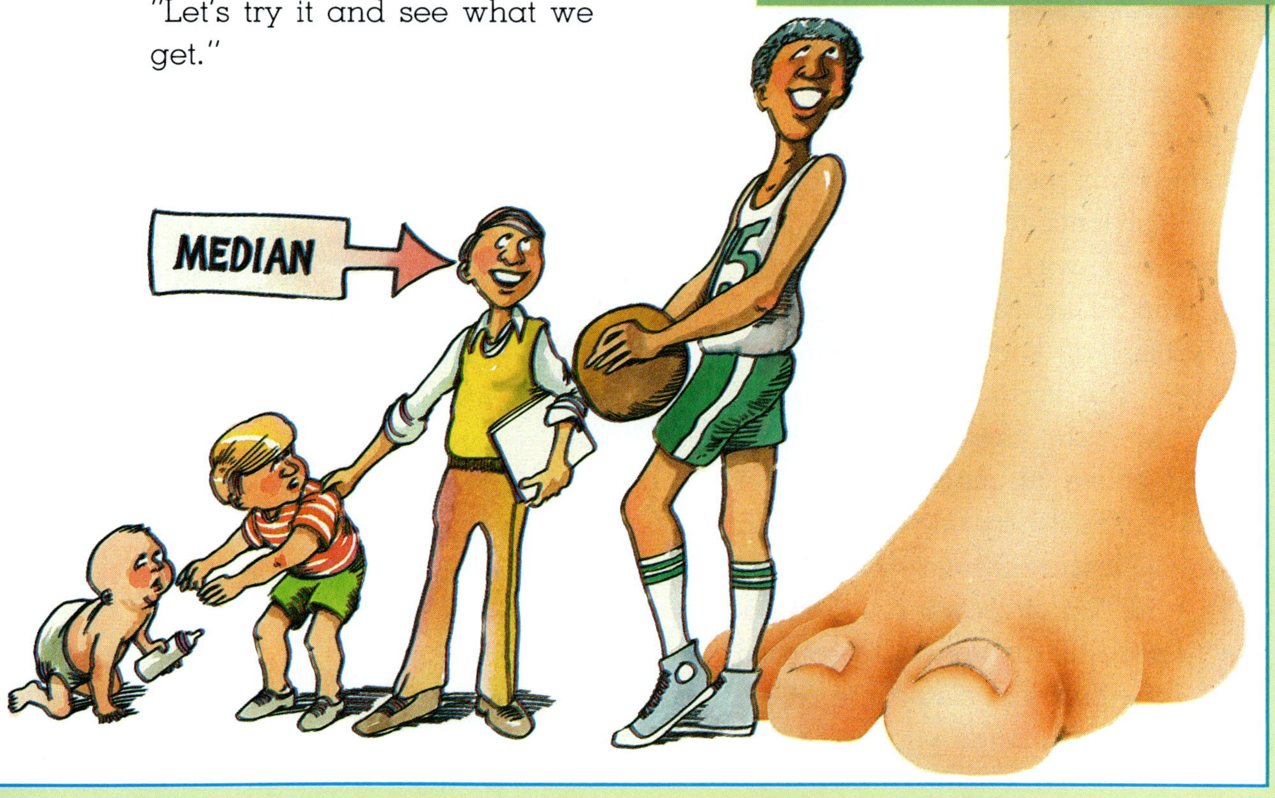

"Hurrah!" cries Harriet. "Jill's allowance is in the middle after all!"

"I don't get it," Steve complains. "How come it's average this time but it wasn't when we found the mean?"

Finding a median is really finding the middle item of a list when the items are put in order. The order is usually based on numerical values —size, price, age, and so on— and it doesn't matter whether it is arranged from low to high or high to low. But unlike a mean, a median can also be found for raw data that do not have numerical values. You can find the median color in a spectrum or the median word or letter in an alphabetical list. As long as there is a way to arrange the data in order, a median can be located.

When you know the median of a group, you know that in the range of raw data there are as many items above the median as below it. This makes it very useful when your raw data are unevenly distributed, as in the list of allowances. The one allowance that is very different from the others cannot distort the picture for the group when you use a median. The U.S. Census uses a median to describe average family income so that the few millionaires won't give a misleading impression of what the average family really has to spend. The mean can give a distorted picture because it is based on the actual numerical values of the raw data. But a median is based on position in the group. It separates the top half of the group from the bottom half.

Don't assume, though, that the mean the campaign committee found was wrong or completely useless. It told them that if all the allowance money for this class were split up evenly, each person would have $3.15 to spend. But that's not the information the committee was looking for. They wanted to know how much allowance the average class member really had to spend. And this information is what the median provided.

As a researcher, it's important for you to know how each kind of measurement works; then you can choose the one that will tell you what you really want to know.

David holds up a sheet of scratch paper. "Here's the list of how many children are in the families of everyone in our class. What do we want to know about the average family?"

"We want to find out how many children the average class member really has in his or her family," replies Harriet.

"That means a median!" Steve exclaims.

children per family	**number of families**	**total children**
1	////	4
2	~~////~~ /	12
3	~~////~~ ////	27
4	///	12
5		0
6	/	6
7	//	14

1111222222333333333444677

↑

median

"Oh, good," Jill says. "There are three children in my family, so I'm average again."

"Let's find the mean too," suggests Harriet. "Then we'll also know the average number of children per family in this class."

"Good idea!" cries David. "Then we can even off the families and give away our extra brothers and sisters."

number of children

1 child × 4 families = 4
2 children × 6 families = 12
3 children × 9 families = 27
4 children × 3 families = 12
5 children × 0 families = 0
6 children × 1 family = 6
7 children × 2 families = <u>14</u>
75

75 ÷ 25 (children in class) = 3

"Look at that! The median and the mean are the same," says David.

Steve thinks a minute. "That must mean that the raw data are spread fairly evenly throughout the range."

As you know, the median locates the midpoint of a range of ordered raw data while the mean indicates the arithmetic average. The mean and the median may be the same, as they are in the example below.

```
    5               3  4  5
    3                  ↑
  + 4                median
12 ÷ 3 = 4   mean
```

But you can see from the next example that when the data are spread very unevenly, these two results give you different information.

```
    2               1  2  9
    1                  ↑
  + 9                median
12 ÷ 3 = 4   mean
```

Remember that to find a mean, you need not put your raw data in order but you have to do some arithmetic; to find a median, no arithmetic is necessary but you do have to put the raw data in order.

Jill is pleased with the results so far. "I wonder whether it's average to be a girl in this class," she says. "Let's find out."

"Well, we can't use a mean," says David, "because there aren't any numerical values to average."

"Okay, let's find the median. You don't need numerical values to do that," says Harriet.

Jill frowns. "We can't do that either. There's no way to put the data in order. After all, it's not like a color spectrum—how can we decide how to arrange them?"

"Let's figure out what question we're asking here," David says. "We want to know which is more common in this class—boys or girls."

Steve is puzzled. "That just sounds as if you're asking whether there are more girls or more boys."

"You've got it, Steve!" cries Jill. "That's exactly what we're asking here! In this case we have to find the mode."

"What's that?" everyone asks.

"Whichever thing you have the most of in a group is the *mode* for that group," says Jill.

"You mean if you have three apples, two oranges, and a banana, apples are the mode for that fruit bowl?" asks David.

"Yes," Jill replies. "So for our class, since we have fourteen girls and eleven boys, girls are the mode. I'm still totally average."

A *mode* is the item that occurs most frequently in a group. When you use the word *average* to mean "usual" or "most common," you are talking about a mode.

You have probably figured out that to find a mode, all you have to do is count. You don't have to do any arithmetic, as you do for a mean; so you can find a mode for data that have no numerical values. You also don't have to put your raw data in order as you do for a median; so you can find a mode for data that have no natural order (like apples and oranges).

Since the mode is defined as the most commonly occurring item in a group, it's obvious that the mode, unlike the mean, must always be the same as an item in the group. But how about the median? Try finding the mean, median, and mode for this range of data:

2
1
6
6
1
1
___
$17 \div 6 = 2.83...$
mean

1 1 1 2 6 6
↑
1.5
median

1 1 1 2 6 6
(first three 1s bracketed) mode

The mean in this case is a number that does not appear in the list. You may remember that this also happened when Jill's campaign committee figured out the mean allowance for their class. This is not an unusual result. But you may have been surprised that the median of 1.5 also does not appear in the list. You can easily see that this will happen whenever you have an even number of items. In this situation you must find the middle two items in the ordered list and then find the point that lies halfway between them. The mode, of course, is always an item that does appear in the list: here you have three ones, two sixes, and one two, so the mode is one.

In the example above, the three results are different from one another. However, look back at the list of the number of children in each family, and figure out the mode. Here is a case where all three results are the same.

"What other kinds of things can we do?" asks Steve.

"Too bad we can't do birthdays," David says. "Mine is tomorrow."

"Why can't we?" replies Harriet. "We can find out the modal month for birthdays. Let's look at the class list."

Jan.	Feb.	Mar.
/	//	
April	May	June
//	/	////
July	Aug.	Sept.
//	////	///
Oct.	Nov.	Dec.
/	//	///

"Uh-oh," says Steve, "we're in trouble. There's no mode."

But Jill is smiling. "Oh, yes, there is. In fact, there are two modes—June and August. And my birthday is August fifteenth."

"Can you really do that?" asks Harriet. "I thought there could only be one mode."

Jill is right. There can be more than one mode for a list of data. If two items occur the same number of times in a list, and no other items occur as often, then both these items are modes.

Sometimes there are a lot of modes, but sometimes you may not be able to find any mode. How is this possible? When no items in the list of data are the same, there is no mode. If each person in your class gets a different score on a test, there is no modal score.

Modes can be used in a number of situations where a mean or median isn't very helpful. When a television commercial informs you that most people prefer Brand X toothpaste, do you recognize this toothpaste preference as a mode? Many products are advertised in this fashion. The advertisers are using *average* in the sense of "most common" or "most popular." So, the next time you hear that Yo-Yo Wax makes the average kitchen floor really sparkle, you'll know what to think!

"Well, Jill, it looks as if you really are average," says David.

Several weeks go by. Jill campaigns hard on the issues. Finally election day arrives. Jill and her campaign committee are sitting outside the school library awaiting the election results.

"Your speech was wonderful, Jill," says Harriet.

"You really convinced me to vote for you," David adds.

Jill crosses her fingers. "I just hope I convinced the average voter."

"We'll know before long. They're counting the ballots now," Steve says.

Just then the library door opens and Bob, this year's Student Council president, comes out.

"Gosh, good luck, Jill," whispers Steve.

Bob smiles. "Hope you'll like the job, Jill. You'll have it for a whole year."

Jill jumps up. "You mean I won?!"

"By a landslide—ninety-seven percent!" says Bob.

"Congratulations, Jill!" shouts David. "But now that you're president, you're not average anymore."

"Oh, yes I am," says Jill. "It just goes to show what the average person can do!"

Thinking and Writing About the Selection

1. Why did Jill want to prove that she was the most average person in the school?
2. If you were trying to determine the average number of books checked out of your school library for one week, what would your raw data be?
3. How does a median differ from a mean? How does a mode differ from a mean?
4. Find the mean, median, and mode for this data:
   4 5 6 7 7 8

Applying the Key Skill

Context Clues

Use context clues to choose the meaning of each underlined word in the sentences below.

1. Jill's friends conferred all afternoon in an attempt to come up with a way to convince voters to support her campaign.
   a. argued b. volunteered
   c. persuaded d. had a discussion
2. David objected vehemently to the use of any corny slogans, declaring that he would leave the group if they decided to use them.
   a. quietly b. unexpectedly
   c. forcefully d. shyly
3. Steve was convinced that something innovative was needed because the entire campaign process had become too ordinary.
   a. remarkable b. new
   c. serious d. powerful
4. Harriet, who was unusually reticent throughout the meeting, finally expressed her views.
   a. talkative b. uninterested
   c. creative d. reserved

Numbers

I hate and like math.
The letter O
and the number zero sound like
poems about O snowflakes. Zero
makes me hungry. It is the emptiest
number in the universe
which is—and is not—round.
The wonder of zero, O snowflake
and the universe
will never be solved.
I want my lunch.

Aliki Barnstone

MAIN IDEA

You know that the most important idea of a paragraph is called **main idea**. Sometimes the main idea is stated in a single sentence. At other times, you must combine information from two or more sentences to state the main idea.

> Sometimes raw data are spread out very unevenly. That is, while most of the data are grouped in a small range, one or two items are very much higher or very much lower than all the others. In such a group of data, the few higher or lower items will pull the mean up or down. In such a situation, the mean doesn't give the most useful information.

Part of the main idea is found in the first sentence, and part is found in the last sentence. Information from both sentences must be combined to state the main idea: *When raw data are spread out very unevenly, the mean doesn't give the most useful information.*

ACTIVITY A Read the paragraph below. Then write the sentence that best states the main idea.

> The gross national product (GNP) is the total value of a country's goods and services. The value is determined every year. To arrive at a figure for the GNP, the value of all the goods produced in one year is determined. The value of all the services performed is added to the value of the goods. The total is called the gross national product.

a. The gross national product is determined on a yearly basis.

b. The gross national product is also referred to as the GNP.
c. To determine a country's gross national product the value of all goods and services produced in one year are added together.
d. The GNP is a total figure.

ACTIVITY B Read the paragraphs below. Then write the main idea of each paragraph on your paper.

1. The study of populations is called demography (di mog′ rə fē). People called demographers study records of births and deaths. They also study census reports. A census can provide information about such things as jobs, language, housing, income, and education. Using these sources, demographers describe population patterns over time and make predictions about future populations.

2. People who migrate, or move from one country to another, affect population growth rates. They decrease the population of the country they leave and increase the population of the country they go to. The population growth rate must take migration into account. Natural increase or decrease also affects the population growth rate. The natural increase is based on birth rate and death rate.

3. You may have seen a listing in a bank or newspaper with the title "Foreign Currency Exchange Rates." The value of one nation's money, or currency, is expressed in terms of another nation's money by an exchange rate. For example, a recent exchange rate showed that a Canadian dollar had about the same value as $1.20 in United States currency. Exchange rates vary, depending on whether the currency is being bought or sold.

LIFE IN FLATLAND

ADAPTED FROM FLATLAND BY A. SQUARE

We live in a world of three dimensions—length, height, and width. What would it be like if the world had only two dimensions?

The book *Flatland* was written nearly one hundred years ago. The author, A. Square (his real name was Edwin Abbott) had a unique viewpoint. In his imaginary world, all the people are Triangles, Squares, Circles, and other flat shapes.

I call our world Flatland—not because this is what we call it, but so that you will know what it is like. You must understand at once that in my country there is nothing of the kind you call a solid shape. As you know, a solid, or three-dimensional shape, has length, width, and thickness. But in Flatland, *everything* is flat. That is, there are only two dimensions—length and width.

Imagine a huge sheet of paper on which Straight Lines, Triangles, Squares, Pentagons, Hexagons, and

other shapes move freely about, very much like shadows. You will then have a pretty correct idea of what my country and countrymen look like. You might think that we can tell Triangles, Squares, and other flat shapes by sight. But this is not so. We cannot tell one shape from another. We can see only Straight Lines. Let me show you why this is so.

Place a penny in the middle of a table. Now, lean over the table and look straight down upon the penny. It will appear to be a Circle.

But, move back to the edge of the table and lower your head. When your eyes are exactly level with the edge of the table (so that you are, as it were, a Flatlander) the penny will no longer look like a Circle. It will seem to have become, so far as you can see, a Straight Line.

The very same thing will happen if you take a piece of cardboard and cut out a Triangle, or Square, or any other shape. Put the shape on a table and look at it from the edge of the table. You will find that you see only a Straight Line.

Well, that is exactly what we see in Flatland when we meet a friend. As our friend comes ever closer to us, the line becomes larger and brighter. When our friend goes away from us, the line becomes smaller and dimmer. Our friend may be a Triangle, Square,

Pentagon, Hexagon, or any other shape, but all we see is a Straight Line.

You may wonder how we can tell one friend from another. I will explain in a moment. But first, let me now tell you about the kinds of people there are in Flatland.

Our Soldiers are Straight Lines. I shall have more to say about them shortly.

All our Farmers are Isosceles Triangles, with two equal sides, each about eleven inches (27 centimeters) long. The third side is quite short, often not much more than half an inch (12 millimeters). This causes the two equal sides to form a very sharp angle that is most useful for plowing.

Our Merchants and Shopkeepers, of whom there are many, are Equilateral, or Equal-Sided, Triangles.

Most of our fine Doctors and Lawyers are Squares, like myself. But a few, who have risen to the top of their profession, are Five-Sided shapes, or Pentagons.

There are several degrees of School Teachers, beginning with Six-Sided shapes, or Hexagons, and going on to shapes that have many more sides. Finally, we have our Philosophers, who are the wisest of all our people. They have so many sides, and the sides are so small, that they cannot be distinguished from a Circle.

There are many dangers in Flatland, just as there are in your world. The greatest of these dangers is our shapes. We have to be careful not to bump into one

another. A Flatlander who has a sharp shape can easily hurt another person. For this reason, our sharply pointed Farmer Triangles are quite dangerous.

This being so, you can see that our Soldiers are far more dangerous. If a Farmer is like an arrowhead, a Soldier is like a needle, inasmuch as a Soldier is all point (for a line, as you know, is made up entirely of points). Add to this the power Soldiers have of making themselves almost invisible and you can easily see that a Soldier of Flatland is not a person to trifle with!

Perhaps you are wondering how our Soldiers can make themselves invisible. Let me explain.

Place a needle on a table. Then, with your eye at the edge of the table, look at the needle sideways. You will see the whole length of it. But look at it end-ways and you see nothing but a point. It has become practically invisible. This is how it is with all of our Soldiers. When a Soldier's side is turned toward us, we see a Straight Line. When the end containing the Soldier's eye faces us, we see nothing but a rather gleaming point. But when a Soldier's back is to us, it is a dim point that is almost impossible to see.

You can understand, then, how dangerous our Soldiers are. You can get a gash by running into a Merchant Triangle. And you can be quite badly wounded in a collision with a Farmer Triangle. But it is nothing less than absolute death to bump into a Soldier! And when a Soldier is seen only as a dim

point, it is difficult, even for the most cautious, to avoid a collision!

For this reason, our Soldiers must be careful. When any Soldiers are out in the street, either standing or walking about, they must move their backs constantly from side to side so that anyone behind them will be able to see them.

You lucky people who live in a world of three dimensions are blessed with shade as well as light. You enjoy many colors. You can see an angle and the complete shape of a Circle. But in Flatland, we do not have these blessings. How, then, can I make you understand the difficulty we have recognizing one another?

The first means of recognition is the sense of hearing. Our hearing is keener and more highly developed than is yours. It enables us not only to tell the voices of our friends, but even to tell the difference between shapes, at least for the Triangle, the Square, and the Pentagon.

But feeling is the best way of recognizing another Flatlander. What an "introduction" is to you, feeling is with us. However, you must not think that feeling is as slow and difficult for us as it might be for you. Long practice and training, which begins in school and goes on throughout life, make it possible for us to quickly tell the difference between the angles of an Equal-Sided Triangle, a Square, or a Pentagon.

It is not necessary, as a rule, to do more than feel a single angle to tell a person's shape, unless he or she belongs to the higher class of shapes. That makes it much more difficult. Even the professors in our University of Wentbridge have been known to confuse a Ten-Sided Polygon with a Twelve-Sided one. And there is hardly a Doctor of Science anywhere in Flatland who would know at once, just by feeling a single angle, the difference between a Twenty-Sided and a Twenty-Four-Sided shape.

Many of us prefer still a third method, which is recognition by the sense of sight.

That this power exists anywhere, and for any class, is the result of Fog. For Fog is present everywhere during most of the year, except in the very hot parts of Flatland. For you, Fog is a bad thing that hides the landscape, makes you feel poorly, and damages your health. But for us, Fog is a blessing, nearly as important as the air itself!

If there were no Fog, all our friends would look like exactly the same kind of Straight Line. But wherever there is a rich supply of Fog, an object only slightly farther away than another is a bit dimmer than the nearer object. So, by carefully examining the dimness and brightness of things, we are able to tell the exact shape of an object.

For example, suppose I were to see two people coming toward me. Let us say that one is a Merchant

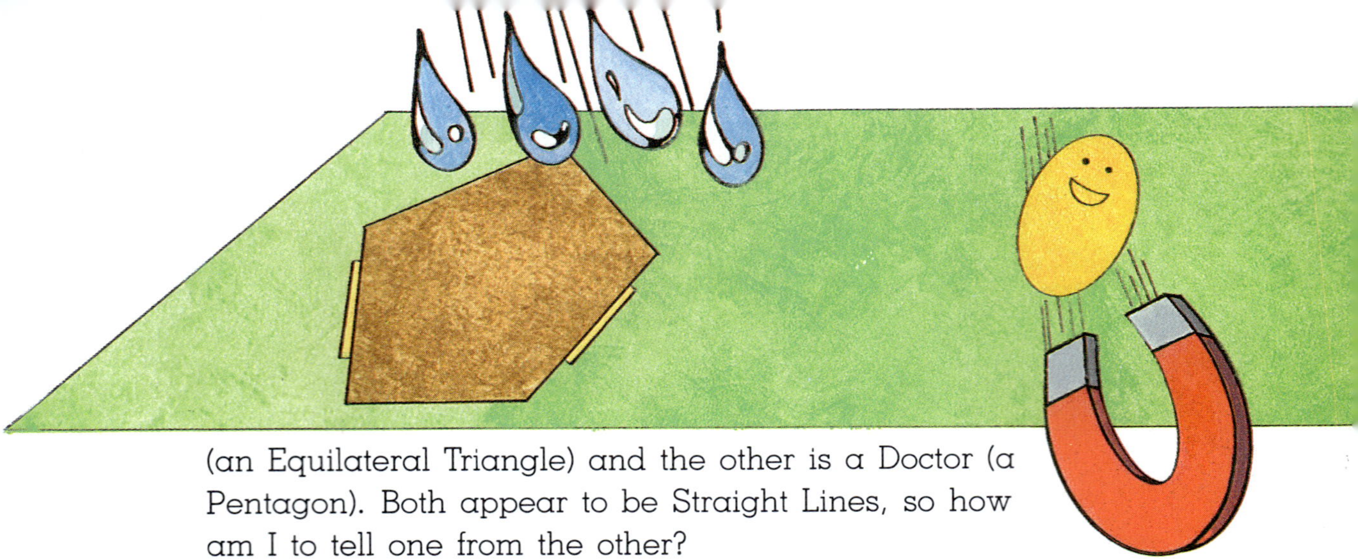

(an Equilateral Triangle) and the other is a Doctor (a Pentagon). Both appear to be Straight Lines, so how am I to tell one from the other?

In the case of the Merchant, I see a Straight Line, of course. The center of this line, which is the part nearest to me, is very bright. But on either side, the line fades away rapidly into the Fog. I can tell at once, then, that the line slants back quite sharply from the center.

On the other hand, the Doctor has a slightly different appearance. As with the Merchant, I see only a Straight Line with a very bright center. On either side, the Doctor's line also fades into the Fog, but not as rapidly as the Merchant's line. Thus I can tell at once that the Doctor's line does not slant back as sharply. Because of the slight difference in brightness, I know that one shape is an Equilateral Triangle and that the other is a Pentagon.

But enough about how we recognize one another. Let me now say a word or two about our climate and our houses.

Just as you do, we have four points of the compass: North, South, East, and West. But because there is no sun—or, indeed, any other heavenly body—in Flatland, it is impossible for us to tell North in the way you do. However, we have a method of our own.

By a Law of Nature in Flatland, there is a constant pull from the South. This pull is quite enough to serve

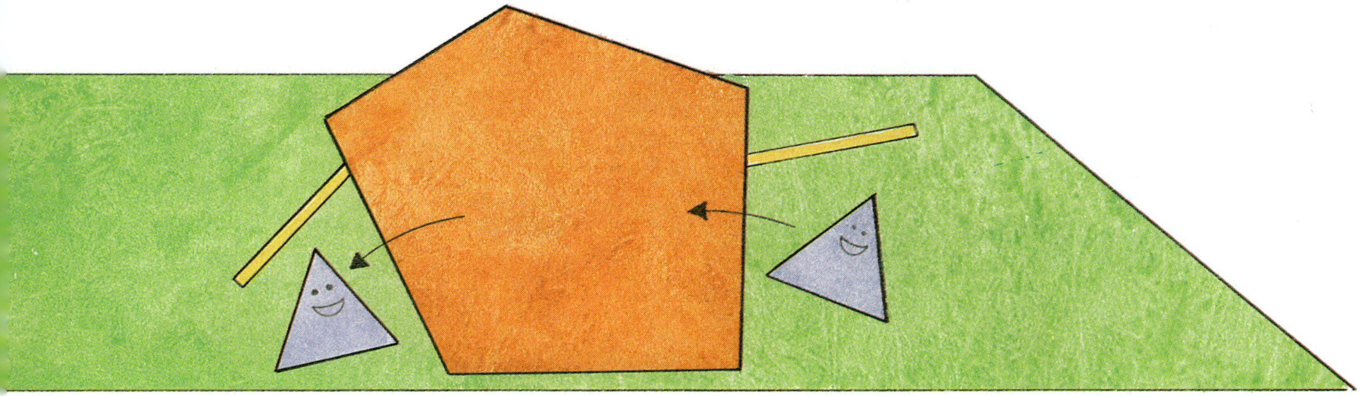

as a compass in most parts of Flatland. Moreover, the rain, which falls at regular times each day, comes always from the North, so this is an additional help. And in the towns we have the help of the houses, for every house is built with the roof pointing North, to keep off the rain.

However, in our more northern regions, the pull of the South is hardly felt. Sometimes, when walking across an open plain where there have been no houses to guide me, I have had to stand and wait for hours until the rain came. Only then could I be sure of the direction in which I was going.

Our houses are quite comfortable and very well-suited to our climate and way of life. The most common form of house construction in Flatland is Five-Sided, or Pentagon-Shaped.

The two northern sides make up the roof, and usually have no doors. On the east, there is the door by which we go in. On the west side, there is another door by which we go out. In this way, we are able to go in and out without bumping into and hurting one another. The south side, or floor, is usually doorless.

Square and Triangular houses are not allowed. There is a good reason for this. The angles of a Square (and still more of a Triangle) are much more pointed than the angles of a Pentagon. The lines of houses and almost all other objects are dimmer than the lines of Men and Women. Therefore, there is a

danger that the points of a Square or Triangular house might do serious injury to an absent-minded traveler suddenly running against them.

As early as the eleventh-century of our era, Triangular houses were forbidden by law. The only exceptions were forts and similar kinds of buildings, where the sharp points might serve a useful purpose. At this period, Square houses were still permitted. But about three centuries later, the Law decided (for reasons of public safety) that in all towns with a population above ten thousand, the angle of the Pentagon was the smallest house angle that could be allowed. It is only now and then, in some very remote and backward farming district, that one may still discover a Square house.

We have no windows in our houses. This is because light comes to us both inside and outside, by day and by night, equally at all times and in all places. But where light comes from, we do not know. In the old days, our wise men liked to try to discover the cause of light, but this filled our hospitals with those who went mad trying to solve the problem.

I—alas, I alone in Flatland—know the true solution to this mysterious problem. But I cannot make my knowledge understandable to a single one of my countrymen. I am mocked at—I, the only one who knows the truth: that light comes from your strange world of three dimensions!

Thinking and Writing About the Selection

1. What are the three dimensions of a solid object?
2. How do isosceles triangles differ from equilateral triangles?
3. What senses are most important to Flatlanders? Why?
4. If you lived in Flatland, what shape would you choose to have? What would be the advantages of that shape? What would be the disadvantages?

Applying the Key Skill
Author's Purpose and Point of View

Choose the best answer or answers to each of the following questions about "Life in Flatland."

1. The author probably wrote the story to ____.
   a. entertain
   b. inform
   c. describe
   d. persuade
   e. give factual information
2. With which of the following statements do you think the author would probably agree?
   a. It is interesting and worthwhile to think about different points of view.
   b. Flatland is a real place.
   c. Mathematics has nothing to do with fantasy.
   d. Mathematics can be fun.
   e. It is a waste of time to think about places that do not even exist.

WRITING ACTIVITY

MATHEMATICS PROBLEM

Prewrite

Mathematics is an important part of your daily life. The selections in this unit show how mathematics can help you solve fanciful as well as practical problems.

Solving word problems is an important part of many of your math lessons. Suppose you were a writer of a mathematics textbook. Your assignment is to write word problems that involve the operations of addition, subtraction, multiplication, and division.

A word problem is a little like a one-paragraph short story. The problem has characters and a setting. The main idea of the plot is the math question to be answered. The details of the plot are the facts that help solve the problem. Some facts are necessary for solving the problem and some are not.

You are going to write two word problems. Choose information from the list below to use in writing one problem. For the second problem, develop your own information and then write the problem.

MATH OPERATIONS: Addition, Subtraction, Multiplication, Division
CHARACTERS: Matt and Beth SETTING: Movies on Saturday
FACTS: Matt has $10.00
Bargain Showtime tickets: $2.00 each
Regular Show tickets: $4.50 each
Popcorn: $.75 per box Drinks: $.50 per drink
Bus fare: $.65 per person, one way
MAIN IDEA: Find how much money Matt has left.

Write

These steps can be helpful in writing both word problems.

1. Write a sentence introducing the characters, the setting, and what the characters are doing. Here is an example:

   > Matt asked Beth to go to the Bargain
   > Showtime at the movies on Saturday.

2. Now write detail sentences that give the facts in the problem.
3. Write the main idea of the problem as a question.
4. Now write the first draft of your word problem.

Revise

Read your word problems. Have a friend read and solve them, too. Think about this checklist as you revise.

1. Did you include the facts that were necessary for solving the problem?
2. Did you include some facts that were not necessary for solving the problem so your reader had to think carefully?
3. Would your reader know exactly what solution the problem called for by reading the main idea question? If not, rewrite your question.
4. Did you use the operations of addition, subtraction, multiplication, or division in both problems? You could use one operation or a combination.
5. Check the numbers in your facts after you rewrite to make sure you made no changes.
6. Now rewrite your word problems to share.

SKILLS ACTIVITY

GENERALIZATIONS

A **generalization** is a general statement reached as a conclusion. Generalizations are based on many facts, or particular examples. In making a generalization, you identify all the facts. Then you evaluate those facts and form a general, or broad, statement that you believe tells the most important ideas.

In "Life in Flatland," you were told that soldiers were straight lines, farmers were isosceles triangles, merchants and shopkeepers were equilateral triangles, doctors and lawyers were squares or pentagons, and so on. You could use these specific examples to make this generalization: *The people in Flatland have particular shapes according to the kind of work they do.*

A generalization based on facts or evidence is said to be valid. A valid generalization is supported by many specific facts, or details. Sometimes people make generalizations that are *not* supported by facts or details. Such generalizations are said to be invalid.

There are very few times when you know all the details about a particular subject. Therefore, it's a good idea to avoid such words as *all*, *every*, *always*, and *never* when making a generalization. Remember that generalizations, like rules, usually have exceptions. For example, there are hundreds of kinds of mammals that bear living young. However there are a few kinds that lay eggs. Therefore, a valid generalization based on this information would be *Most mammals bear living young.*

ACTIVITY Read the paragraphs below. Then choose the generalization that is supported by the information.

1. What would we do without paper? Books, newspapers, and magazines are printed on paper. We use paper to write letters and notes. And think of all the paper you use in your school work! Then there are paper towels and paper napkins, and even paper tablecloths. Some people wear clothing made of paper. What would a party be without paper favors and decorations? We use paper to wrap packages and to cover walls. You can probably think of dozens of other uses for paper.

   a. Paper has many uses.
   b. The most important use of paper is in printing.
   c. People use too much paper.

2. Augusta Stance has written a dozen books about "geometric people." More than 100,000 copies of each of the books have been sold, and two have had sales of more than 200,000 copies. Three books—*Isosceles Island*, *Planet Pentagon*, and *Cube Country*—were awarded the Hunicutt Literary Award in three successive years. Several of the books have been made into movies. Mrs. Stance often lectures on her books to large audiences. She has also helped organize many writing conferences.

   a. Mrs. Stance is a very good writer.
   b. Most people like Mrs. Stance's books.
   c. Mrs. Stance is a successful author.

Stonehenge (below) may have been an astronomical calendar.

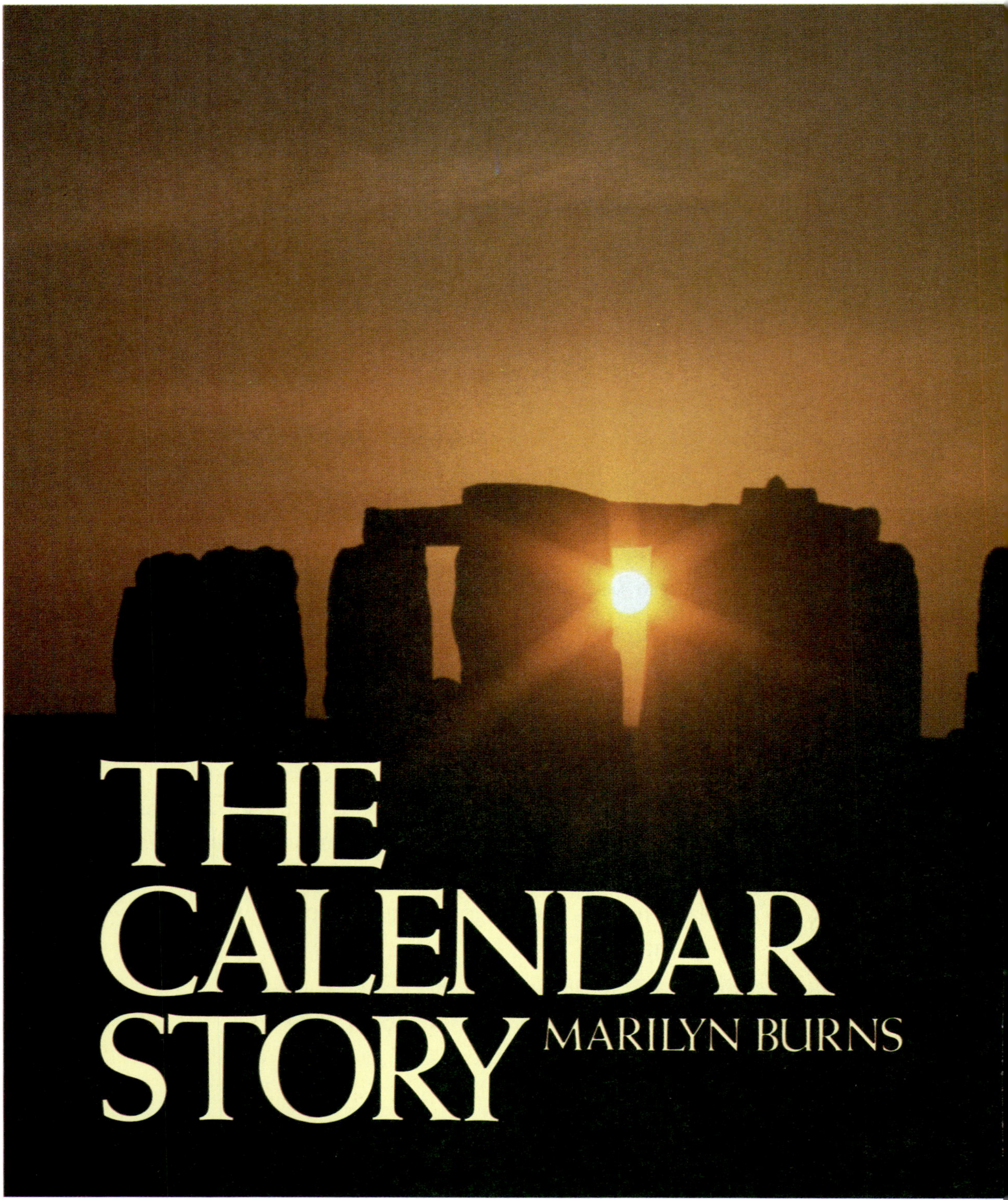

THE CALENDAR STORY

MARILYN BURNS

The days and weeks and seasons go by, year after year. Did you ever wonder how people began keeping track of time?

People had some specific needs for keeping track of time thousands of years ago. They needed to know when it was time to plant seeds. They needed to know when certain religious holidays came. These needs sparked the search for an organized calendar, but how did people start this search?

There were clues that people in ancient times found around them. The sun was one clue. It was a reliable way of watching time. People counted off the days by suns. But that didn't help tell which day was the one to get out and start the year's planting or which was the right day for a religious holiday.

Then there was the moon. That was another reliable clue. People noticed that the cycle of change from a new moon to full moon and back to new moon was a regular occurrence. When they counted the days, they learned that the sun appeared twenty-nine times between one full moon and the next.

They counted again. This time it took thirty days for the full moon to come around again. After checking this out, they found that the moon's phases averaged about twenty-nine and a half days. Now that's not such a convenient number for calendar making, but it was a start. It's not the same length of time as the months used today, but it's pretty close. Maybe the twenty-nine and a half days of the moon's cycle should be called a "moonth." But they're not—they're called a *lunar month*.

The ancient Babylonians set up a calendar using these lunar months. Their system got them in timekeeping trouble. Their year had twelve lunar months, which adds up to 354 days. They didn't know about the 365 days it takes for the earth to make a complete trip around the sun. So when they picked the month to do the planting, next year that same month came about a little earlier according to the season. If they continued this several years, they'd be out there in the middle of winter trying to turn the soil.

The ancient Babylonian calendar (left), made of dried clay, shows the days between new moons.

The Babylonians noticed this error and they fixed it. They just added some extra days to their calendar to avoid that catastrophe. Adding extra time like that to a calendar is called *intercalation*. That's what's done today when an extra day is added on to leap years.

The months are shown as Egyptian gods in this ancient Egyptian calendar from the tomb of a pharaoh.

The ancient Egyptians used a different clue when they designed their calendar. They noticed that the stars moved across the night sky in a regular pattern. The brightest star you can see is called Sirius, and that's the one they focused on. The Egyptian astronomers would watch for the time each year when Sirius first appeared on the horizon in the morning.

They knew that happened every 365 days. They also knew that the appearance of Sirius meant the floods were on their way and that planting could begin soon after. They marked the beginning of a new year with the reappearance of Sirius.

They divided the year into twelve 30-day months. That made 360 days. Then they tacked on five extra days at the

This Aztec calendar stone (left) was used in ceremonies honoring the sun god. At right, a Mayan calendar stone.

end of the year to make 365. Those were feast days to celebrate the birthdays of five gods.

The Egyptian calendar hit a snag, though. Every fourth year, Sirius appeared one day late. That's because the year is really 365 1/4 days long. The Egyptian astronomers knew this, and they predicted the flood correctly. But they never did change the calendar. So after many years, the calendar was way off base.

In Central America over two thousands years ago, the Mayas (mä′ yəz) had it all figured out. They made it their business not to get all confused about measuring time. Time was so important to their religion that they were careful enough to do it right.

They kept exact observations of the sun and the moon and the stars. Priest-astronomers kept separate records on each of these three time-telling guides in almanacs or on tall stone pillars. Then they would check the three different records against each other. That way they knew when their special religious days occurred and when to plant and harvest.

The Mayas divided their year into eighteen months, with 20 days in each month. That accounted for 360 days. They also added on five more days to make the 365 day year. They weren't holidays, though, like the Egyptian extra days were. These were considered to be bad luck days, kind of like having five Friday-the-13ths all in a row. The Mayas also figured out a clever formula for including that extra one-quarter of a day in their records. The Mayan calendar was more exact than the one you use today.

None of these calendar attempts had anything to do with the calendar we use today. Ours comes from the Roman calendar, though lots of changes have been made in it over the past twenty-five hundred years or so to get it where it is today.

The first Roman calendar was a lunar calendar. There were ten months: Martius, Aprilis, Maius, Junius, Quintilis, Sextilis, September, October, November, and December. Look familiar? What's missing, and what's different from today's calendar? Six of these months had thirty days; four of them (Martius, Maius, Quintilis, and October) had thirty-one days.

So the year added up to 304 days. That's 61 1/4 days short of a full year. The priests responsible for telling time knew about this shortage. They fixed it by not announcing the new year in Martius until it was the right time. Those extra days were there in the dead of winter when nothing much seemed to be happening anyway, so they just didn't count them.

King Numa was one of the leaders of ancient Rome. One thing he did during his reign was to try to fix the calendar. In about 712 B.C. he had two more months added to the calendar, just before Martius. They were called Januarius and Februarius. He also changed the lengths of some of the months.

It seems that even numbers were thought to be unlucky numbers to the Romans. So King Numa made all the 30-day months 29-day months. He also gave twenty-nine days to Januarius but made Februarius a 28-day month. Februarius was an odd-ball month even way back then. By giving Februarius twenty-eight days, he made the total number of days in the year an odd number instead of an even number. The year was now 355 days. That wasn't an unlucky number. It was just wrong. The King's calendar experts pointed this out to him. "Listen," they said, "we're short about 22 days every two years."

That didn't bother the King. His solution was intercalation. "So add an extra 22-day month every two years," he said. It seems that kings could do just about anything. But the experts weren't so expert. Those 22 days didn't make good calendar sense. They made each year 11 days longer, which brought it up to 366 days. Not good.

A medieval woodcut shows astronomers with their instruments studying the phases of the moon.

By the time Julius Caesar came into power, the calendar was a total mess. Not only was the plan wrong, but the priest-astronomers didn't even follow their plan regularly. It was a calendar disaster.

"Enough of this," was Julius Caesar's opinion. In the year 46 B.C., he decided to get this calendar back in line with the seasons and figure a way to keep it in line with the seasons. The new plan was called the

Below left, a detail from one of the earliest printed calendars showing dials used to figure the position of the sun and moon. Center, the month of September from a medieval calendar.

JANUARIUS	**31 DAYS**
FEBRUARIUS	**29 DAYS***
MARTIUS	**31 DAYS**
APRILIS	**30 DAYS**
MAIUS	**31 DAYS**
JUNIUS	**30 DAYS**
JULIUS	**31 DAYS**
SEXTILIS	**30 DAYS**
SEPTEMBER	**31 DAYS**
OCTOBER	**30 DAYS**
NOVEMBER	**31 DAYS**
DECEMBER	**30 DAYS**

except 30 every fourth year

Julian calendar. It had twelve months, starting with Januarius. The months were thirty or thirty-one days long. Except for Februarius, of course. An extra day was added every four years, just like today. What a relief. Caesar was proud of this reform. He was so proud that he made one more change. The name of the seventh month was changed from Quintilis to Julius. The chart above shows how the calendar stood.

Compare that with today's calendar. There are some differences in the lengths of the months, and there's one difference in the names of the months. Sextilis is now called August.

This is because of the next emperor after Julius Caesar. His name was Caesar Augustus. He wasn't going to get the short end of the calendar changing. Not only did a month get named after him, it got an extra day

This detail from the calendar on the previous page shows Virgo and Libra, constellations visible in the September sky.

added so his month had as many days as Julius Caesar's month did. The extra day was taken from Februarius, which seems to get pushed around a lot. In the shuffle, the days in the last four months were switched too.

All was fine for a long, long time—for over fifteen hundred years. Then a problem that had been building all those years demanded some attention. It turns out that the year really isn't exactly 365 1/4 days long. It's just a little bit shorter than that.

A 365 1/4-day year would be 365 days and six hours. But the actual year is only 365 days, five hours, forty-eight minutes and forty-six seconds long, give or take a bit. The Julian calendar year was a little over eleven minutes too long. And eleven minutes a year can add up. The calendar was out of whack with the seasons again.

In 1582 Pope Gregory XIII decided to get the calendar back in step. By that time, those eleven minutes a year had added up to ten days' worth. So Pope Gregory had ten days cut out of the calendar. He did this on October 4, 1582. On October 4, he just ripped ten days off the calendar instead of one. Then next came October 15, instead of October 5.

To stop this accumulation of days from happening again, Pope Gregory changed the leap-year rule. The rule had been that all the years that could be divided evenly by four were leap years. The new rule applied to all years except the century years: 1600, 1700, 1800, 1900, 2000, and so on. In order for those to be leap years, they have to be divisible by four hundred instead of by four. This eliminates some of them. Now this new calendar, the Gregorian calendar, is off by only twenty-six seconds a year, which means it will only go out of step one day every 3,323 years. That won't happen until the year 4905. Then the nearest leap day will have to be dropped.

It took some time for other countries to go along with Pope Gregory's changes. The Roman Catholic church countries all adopted it immediately, but the European Protestant countries didn't do so until the 1700s. By that time, the old Julian calendar was eleven days off instead of ten. That's because by Pope Gregory's leap year rule, 1700 didn't get an extra day because it can't be divided evenly by four hundred.

It was no easy switch in Great Britain. They waited until 1752 to make it. People were furious. "You're robbing us of time," some said. "We're going to lose almost two weeks rent," landlords complained. "We're losing wages," workers cried. A mob formed outside the Houses of Parliament shouting, "Give us back our eleven days! Give us back our eleven days!" But the change was made. After September 2, 1752, came September 14. And after a while, the fuss died down.

In 1752, Great Britain still controlled the American colonies, so the calendar change was made here too. Japan adopted it in 1873. China did in 1912. The Russians waited until 1918. Today, this is the calendar used for most business and daily dealings, even though other calendars are still used in various parts of the world. It's called the Gregorian calendar.

Thinking and Writing About the Selection

1. What did people in ancient times notice about the moon?
2. Why did the first Babylonian calendar have only 354 days?
3. Why do you think countries all over the world agreed to use the Gregorian calendar? What problems would result if they hadn't agreed?
4. If an American had created the calendar, what might the names of each of the months be?

Applying the Key Skill

Cause and Effect

Copy the chart below on your paper. Then use the information in "The Calendar Story" to complete the chart.

CAUSE	EFFECT
	The Egyptians added 5 days at the end of every year.
Time was important to the religion of the Mayas.	
	Numa told the astronomers to add an extra 22-day month every two years.
Julius Caesar wanted people to remember his contribution to the calendar.	
	In 4905, a day will be dropped from the calendar.

The Months

January cold and desolate;
February dripping wet;
March wind ranges;
Birds sing in tune
To flowers of May
And sunny June
Brings longest day;
In scorched July
The storm-clouds fly
Lightning-torn;
August bears corn,
September fruit;
In rough October
Earth must disrobe her;
Stars fall and shoot
In keen November;
And night is long
And cold is strong
In bleak December.

Christina G. Rossetti

THE LOST HALF-HOUR

HENRY BESTON

What happens to lost time? Bobo the simpleton found out when he set off to find the princess's lost half-hour.

Once upon a time there was an old widow woman who had three sons; the first two were clever enough, but the third, Bobo by name, was little better than a silly simpleton. All his mother's scoldings did him no good whatever.

Now it came to pass that one morning Princess Zenza, the ruler of the land, happened to pass by the cottage and heard Bobo being given a terrible tongue-lashing. Curious as to the cause of all the noise, the Princess drew rein and summoned Bobo's mother to come near. On hearing her story, it occurred to the Princess that so silly a lad might amuse her; so she gave the mother a golden florin and took poor silly Bobo with her to be her page.

You may be sure that it did not take the wise folk at the castle long to discover how great a simpleton had arrived. Courtiers, footmen, lackeys, turnspits even, were forever sending him off on ridiculous errands. Now he would be sent to find a white crow's feather or a spray of yellow bluebells; now he was ordered to look for a square wheel or a glass of dry water. Everybody laughed at him and made fun of him—that is, everybody except little Tilda, the kitchen maid. When poor Bobo used to return from some wild-goose chase, tired out, mud-stained, and often enough wet to the skin, instead of laughing, little Tilda would find him a glass of warm milk, hang his coat by the fire to dry, and tell him not to

be such a simpleton again. Thus, after a while, Bobo learned to ask Tilda's advice before going away on a wild-goose chase and was in this way saved from many a jest.

Tilda, the kitchen-maid, was as sweet and pretty as she was kind and good. She was said to be the daughter of an old crone who had come to the castle one day, asking for help.

One pleasant midsummer morning, when Bobo had been nearly a year at the castle, Princess Zenza overslept half an hour and did not come down to breakfast at the usual time. When she did get up, she found her court waiting for her in the castle gardens. As she came down the steps of the garden terrace, the Princess looked up at the castle clock to see how late she was and said to her lady in waiting—

"Dear me,—why I've lost half an hour this morning!"

At these words, Bobo, who was in attendance, pricked up his ears and said—

"Please Your Highness, perhaps I can find it."

At this idea of finding a lost half-hour, the Princess laughed and found herself echoed by the company.

"Shall we send Bobo in search of the lost half-hour?" said the Princess to the courtiers.

"Yes! Yes!" cried the courtiers. "Bobo shall look for the lost half-hour."

"I'll give him a horse," said one. "I'll give him my old hat," said another. "He can have an old sword I broke last week," said still another.

And so, in less time than it takes to tell about it, poor simpleton Bobo was made ready for his journey.

Before he left the castle, Bobo went down to the kitchen to say good-bye to Tilda.

"What, off again?" said the little kitchen-maid. "Where are you going now?"

"The Princess has lost a half-hour, and I am going in search of it," said Bobo proudly. And he told how the Princess herself had commanded him to seek the half-hour through the world, and promised to bring Tilda a splendid present when he returned.

The good kitchen-maid said little, for she feared lest some misadventure overtake the poor simpleton; but when the chief cook was not looking, she tucked a fresh currant-bun into Bobo's pocket and wished him the best of good fortune.

So Bobo went to the castle gate and mounted his old horse, which stumbled and was blind in one eye.

"Good-bye, Bobo," cried the assembled courtiers, who were almost beside themselves with laughter at the simpleton and his errand. "Don't fail to bring back the lost half-hour!"

So Bobo rode over the hills and far away. Every now and then he would stop a passer-by and ask him if he had seen a lost half-hour.

The first person whom he thus questioned was an old man who was wandering down the high road that leads from the Kingdom of the East to the Kingdom of the West.

"A lost half-hour?" said the old man. "I've lost something much more serious; I've lost my reputation. You haven't seen a lost reputation lying about here, have you? It was very dignified and wore tortoise-shell glasses."

But Bobo had to answer "No," and the old man wandered on again.

Another day the simpleton encountered a tall, fierce kind of fellow, who answered his polite question with a scream of rage.

"A half-hour," he roared. "No, I haven't seen your half-hour; I wouldn't tell you if I had; what's more, I don't want to see it. I'm looking for something I've lost myself. I've lost my temper. I lost it two years ago at home and haven't been able to find it anywhere since. Answer me, you silly; have you seen a lost temper anywhere? It's the size of a large melon and has sharp little points."

On Bobo's answering "No," this dreadful person uttered so awful a screech of rage that Bobo's horse took fright and ran away with him, and it was all that Bobo could do to rein him in three miles down the road.

Still farther along, Bobo came to Zizz, the capital city of the Kingdom of the Seven Brooks, and was taken before the King himself.

"A lost half-hour?" said the King. "No, I am quite sure it has not been seen in my dominions. Would you mind asking, as you go through the world, for news of my little daughter?" (Here the poor old King took out a great green handkerchief and wiped his eyes.) "She was stolen by the fairies on midsummer eve fifteen years ago. Find her, worthy Bobo, and an immense reward will be yours."

So Bobo left the proud city of Zizz and once again rode over the hills and far away. But never a sign of the lost half-hour did he find, although he asked thousands of people. His faithful white horse died, and he continued his way on foot.

Three long years passed, and Bobo grew into a handsome lad, but remained a simpleton still. Finally, after he had wandered all about Fairyland, he came to the edge of the sea. Finding a ship moored in a little harbor, Bobo asked the sailors if they had seen a lost half-hour.

"No," said the sailors, "but we are going to the Isles of Iron; suppose you go with us. The lost half-hour may be there."

So Bobo went aboard the ship and sailed out upon the dark sea.

For two days the weather was warm and clear, but on the third day, there came a dreadful storm, and on the third night the vessel was driven far off her course into the unknown ocean and was wrecked upon a mysterious island of rocks that shone in the night like wet matches. A great wave swept the decks, and Bobo was borne away from his companions and carried toward the shining land. Though pounded and battered by the foaming waves, the simpleton at length managed to reach the beach and took refuge in a crevice of the cliff during the night.

When the dawn broke, all sign of the ship had disappeared. Looking about, Bobo found himself on a lovely island whose heart was a high mountain mass hidden in the fog still sweeping in from the sea. There was not a house, a road, or a path to be seen. Suddenly Bobo noticed a strange little door in the bark of a great lonely tree, and opening this door, he discovered a little cupboard in which were a pair of wooden shoes. Above the shoes was a card, saying simply—

PUT US ON

So Bobo sat down on a stone by the foot of the tree and put on the wooden shoes, which fitted him very nicely. Now these shoes were magic shoes, and Bobo had hardly stepped into them before they turned his feet inland. So Bobo obediently let the shoes guide him. At corners the shoes always turned in the right direction, and if Bobo forgot and

blundered the wrong way, the shoes began to pinch his toes.

For two days Bobo walked inland toward the great mountain. A warm wind blew the clouds and rain away; the sun shone sweet and clear. On the morning of the third day, the simpleton entered a wood of tall silent trees, and as that day was drawing to a close, turrets of a magnificent castle rose far away over the leaves of the forest.

Bobo arrived at twilight.

He found himself in a beautiful garden, lying between the castle walls and the rising slopes of a great mountain. Strange to say, not a living creature was to be seen, and though there were lights in the castle, there was not even a warder at the gate. Suddenly a great booming bell struck seven o'clock; Bobo began to hear voices and sounds; and then, before the humming of the bell had died away, a youth mounted on a splendid black horse dashed at lightning speed out of the castle and disappeared in the wood. An old man with a white beard, accompanied by eleven young men—whom Bobo judged, from their expressions, to be brothers—stood by the gate to see the horseman ride away.

Plucking up courage, Bobo came forward, fell on his knees before the old man, and told his story.

"Truly you should thank the storm fairies," said the old man, "for had you not been wrecked upon this island, never would you have discovered the lost half-hour. I am Father Time himself, and these are my twelve sons, the Hours. Every day, one after the other, they ride for an hour round the whole wide world. Seven O'Clock has just ridden forth. Yes, you shall have the lost half-hour, but you must look after my sons' horses for the space of a whole year."

To this Bobo willingly agreed. So Twelve O'Clock, who was the youngest of the Hours, took him to the stables and showed him the little room in the turret that he was to have. And thus for a year Bobo served Father Time and his sons. He took such good care of the great black horses of the Hours of the Night, and the white horses of the Hours of the Day, that they were never more proud and strong, nor their coats smoother and more gleaming.

When the year was up, Bobo again sought out Father Time.

"You have served faithfully and well," said Father Time. "Here is your reward." And, with these words, he placed in Bobo's hands a small square casket made of ebony. "The half-hour lies inside. Don't try to peek at it or open the box until the right time has come. If you do, the half-hour will fly away and disappear forever."

"Farewell, Bobo," said kind young Twelve O'Clock, who had been the simpleton's good friend. "I, too, have a gift for thee. Drink this cup of water to the last drop." And the youth handed the simpleton a silver cup full to the brim of clear shining water.

Now this water was the water of wisdom, and when Bobo had drunk of it, he was no longer a simpleton. And being no longer a simpleton, he remembered the man who had lost his reputation, the man who had lost his temper, and the King whose daughter had been stolen by the fairies. So Bobo made so bold as to ask Father Time about them, for Father Time knows everything that has happened in the whole wide world.

"Tell the first," said Father Time, "that his reputation has been broken into a thousand pieces which have been picked up by his neighbors and carried

home. If he can persuade neighbors to give them up, he should be able to piece together a pretty good reputation again. As for the man who lost his temper, tell him that it is to be found in the grass by the roadside close by the spot where you first met him. As for the missing daughter, she is the kitchen-maid in Princess Zenza's palace who is known as Tilda."

So Bobo thanked Father Time, and at noon, Twelve O'Clock placed Bobo behind him on the white charger and hurried away. So fast did they fly that Bobo, who was holding the ebony casket close against his heart, was in great danger of falling off. When they got to the seashore, the white horse hesitated not an instant, but set foot upon the water, which bore him up as if it had been, not water, but earth itself. Once they arrived at the shore of Fairyland, Twelve O'Clock stopped, wished Bobo good-speed, and, rising in the air, disappeared into the glare of the noonday sun. Bobo, with the precious ebony casket in his hand, continued on foot in the direction of Princess Zenza's palace.

On the second morning of his journey, he happened to see far ahead of him on the highway the unfortunate aged man who had lost his reputation. To him therefore, Bobo repeated the counsel of Father Time and sent him hurrying home to his neighbors' houses. Of the man who had lost his temper, Bobo found no sign. In the grass by the roadside, however, he did find the lost temper—a queer sort of affair like a melon of fiery red with uneven spines and brittle thorns. Bobo, with great goodness of heart, took along this extraordinary object in the hope of finding its angry possessor and returning it to him.

Further on, the lad encountered Tilda's father, the unhappy King, and delivered his message. The joy of the monarch knew no bounds, and Bobo, the one-time simpleton, became on the spot Lord Bobo of the Sapphire Hills, Marquis of the Mountains of the Moon, Prince of the Valley of Golden Apples, and Lord Seneschal of the proud city of Zizz—in a word, the greatest nobleman in all Fairyland. Then, having got together a magnificent cohort of dukes, earls, and counts, all in splendid silks, and soldiers in shining armor, the delighted King rode off to claim his missing daughter from Princess Zenza.

So on they rode, the harnesses jingling, the bridle-bells ringing, and the breastplates of the armed men shining in the sun. After a week of almost constant progress (for the King was so anxious to see his beloved daughter that he would hardly give the cavalcade time to rest), they came to the frontiers of Princess Zenza's kingdom.

Strange to say, black mourning banners hung from the trees and every door which the travelers saw was likewise hung with black streamers. On the steps of one of the cottages sat an old woman, all alone and weeping with all her might.

"What *is* the matter, my good woman?" said the King.

"O sir," said the peasant woman, "evil days have fallen upon our unhappy kingdom. Three days ago a terrible dragon alighted in the gardens of the palace and sent word to Princess Zenza that if within three days she did not provide him with someone brave enough to go home with him and cook his meals and keep his cavern tidy, he would burn our fields with his fiery breath. Yet who, I ask you, would be housekeeper for a

dragon? Suppose he didn't like the puddings you made for him—why he might eat you up! All would have been lost had not a brave little kitchen-maid named Tilda volunteered to go. It is for her that we are mourning. At two o'clock she is to be carried off by the dragon. It is almost two now. Alas! Alas!"

Hardly were the words out of her mouth, when the town bell struck twice, solemnly and sadly.

"Quick, quick!" cried the King and Bobo in the same breath. "Let us hurry to the castle. We may save her yet."

But they knew in their hearts that they were too late and that poor Tilda had given herself to the dragon. And so it proved. In spite of his mad dash, Bobo, who had spurred on ahead, arrived exactly half an hour late. The monstrous dragon with Tilda in its claws was just a little smoky speck far down the southern sky. Princess Zenza and her court stood by wringing their jeweled hands.

Suddenly Bobo thought of the half-hour. He had arrived half an hour late, *but he could have that half-hour back again!* Things should be exactly as they were half an hour before.

He opened the cover of the ebony box. Something like a winged white flame escaped from it and flew hissing through the air to the sun. As for the sun itself, turning round like a cart-wheel and hissing like ten thousand rockets, it rolled back along the sky to the east. The hands of the clocks, which marked half-past two, whirred back to two o'clock in a twinkling. And, sure enough, there was brave little Tilda standing alone in a great field waiting for the dragon to come and take her away. Lumbering along like a monstrous turtle and snorting

blue smoke, the dragon was advancing toward her.

Bobo ran down into the field and stood beside Tilda, ready to defend her to the end.

The dragon came nearer and nearer. Suddenly, angered by the sight of Bobo and his drawn sword, he roared angrily but continued to approach. Bobo struck at him with his sword. The blade broke upon his steely scales. The dragon roared again. Now just as the dragon's mouth was its widest, Bobo, who had been searching his pockets desperately, hurled into it *the lost temper*.

There was a perfectly terrific bang! as if a million balloons had blown up all at once, for the dragon had blown up. The lost temper had finished him. Only one fragment of him, a tiny bit of a claw, was ever found.

Everybody, you may be sure, began to cry "Hurrah" and "Hooray," and soon they were firing off cannon and ringing all the bells. Then Tilda's father took her in his arms and told her that she was a real Princess. The Grand Cross of the Order of the Black Cat was conferred upon Bobo by Princess Zenza, who also asked his pardon for having treated him so shabbily. This Bobo gave readily. A wonderful fete was held. When the rejoicings were over, Bobo and Tilda were married and lived happily together all their days.

Thinking and Writing About the Selection

1. How did Tilda help Bobo? Why did he need her help?
2. What events led to Bobo's meeting with Father Time?
3. Why would Twelve O'Clock be the youngest of the Hours?
4. If you could convince Father Time to grant you a favor, what would it be? Would you ask to go back in time or to go forward? Why?

Applying the Key Skill
Context Clues

Find the following words in "The Lost Half-Hour." List the words, phrases, or other context clues that helped you to figure out the meaning of each word. Then write a definition of the word.

a. simpleton b. florin
c. courtiers d. dominions
e. moored f. turret
g. casket h. fete

**The clock
on the bookcase ticks,
the watch on the table ticks—
these busy insects
are eating away my world.**

Charles Reznikoff

LANGUAGE ACTIVITY

TIME OUT

Although a day is 24 hours long, we usually divide it into two 12-hour periods. The hours from midnight to noon are designated A.M., those from noon to midnight as P.M. **A.M.** is the abbreviation for *ante* ("before") *meridian;* **P.M.** is the abbreviation for *post* ("after") *meridian.* **Meridian** is an old word for "noon" (from Latin *medius,* "middle" + *dies,* "day").

Because of the earth's rotation, the sun is always directly overhead somewhere—it is noon there. Can you imagine how confusing it would be if every place kept "sun time," or local time? To avoid this confusion, 24 standard time zones (corresponding to the 24 hours in a day) were established throughout the world in 1884. The boundaries of the time zones coincide closely with every 15° of longitude (the earth rotates through 15° of longitude in one hour). Lines of longitude are also called meridians—do you know why? They are numbered in degrees up to 180° east and west of the 0° meridian.

The 0° meridian, which passes through Greenwich, England, is called the **prime** ("first") **meridian.** Because the time at Greenwich is used for calculating time throughout most of the world, the time there is called **Greenwich mean time.**

Princess Zenza lost a half-hour. Can you see that you can lose or gain an hour just by crossing a time zone boundary?

SKILLS ACTIVITY

CAUSE AND EFFECT

To understand what you read, you should try to think about how things are related. One way in which things are related is called cause and effect. A **cause** is the reason something happens. An **effect** is the result or the thing that happens. The sentence below is an example of a cause-and-effect relationship.

> Because she was curious about the noise, the Princess summoned Bobo's mother to come near.

The part of the sentence that states the cause is underlined once. The part that states the effect is underlined twice. It is easy to understand how the parts of this sentence are related because the signal word *because* is used to introduce the cause. Other words that signal a cause-and-effect relationship are *so*, *so that*, *in order to*, and *as a result*.

Writers do not always use signal words. You must figure out relationships by thinking about how two events are connected. Ask yourself, "What happened?" The answer is the effect. Then ask yourself, "Why did it happen?" The answer is the cause. See if you can figure out the cause-and-effect relationship between the sentences below.

> Bobo learned to ask Tilda's advice before going on a wild-goose chase.
>
> He was saved from many a jest.

ACTIVITY A Copy the sentences below on your paper. Draw one line under the cause. Draw two lines under the effect.

1. The dreadful person uttered so awful a screech of rage that Bobo's horse took fright and ran away with him.
2. A great wave swept the decks, and Bobo was borne away from his companions.

Sometimes there is more than one cause for an effect. There can also be more than one effect of a single cause.

ACTIVITY B

1. On your paper, write two effects of the underlined cause.

   Suddenly Bobo thought of the half-hour. He had arrived half an hour late, but he could have that half-hour back again! Things could be exactly as they were half an hour before. He opened the cover of the ebony box. Something like a winged white flame escaped from it and went hissing through the air to the sun. As for the sun itself, it rolled back along the sky to the east. The hands of the clocks, which marked half-past two, whirred back to two o'clock in a twinkling. And, sure enough, there was brave little Tilda standing alone in a great field waiting for the dragon to come and take her away.

2. On your paper, write two causes of the underlined effect.

   For two days the weather was warm and clear, but on the third day, there came a dreadful storm. The wind lashed furiously at the sails. Great waves beat against the sides of the ship. The little vessel was driven far off her course into the unknown ocean.

EINSTEIN'S IDEAS

DAVID E. FISHER

Albert Einstein is considered to be one of the greatest scientists of the twentieth century. His ideas about light, speed, and time have changed the way we view our world.

When Albert Einstein was a young boy, he wondered about a very simple question: What is light? No one could give him an answer that would satisfy him. He thought about it so much in school that his teachers became angry. Whenever the rest of the class was studying history or singing or learning grammar, Albert was staring out the window daydreaming.

"Albert! What are you doing now?"

"I was looking at the sunlight. I was wondering, what if I could ride along on that sunbeam, go just as fast as it is going—"

"Albert! Such nonsense! You must learn to concentrate on your lessons!"

But he never did. As he grew up, as he passed through his teenage years and into adulthood, he kept thinking about that question.

During Einstein's childhood, other scientists had begun to think about similar questions. When Einstein was eight years old, two American scientists, Albert Michelson and Edward Morley, did an experiment to actually measure the speed of light.

They bounced a beam of light back and forth between two mirrors and measured how long it took to go the distance between the mirrors. From this they could calculate how fast the light was traveling: its speed. They found that light moves at exactly 186,283 miles per second (or 299,793 kilometers per second). They found that it *always* moves at this speed, even if they themselves were moving along in the same direction as the beam of light or in the opposite direction.

Now, this is very strange. Nothing else moves in this manner. Everything else moves with a speed that depends on the motion of the observer, the person watching. Think of it this way:

Suppose you were standing next to a railroad track and a train came whizzing by. Suppose you knew that the length of a railroad car was exactly 50 feet, and suppose that you wanted to measure how fast it was going, how would you do it?

You would simply measure the time it took for one railroad car to pass you. If it took exactly one-half of a second (that is, one-half second between the time the front of the car passed you and the rear of the car passed you), the train would be moving at a speed of 50 feet every half-second, which is 100 feet every second, right? Then you could figure out that that meant the train had a speed of 68 miles per hour.

100 feet per second is 6,000 feet per minute:

$$100 \times 60 = 6{,}000$$

6,000 feet per minute is 360,000 feet per hour:

$$6{,}000 \times 60 = 360{,}000$$

Since there are 5,280 feet in a mile, 360,000 feet per hour is 68 miles per hour:

$$360{,}000 \div 5{,}280 = 68$$

Now, just to make sure you understand all that, figure out how fast the train would be going if it took one second for the railroad car to pass you. (Answer: 34 miles per hour.)

Now suppose you were to do the same experiment while driving along in a car on a road next to the railroad track. Suppose you were driving the car at 34 miles per hour. If you were going in the same direction as the train, which is going at 68 miles per hour, how long would it take for each railroad car to pass you?

If you think about it (or if you get someone to take you for a ride and try it), you will see that it takes each car twice as long to pass you; it will take one second instead of one-half second. So you must say that *compared to you* the train is only going 34 miles per hour, although compared to the street or the railroad tracks it is still going 68 miles per hour.

But what is the *real* speed of the railroad train? You might be tempted to say that the real speed is 68 miles per hour, but if you are, try to resist that temptation. Because you would be wrong.

What if there were a man on Mars looking at the train through a telescope? He would agree that it was going 34 miles per hour relative to you in your car or 68 miles per hour relative to the earth, but he can see that the earth itself is zooming around the sun at a speed at 67,000 miles per hour. So, relative to the sun, the train is zipping along at 67,068 miles per hour (if it is moving in the same direction as the earth). And compared to himself on Mars, which is itself speeding around the sun at 54,000 miles per hour, the train would be moving at a speed of—well, you

see it gets very complicated. And even if you went ahead and figured that out, what if the train were also being observed by somebody standing on Venus? Or Saturn? Or in a spaceship?

All of these people would measure different speeds for the train *relative to themselves*. How could they agree on which is the *real* speed?

So Einstein said there is no such thing as a real speed: all motion is relative. By this he meant that the speed of anything is relative to the person making the measurement. Different people who measure the speed of the train—the person standing near the track, the person in the car, and so on—will get different speeds, and none is the "real" speed.

Now Einstein came back to the question of light. What would happen if you did the same kind of experiment with a beam of light? Suppose you go with your friend Bill to an empty field in the middle of the night. You each have a watch, and each watch is set to exactly the same time. Then you leave Bill there in the middle of the field and you measure off a certain distance; let's say you measured off exactly 186,283 miles (or 299,793 kilometers) from him. Then, at exactly midnight, you shine a flashlight at him. If the speed of light is really constant with a value of 186,283 miles per second, as Michelson and Morley claimed, your friend would see the flash of light exactly one second later, at one second past midnight.

But suppose Bill has a twin sister. And his twin sister, Sandy, owns a rocket ship! And suppose that Sandy's rocket ship could whiz along at a speed of 186,283 miles per second.

Now let's do the experiment again, but this time, when you shine your flashlight at Bill, Sandy will zoom off in her rocket ship from you to him. How long will it take her to go from you to Bill?

If she is traveling 186,283 miles per second, that means that in one second she will travel 186,283 miles, right? And since Bill is standing 186,283 miles away, it will take her exactly one second to get there.

Now, what if Sandy had also measured the speed of the light beam from your flashlight? Wouldn't she find that relative to herself it hadn't moved at all? (Since both she and the beam of light started together at you and finished together at Bill.)

That would mean that relative to her the speed of light was zero. But Michelson and Morley proved that the speed of light is always the same for everybody! So what *would* happen if Sandy measured the speed of the beam of light?

Einstein couldn't actually do the experiment, and neither could anyone else, because nobody really has a rocket ship that can go 186,283 miles per second. Our fastest jets and rockets can't go anywhere near that fast. But Einstein could *think* about it. He could think about what would happen if we really had a rocket ship that could go as fast as light.

And so he sat there and thought about it. He thought about it and wondered about it, and so did the world's greatest physicists in every country on earth. None of them could figure out what would happen. Finally Einstein suggested that perhaps there is no solution to this problem. Perhaps they should stop worrying about it and instead start over in thinking about the laws of motion.

But where should they start? Well, what did they actually *know*? They knew that ordinary motion, like the speed of an automobile or a jet or a train, is relative to whomever is observing it. They also knew that the Michelson-Morley experiment showed that the speed of light is *not* relative, but is *absolute*: it is always 186,283 miles per second. Perhaps we should just accept those two statements as basic truths, and go on from there.

And that is what Einstein did. He said that there are two rules for motion. Rule #1: All motion is relative. Rule #2: *Except* the speed of light, which is absolute and always constant.

How did this explain anything? If Einstein were right, then the beam of light from your flashlight would still reach Bill at exactly one second past midnight, and so would Sandy in her rocket ship. But now Sandy in her rocket ship would say that *relative to her* the light was still moving at the same speed! And if the light were moving ahead faster than she was, then certainly it would have had to reach Bill before she did!

But Bill would say: "No, the light and Sandy both reached me at the same time."

Who would be right? Would the light reach Bill at the same time or before her? It couldn't do *both*!

Or could it?

Actually, Einstein said that this question has no "real" answer—that the question of when the light reaches Bill has *different* answers. Sandy's answer is that the light reaches Bill first, and Bill's answer is that both the light and Sandy reach him at the same time—and they're both right!

How can that be? Because, Einstein explained, the very nature of space and time are changed when Sandy—or anyone else—travels at speeds near the speed of light. Space and time are not "real," as we always thought, but instead they are *relative* to different people moving at different speeds.

But then what *is* "real"? Is *anything* real? When Einstein finally found the answer to that question, he changed our whole world.

THE THEORY OF RELATIVITY

Einstein thought and thought about this problem for a long time. If the speed of light is 186,283 miles per second for everyone, then Sandy and the beam of light could not arrive at Bill at the same time: because that would mean that *relative to Sandy* the beam of light hadn't moved. But *relative to Bill* both Sandy and the beam of light were moving with the same speed, so they'd *have* to get there at the same time! This was certainly a puzzle.

Finally Einstein was forced to accept the conclusion that if the world around us really behaved the way we thought it did, his two rules were impossible. The speed of light could *not* be constant for everybody. But Michelson and Morley had proven that it was!

Slowly he began to wonder if perhaps the world is *not* the way we think it is. Perhaps all the rules of space and time and speed should be changed. Perhaps he could discover a whole new set of laws or rules which would allow his two rules to be possible. This was an exciting thought!

At this time he was a clerk in the patent office in Berne, a lovely little town in Switzerland. Every day, when he had finished his work, he would sit and think about this problem.

Finally, after years of struggling, he came upon the solution. And once he did, our world was never the same again.

Einstein solved the problem by using mathematics. He realized that mathematics may be hard to learn, but once you learn it, it's really useful for solving problems because it always gives you the right answer. Always.

For example, once you learn that one plus one is two, you know that one anything plus one anything is *always* two anythings. If someone asks you how many apples are one apple plus one apple, you don't have to ask if the apples are red or green or fresh or rotten. You know the answer: two apples.

So Einstein decided he would use mathematics to try to answer his tough problem. In his spare time after work he studied more and more mathematics, and finally, after years of struggling, he came upon the solution.

He called his solution the *theory of relativity*. He called it that because he found that, except for the constant speed of light, all other motion is relative to whoever is measuring. Except for light, there is no such thing as *real* motion.

Then he said that time and space are relative too!

But what does that mean?

It means that in the experiment, when you and Bill were standing in the field in the middle of the night, you both agreed that it took the beam of light from your flashlight one second to travel the measured distance. But according to Einstein's theory, Sandy, in her rocket ship, would agree with nothing except that the speed of light was constant! She would say that it took much less than one second for her trip, and that the distance was much less than 186,283 miles. That is because her space and time are different from yours! And if you checked her watch, you would find that it no longer agreed with yours, even though you had set them together just before the experiment. And as she zipped past you, you would say that her whole rocket ship looked shorter than it did when it was sitting on the ground!

Hey, what's going on?!

What's going on, Einstein explained, is that time and space behaved differently for Sandy because she was in motion. The behavior of time and space is not *real* (he used the word *absolute*) but *relative*.

What does that mean? Well, you already know that some things are *relative*. Wind, for example: if you are standing still on a calm day you feel no wind, but if you run down the street you will feel a breeze on your face. The question of whether or not there is a wind depends on whether you are standing still or are in motion: there is *no absolute* answer to that question. The answer is relative. And don't forget, the faster you are in motion, the greater the wind.

Other things are *absolute*, like rain: it doesn't matter whether you are standing still outside or running around. If it's raining you are going to get wet. The question whether or not it's raining does not depend on your motion. It is not *relative*.

Einstein's mathematics now told us that time and space, which we had always believed were *absolute* (like the rain), were in fact *relative* (like the wind): their effect on us depends on whether or not we are in motion, and how fast we are going. For example, since time is relative, people don't get older at the same rate. Sandy in the rocket ship—or any person in motion—would not get older as fast as you and Bill standing still on the ground!

This result of relativity—that time is not real but is relative—is called *time dilatation*: it says that time flows more slowly for a person in motion, so that all his clocks and calendars run slow, and therefore he will get older more slowly.

Let's take the twins Bill and Sandy again. Bill stays on earth while Sandy goes off in her rocket ship to the stars. If the rocket ship travels at 99.99 percent the speed of light, and if the rocket trip to the stars and back takes fifty years, do you know what will happen when Sandy comes home? Bill will be fifty years older, of course. But Sandy will still be a little kid! She'll only be half a year older than when she started!

In fact, Einstein said her clocks on the rocket ship (and her calendar) will have told her that the trip took only six months. Unless she knows all about Einstein's theory of relativity, she would be shocked that her twin brother Bill—and *everyone* on earth—is so much older.

Sounds silly, doesn't it? If your father were forty years old and you were ten, and if he went on such a trip, when he came back he would still be forty years old but you would be sixty! You'd be older than your own father!

But is it really so silly, Einstein asked? It *sounds* silly, but do we *know* that it is silly? The only way to know for

sure is to do the experiment—fly off in a rocket ship—and see what happens. The problem is that the rocket ship has to go at nearly the speed of light, and we can't yet make anything that will fly that fast.

Einstein suggested time dilatation in 1905. It was not possible to test it by experiment then. But by 1971, nearly seventy years later, scientists had learned to make atomic clocks that could measure time accurately to a few billionths of a second, and with such accurate clocks they were able to test Einstein's idea. One of the clocks they set on the ground at the U.S. Naval Observatory, and the other they flew around the world on a jet airliner at a speed of about 600 miles per hour. Now 600 miles per hour is nowhere near as fast as the speed of light, but it's fast enough that if Einstein was correct they should see a very small effect. If Einstein was right, when the two clocks came back together again at the Naval Observatory (after one of them had flown around the world) they would no longer show the same time. Their times should be different by a few billionths of a second.

And when the scientists looked, the clocks *were* different. By a few billionths of a second!

They could calculate that this change meant that, if the clock had been traveling at a speed 99.99 percent the speed of light, when fifty years had gone by on earth only a half year would have gone by for the traveling clock.

Einstein's theory of relativity was correct!

Thinking and Writing About the Selection

1. What is the speed of light? How was it calculated?
2. Why did Einstein say that all motion is relative?
3. How did the 1971 experiments involving two clocks prove that Einstein's theory of relativity was correct even though the jet airliner did not go at a speed even close to the speed of light?
4. After reading "Einstein's Ideas," have any of your ideas about things changed? Explain your answer.

Applying the Key Skill

Cause and Effect

Choose or provide the answers to the following questions about cause-and-effect relationships in "Einstein's Ideas."

1. Why would an observer on Mars say that relative to the sun, a person who is sitting quietly in a chair on the Earth is moving at a speed of 67,000 miles per hour?
2. The speed of light on a rocket traveling at 1,000 miles per hour is ____.
   a. the same as the speed of light to a person moving in a jet-propelled cart at 1,000 miles per hour
   b. the same as the speed of light to someone who is not moving
   c. the same as the speed of light anywhere
   d. greater than the speed of light on a rocket that is not moving
3. To an observer standing by the side of the road, a jet-propelled car that zooms by at tremendous speed looks ____.
   a. longer than it would if it were standing still
   b. shorter than it would if it were standing still
   c. the same length it looks moving at any speed
   d. the same length it would if it were standing still

MADELEINE L' ENGLE

A WRINKLE IN TIME

AWARD CLASSICS WINNERS

Meg Murry's father, a prominent physicist, had been doing secret government research when he mysteriously disappeared. For several years his family had no word from him. Then Meg Murry and her five-year-old brother, Charles Wallace, met a strange trio—Mrs. Whatsit, Mrs. Which, and Mrs. Who. The women told them that their father was being held prisoner on the distant planet of Camazotz and that only they could rescue him. The children had to travel to Camazotz by means of a tesseract—a fifth dimension which reduces the distance between two points by creating a "wrinkle" in time.

Meg, Charles Wallace, and their friend Calvin O'Keefe reached Camazotz with their three strange companions. Then the children went on alone. Meg was able to rescue her father from the CENTRAL Central Intelligence building, headquarters of IT, the Power of Darkness which controls all minds on Camazotz. But Charles Wallace fell under IT's power, and became another of IT's robot-like followers. Just before Meg could be sucked into IT's power, Mr. Murry tessered them away. Charles Wallace was left behind, his mind under the control of IT.

Mr. Murry, Meg, and Calvin escaped to the friendly planet Ixchel, inhabited by tall, tentacled, furry creatures. As they passed through the Black Thing (the cloud of evil that surrounds Camazotz), Meg was injured. One of the creatures nursed her back to health, however, and Meg nicknamed her Aunt Beast.

As the group met to decide how to rescue Charles Wallace, Mrs. Whatsit, Mrs. Who, and Mrs. Which reappeared.

Meg could see nothing, but she felt her heart pounding with hope. With one accord all the beasts rose to their feet, turned toward one of the arched openings, and bowed their heads and tentacles in greeting. Mrs. Whatsit appeared, standing between two columns. Beside her came Mrs. Who, behind them a quivering of light. The three of them were somehow not quite the same as they had been when Meg had first seen them. Their outlines seemed blurred; colors ran together as in a wet watercolor painting. But they were there; they were recognizable; they were themselves.

Meg pulled herself away from Aunt Beast, jumped to the floor, and rushed at Mrs. Whatsit. But Mrs. Whatsit held up a warning hand and Meg realized that she was not completely materialized, that she was light and not substance, and embracing her now would have been like trying to hug a sunbeam.

"We had to hurry so there wasn't quite time. . . .You wanted us?" Mrs. Whatsit asked.

The tallest of the beasts bowed again and took a step away from the table and towards Mrs. Whatsit. "It is a question of the little boy."

"Father left him!" Meg cried. "He left him on Camazotz!"

Appallingly, Mrs. Whatsit's voice was cold. "And what do you expect us to do?"

Meg pressed her knuckles against her teeth so that her braces cut her skin. Then she flung out her arms pleadingly. "But it's Charles Wallace! IT has him, Mrs. Whatsit! Save him, please save him!"

"You know that we can do nothing on Camazotz," Mrs. Whatsit said, her voice still cold.

"You mean you'll let Charles be caught by IT forever?" Meg's voice rose shrilly.

"Did I say that?"

"But we can't do anything! You know we can't! We tried! Mrs. Whatsit, you have to save him!"

"Meg, this is not our way," Mrs. Whatsit said sadly. "I thought you would know that this is not our way."

Mr. Murry took a step forward and bowed, and to Meg's amazement the three ladies bowed back to him. "I don't believe we've been introduced," Mrs. Whatsit said.

"It's Father, you know it's Father," Meg's angry impatience grew. "Father—Mrs. Whatsit, Mrs. Who, and Mrs. Which."

"I'm very glad to—" Mr. Murry mumbled, then went on. "I'm sorry, my glasses are broken, and I can't see you very well."

"It's not necessary to see us," Mrs. Whatsit said.

"If you could teach me enough more about the tesseract so that I could get back to Camazotz—"

"Wwhat tthenn?" came Mrs. Which's surprising voice.

"I will try to take my child away from IT."

"Annd yyou kknoww tthatt yyou wwill nnott ssucceeedd?"

"There's nothing left except to try."

Mrs. Whatsit spoke gently. "I'm sorry. We cannot allow you to go."

"Then let me," Calvin suggested. "I almost got him away before."

Mrs. Whatsit shook her head. "No, Calvin. Charles has gone even deeper into IT. You will not be permitted to throw yourself in with him, for that, you must realize, is what would happen."

There was a long silence. All the soft rays filtering into the great hall seemed to concentrate on Mrs. Whatsit, Mrs. Who, and the faint light that must be Mrs. Which. No one spoke. One of the beasts moved a tendril slowly back and forth across the stone table top. At last Meg could stand it no longer and she cried out despairingly, "Then what are you going to do? Are you just going to throw Charles away?"

Mrs. Which's voice rolled formidably across the hall. "Ssilencce, cchilldd!"

But Meg could not be silent. She pressed close against Aunt Beast, but Aunt Beast did not put the protecting tentacles around her. "*I* can't go!" Meg cried. "I can't! You know I can't!"

"Ddidd annybbodyy asskk yyou ttoo?" The grim voice made Meg's skin prickle into gooseflesh.

She burst into tears. She started beating at Aunt Beast like a small child having a tantrum. Her tears rained down her face and spattered Aunt Beast's fur. Aunt Beast stood quietly against the assault.

"All right, I'll go!" Meg sobbed. "I know you want me to go!"

"We want nothing from you that you do without grace," Mrs. Whatsit said, "or that you do without understanding."

Meg's tears stopped as abruptly as they had started. "But I do understand." She felt tired and unexpectedly peaceful. Now the coldness that, under Aunt Beast's ministrations, had left her body had also left her mind. She looked toward her father and her confused anger was gone and she felt only love and pride. She smiled at him, asking forgiveness, and then pressed up against Aunt Beast. This time Aunt Beast's arm went around her.

Mrs. Which's voice was grave. "Wwhatt ddoo yyou unnddderrsstanndd?"

"That it has to be me. It can't be anyone else. I don't understand Charles, but he understands me. I'm the one who's closest to him. Father's been away for so long, since Charles Wallace was a baby. They don't know each other. And Calvin's only known Charles for such a little time. If it had been longer then he would have been the one, but—oh, I see, I see, I understand, it has to be me. There isn't anyone else."

Mr. Murry, who had been sitting, his elbows on his knees, his chin on his fists, rose. "I will not allow it!"

"Wwhyy?" Mrs. Which demanded.

"Look, I don't know what or who you are, and at this point I don't care. I will not allow my daughter to go alone into this danger."

"Wwhyy?"

"You know what the outcome will probably be! And she's weak, now, weaker than she was before. She was almost killed by the Black Thing. I fail to understand how you can even consider such a thing."

Calvin jumped down. "Maybe IT's right about you! Or maybe you're in league with IT. *I'm* the one to go if anybody goes! Why did you bring me along at all? To take care of Meg! You said so yourself!"

"But you have done that," Mrs. Whatsit assured him.

"I haven't done anything!" Calvin shouted. "You

can't send Meg! I won't allow it! I'll put my foot down! I won't permit it!"

"Don't you see that you're making something that is already hard for Meg even harder?" Mrs. Whatsit asked him.

Aunt Beast turned tentacles toward Mrs. Whatsit. "Is she strong enough to tesser again? You know what she has been through."

"If Which takes her she can manage," Mrs. Whatsit said.

"If it will help I could go too, and hold her." Aunt Beast's arm around Meg tightened.

"Oh, Aunt Beast—" Meg started.

But Mrs. Whatsit cut her off. "No."

"I was afraid not," Aunt Beast said humbly. "I just wanted you to know that I *would*."

"Mrs.—uh—Whatsit." Mr. Murry frowned and pushed his hair back from his face. Then he shoved with his middle finger at his nose as though he were trying to get spectacles closer to his eyes. "Are you remembering that she is only a child?"

"And she's backward," Calvin bellowed.

"I resent that," Meg said hotly, hoping that indignation would control her trembling. "I'm better than you at math and you know it."

"Do you have the courage to go alone?" Mrs. Whatsit asked her.

Meg's voice was flat. "No. But it doesn't matter." She turned to her father and Calvin. "You know it's the only thing to do. You know they'd never send me alone if—"

"How do we know they're not in league with IT?"

Mr. Murry demanded.

"Father!"

"No, Meg," Mrs. Whatsit said. "I do not blame your father for being angry and suspicious and frightened. And I cannot pretend that we are doing anything but sending you into the gravest kind of danger. I have to acknowledge quite openly that it may be a fatal danger. I know this. But I do not believe it. And the Happy Medium doesn't believe it, either."

"Can't she see what's going to happen?" Calvin asked.

"Oh, not in this kind of thing." Mrs. Whatsit sounded surprised at his question. "If we knew ahead of time what was going to happen we'd be—we'd be like the people of Camazotz, with no lives of our own, with everything all planned and done for us. How can I explain it to you? Oh, I know. In your language you have a form of poetry called the sonnet."

"Yes, yes," Calvin said impatiently. "What's that got to do with the Happy Medium?"

"Kindly pay me the courtesy of listening to me." Mrs. Whatsit's voice was stern, and for a moment Calvin stopped pawing the ground like a nervous colt. "It is a very strict form of poetry, is it not?"

"Yes."

"There are fourteen lines, I believe, all in iambic pentameter. That's a very strict rhythm or meter, yes?"

"Yes." Calvin nodded.

"And each line has to end with a rigid rhyme pattern. And if the poet does not do it exactly this way, it is not a sonnet, is it?"

"No."

"But within this strict form the poet has complete freedom to say whatever he wants, doesn't he?"

"Yes." Calvin nodded again.

"So," Mrs. Whatsit said.

"So what?"

"Oh, do not be stupid, boy!" Mrs. Whatsit scolded. "You know perfectly well what I am driving at!"

"You mean you're comparing our lives to a sonnet? A strict form, but freedom within it?"

"Yes." Mrs. Whatsit said. "You're given the form, but you have to write the sonnet yourself. What you say is completely up to you."

"Please," Meg said. "Please. If I've got to go I want to go and get it over with. Each minute you put it off makes it harder."

"Sshee iss rright," boomed Mrs. Which's voice. "Itt iss ttime."

"You may say good-bye." Mrs. Whatsit was giving her not permission, but a command.

Meg curtsied clumsily to the beasts. "Thank you all. Very much. I know you saved my life." She did not add what she could not help thinking: Saved it for what? So that IT could get me?

She put her arms about Aunt Beast, pressed up against the soft, fragrant fur. "Thank you," she whispered. "I love you."

"And I, you, little one." Aunt Beast pressed gentle tendrils against Meg's face.

"Cal—" Meg said, holding out her hand.

Calvin came to her and took her hand, then drew her roughly to him and kissed her. He didn't say anything, and he turned away before he had a chance to see the surprised happiness that brightened Meg's eyes.

At last she turned to her father. "I'm—I'm sorry, Father."

He took both her hands in his, bent down to her with his short-sighted eyes. "Sorry for what, Megatron?"

Tears almost came to her eyes at the gentle use of the old nickname. "I wanted you to do it all for me. I wanted everything to be all easy and simple. . . . So I tried to pretend that it was all your fault. . . because I was scared, and I didn't want to have to do anything myself—"

"But I wanted to do it for you," Mr. Murry said. "That's what every parent wants." He looked into her dark, frightened eyes. "I won't let you go, Meg. I am going."

"No." Mrs. Whatsit's voice was sterner than Meg had ever heard it. "You are going to allow Meg the privilege of accepting this danger. You are a wise man, Mr. Murry. You are going to let her go."

Mr. Murry sighed. He drew Meg close to him. "Little Megaparsec. Don't be afraid. We will try to have courage for you. That is all we can do. Your mother—"

"Mother was always shoving me out in the world," Meg said. "She'd want me to do this. You know she would. Tell her—" she started, choked, then held up her head and said, "No. Never mind. I'll tell her myself."

"Good girl. Of course you will."

Now Meg walked slowly around the great table where Mrs. Whatsit was still posed between the columns. "Are you going with me?"

"No. Only Mrs. Which."

"The Black Thing—" Fear made her voice tremble.

"When Father tessered me through it, it almost got me."

"Your father is singularly inexperienced," Mrs. Whatsit said, "though a fine man, and worth teaching. At the moment he still treats tessering as though he were working with a machine. We will not let the Black Thing get you. I don't think."

This was not exactly comforting.

The momentary vision and faith that had come to Meg dwindled. "But suppose I can't get Charles Wallace away from IT—"

"Stop." Mrs. Whatsit held up her hand. "We gave you gifts the last time we took you to Camazotz. We will not let you go empty handed this time. But what we can give you now is nothing you can touch with your hands. I give you my love, Meg. Never forget that. My love always."

Mrs. Who, eyes shining behind spectacles, beamed at Meg. Meg felt in her blazer pocket and handed back the spectacles she had used on Camazotz.

"Your father is right," Mrs. Who took the spectacles and hid them somewhere in the folds of her robes. "The virtue is gone from them. And what I have to give you this time you must try to understand not word by word, but in a flash, as you understand the tesseract. Listen, Meg. Listen well. *The foolishness of God is wiser than men; and the weakness of God is stronger than men. For ye see your calling, brethren, how that not many wise men after the flesh, not many mighty, not many noble, are called, but God hath chosen the foolish things of the world to confound the wise; and God hath chosen the weak things of the world to confound the things which are mighty. And base things of the world, and things which are despised, hath God chosen, yea, and things which are not, to bring to nought things that are.*" She paused, and then she said, "May the right prevail." Her spectacles seemed to flicker. Behind her, through her, one of the columns became visible. There was a final gleam from the glasses, and she was gone. Meg looked nervously to where Mrs. Whatsit had been standing before Mrs. Who spoke. But Mrs. Whatsit was no longer there.

"No!" Mr. Murry cried, and stepped toward Meg.

Mrs. Which's voice came through her shimmer. "I ccannott hhollldd yyourr hanndd, chilldd."

Immediately Meg was swept into darkness, into nothingness, and then into the icy devouring cold of the Black Thing. Mrs. Which won't let it get me, she thought over and over while the cold of the Black Thing seemed to crunch at her bones.

Then they were through it, and she was standing breathlessly on her feet on the same hill on which they had first landed on Camazotz. She was cold and a little numb, but no worse than she had often been in the winter in the country when she had spent an afternoon skating on the pond. She looked around. She was completely alone. He heart began to pound.

Then, seeming to echo from all around her, came Mrs. Which's unforgettable voice. "I hhave nnott ggivenn yyou mmyy ggiifftt. *Yyou hhave ssomethinngg thatt ITT hhass nnott.* Thiss ssomethinngg iss yyourr onlly wweapponn. Bbutt yyou mmusstt ffinndd itt fforr yyourrssellff."

Then the voice ceased, and Meg knew that she was alone.

She walked slowly down the hill, her heart thumping painfully against her ribs. There below her was the same row of identical houses they had seen before, and beyond these the linear buildings of the city. She walked along the quiet street. It was dark and the street was deserted. No children playing ball or skipping rope. No mother figures at the doors. No father figures returning from work. In the same window of each house was a light, and as Meg walked down the street all the lights were extinguished simultaneously. Was it because of her presence, or was it simply that it was time for lights out?

She felt numb, beyond rage or disappointment or even fear. She put one foot ahead of the other with precise regularity, not allowing her pace to lag. She was not thinking; she was not planning; she was simply walking slowly but steadily toward the city and the domed building where IT lay.

Now she approached the outlying buildings of the city. In each of them was a vertical line of light, but it was a dim, eerie light, not the warm light of stairways in cities at home. And there were no isolated brightly lit windows where someone was working late, or an office was being cleaned. Out of each building came one man, perhaps a watchman, and each man started walking the width of the building. They appeared not to see her. At any rate they paid no attention to her whatsoever, and she went on past them.

What have I got that IT hasn't got? she thought suddenly. What have I possibly got?

Now she was walking by the tallest of the business buildings. More dim vertical lines of light. The walls glowed slightly to give a faint illumination to the streets. CENTRAL Central Intelligence was ahead of her. Was the man with red eyes still sitting there? Or was he allowed to go to bed? But this was not where she must go, though the man with red eyes seemed the kind old gentleman he claimed to be when compared with IT. But he was no longer of any consequence in the search for Charles Wallace. She must go directly to IT.

IT isn't used to being resisted. Father said that's how he managed, and how Calvin and I managed as long as we did. Father saved me then. There's nobody here to save me now. I have to do it myself. I have to resist IT by myself. Is that what I have that IT hasn't got? No, I'm sure IT can resist. IT just isn't used to having *other* people resist.

CENTRAL Central Intelligence blocked with its huge rectangle the end of the square. She turned to walk around it, and almost imperceptibly her steps slowed.

It was not far to the great dome which housed IT.

I'm going to Charles Wallace. That's what's important. That's what I have to think of. I wish I could feel numb again the way I did at first. Suppose IT has him somewhere else? Suppose he isn't there?

I have to go there first, anyhow. That's the only way I can find out.

Her steps got slower and slower as she passed the great bronzed doors, the huge slabs of the CENTRAL Central Intelligence building, as she finally saw ahead of her the strange, light, pulsing dome of IT.

Father said it was all right for me to be afraid. He said to go ahead and be afraid. And Mrs. Who said—I don't understand what she said but I think it was meant to make me not hate being only me, and me being the way I am. And Mrs. Whatsit said to remember that she loves me. That's what I have to think about. Not about being afraid. Or not as smart as IT. Mrs. Whatsit loves me. That's quite something, to be loved by someone like Mrs. Whatsit.

She was there.

No matter how slowly her feet had taken her at the end, they had taken her there.

Directly ahead of her was the circular building, its walls glowing with violet flame, its silvery roof pulsing with a light that seemed to Meg to be insane. Again she could feel the light, neither warm nor cold, but reaching out to touch her, pulling her toward IT.

There was a sudden sucking, and she was within.

It was as though the wind had been knocked out of her. She gasped for breath, for breath in her own rhythm, not the permeating pulsing of IT. She could feel the inexorable beat within her body, controlling her heart, her lungs.

But not herself. Not Meg. It did not quite have her.

She blinked her eyes rapidly and against the rhythm until the redness before them cleared and she could see. There was the brain, there was IT, lying pulsing and quivering on the dais, soft and exposed and nauseating. Charles Wallace was crouched beside IT, his eyes still slowly twirling, his jaw still slack, as she had seen him before, with a tic in his forehead reiterating the revolting rhythm of IT.

As she saw him it was again as though she had been punched in the stomach, for she had to realize afresh that she was seeing Charles, and yet it was not

Charles at all. Where was Charles Wallace, her own beloved Charles Wallace?

What is it I have got that IT hasn't got?

"You have nothing that IT hasn't got," Charles Wallace said coldly. "How nice to have you back, dear sister. We have been waiting for you. We knew that Mrs. Whatsit would send you. She is our friend, you know."

For an appalling moment Meg believed, and in that moment she felt her brain being gathered up into IT.

"No!" she screamed at the top of her lungs. "No! You lie!"

For a moment she was free from ITs clutches again.

As long as I can stay angry enough IT can't get me.

Is that what I have that IT doesn't have?

"Nonsense," Charles Wallace said. "You have nothing that IT doesn't have."

"You're lying," she replied, and she felt only anger toward this boy who was not Charles Wallace at all. No, it was not anger, it was loathing; it was hatred, sheer and unadulterated, and as she became lost in hatred she also began to be lost in IT. The red miasma swam before her eyes; her stomach churned in IT's rhythm. Her body trembled with the strength of her hatred and the strength of IT.

With the last vestige of consciousness she jerked her mind and body. Hate was nothing that IT didn't have. IT knew all about hate.

"You are lying about that, and you were lying about Mrs. Whatsit!" she screamed.

"Mrs. Whatsit hates you," Charles Wallace said.

And that was where IT made IT's fatal mistake, for

as Meg said, automatically, "Mrs. Whatsit loves me; that's what she told me, that she loves me," suddenly she knew.

She knew!

Love.

That was what she had that IT did not have.

She had Mrs. Whatsit's love, and her father's, and her mother's, and the real Charles Wallace's love, and the twins', and Aunt Beast's.

And she had her love for them.

But how could she use it? What was she meant to do?

If she could give love to IT perhaps it would shrivel up and die, for she was sure that IT could not withstand love. But she, in all her weakness and foolishness and baseness and nothingness, was incapable of loving IT. Perhaps it was not too much to ask of her, but she could not do it.

But she could love Charles Wallace.

She could stand there and she could love Charles Wallace.

Her own Charles Wallace, the real Charles Wallace, the child for whom she had come back to Camazotz, to IT, the baby who was so much more than she was, and who was yet so utterly vulnerable.

She could love Charles Wallace.

Charles. Charles, I love you. My baby brother who always takes care of me. Come back to me, Charles Wallace, come away from IT, come back, come home. I love you, Charles. Oh, Charles Wallace, I love you.

Tears were streaming down her cheeks, but she was unaware of them.

Now she was even able to look at him, at this animated thing that was not her own Charles Wallace at all. She was able to look and love.

I love you. Charles Wallace, you are my darling and my dear and the light of my life and the treasure of my heart. I love you. I love you. I love you.

Slowly his mouth closed. Slowly his eyes stopped their twirling. The tic in the forehead ceased its revolting twitch. Slowly he advanced toward her.

"I love you!" she cried. "I love you, Charles! I love you!"

Then suddenly he was running, pelting, he was in her arms, he was shrieking with sobs. "Meg! Meg! Meg!"

"I love you, Charles!" she cried again, her sobs almost as loud as his, her tears mingling with his. "I love you! I love you! I love you!"

A whirl of darkness. An icy cold blast. An angry, resentful howl that seemed to tear through her. Darkness again. Through the darkness to save her came a sense of Mrs. Whatsit's presence, so that she knew it could not be IT who now had her in its clutches.

And then the feel of earth beneath her, of something in her arms, and she was rolling over on the sweet smelling autumnal earth, and Charles Wallace was crying out, "Meg! Oh, Meg!"

Now she was hugging him close to her, and his little arms were clasped tightly about her neck. "Meg, you saved me! You saved me!" he said over and over.

CONCLUDING LEVEL 12, UNIT 4

Viewpoints

As Alec Bings in "The Road to Digitopolis" said, "You certainly can't always look at things from someone else's Point of View." In *Viewpoints*, you had an opportunity to try it for just a little while. The Dodecahedron and the Mathemagician revealed a kingdom in which numbers were more precious than jewels. They both would have felt right at home with the Möbius strips and magic squares you read about. Would you feel at home on the tiny planet of the little prince or in Flatland? You may have had certain ideas about clocks and calendars and space and time, but have your viewpoints changed after reading this unit?

Thinking and Writing About *Viewpoints*

1. The Dodecahedron in "The Road to Digitopolis" had twelve different faces. How many faces did the inhabitants of Flatland have? Why?
2. In what ways was Jill of "What Do You Mean by *Average?*" not average at all?
3. Which of the characters in *Viewpoints* would probably understand the drawings done by the author of "The Little Prince"? Explain your choices.
4. Could the little prince use the same kind of clock we use? Could he use the same kind of calendar? Explain your answers.
5. Imagine that Bobo of "The Lost Half-Hour" had met Einstein instead of Father Time. What might Einstein have said about trying to find time?
6. Imagine that you have been chosen to work as an assistant in Einstein's laboratory. Write a report summarizing your first day on the job.

Glossary

This glossary can help you to pronounce and find out the meanings of words in this book that you may not know.

The words are listed in alphabetical order. Guide words at the top of each page tell you the first and last words on the page.

Each word is divided into syllables. The way to pronounce each word is given next. You can understand the pronunciation respelling by using the key below. A shorter key appears at the bottom of every other page.

When a word has more than one syllable, a dark accent mark (′) shows which syllable is stressed. In some words, a light accent mark (′) shows which syllable has a less heavy stress.

Information about the history, or etymology, of selected words is presented in brackets following the definition.

The following abbreviations are used in this glossary:

n. noun　　*v.* verb　　*adj.* adjective　　*adv.* adverb　　*pl.* plural

Glossary entries were adapted from the *Macmillan School Dictionary* and the *Macmillan Dictionary.*

PRONUNCIATION KEY

Vowel Sounds

/a/	bat	/i/	bib	/ou/	out, cow
/ā/	cake, rain, day	/ī/	kite, fly, pie, light	/u/	sun, son, touch
/ä/	father	/ir/	clear, cheer, here	/u̇/	book, pull, could
/är/	car	/o/	top, watch	/ü/	moon
/ãr/	dare, hair	/ō/	rope, soap, so, snow	/ū/	cute, few, music
/e/	hen, bread	/ô/	saw, song, auto	/ə/	about, taken, pencil apron, helpful
/ē/	me, meat, baby, believe	/oi/	coin, boy		
/ėr/	term, first, worm, turn	/ôr/	fork, ore, oar	/ər/	letter, dollar, doctor

Consonant Sounds

/b/	bear	/m/	map	/y/	yo-yo
/d/	dog	/n/	nest	/z/	zoo, eggs
/f/	fish, phone	/p/	pig	/ch/	chain , match
/g/	goat	/r/	rug, wrong	/sh/	show
/h/	house, who	/s/	city, seal	/th/	thin
/j/	jar, gem, fudge	/t/	tiger	/t̲h̲/	those
/k/	car, key	/v/	van	/hw/	where
/l/	lamb	/w/	wagon	/ng/	song

A

ab·duct (ab dukt') *v.* to carry off someone unlawfully by force. [Latin *abductus*, past participle of *abdūcere* to lead away.]

a·beam (ə bēm') *adv.* straight across a ship; at right angles to a ship's length.

a·bound (ə bound') *v.* to exist in great quantity or large numbers; to be filled with; teem with. [Old French *abonder*, from Latin *abundare* to overflow, going back to Latin *ab* from + *unda* wave.]

a·brupt (ə brupt') *adj.* sudden; unexpected; hasty. [Latin *abruptus*, past participle of *abrumpere* to break off.]

ab·so·lute (ab' sə lüt') *adj.* certain; unchanging; positive.

ab·surd (ab sėrd', ab zėrd') *adj.* contrary to reason, common sense, or truth; ridiculous. [Latin *absurdus* out of tune, senseless.]

ac·ces·so·ry (ak ses' ər ē) *n.*, *pl.* **ac·ces·so·ries.** something that is not a necessity, but adds to appearance or usefulness; extra thing that is helpful in a secondary way.

ac·cu·rate (ak' yər it) *adj.* exact; precise.

ac·cus·tom (ə kus' təm) *v.* to familiarize by use, custom, or habit. **to become accustomed to**. to become used to; become familiar with.

a·chieve (ə chēv') *v.* **a·chieved, a·chiev·ing.** **1.** to succeed in gaining; attain. **2.** to carry out successfully; accomplish. [Old French *achever* to bring to an end, accomplish, from the phrase *a chief* to a head, to an end, from the Latin phrase *ad caput* to a head.]

ac·knowl·edge (ak nol' ij) *v.* **ac·knowl·edged, ac·knowl·edg·ing. 1.** to admit the truth or fact of. **2.** to recognize the authority, rights, or claims of.

ad·mon·ish (ad mon' ish) *v.* to caution against some action; warn. [Old French *amonester* to warn, going back to Latin *admonere* to remind, warn.]

ad·mo·ni·tion (ad' mə nish' ən) *n.* **1.** advice or counsel. **2.** warning.

ag·ile (aj' əl) *adj.* able to move quickly or easily; nimble.

a·light (ə līt') *v.* **a·light·ed** or **a·lit, a·light·ing. 1.** to land on. **2.** to step down from; get off. [Old English *alīhtan* to remove weight from, descend.]

al·ti·tude (al' tə tüd', al' tə tūd') *n.* height or elevation above the earth's surface. [Latin *altītūdo* height.]

am·e·thyst (am' ə thist) *n.* purple or violet quartz, used as a gem.

am·ple (am' pəl) *adj.* **1.** more than enough; abundant. **2.** of great size or extent.

an·ces·tor (an' ses tər) *n.* a person from whom one is descended. [Old French *ancestre* forefather, from Latin *antecessor* one who goes before, predecessor.]

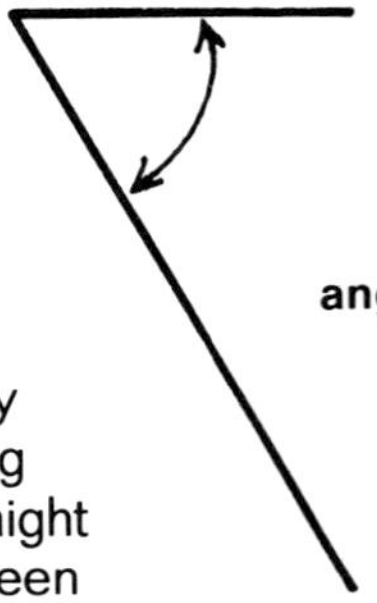

angle

an·gle (ang' gəl) *n.* **1.** figure formed by two lines extending from the same straight line. **2.** space between these two lines.

an·i·mat·ed (an' ə mā' tid) *adj.* stimulated; activated; lively; spirited. [Latin *animātus*, past participle of *animāre* to give life to.]

an·tic·i·pa·tion (an tis' ə pā' shən) *n.* **1.** feeling of excited expectation. **2.** act of looking forward to or expecting.

a·pace (ə pās') *adv.* *Archaic.* swiftly; quickly; rapidly. [Old French *a pas* at a (fast) pace, going back to Latin *ad* to, at + *passus* step, pace.]

ap·pa·ri·tion (ap' ə rish' ən) *n.* **1.** something strange, startling, or unexpected which comes suddenly into view. **2.** ghost; phantom. [Late Latin *appāritiō* appearance, from Latin *appārēre* to appear.]

ap·pen·dix (ə pen′ diks) *n., pl.* **ap·pen·dix·es** or **ap·pen·di·ces.** (ə pen′ də sēz′). **1.** tube located at the bottom of the bag of a dirigible or balloon, by which it is inflated or deflated. **2.** thin, saclike structure attached to the upper part of the large intestine.

ap·pren·tice (ə pren′ tis) *n.* in the Middle Ages, a person who was bound by contract to serve a master for a specified time, in return for instruction in a craft or trade and room and board. [Old French *aprentis* one who learns a trade, from *aprendre* to learn, from Latin *apprehendere* to seize, grasp mentally.]

ar·chi·tec·tur·al (är′ kə tek′ chər əl) *adj.* relating to or characteristic of architecture, the science or profession of designing and constructing buildings or other structures.

ar·du·ous (är′ jü əs) *adj.* requiring great effort or energy.

ar·ma·da (är mä′ də) *n.* fleet of warships. [Spanish *armada* fleet, from *armar* to arm, from Latin *armare* to furnish with weapons.]

armada

ar·mor·y (är′ mər ē) *n., pl.* **ar·mor·ies.** place where weapons are kept; arsenal.

ar·ro·gance (ãr′ ə gəns) *n.* too much pride or confidence mixed with lack of respect for others; conceit; haughtiness.

ar·til·ler·y (är til′ ər ē) *n.* branch of a military force using large weapons such as cannon, howitzers, and mortars, that fire projectiles and are mounted on stationary or movable platforms. [Old French *artillerie* war equipment, from *artiller* to fortify, possibly going back to Latin *ars* skill.]

A·sia Mi·nor (ā′ zhə mī′ nər) *n.* peninsula in western Asia, bounded by the Black and Mediterranean seas, comprising most of Asiatic Turkey.

as·sault (ə sôlt′) *n.* violent or vigorous attack. —*v.* to make an assault on; attack.

as·si·mi·late (ə sim′ ə lāt) *v.* **as·si·mi·lat·ed, as·sim·i·lat·ing.** to take into a larger group and make part of. [Latin *assimilātus*, past participle of *assimilāre* to make like.]

as·sur·ance (ə shür′ əns) *n.* confidence.

as·ter·oid (as′ tə roid′) *n.* any of thousands of minor planets that revolve around the sun. [Greek *asteroeides* starlike, from *aster* star.]

as·trol·o·ger (ə strol′ ə jər) *n.* a person who attempts to predict events by studying the movement of stars, planets, and other heavenly bodies.

as·tute (ə stüt′, ə stūt′) *adj.* having or showing a keen mind; shrewd.

A·the·na (ə thē′ nə) *n. Greek Mythology.* goddess of wisdom and the arts, the daughter of Zeus.

at·tend (ə tend′) *v.* to be present at. **to attend to.** to take care of; serve.

at·tire (ə tīr′) *n.* clothes; dress.

au·da·cious (ô dā′ shəs) *adj.* bold; daring; courageous.

a·venge (ə venj′) *v.* **a·venged, a·veng·ing.** to get revenge for. [Old French *avengier*, from *a* to (from Latin *ad* to) + *vengier* to take vengeance, from Latin *vindicāre* to punish.]

a b**a**t, ā c**a**ke, ä f**a**ther, är c**ar**, ãr d**are**; e h**e**n, ē m**e**, ėr t**er**m; i b**i**b, ī k**ī**te, ir cl**ear**; o t**o**p, ō r**o**pe, ô s**aw**, oi c**oi**n, ôr f**or**k, ou **ou**t; u s**u**n, ů b**oo**k, ü m**oo**n, ū c**u**te; ə **a**bout, tak**e**n

B

Bab·y·lo·ni·an (bab′ ə lō′ nē ən) *n.* member of the people of Babylonia, an ancient empire in Mesopotamia, an area in southwestern Asia between the Tigris and Euphrates rivers, that flourished from about 1900 B.C. until about 500 B.C.

badg·er (baj′ ər) *v.* to annoy or harass persistently; pester; torment.

ba·gel (bā′ gəl) *n.* doughnut-shaped roll made of yeast dough, cooked in simmering water and then baked.

ba·leen (bə lēn′) *n.* an elastic, horny, material similar to fingernails, forming thin plates that grow in place of teeth in the upper jaw of certain whales; whalebone.

bal·last (bal′ əst) *n.* heavy material placed in the bottom of a boat or ship to maintain stability.

bal·lot (bal′ ət) *n.* written or printed form used to cast a vote.

ban·nock (ban′ ək) *n. Scottish.* round, flattened cake made of oatmeal or flour. [Old English *bannuc* a cake, from Gaelic *bonnach*, possibly going back to Latin *panicium* something baked.]

ba·o·bab (bā′ ō bab′) *n.* tree found mostly in tropical Africa, having a broad trunk, thick spreading branches, and a fruit resembling a gourd.

baobab

bar (bär) *n.* mass or ridge of sand, gravel, or other material deposited in a river or bay, or along the shore, built up by the action of waves and currents.

bar·on (bâr′ ən) *n.* in the Middle Ages, a lord who held lands as a vassal of a king or other high-ranking nobleman. [Middle English from Latin *barōn* from Germanic *barō* man.]

bas·tion (bas′ chən, bas′ tē ən) *n.* part of a fortification that extends outward from the main fort and has five sides.

bat·ter·y (bat′ ər ē) *n., pl.* **bat·ter·ies.** two or more guns or other weapons together with the men and equipment for them.

beck·on (bek′ ən) *v.* to signal, summon, or direct (someone) by a sign or gesture. [Old English *biecnan, bēcnan* to signify.]

be·like (bi līk′) *adv. Archaic.* perhaps.

bel·low (bel′ ō) *v.* to cry out in a loud deep voice; roar. [Old English *bylgean* to roar like a bull, or Old English *bellan* to make a loud noise, from German *bellen* howl.]

berth (bėrth) *n.* **1.** place for a ship to moor. **2.** built-in bed or bunk, especially in a ship or train.

be·seech·ing·ly (bi sē′ ching lē) *adv.* in a pleading way; imploringly.

be·siege (bi sēj′) *v.* **be·sieged, be·sieg·ing.** to overwhelm or harass.

be·tray·al (bi trā′ əl) *n.* an act of betraying, or being a traitor; treachery; disloyalty.

bil·let (bil′ it) *n.* small thick stick of wood, especially one used for fuel.

bi·ol·o·gy (bī ol′ ə jē) *n.* the science of living organisms. Its two major divisions are botany, the science of plants, and zoology, the science of animals. [German *biologie*, from Greek *bios* life.]

block and tack·le (blok′ ənd tak′ əl) arrangement of pulleys and ropes used for lifting and hauling.

block·ad·ing (blo kā′ ding) *adj.* shutting off an area by ships to prevent people or supplies from going into or out of it.

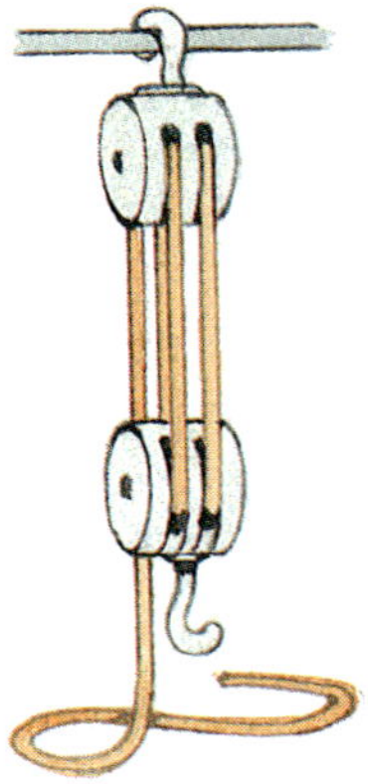
block and tackle

boar (bôr) *n., pl.* **boars** or **boar**. a male pig or hog.

board·er (bôr′ dər) *n.* a person who receives regular meals, or meals and lodging, for a fixed price.

boo·ty (bü′ tē) *n., pl.* **boo·ties.** **1.** goods seized by violence and robbery; plunder. **2.** goods taken from an enemy in combat; spoils of war.

brace (brās) *adj.* pair; couple.

bran·dish (bran′ dish) *v.* to wave, shake, or swing threateningly, as a weapon. [Old French *brandiss-*, a stem of *brandir* to brandish, from Anglo-Norman *brand* sword, from Old Norse *brandr* torch, sword.]

bra·zen (brā′ zən) *adj.* **1.** loud; harsh; forthright. **2.** made of brass.

brim·stone (brim′ stōn′) *n.* sulfur. [Middle English *brinston* literally burn stone, from Germanic *brennen* to burn + *stein* stone.]

bro·chure (brō shůr′) *n.* pamphlet; booklet.

bu·bon·ic plague (bū bon′ ik, bü bon′ ik plāg′) *n.* a very serious and dangerous disease marked by a high fever and swelling of the lymph glands. It is carried to humans by flea infected rats. [Late Latin *būbo* swelling, from Greek *boubōn*, swollen gland.]

buck·ler (buk′ lər) *n.* small, round shield.

buoy (bü′ ē, boi) *v.* **1.** to prevent from sinking; keep afloat. **2.** to furnish or mark with a buoy or buoys.

C

Cae·sar (sē′ zər) **Ga·ius Jul·ius** (gā′ əs jül′ yəs) 100?-44 B.C. Roman statesman and general. The name *Caesar* was used by the Roman emperors from Augustus to Hadrian, and also by certain later rulers.

calm (käm) *adj.* without or nearly without motion; not stormy. [French *calme* quiet, from Italian *calma* rest, going back to Greek *kauma* heat of the sun or the day (at which time people rested in the shade).]

cam·paign (kam pān′) *n.* organized series of actions carried on for a particular purpose.

can·di·date (kan′ də dāt′) *n.* a person who seeks a position, office, or honor. [Latin *candidātus* a person dressed in white, candidate for office, from *candidus* white; in ancient Rome, those seeking political office wore white togas to symbolize purity.]

can·is·ter (kan′ i stər) *n.* small box, can, or other container, usually made of metal.

can·o·py (kan′ ə pē) *n., pl.* **can·o·pies.** covering of cloth or other material, hung over a bed, throne or entrance of a building, or supported on poles over a person or sacred object. [Medieval Latin *canopēum* mosquito net, going back to Greek *kōnōpeion* mosquito net, bed with a mosquito net, from *knops* mosquito.]

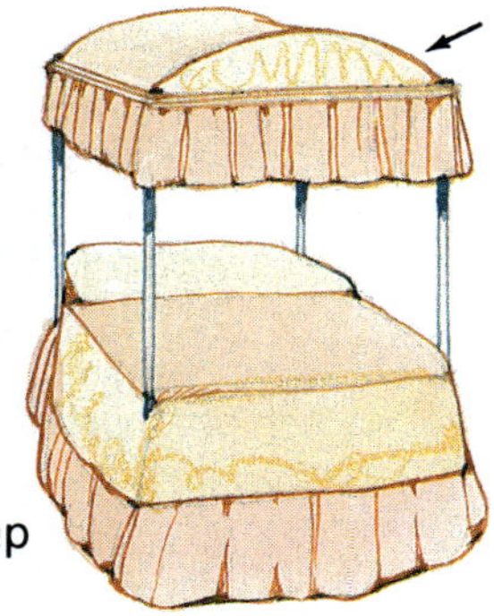

canopy

cap·size (kap′ sīz, kap sīz′) *v.* **cap·sized, cap·siz·ing.** to overturn; sink.

cas·ket (kas′ kit) *n.* **1.** small box or chest, as for jewels. **2.** coffin. [Modification of French *cassette* small box, from *casse* box, chest, from Latin *capsa*.]

cat·a·pult (kat′ ə pult) *v.* to leap or be thrown; hurl; eject.

a bat, ā cake, ä father, är car, ãr dare; e hen, ē me, ėr term; i bib, ī kīte, ir clear; o top, ō rope, ô saw, oi coin, ôr fork, ou out; u sun, ů book, ü moon, ū cute; ə about, taken

ca·tas·tro·phe (kə tas′ trə fē′) *n.* great and sudden disaster or misfortune. [Greek *katastrophē* overturning.]

ca·the·dral (kə thē′ drəl) *n.* **1.** any large or important church. **2.** official church of a bishop, containing his throne. [Medieval Latin (*ecclesia*) *cathedrālis* (church) having a cathedra, or a bishop's throne, from Latin *cathedra* chair.]

cav·al·cade (kav′ əl kād′) *n.* procession, especially of people on horseback. [Middle French *cavalcade* riding on a horse, from Italian *cavalcata* band of horsemen, going back to Latin *cavallo* horse.]

cavalcade

cav·al·ry (kav′ əl rē) *n., pl.* **cav·al·ries.** military unit trained to fight on horseback. [Middle French *cavallerie* horsemen, from Italian *cavalleria* knighthood, troop of horses from *cavaliere* knights from Italian *cavallo* horse.]

cen·tu·ry (sen′ chər ē) *n., pl.* **centuries.** period of one hundred years. [Latin *centuria* division of a hundred units, from *centum* hundred.]

cer·e·mo·ni·al (sãr′ ə mō′ nē əl) *adj.* having to do with ceremony, a formal act or set of acts done on a special or important occasion; ritual; formal.

cha·let (sha lā′) *n.* house having a wide, sloping roof with overhanging eaves, commonly found in Switzerland and other nearby regions. [Swiss French *chalet* cottage, from a pre-Latin word for "shelter."]

cham·ber (chām′ bər) *n.* room, especially a bedroom.

charg·er (chär′ jər) *n.* horse trained for use in battle.

chiv·al·ry (shiv′ əl rē) *n.* qualities of an ideal knight, such as honor, courtesy, generosity, respect for women, protection of the weak, and skill in battle. [Old French *chevalerie* knighthood, from *chevalier* knight.]

cir·cum·fer·ence (sər kum′ fər əns) *n.* line bounding any rounded figure, especially a circle; distance around something. [Latin *circumferentia*, from *circumferēns*, present participle of *circumferre*, from *circum* around + *ferre* bear.]

civ·ic (siv′ ik) *adj.* of or relating to a city or citizenship. [Latin *civicus* relating to a citizen, from *civis* citizen.]

civ·il (siv′ əl) *adj.* **1.** polite; courteous; showing good manners. **2.** of or relating to a citizen or citizens. [Latin *cīvīlis* relating to a citizen, polite, from *cīvis* citizen.]

clas·sic (klas′ ik) *n.* work of art of such high quality that it serves as a model.

coax (kōks) *v.* to persuade.

cof·fer (kô′ fər) *n.* box or chest for holding money or other valuables; strongbox.

co·hort (kō′ hôrt′) *n.* any band, company, or group.

coin (koin) *v.* **1.** to make up; devise. **2.** to make money by stamping metal.

col·li·sion (kə lizh′ ən) *n.* the act of coming together with force.

col·umn (kol′ əm) *n.* written or printed group of items arranged one above the other. [Latin *columna* pillar.]

com·mon (kom′ ən) *n.* piece of land, as a pasture or park, owned or used by the public. [Old French *comun* general, mutual, from Latin *commūnis* general, universal.]

com·pact (kəm pakt′) *adj.* taking up a small space or area. [Latin *compactus* joined together, past participle of *compingere* to join together.]

com·po·si·tion (kom′ pə zish′ ən) *n.* **1.** act, process, or art of creating a musical, literary, or artistic work. **2.** act of combining parts or elements in order to form a whole. [Old French *composition* a making, framing, from Latin *compositio* a putting together, connection.]

com·post·ing (kom′ pōs ting) *n.* the act or process of mixing various natural substances as dung, dead leaves, or the like in order to make a rich soil fertilizer.

com·pound (kom′ pound′) *n.* an enclosed area containing a house or other building.

com·rade (kom′ rad) *n.* friend or companion. [French *camarade* roommate, companion, from Spanish *camarada*, from *camara* room, from Late Latin *camera*.]

con·ceit·ed (kən sē′ tid) *adj.* having a very high opinion of oneself or of one's achievements or abilities; vain.

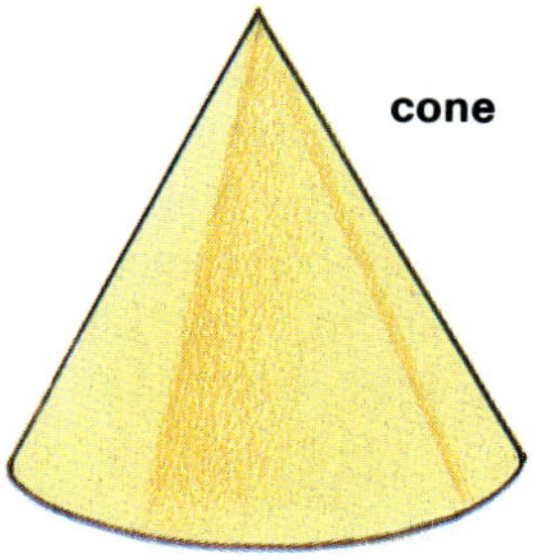

cone (kōn) *n.* a solid that narrows to a point from a circular base.

Con·fed·er·ate (kən fed′ ər it) *adj.* relating to the Confederate States of America, the union of the eleven southern states that seceded from the United States in 1860 and 1861.

con·fi·dent·ly (kon′ fə dənt le) *adv.* with a feeling of faith in one's own ability or competence.

con·fines (kon′ fīnz) *n. pl.* limits; boundaries; borders.

con·found (kən found′, kon found′) *v.* confuse; bewilder; perplex. [Old French *confondre* to overturn, destroy, from Latin *confundere* to pour together, mix, overwhelm.]

con·fus·ti·cate (kən fus′ tə kāt′) *v.* **con·fus·ti·cat·ed, con·fus·ti·cat·ing.** to confuse; confound.

con·se·quence (kon′ sə kwens′, kon′ sə kwəns) *n.* **1.** importance; significance. **2.** something which results from an earlier action or condition; effect.

con·sign·ment (kən sīn′ mənt) *n.* **1.** shipment of goods. **2.** act of handing over.

con·spir·a·tor (kən spir′ ə tər) *n.* person who secretly plans with another or others the performance of some evil or illegal act.

con·spire (kən spīr′) *v.* **con·spired, con·spir·ing.** to plan a conspiracy; plot against. [Latin *conspīrāre* to breathe together, agree, plot.]

con·ster·na·tion (kon′ stər nā′ shən) *n.* a feeling of alarm or amazement leading to confusion or fear.

con·sult (kən sult′) *v.* to look to for information or advice. [Latin *consultare* to take counsel, reflect.]

con·sum·er (kən sü′ mər) *n.* someone who buys or uses up things for sale.

con·tem·pla·tion (kon′ təm plā′ shən) *n.* act of looking at or thinking about something long and intensely.

con·tra·dict (kon′ trə dikt′) *v.* to say the opposite of or deny (a statement); declare to be untrue. [Latin *contrādictus*, past participle of *contrādīcere* to speak against.]

con·trol group (kən trōl′ grüp′) *n.* in a scientific experiment, a group of animals, plants, or the like that receives no particular treatment, and as such is used as a basis for comparison to another group that does receive particular treatment.

con·ven·ient (kən vēn′ yənt) *adj.* suited to one's needs. [Latin *conveniēns*, present participle of *convenīre* to come together, suit.]

a b**a**t, ā c**a**ke, ä f**a**ther, är c**ar**, ãr d**are**; e h**e**n, ē m**e**, ėr t**er**m; i b**i**b, ī k**ī**te, ir cl**ear**; o t**o**p, ō r**o**pe, ô s**aw**, oi c**oi**n, ôr f**or**k, ou **ou**t; u s**u**n, u̇ b**oo**k, ü m**oo**n, ū c**u**te; ə **a**bout, tak**e**n

con·vey (kən vā′) *v.* to express or communicate; transport. [Anglo-Norman *conveier* to conduct, going back to Latin *cum* with + *via* road, way.]

con·voy (kon′ voi) *n.* group of persons traveling together; protective escort. [Old French *convoier* to accompany on the way, going back to Latin *cum* with + *via* road, way.]

Cook, James 1728-1779, English navigator.

cor·o·na·tion (kôr′ ə nā′ shən) *n.* act of crowning a king or queen.

couch (kouch) *v.* **1.** to lower (a spear, gun, or other weapon) to a position of attack. **2.** to put into words; express.

coun·sel (koun′ səl) *n.* advice.

coun·sel·lor (koun′ sə lər) *n.* person who gives advice; adviser.

cour·ti·er (kôr′ tē ər) *n.* person who attends the court of a king, queen, or other royal ruler.

cove (kōv) *n.* small, sheltered bay. [Old English *cofa* chamber.]

craft (kraft) *n.* **1.** boat, ship, or aircraft. **2.** special skill or ability. [Old English *craft* strength, skill, ability.]

crevice

crev·ice (krev′ is) *n.* crack; fissure; chink. [Old French *crevace* fissure, ravine, from *crever* to split, from Latin *crepāre* to rattle, crack.]

croon (krün) *v.* to sing or hum in a soft, low tone. [Middle Low German *kronen* to mourn; groan.]

cro·quet (krō kā′) *n.* an outdoor game in which each player uses a mallet to drive a ball through small, bent wickets that are arranged in a particular order to form a course.

cub·by·hole (kub′ ē hol′) *n.* small, enclosed space.

cube (kūb) *n.* **1.** solid figure with six equal, square sides. **2.** The product of a number multiplied by itself twice.

cu·bic (kū′ bik) *adj.* **1.** of or relating to the third power of a number. **2.** of or having three dimensions.

cum·ber (kum′ bər) *v.* to hinder or obstruct; hold back.

cum·ber·some (kum′ bər səm) *adj.* not easily managed or carried; unwieldy.

cur·rent (kėr′ ənt) *n.* part of a body of water or air moving along in a path.—*adj.* belonging to the present time; existing.

cy·cle (sī′ kəl) *n.* complete series of events that occur over and over again in a definite order. [Late Latin *cyclus* circle, recurring period, from Greek *kyklos* circle, wheel.]

D

da·is (dā′ is, dī′ is, dās) *n.* slightly raised platform, as for a throne or speaker's desk.

dais

dam·sel (dam′ zəl) *n.* young, unmarried woman; maiden. [Old French *dameisele*, going back to Latin *domina* lady, mistress.]

da·ta (da′ tə, dāt′ ə) *n.* information from which conclusions can be drawn; facts and figures. [Plural of Latin *datum* something given, from neuter of *datus*, past participle of *dare* to give.]

de·bris (də brē′) *n.* scattered remains, as of something broken or destroyed; rubbish.

deft·ly (deft′ lē) *adv.* skillfully; nimbly; dexterously.

de·gree (di grē′) *n.* stage or step in a process. [Old French *degre* step, stair, rank, going back to Latin *dē* down + *gradus* step, rank, grade.]

del·i·ca·tes·sen (del′ i kə tes′ ən) *n.* store that specializes in prepared foods, as cooked meats. [German *Delikatessen*, plural of *Delikatesse* choice food, through French, going back to Latin *dēlicātus*, dainty, luxurious.]

dem·on·stra·tion (dem′ ən strā′ shən) *n.* the act of showing the use of something.

dense (dens) *adj.* having parts closely packed together; thick.

de·pict (di pikt′) *v.* to represent by drawing; portray.

dep·re·da·tion (dep′ rə dā′ shən) *n.* act of laying waste; plundering; ravaging. [French *depredation*, Late Latin *dēpraedātiō*, going back to Latin *dē* + *praeda* booty.]

der·i·va·tion (dãr′ ə vā′ shən) *n.* source or origin.

des·o·late (des′ ə lit) *adj.* **1.** deserted. **2.** left alone; lonely.

de·tract (di trakt′) *v.* to lessen in value or importance.

de·vo·tion (di vō′ shən) *n.* loyalty; faithfulness.

de·vour (di vour′) *v.* to eat up with great greed.

di·ag·o·nal (dī′ ag′ ə nəl) *adj.* having a slanting direction.

di·am·e·ter (dī am′ ə tər) *n.* straight line passing through the center of a circle or sphere, from one side to the other. [Old French *diametre* diameter of a circle, from Latin *diametros* a diagonal, diameter of a circle, from *dia* through + *metron* measure.]

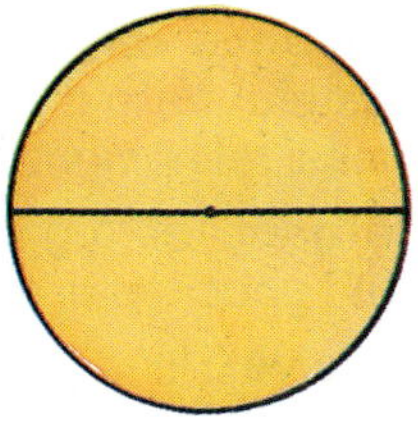

diameter

di·a·ry (dī′ ə rē) *n., pl.* **di·a·ries.** a daily record of a writer's personal feelings or experiences. [Latin *diārium* daily allowance, daily record, from *diēs* day.]

dic·tate (dik′ tāt) *v.* **dic·tat·ed, dic·tat·ing.** to say or read aloud something to be recorded.

dig·it (dij′ it) *n.* **1.** finger or toe. **2.** any of the ten Arabic numerals from 0 through 9. Sometimes 0 is excluded. [Latin *digit(us)* finger or toe, from the ancient practice of counting on one's fingers and/or toes.]

dil·a·ta·tion (dil′ ə tā′ shən, dī′ lə tā′ shən) *n.* to become large or wider; expand.

dim (dim) *adj.* not clear or distinct.

di·men·sion (di men′ shən) *n.* extent that can be measured, such as length, width, thickness, and height.

dip·lo·mat·i·cal·ly (dip′ lə mat′ ik lē) *adv.* with sensitivity to the feelings of others; tactfully.

dis·ci·pline (dis′ ə plin) *n.* **1.** orderly and restrained behavior; self-control; self-restraint. **2.** training that molds, corrects, or improves something, as mental ability or character. [Latin *disciplīna* instruction, knowledge.]

dis·crim·i·nat·ing (dis krim′ ə nā′ ting) *adj.* attentive to small details; particular.

dis·heart·en (dis härt′ ən) *v.* to discourage; depress.

dis·mayed (dis mād′) *adj.* troubled; discouraged.

dis·tin·guish (dis ting′ gwish) *v.* to recognize or indicate as different. [Latin *distinguere* to separate.]

dis·tin·guished (dis ting′ gwisht) *adj.* famous for excellent qualities; worthy of special notice.

a bat, ā cake, ä father, är car, ãr dare; e hen, ē me, ėr term; i bib, ī kīte, ir clear, o top,
ō rope, ô saw, oi coin, ôr fork, ou out; u sun, u̇ book, ü moon, ū cute; ə about, taken

dis·tort (dis tôrt′) *v.* to change so as to give a false impression; misrepresent. [Latin *distortus*, past participle of *distorquēre* to twist.]

dis·trib·ute (dis trib′ ūt) *v.* **dis·trib·ut·ed, dis·trib·ut·ing.** to spread out, classify, or arrange into groups.

do·dec·a·he·dron (dō dek′ ə hē′ drən) *n.* a solid figure having twelve faces. [Greek *dōdeka*, combining form of *dōdekas* twelve, *dō-* two + *-dekas* ten.]

dol·phin (dol′ fin, dôl′ fin) *n.* any of a group of highly intelligent animals related to the whale, found in all seas and in some freshwater rivers. Dolphins have scaleless black, brown, or gray skin, two flippers, and usually a beaklike snout.

dolphin

dom·i·nate (dom′ ə nāt′) *v.* **dom·i·nat·ed, dom·i·nat·ing. 1.** to have a commanding or towering position over; loom over. **2.** to exercise control or rule over; govern. [Latin *dominātus*, past participle of *dominārī* to be master.]

do·min·ion (də min′ yən) *n.* territory or country under the authority of a particular ruler or government.

down (doun) *n.* rolling grassy piece of land, especially in southern and southeastern England. [Old English *dūn* hill.]

dow·ry (dour′ ē) *n., pl.* **dow·ries.** money or property that a woman brings to her husband at the time of their marriage.

Drake, Sir Fran·cis (drāk′, sėr fran′ sis) c. 1540-1596, English admiral and explorer, commander of the first English voyage around the world.

duct (dukt) *n.* tube, pipe, or channel which conveys or conducts something, as a liquid or gas.

Dü·rer, Al·brecht (dür′ ər, dūr′ ər, ôl′ brekt) 1471-1528, German artist and engraver.

E

earl (ėrl) *n.* British nobleman ranking below a marquis and above a viscount. [Old English *eorl*, warrior, nobleman.]

eaves·drop (ēvz′ drop′) *v.* **eaves·dropped, eaves·drop·ping.** to listen secretly to a private conversation. [Earlier *eavesdrip*, from Old English *yfesdrype* water that drips from the eaves, referring to standing under the eaves from which rainwater dripped in order to hear a conversation in a house.]

eb·on·y (eb′ ə nē) *n., pl.* **eb·on·ies.** hard, black wood, used especially for piano keys, knife handles, and cabinets.

ed·dy (ed′ ē) *v.* **ed·died, ed·dy·ing.** to move with a circular motion; whirl. [Possibly from Old Norse *itha* whirlpool.] —*n., pl.* **ed·dies.** circular or whirling current of air or water; small whirlwind or whirlpool.

ed·i·to·ri·al (ed′ ə tôr′ ē əl) *n.* an article in a newspaper or magazine expressing the viewpoint of the editor, publisher, or writer on a certain topic.

ee·rie (ir′ ē) *adj.* strange and frightening.

ef·fect (i fekt′) *n.* something that is produced by a cause; result. [Latin *effectus*, from *efficere* to work out, accomplish, from *ex-* out + *facere* to make.]

el·e·gance (el′ ə gəns) *n.* quality of being tasteful, as in dress or furnishings; tastefulness; refinement; culture; polish.

el·e·gant (el′ ə gənt) *adj.* showing richness and good taste; dignified; refined; polished.

e·lu·sive (i lü′ siv) *adj.* difficult to capture.

em·bark (em bärk′) *v.* to go aboard a ship or boat for a trip. [Old French *embarquer* to put on a boat, going back to Latin *in* in + Late Latin *barca* small boat.]

em·bod·y (em bod′ ē) *v.* **em·bod·ied, em·bod·y·ing.** to give concrete or visible form to.

e·mo·tion (i mō′ shən) *n.* strong feeling, as love, hate, or sorrow. [French *emotion*, from *emouvoir* to move, stir up, going back to Latin *ēmovēre* to move out, stir up.]

en·deav·or (en dev′ ər) *n.* serious attempt.

en·hance (en hans′) *v.* **en·hanced, en·hanc·ing.** to make greater in value.

en·ter·prise (en′ tər prīz′) *n.* project or undertaking, especially one of a difficult, dangerous, or important nature. [Old French *entreprise* undertaking, from *entreprendre* to undertake, going back to Latin *inter* among + *prehendere* to take, seize.]

en·tic·ing (en tī′ sing) *adj.* tempting; attracting; alluring.

en·ve·lope (en′ və lōp′, än′ və lōp′) *n.* **1.** outer covering of a balloon or airship, usually made of fabric. **2.** flat paper wrapper used for mailing letters.

ep·ic (ep′ ik) *adj.* heroic. [Latin *epicus* epic poem, from Greek *epikos*, from *epos* word, song, story.]

e·qua·tion (i kwā′ zhən) *n.* *Mathematics.* a statement of equality between two quantities or expressions, especially one using an equal sign. $9 + 6 = 15$ is an equation.

e·qui·lat·er·al tri·an·gle (ēk′ wə lat′ ər əl trī′ ang′ gəl) *n.* triangle whose sides are of equal length. [Late Latin *aequilatenalis* having all sides equal, from Latin *aequus* even, equal + *later-*, stem of *latus* side.]

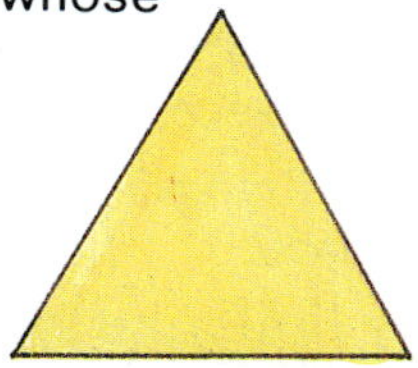

equilateral triangle

e·qui·lib·ri·um (ē′ kwə lib′ rē əm) *n.* state of balance. [Latin *aequilibrium* level position, from *aequus* even, equal + *lībra* balance.]

e·ra (ir′ ə, ãr′ ə) *n.* period of time marked by certain events, conditions, ideas, persons, or things. [Late Latin *aera* number, epoch (from which time is calculated), from Latin *aera* counters (for calculating), plural of *aes* brass.]

ere (ãr) *Archaic. prep.* before (in time).

es·say (es′ ā) *n.* a short written composition on a particular subject or topic.

E·thi·o·pi·a (ē′ thē ō′ pē ə) *n.* **1.** ancient country in northeastern Africa, south of Egypt. **2.** country in eastern Africa, whose capital is Addis Ababa.

Ethiopia

e·volve (i volv′) *v.* **e·volved, e·volv·ing.** to develop gradually. [Latin *ēvolvere* to unroll]

ex·ag·ger·a·tion (eg zaj′ ə rā′ shən) *n.* the result of making something seem more, larger, or greater than it is; overstatement.

ex·cep·tion·al (ek sep′ shən əl) *adj.* out of the ordinary; unusual; extraordinary.

ex·ces·sive (ik ses′ iv) *adj.* beyond what is necessary, usual, just, or proper.

ex·ot·ic (eg zot′ ik) *adj.* not native; foreign; strangely beautiful or fascinating. [Latin *exōticus* foreign, from Greek *exōtikós*, from *exo* outside.]

ex·ploit (eks′ ploit) *n.* heroic deed or act, bold feat. [Old French *exploit* achievement, deed, from Latin *explicitum* something unfolded or settled, from *explicāre* to unfold, explain.]

a bat, ā cake, ä father, är car, ãr dare; e hen, ē me, ėr term; i bib, ī kīte, ir clear; o top, ō rope, ô saw, oi coin, ôr fork, ou out; u sun, ů book, ü moon, ū cute; ə about, taken

ex·tin·guish (iks ting' gwish) *v.* to put out.

ex·tra·ter·res·tri·al (eks' trə tə res' trē əl) *adj.* coming from or living in regions outside the earth and its atmosphere.

F

face (fās) *n. Geometry.* one of the surfaces or sides of a solid: *a cube has six faces.*

falconry

fad (fad) *n.* popular pastime or interest pursued enthusiastically for a short time.

fal·con·ry (fôl' kən rē, fal' kən rē) *n.* the sport of hunting with falcons; hawking.

fal·ter (fol' tər) *v.* to act with hesitation or uncertainty; waver.

fan·fare (fan' fãr') *n.* call or short tune sounded by bugles, trumpets, or other brass instruments, used especially for military or ceremonial occasions.

fath·om (fath' əm) *n.* unit of measure equal to six feet. [Old English *fæthm* length of the outstretched arms, grasp.]

fa·tigue (fə tēg') *n.* loss of strength resulting from physical or mental effort; weariness; exhaustion.

feat (fēt) *n.* an act or deed, especially one displaying great skill, strength, or courage. [Old French *fait* deed, exploit, from Latin *factum*, thing done, deed, from *facere* to do.]

feint (fānt) *v.* to make a false movement to trick an opponent.

fell (fel) *n.* tract of high wasteland; moor; down.

fete (fāt) *n.* festival or large celebration.

fi·ber (fī' bər) *n.* a fine, threadlike part of a substance such as cloth.

Fi·bo·nac·ci, Le·o·nar·do (fē bə nä' chē, lā' ə när' dō) 1180?-1250? Italian mathematician and author.

fig·ure (fig' yər) *n.* **1.** symbol representing a number as 0, 1, 2, 3. **2.** drawing; diagram. **3.** *Geometry.* bounded surface or space; series of lines, solids, or surfaces having a definite shape: *a circle is a plane figure; a sphere is a solid figure.*

flad·bröd (flät' brōd) *n.* a hard, flat, unrisen bread.

flag·on (flag' ən) *n.* large bottle used to hold alcoholic drinks.

flex (fleks) *v.* to tighten or contract a muscle or muscles.

flor·in (flôr' in) *n.* formerly, any of various gold or silver coins issued in different European countries since 1252.

foe (fō) *n.* enemy. [Old English *fāh* hostile, *gefāh* adversary.]

for·bear·ance (fôr bãr' əns) *n.* act of controlling oneself, as when angered; patience.

fore·fin·ger (fôr' fing' gər) *n.* index finger.

fore·mast (fôr' mast') *n.* mast nearest the bow of a ship.

for·mu·la (fôr' myə lə) *n., pl.* **for·mu·las** or **for·mu·lae.** a set method for doing something.

frag·ment (frag' mənt) *n.* part broken off; chip; piece; scrap.

franc (frangk) *n.* the unit of money used in France.

fray (frā) *n.* noisy quarrel, fight, or disturbance; brawl.

free·boot·er (frē' bü' tər) *n.* one who plunders; pirate. [Dutch *vrijbuiter* robber, going back to *vrij* free + *buit* booty.]

French Revolution revolution in France from 1789 to 1799 which overthrew the monarch and aristocracy and gave rise to the First French Republic.

fret (fret) *v.* **fret·ted, fret·ting.** to worry. [Old English *fretan* to eat up, from German *fressen* to eat.]

fric·tion (frik′ shən) *n.* the rubbing of one thing against another. [Latin *frictiō* a rubbing.]

Fro·bish·er, Sir Mar·tin (frō′ bi shər, sėr märt′ ən) c. 1535-1594, English explorer and navigator.

frus·trate (frus′ trāt) *v.* **frus·tra·ted, frus·trat·ing.** to keep (someone) from doing or achieving something; disappoint; thwart. [Latin *frustrātus*, past participle of *frustrārī* to disappoint, render vain, from *frustra* in vain.]

fume (fūm) *v.* **fumed, fum·ing. 1.** to feel great anger or irritation. **2.** to give off smoke, gas, or vapor.

fu·nic·u·lar rail·way(fū nik′ yə lər rāl′ wā′) *n.* railway system in which two cars attached ends of a cable along a steep slope move alternately up and down the slope by counterbalancing and pulling each other. [Latin *fūniculus* small rope, diminutive of *fūnis* rope.]

funicular railway

fust·y (fus′ tē) *adj.* **1.** not up-to-date; old-fashioned; timeworn. **2.** having a stale smell; musty; moldy. [Old French *fuste* odor of a cask, from *fust* tree trunk, cask, from Latin *fūstis* stick, staff.]

G

gal·lant (gal′ ənt) *adj.* brave or noble in spirit or conduct; heroic. [Old French *galant* brave, gay, present participle or *galer* to make merry, rejoice, from *gale* mirth, pleasure; of Germanic origin.]

gar·net (gar′ nit) *n.* any of a group of hard minerals found in various colors. The deep red variety is most commonly used as a gem.

gaunt (gont) *adj.* very thin and hollow-eyed; haggard.

ge·om·e·try (jē om′ ə trē) *n., pl.* **ge·om·e·tries.** branch of mathematics that deals with the properties, measurements, and relationships of points, lines, angles, planes, and solid figures.

gird (gėrd) *v.* **girt** or **gird·ed, gird·ing.** to encircle, as with a belt; enclose; surround. [Old English *gyrdan* to surround, encircle.]

glade (glād) *n.* open space in a wood or forest.

glee·ful·ly (glē′ fə lē) *adv.* with a feeling of joy or gladness.

goat·ee (gō tē′) *n.* small pointed beard on a man's chin. [From goat; because it resembles a goat's beard.]

goatee

gob·let (gob′ lit) *n.* drinking glass with a base and a stem.

grade (grād) *n.* **1.** slope, as of a road or railroad track. **2.** step or degree in a scale, as of quality, merit, or value.

grad·u·ate stu·dent (graj′ ü it stüd′ ənt) *n.* a college student who is engaged in postgraduate work or studies.

grap·nel (grap′ nəl) *n.* grappling iron, a device having one or more hooks or clamps, used especially for grasping or holding something.

a **b**at, ā **c**ake, ä f**a**ther, är c**ar**, ãr d**are**; e h**e**n, ē m**e**, ėr t**er**m; i b**i**b, ī k**ī**te, ir cl**ear**; o t**o**p, ō r**o**pe, ô s**aw**, oi c**oi**n, ôr f**or**k, ou **ou**t; u s**u**n, u̇ b**oo**k, ü m**oo**n, ū c**u**te; ə **a**bout, tak**e**n

green·wood (grēn′ wu̇d′) *n.* forest when green, as in the summer.

griev·ance (grē′ vəns) *n.* real or imagined wrongs that cause anger or resentment.

grim (grim) *adj.* without mercy; harsh; fierce; forbidding.

gri·mace (grim′ əs, gri mās′) *n.* twisted facial expression, especially one indicating pain or displeasure; wry face.

gross (grōs) *adj.* very easy to see or perceive; glaring; flagrant.

grove (grōv) *n.* small forested areas or groups of trees without underbrush.

gun·wale (gun′ əl) *n.* upper edge of the side of a boat or ship. [From gun + Old English *walu* ridge, welt. So called because it once supported a ship's guns.]

H

hab·i·ta·tion (hab′ ə tā′ shən) *n.* place where one lives; living quarters.

haugh·ty (hô′ tē) *adj.* having or showing excessive pride in oneself and contempt for others. [From Old French *haut* high, from Latin *altus*.]

head·land (hed′ lənd) *n.* high point of land extending out into the water; cape.

hearth (härth) *n.* floor of a fireplace, often extending out into the room.

heath (hēth) *n.* open wasteland overgrown with evergreen shrubs or other low bushes; moor.

hedge·row (hej′ rō′) *n.* row of shrubs or small trees planted close together, forming a fence or barrier; hedge.

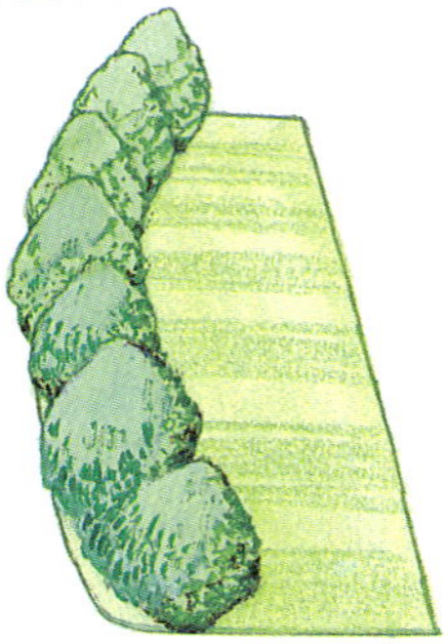

hedgerow

heir (ãr) *n.* person who inherits or is entitled to inherit money, property, or the like after the death of the owner.

helm (helm) *n.* handle or wheel by which a ship is steered.

hence·forth (hens′ forth′) *adv.* from this time on; from now on.

her·ald (hãr′ əld) *n.* **1.** a person who proclaims or announces; messenger. **2.** formerly, an officer who carried messages between princes or rulers.

Her·mes (hėr′ mēz) *n. Greek Mythology.* god of science and invention, who was the swift messenger of the gods, usually pictured with winged sandals and helmet.

Hermes

her·mit (hėr′ mit) *n.* a person who lives alone, away from society, often for religious reasons. [Old French, *(h)ermite*, from Late Latin *(h)erēmīta*, from Greek *erēmites*, literally, dweller in a desert.]

hes·i·ta·tion (hez′ ə tā′ shən) *n.* a delay due to fear, uncertainty, or doubt.

hex·a·gon (hek′ sə gon′) *n.* closed figure lying in a plane, having six sides and six angles. [Latin *hexagōnum*, from Greek *hexagōnos* having six angles, from *hex* six + *gōnia* angle, corner.]

hith·er (hith′ ər) *adv.* to or toward this place.

hoard (hôrd) *n.* thing or things stored or hidden away for future use.

ho·ly or·ders (hō′ le ôr′ dərz) *n.* pl. **1.** the higher grades of the ministry, as in the Roman Catholic or Anglican Church. **2.** rite or sacrament of ordination, or being installed as a religious minister.

hon·or·a·ble men·tion (on′ ər ə bəl men′ shən) *n.* an honorary award or distinction, generally next below those that win prizes.

Hook, James fictional character, also known as Captain Hook, in the book *Peter Pan* by James M. Barrie.

ho·ri·zon (hə rī′ zən) *n.* the line where the sky seems to meet the earth or sea. [Old French *horizon* line of apparent meeting of the sky and the earth or sea, from Late Latin *horīzōn*, from Greek *horīzōn* (kuklos) bounding (circle), going back to *horōs* limit.]

horn (hôrn) *n.* hard, bony growth on the head of various hoofed animals, including cattle, sheep, antelope, and rhinoceroses.

horn·book (hôrn′ bu̇k′) *n.* a primer consisting of a page with the alphabet and a prayer or numerals on it, covered with a sheet of horn and fastened in a frame with a handle, formerly used to teach children to read.

hos·tile (hos′ təl, hos′ tīl) *adj.* feeling or showing unfriendliness or antagonism. [Latin *hostīlis* relating to an enemy, from *hostis* enemy.]

hov·er (huv′ ər, hov′ ər) *v.* to remain as if suspended in the air over a particular spot.

hull (hul) *n.* **1.** frame or body of a ship. **2.** outer covering of a seed.

hy·dro·gen (hī′ drə jən) *n.* highly flammable gas that is colorless, tasteless, and odorless, and is the lightest chemical element. [French *hydrogene*, going back to Greek *hydor* water + *gennan* to produce, because water is produced when hydrogen is burned.]

hy·po·der·mic (hī′ pə dėr′ mik) *n.* instrument used to give injections beneath the skin; syringe. [Greek *hypo* under, below + *derma* skin.]

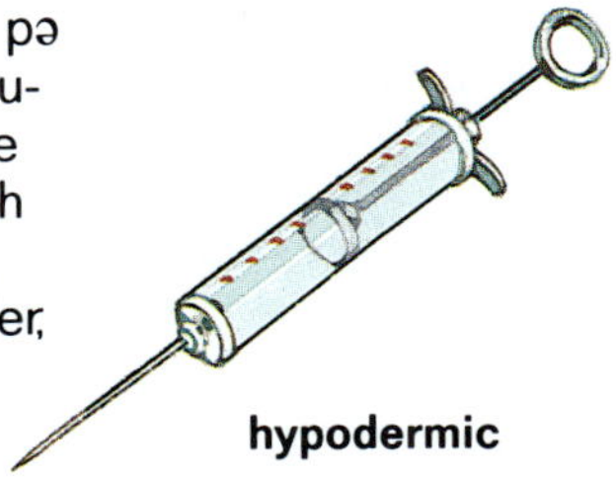

hypodermic

I

i·am·bic pen·tam·e·ter (ī am′ bik pen tam′ ə tər) *n.* line of verse consisting of five metrical feet, each foot consisting of two syllables, the first one unstressed and the second stressed: *To*day′/to*day*′/we all′/should stay′/away′.

ice floe (īs′ flō′) *n.* sheet of floating ice.

il·lu·sion (i lü′ zhən) *n.* a false or misleading idea or belief; misconception. [Latin *illusio* mocking; deception.]

il·lus·tra·tor (il′ ə strā′ tər) *n.* an artist who makes illustrations for books or magazines.

im·mense (i mens′) *adj.* huge; vast; enormous. [Latin *immensus* literally, not measured.]

im·pact (im′ pakt) *n.* strong effect or influence. [Latin *impactus*, past participle of *impingere* to strike against.]

im·pen·e·tra·ble (im pen′ ə trə bəl) *adj.* **1.** incapable of being understood; unfathomable. **2.** that cannot be pierced, entered, or passed through.

im·per·cep·ti·bly (im′ pər sep′ tə blē) *adv.* in a way that can barely be seen or perceived; almost beyond notice.

in·as·much (in′ əz much′) *conj.* in view of the fact that; since.

in·cog·ni·to (in′ kog nē′ tō) *adv.* having one's identity hidden so as to be unknown; in disguise. [Italian *incognito* unknown, from Latin *incognitus*.]

in·cred·u·lous·ly (in krej′ ə ləs′ lē) *adv.* doubtfully; unbelievingly.

in·cur (in kėr′) *v.* **in·curred, in·cur·ring.** to bring something on oneself through one's own actions.

a b**a**t, ā c**a**ke, ä f**a**ther, är c**ar**, ãr d**are**; e h**e**n, ē m**e**, ėr t**er**m; i b**i**b, ī k**ī**te, ir cl**ear**; o t**o**p, ō r**o**pe, ô s**aw**, oi c**oi**n, ôr f**or**k, ou **ou**t; u s**u**n, u̇ b**oo**k, ü m**oo**n, ū c**u**te; ə **a**bout, tak**e**n

in·de·ci·pher·a·ble (in′ di sī′ fər əb əl) *adj.* illegible; difficult to read.

in·dig·na·tion (in′ dig nā′ shən) *n.* restrained, dignified anger aroused by something unfair, cruel, or evil.

in·dul·gent·ly (in dul′ jənt lē) *adv.* patiently; tolerantly; considerately; permissively.

in·ex·o·ra·ble (i nek′ sər ə bəl) *adj.* unchanging or unyielding, no matter what is done or said; relentless. [Latin *inexōrābilis*, going back to *in-* not + *exōrāre* to gain by pleading.]

in·fan·try (in′ fən trē) *n., pl.* **in·fan·tries.** soldiers trained and equipped to fight on foot.

in·fest (in fest′) *v.* to overrun or occur in large numbers so as to be harmful or troublesome.

in·fi·nite·ly (in′ fə nit lē) *adv.* greatly; immensely; boundlessly.

in·ge·nu·i·ty (in′ jə nü′ ə tē, in′ jə nū′ ə tē) *n., pl.* **in·ge·nu·i·ties.** cleverness or originality.—*adj.* **in·gen·ious.**

in·scrip·tion (in skrip′ shən) *n.* message or note written on something.

in·spir·ing (in spīr′ ing) *adj.* exerting a creative influence on; animating; stimulating; stirring.

in·stinc·tive·ly (in stingk′ tiv lē) *adj.* by instinct; without thinking; automatically; unconsciously; spontaneously.

in·su·lat·ed (in′ sə lā′ tid) *adj.* covered or surrounded with material, such as rubber, that does not conduct electricity.

in·tent·ly (in tent′ lē) *adv.* fixedly; in a concentrated manner.

in·ter·val (in′ tər vəl) *n.* time or space between. [Latin *intervallum* space between ramparts, space between, from *inter* between + *vallum* rampart.]

in·tim·i·date (in tim′ ə dāt′) *v.* **in·tim·i·dat·ed, in·tim·i·dat·ing.** to make fearful or timid. [Medieval Latin *intimidātus*, past participle of *intimidāre* to frighten, from Latin *in* in + *timidus* fearful.]

ire (īr) *n.* anger; wrath.

i·so·lat·ed (ī′ sə lā′ tid) *adj.* set apart; separated from others. [From Italian *isolato* detached, from *isola* island, from Latin *insula.*]

i·sos·ce·les tri·an·gle (ī sos′ ə lēz trī′ ang′ gəl) *n.* triangle having two sides whose lengths are equal. [Late Latin *isoscelēs* having equal legs, from Greek *isoskelēs*, from *isos* equal + *skelos* leg.]

is·sue (ish′ ü) *v.* **is·sued, is·su·ing.** to send or give out. [Old French *issue* way out, event, from *issir* to go out, from Latin *exīre.*]

J

jest (jest) *n.* prank; joke. —*v.* to speak or act in a playful manner; speak or act without seriousness.

jet·ti·son (jet′ ə sən) *v.* to throw overboard to lighten an aircraft.

Jones, John Paul 1747-1792, Scottish-born U.S. naval hero of the American Revolution.

jour·nal·ist (jėrn′ ə list) *n.* a person who edits or writes for a newspaper or magazine.

joust·ing (jous′ ting) *n.* formal combat, often part of a tournament, between two mounted knights armed with lances and other weapons. [Old French *jouste*, from *jouster* to meet, joust, tourney, from Late Latin *iuxtāre* to approach, join, from Latin *iuxtā* near.]

jousting

jo·vi·al (jō′ vē əl) *adj.* characterized by hearty, good-natured humor; merry; jolly. [From Latin *Joviālis* relating to Jove or Jupiter, from the belief that people born under the sign of the planet Jupiter were happy and jolly.]

K

keel (kēl) *n.* main timber or steel piece extending lengthwise along the center of the bottom of a ship or boat and supporting the entire frame.

keen (kēn) *adj.* **keen·er, keen·est.** sensitive or sharp.

kelp (kelp) *n.* any of a large group of brown seaweeds, growing in great masses along the coasts of the Atlantic and Pacific oceans.

kelp

knave (nāv) *n.* deceitful, dishonest or disloyal man; scoundrel.

L

lack·ey (lak′ ē) *n.* low-ranking male servant.

lad·en (lād′ ən) *adj.* loaded.

lance (lans) *n.* long spear, usually consisting of a wooden shaft with a sharp metal head, carried by mounted soldiers or knights.

lan·tern bat·ter·y (lan′ tərn bat′ ər ē) *n.* **bat·ter·ies.** a large, rectangular six-volt battery commonly used to power such things as a lantern flashlight.

Lapp (lap) *n.* member of a people living in Lapland, a region in northern Europe that includes the northernmost sections of Norway, Sweden, and Finland.

la·ser (lā′ zər) *n. Physics.* device that generates and increases light energy, producing an extremely powerful beam consisting of light waves which are of the same wavelength. [Abbreviation of **l**(ight) **a**(mplification by) **s**(timulated) **e**(mission of) **r**(adiation.]

league (lēg) *n.* **1.** an association of people or countries to further their common interests. **in league with.** associated with others in some plan. **2.** measure of distance equal to three nautical miles.

lev·er (lev′ ər, lē′ vər) *n.* rod or bar that transmits force or motion from one point to another.

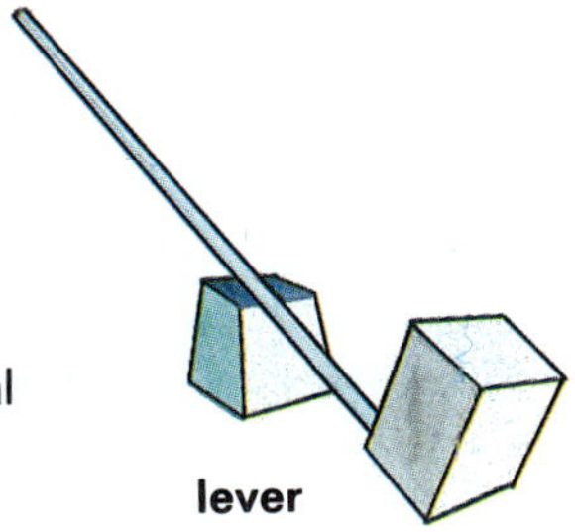

lever

Li·bra·ry of Con·gress, national library of the U.S., located in Washington, D.C.

lift (lift) *n. British.* elevator.

lim·bo (lim′ bō) *n.* place for people and things cast aside, forgotten, or out of date.

limp (limp) *adj.* weak; unable to support oneself.

li·nen (lin′ ən) *n.* a strong cloth woven from flax fibers, used for dresses, suits and tablecloths.

lin·go (ling′ gō) *n., pl.* **lin·goes.** language peculiar to a particular group of people. [Latin *lingua* tongue.]

list·less·ly (list′ lis lē) *adv.* without energy or vigor; numbly; indifferently.

loath·ing (lō′ thing) *n.* extreme disgust or distaste; abhorrence; repugnance.

log (lôg, log) *n.* book containing the official daily record of a ship's voyage.

loi·ter (loi′ tər) *v.* to linger idly or aimlessly about a place.

a bat, ā cake, ä father, är car, ãr dare; e hen, ē me, ėr term; i bib, ī kīte, ir clear; o top, ō rope, ô saw, oi coin, ôr fork, ou out; u sun, ů book, ü moon, ū cute; ə about, taken

Long John Sil·ver fictional character, a pirate, in the book *Treasure Island* by Robert Louis Stevenson.

loom (lüm) *n.* machine for weaving thread into cloth. —*v.* to appear as a large threatening shape.

loy·al·ly (loi′ ə lē) *adv.* faithfully; constantly.

lum·ber (lum′ bər) *v.* to move in a clumsy or noisy manner.

lu·nar (lü′ nər) *adj.* **1.** of or relating to the moon. **2.** measured by the moon's revolutions: *a lunar month.* [Latin *luna* moon.]

lunge (lunj) *v.* **lunged, lung·ing.** to make a sudden forward thrust or movement. [Short for obsolete *allonge*, going back to Latin *ad* to + *longus* extended; referring to the extension of the body when lunging.]

lure (lür) *v.* **lured, lur·ing.** to attract powerfully; tempt. [Old French *loirre* bait; of Germanic origin.]

M

mace (mās) *n.* heavy war club, usually having a spiked metal head, used especially in the Middle Ages for crushing armor.

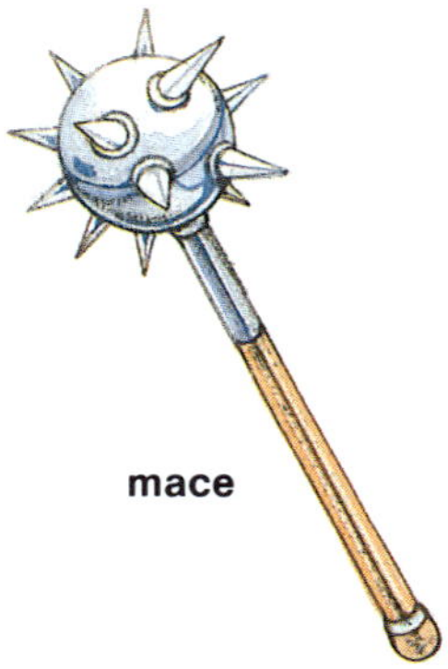
mace

main·land (mān′ land′, mān′ lənd) *n.* the body of land forming the principal or largest land mass of a region, country, or continent, as distinguished from an island or a peninsula.

make·shift (māk′ shift′) *n.* something used temporarily in place of the proper or usual thing.

ma·nip·u·late (mə nip′ yə lāt′) *v.* **ma·nip·u·lat·ed, ma·nip·u·lat·ing. 1.** to work with the hands, especially with dexterity and skill. **2.** to try to influence or adapt to one's own advantage.

mar·i·ner (mãr′ ə nər) *n.* person who navigates a ship; sailor. [Anglo-Norman *mariner*, from Medieval Latin *marinarius*, from Latin *marinus* relating to the sea, from *mare* sea.]

mariner

mar·quis (mär kē′) *n.* nobleman ranking next below a duke and above an earl or count. [Old French *marquis, marchis* originally, governor of a frontier, from *marche* frontier; of Germanic origin.]

mas·ter (mas′ tər) *n.* **1.** a male teacher, especially in a private school. **2.** a person who has power, control, or authority over someone or something. [Partly from Old English *maegister* chief, teacher; partly from Old French *maistre* one in charge, chief; both from Latin *magister* superior, chief, teacher.]

mate (māt) *n.* **1.** assistant to an officer in the U.S. Navy. **2.** one of a pair.

maul (môl) *v.* to injure as by beating, bruising, or knocking about.

May·a (mä′ yə) *n.* member of a highly civilized group of American Indians who lived in southern Mexico and parts of South America at the time of the Spanish conquest in the sixteenth century.

may·hap (mā′ hap′, mā′ hap′) *adv. Archaic.* perhaps.

me·die·val (mid ē′ vəl) *adj.* of, relating to, or belonging to the Middle Ages, the period in European history from about A.D. 500 to 1450. [Latin *medius* middle + *aevum* age.]

mer·it (mãr′ it) *n.* good quality.

met·ro (me′ trō) *n.* subway system in Paris, France.

mi·as·ma (mī az′ mə, mē az′ mə) *n., pl.* **mi·as·mas** or **mi·as·ma·ta** (mī az′ mə tə) poisonous vapor formerly thought to rise from the earth and pollute the air. [Greek *miasma* pollution.]

Mid·dle Ag·es (mid′ əl ā′ jəz) *n. pl.* period of European history between the fall of the Western Roman Empire and the beginning of the Renaissance, from about the fifth century to the middle of the fifteenth century.

Mid·dle Eng·lish, English language from 1100-1500.

midst (midst) *n.* **1.** gathering or association of people; company. **2.** condition or position of being surrounded by, involved in, or beset by.

mil·li·ner (mil′ ə nər) *n.* a person who designs, makes, trims, or sells women's hats.

mim·e·o·graphed (mim′ ē ə graft′) *adj.* reproduced by a mimeograph machine.

min·i·a·ture (min′ ē ə chər, min′ ə chər) *adj.* very small. [Latin *miniatura* small picture, illumination of manuscripts, going back to Latin *miniare* to paint with read lead, from *minium* red lead; referring to the decorating of medieval manuscripts with *minium* and to the small size of the illustrations so done.]

min·is·tra·tion (min′ is trā′ shən) *n.* act of helping or giving aid.

mi·nor (mī′ nər) *adj.* of lesser importance, seriousness, or danger.

min·strel (min′ strəl) *n.* in the Middle Ages, a traveling musician who sang or recited poems, usually to the accompaniment of a harp, lute, or similar instrument. [Old French *menestrel* entertainer, servant, from Late Latin *ministerialis* official, servant, from Latin *ministerium* service.]

minstrel

mis·ad·ven·ture (mis′ əd ven′ chər) *n.* mishap; misfortune.

mis·lead·ing (mis lē′ ding) *adj.* causing or tending to cause a mistaken or wrong thought or action.

Mö·bi·us, Au·gust F. (mō′ bē əs, ô güst′) 1790-1868, German mathematician.

mock (mok) *adj.* not real; pretended; sham.

mod·est·ly (mod′ ist lē) *adv.* in a simple manner; not boastfully.

mon·arch (mon′ ərk) *n.* **1.** a hereditary ruler of a state or country, such as a king or queen. **2.** monarch butterfly. A large orange and black butterfly found in North America that is known for its fall migrations southward of several thousand miles.

mon·ar·chy (mon′ ər kē) *n., pl.* **mon·ar·chies.** government by a monarch, a hereditary ruler of a nation, as a king or queen. [Late Latin *monarchia*, absolute rule, going back to *monas* alone + *archein* to rule.]

mon·o·tone (mon′ ə tōn′) *n.* saying or uttering of words or sounds with no change in pitch; single, unchanging tone in speaking.

moon·stone (mün′ stōn) *n.* a pearly gemstone.

moor·ing (mür′ ing) *n.* device, such as a cable line or anchor, by which a boat or ship is secured in place.

mor·al·ist (môr′ ə list) *n.* one who teaches or writes about morality, or standards of right conduct.

mo·roc·co (mə rok′ ō) *n.* leather that originally came from Morocco, made from goatskin tanned with sumac.

mor·tal (môrt′ əl) *adj.* subject to death; not living forever. [Latin *mortālis* subject to death, human, from *mors* death.]

a bat, ā cake, ä father, är car, ãr dare; e hen, ē me, ėr term; i bib, ī kīte, ir clear; o top, ō rope, ô saw, oi coin, ôr fork, ou out; u sun, ů book, ü moon, ū cute; ə about, taken

mot·to (mot' ō) *n., pl.* **mot·toes** or **mot·tos.** brief saying or proverb that expresses a guiding idea or principle. [Italian *motto* word, saying, going back to Latin *muttum* grunt, mutter.]

mourn·ing (môr' ning) *adj.* of or relating to the display of expression of sorrow or grief over someone's death.

mouth (mouth) *n.* part of a river where it empties into another body of water.

muf·fler (muf' lər) *n.* a scarf of wool or other material, worn around the neck for warmth.

mus·ket (mus' kit) *n.* gun introduced in the 1500s and widely used before the development of the rifle. [Middle French *mousquet*, from Italian *moschetto* musket; earlier, arrow for a crossbow, from *mosca* fly, from Latin *musca*.]

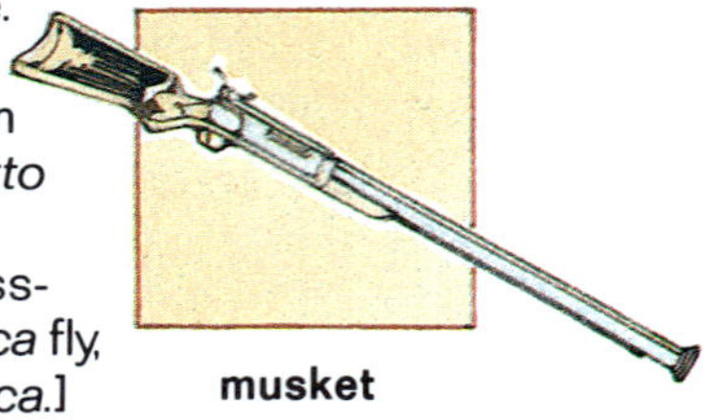

musket

mu·ta·tion (mū tā' shən) *n.* a change in a gene that affects the offspring and is inheritable. [Latin *mutatio* change.]

my·thol·o·gy (mi thol' ə jē) *n., pl.* **my·thol·o·gies.** myths and legends as a group, especially a body of myths belonging to a particular ancient religion or culture. [Late Latin *mȳthologia* from Greek *mythologia*, legend, storytelling, from *mythos* word, fable, story + *logos* word, discourse.]

N

Nan·sen, Fridt·jof (nän' sən, frit' yof) 1861-1930, Norwegian arctic explorer, scientist, and statesman.

Na·tion·al Aer·o·nau·tics and Space Ad·min·is·tra·tion (NASA) civilian agency of the U.S. government with the mission of performing research and carrying out operations in the areas of space exploration, artificial satellites, and rocketry.

Na·tion·al O·cean·o·graph·ic and At·mos·pher·ic Ad·min·is·tra·tion (NOAA) an agency of the U.S. Department of Commerce that works to improve knowledge and use of the environment.

na·tion·al·i·ty (nash' ə nal' ə tē) *n., pl.* **na·tion·al·i·ties. 1.** group of persons sharing a common origin, language, and history. **2.** fact or state of belonging to a particular nation, especially by birth.

nau·se·at·ing (nô' zē ā' ting) *adj.* producing a sick feeling in the stomach; disgusting; revolting.

nav·i·gate (nav' i gāt') *v.* **nav·i·gat·ed, nav·i·gat·ing.** to direct the course of or operate a ship, boat, or aircraft. [Latin *nāvigātus*, past participle of *nāvigāre* to sail, from *navis* ship + *agere* to drive.]

Na·zi (nät' sē) member or follower of the party that controlled Germany under the leadership of Adolf Hitler from 1933 to 1945.

nec·ro·man·cer (nek' rə man' sər) *n.* person who is believed to predict the future by communicating with the dead. [Late Latin *necromantīa* prophecy by invoking the dead, from Greek *nekromanteia*, from *nekros* corpse + *manteia* prophecy.]

Nel·son, Ho·ra·ti·o (nel' sən, hə rā' shē ō') 1758-1805, English admiral.

nom·i·nate (nom' ə nāt') *v.* **nom·i·nat·ed, nom·i·nat·ing.** to put forward as a candidate for an office or honor. [Latin *nōminātus*, past participle of *nōmināre* to name, from *nōmen* name.]

no·tion (nō' shən) *n.* idea; opinion.

no·to·ri·ous (nō tôr' ē əs) *adj.* well-known for something bad; infamous. [Medieval Latin *notorious* well-known, from Latin *nōtus* known.]

nought (nôt) *also,* **naught.** *n.* nothing. [Old English *nāwiht* mischief, nothing, from *nā* no + *wiht* thing.]

nu·cle·ar en·er·gy (nü' klē ər en' ər jē) *n.* energy obtained from the nucleus of the atom.

nu·mer·i·cal (nü mãr′ i kəl, nū mãr′ i kəl) *adj.* of, relating to, or represented by a number or numbers.

nymph (nimf) *n.* in Greek and Roman mythology, any of various goddesses living especially in forests, hills, or rivers and usually represented as beautiful maidens.

O

oath (ōth) *n.* a formal promise made with an appeal to God to be a witness to the promise.

o·cean·o·graph·ic (ō′ shə nə graf′ ik) *adj.* of or relating to oceanography, the science of the sea.

off·spring (ôf′ spring′) *n., pl.* **off·spring, off·springs.** the young of a person, animal, or plant.

Old Norse, North Germanic language of Scandinavia from 700-1300 A.D.

o·men (ō′ mən) *n.* sign or event that is supposed to foretell good or bad luck.

om·i·nous·ly (om′ ə nəs lē) *adv.* in such a way as to foretell trouble or misfortune; threateningly; menacingly. [Latin *ōminōsus*, from *ōmen* omen.]

on·slaught (ôn′ slôt) *n.* vigorous or destructive attack.

orb and scep·ter, a globe with a cross on top and a staff, the pair symbolizing kingly power and justice.

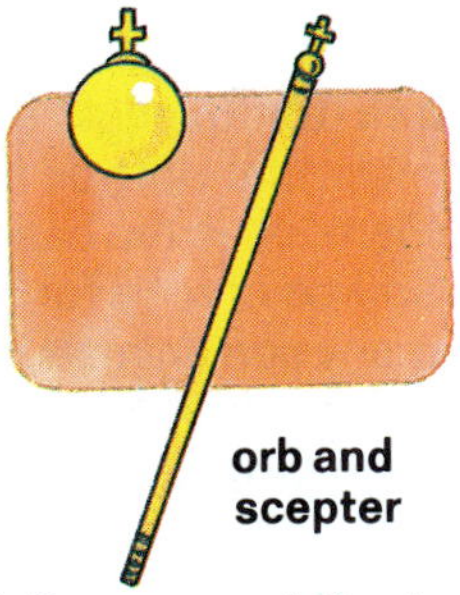
orb and scepter

or·deal (ôr dēl′, ôr′ dēl) *n.* very difficult or painful experience. [Old English *ordāl* form of trial in which the accused is forced to take a test of a dangerous nature.]

out·crop (out′ krop′) *n.* part of a rock layer that sticks out of the ground so as to be seen or easily mined.

o·ver·whelm (ō′ vər hwelm′, ō′ vər welm′) *v.* to completely overcome; overpower.

P

pad·dock (pad′ ək) *n.* small field or enclosure in which an animal can graze and exercise.

page (pāj) *n.* servant or attendant, especially a boy who attends a person of rank, as in a royal household. [Old French *page* young boy, valet, going back to Greek *paidion* young boy, diminutive of *pais* child.]

pag·eant·ry (paj′ ən trē) *n., pl.* **pag·eant·ries.** the act or process of composing and producing an elaborate theatrical presentation, especially one that celebrates historical events.

pal·let (pal′ it) *n.* straw bed or mattress.

pam·phlet (pam′ flit) *n.* a short, unbound printed publication, usually having a paper cover; booklet.

par·a·pet (pãr′ ə pit, pãr′ ə pet′) *n.* low wall of earth or stone to protect troops from observation or fire.

parch·ment (pärch′ mənt) *n.* skin of sheep, goats, or other animals, prepared for writing or painting upon. [Old French *parchemin* such skin, modification of Latin *pergamina*, from Greek *pergamēne*, from *Pergamon*, city in Asia Minor where it was first produced.]

Par·lia·ment (pär′ lə mənt) *n.* the legislature of Great Britain made up of the House of Commons and the House of Lords.

a bat, ā cake, ä father, är car, ãr dare; e hen, ē me, ėr term; i bib, ī kite, ir clear; o top, ō rope, ô saw, oi coin, ôr fork, ou out; u sun, u̇ book, ü moon, ū cute; ə about, taken

par·ry (păr′ ē) *v.* **par·ried, par·ry·ing.** to stop or deflect an opponent's attack in fencing, as with the side of one's own sword. [French *parez*, imperative of *parer* to defend, from Latin *parāre* to make ready.]

par·ti·tion (pär tish′ ən) *n.* **1.** section or part into which a thing is divided. **2.** something that divides a room.

par·tridge (pär′ trij) *n., pl.* **par·tridg·es, par·tridge.** any of several plump game birds of Europe, Asia, and Africa, having gray, brown, and white feathers.

pa·thet·i·cal·ly (pə thet′ ik lē) *adv.* in such a way as to arouse pity, sadness, or compassion, pitifully.

pa·tri·ot·ic (pā′ trē ot′ ik) *adj.* characterized or showing love for one's country. [Middle French *patriote*, from Late Latin *patriōta* fellow countryman, from Greek *patriōtes*.]

pa·tron saint (pā′ trən sānt′) *n.* saint chosen as the special guardian or protector of a person, place, organization, or the like.

pen·ta·gon (pen′ tə gon′) *n.* closed figure lying in a plane, having five sides and five angles. [Late Latin *pentagōnum* this figure, from Greek *pentagōnon*, from *pente* five + *gōnia* angle.]

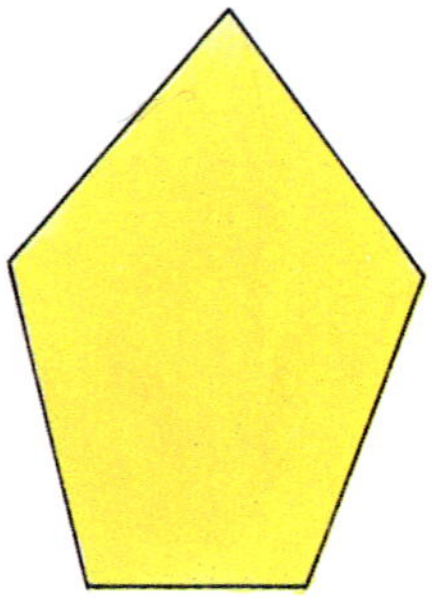

pentagon

per·il·ous (păr′ ə ləs) *adj.* full of peril or danger; hazardous; dangerous. [Old French *perillous*, from Latin *perīculōsus*, from *perīculum* danger.]

per·me·at·ing (pėr′ mē ā ting) *adj.* spreading throughout; filling; pervading.

phase (fāz) *n.* **1.** appearance of the moon at a particular time, depending on how much of its lighted side can be seen from the earth. **2.** stage of development of a person or thing.

phi·los·o·pher (fi los′ ə fər) *n.* person who studies or is an expert in philosophy, the study of the fundamental nature, function, and purpose of human life. [Anglo-Norman *philosofre* one who studies philosophy, from Latin *philosophus*, from Greek *philosophos* lover of wisdom, from *philos* loving + *sophos* wise.]

phys·i·cist (fiz′ ə sist) *n.* person who is an expert in physics, the science that deals with matter and energy, and with the laws governing them.

pi (pī) *n.* **1.** the ratio of the circumference of a circle to its diameter, represented by the Greek letter π. Pi is approximately 3.1416. **2.** the sixteenth letter of the Greek alphabet (Π, π).

pitch (pich) *n.* **1.** dark, thick, sticky substance obtained from such substances as petroleum, coal tar or wood tar, used for waterproofing or paving. **2.** resin from pines.

plac·id (plas′ id) *adj.* calm or peaceful; undisturbed.

plain·tive (plān′ tiv) *adj.* expressing sorrow; mournful; complaining. [going back to Latin *planctus* lamentation.]

plane (plān) *n. Geometry.* flat surface that wholly contains every line connecting any two points on it.

plank·ton (plangk′ tən) *n.* tiny plants and animals that drift or float on a body of water. Plankton is the basic source of food for many sea animals. [German *Plankton*, from Greek *plankton*, neuter of *planktos* wandering; referring to their wandering or drifting habits.]

plankton

plum·met (plum′ it) *v.* to fall or drop straight downward; plunge.

Po·lo, Mar·co (pō′ lō, mär′ kō) c. 1254-1324, Italian traveler.

pol·y·gon (pol′ ē gon′) *n.* closed figure lying in a plane and having three or more straight sides. [Late Latin *polygōnon,* from *polys* much, many + *gōnia* angle.]

pom·mel (pum′ əl) *v.* to strike repeatedly with the fists; pummel.

pon·der (pon′ dər) *v.* to weigh in the mind; think over carefully. [Old French *ponderer* to weigh, balance, from Latin *ponderāre* to weigh, from *pondus* weight, related to *pendere* to hang.]

pope (pōp) *n.* the highest representative of the Roman Catholic Church.

port·cul·lis (pôrt kul′ is) *n.* heavy grating constructed so as to slide up and down in grooves cut in the sides of a gateway of a castle or fortress, capable of being lowered quickly as a defense against attack.

portcullis

por·ter (pôr′ tər) *n.* one who is employed to carry baggage, as at a railroad station, or in a hotel. [Old French *porteur* bearer, from Latin Latin *portator* from Latin *portare* to carry.]

port·hole (pôrt′ hōl′) *n.* small, usually circular opening in the side of a boat or ship for letting in air and light.

Po·sei·don (pə sī′ dən) *n. Greek Mythology.* god of the sea and brother of Zeus and Pluto.

pow·der mon·key (pou′ dər mung′ kē) *n.* a boy formerly employed on warships to carry powder to the guns.

prac·ti·cal (prak′ ti kəl) *adj.* having or showing good judgment or good sense; sensible. [Late Latin *practicus* relating to action, from Greek *praktikos,* from *prassein* to do, accomplish.]

pre·ci·sion (pri sizh′ ən) *n.* accuracy; exactness.—*adj.* **pre·cise.**

pre·oc·cu·pied (prē ok′ yə pīd) *adj.* absorbed in thought.

pre·scribed (pri skrībd′) *adj.* set down or given as a rule or direction to be followed.

pres·er·va·tion (prez′ ər vā′ shən) *n.* the act of maintaining or keeping intact.

pre·vail (pri vāl′) *v.* to prove successful, succeed; win.

pre·vi·ous (prē′ vē əs) *adj.* coming before; earlier.

prey (prā) *n.* any animal hunted or killed for food. [Old French *preie* animal seized by meat-eating animals for food, booty, from Latin *praeda* booty.]

pri·me·val (prī mē′ vəl) *adj.* of, relating to, or belonging to the first or earliest age or ages, especially of the world; primitive. [Latin *prīmaevus* in the first period of life, from *primus* first + *aevum* age.]

prin·ci·ple (prin′ sə pəl) *n.* **1.** rule of personal conduct. **2.** fundamental truth, law, belief, or doctrine. [Modification of Latin *principium* beginning, origin.]

pri·o·ry (prī′ ə rē) *n., pl.* **pri·o·ries.** a religious house governed by a prior or prioress, often dependent on an abbey.

pri·va·teer (prī′ və tir′) *n.* commander or crew member of a privately owned ship hired by a government to attack enemy ships.

pro·ce·dure (prə sē′ jər) *n.* a course of action.

a **b**at, ā **c**ake, ä **f**ather, är **c**ar, ãr **d**are; e **h**en, ē **m**e, ėr **t**erm; i **b**ib, ī **k**īte, ir **c**lear; o **t**op, ō **r**ope, ô **s**aw, oi **c**oin, ôr **f**ork, ou **out**; u **s**un, u̇ **b**ook, ü **m**oon, ū **c**ute; ə **a**bout, tak**e**n

pro·found (prə found′) *adj.* intensely felt. [Old French *profond* deep, from Latin *prō-fundus.*]

prom·on·to·ry (prom′ ən tôr′ ē) *n., pl.* **prom·on·to·ries.** high piece of land extending out into a body of water; headland.

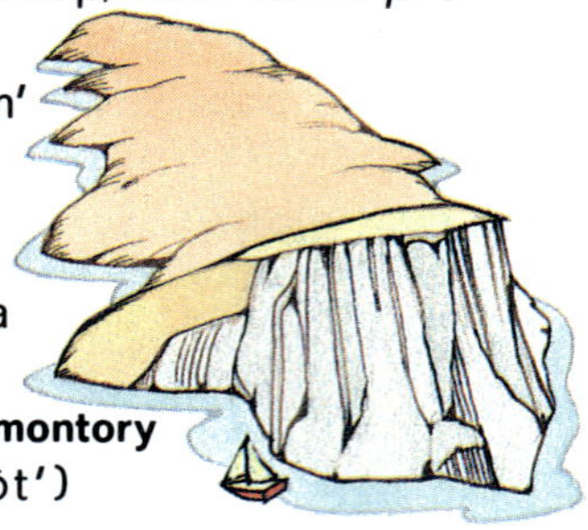
promontory

pro·mote (prə mōt′) *v.* **pro·mot·ed, pro·mot·ing.** to try to sell by advertising.

prose (prōz) *n.* everyday written or spoken language that does not follow poetic meter.

Prot·es·tant (prot′ is tənt) *n.* a Christian who does not belong to the Roman Catholic Church or the Orthodox Church.

ptar·mi·gan (tär′ mi gən) *n.* any of various grouse of northern regions, having brownish feathers and feathered legs and feet.

pub·lic re·la·tions (pub′ lik ri lā′ shənz) *n. pl.* act or process of promoting good will for an individual or corporation.

pub·li·ca·tion (pub′ li kā′ shən) *n.* something, such as a book or a magazine, that has been published.

pum·ice (pum′ is) *n.* light, porous, volcanic rock.

pum·per·nick·el (pum′ pər nik′ əl) *n.* coarse black or dark-brown bread made of unsifted rye flour.

pu·ny (pū′ nē) *adj.* inferior in size, strength, or importance.

Q

quar·ter (kwor′ tər) *n.* one of four equal parts; one-fourth. [Old French *quartier* a fourth part, district, from Latin *quartārius* a fourth part, from *quartus* fourth.]

quest (kwest) *n.* a search or pursuit. [Old French *queste* search, going back to Latin *quaesīta* thing sought, from *quaerere* to seek, inquire.]

R

raf·fi·a (raf′ ē ə) *n.* strong fiber obtained from the leaves of an evergreen palm tree, used to make netting and baskets.

rage (rāj) *n.* violent anger; fury.

Ra·leigh, Sir Wal·ter (rô′ lē, sėr wôl′ tər) c. 1552-1618, English colonizer, statesman, and author.

rank (rangk) *n.* social position.

rapt (rapt) *adj.* deeply absorbed. [Latin *raptus*, past participle of *rapere* to seize.]

rap·tur·ous (rap′ chər əs) *adj.* showing or feeling great joy, love, or other kinds of strong emotion.

rav·aged (rav′ ijd) *adj.* marked by the effects of painful experiences.

ra·vine (rə vēn′) *n.* deep, narrow valley, especially one created by running water; large gully. [French *ravine* violent rush, as of water, from Latin *rapina* violence, plunder.]

ravine

realm (relm) *n.* kingdom.

re·cess (rē′ ses) *n., pl.* **re·cess·es.** part of a wall that is set back or indented.

re·flec·tive (ri flek′ tiv) *adj.* given to or showing serious or careful thinking; thoughtful.

re·form (ri form′) *n.* a change for the better. [Latin *reformāre* to shape again, change.]

ref·u·gee (ref′ ū jē′) *n.* a person who leaves his or her homeland because of war or other dangers and seeks safety in another place.

re·it·er·ate (rē it′ ə rāt′) *v.* **re·it·er·at·ed, re·it·er·at·ing.** to say or do again repeatedly; repeat. [Late Latin *reiterātus*, past participle of *reiterāre* to repeat, going back to Latin *re-* again + *iterum* again.]

re·ject (ri jekt') *v.* to refuse to accept, believe, or approve. [Latin *rejectus*, past participle of *rejicere* to throw back, scorn.]

rel·a·tive (rel' ə tiv) *adj.* resulting from or judged by comparison; comparative; having meaning only in relation to something else. [Late Latin *relātīvus* having reference to, from Latin *relātus*, past participle of *referre* to carry back, report.]

re·li·a·ble (ri lī' ə bəl) *adj.* able to be depended on; trustworthy.

re·mit·tance (ri mit' əns) *n.* money that is sent.

re·mote (ri mōt') *adj.* not near; far away; out of the way; secluded. [Latin *remōtus* far off, past participle of *removēre* to move back.]

rep·u·ta·tion (rep' yə tā' shən) *n.* a general or public estimation of someone.

re·signed (ri zīnd') *adj.* submissive; showing acceptance or resignation.

re·sist (ri zist') *v.* to keep from yielding or giving in to.

re·solve (ri zolv') *v.* **re·solved, re·sol·ving.** to decide (to do something).

reti·nue (ret' ən ü') *n.* group of servants accompanying a person of rank or authority.

ret·ri·bu·tion (re' trə bū' shən) *n.* act of paying back or punishing for wrongdoing. [Latin *retribūtiō* repayment.]

re·trieve (ri trēv') *v.* **re·trie·ved, re·triev·ing.** to get back; recover.

rev·eil·le (rev' ə lē) *n.* signal on a bugle to awaken troops. [French *reveillez* wake up, imperative of *reveiller* to awaken, going back to Latin *re-* again + *vigilāre* to keep watch.]

rev·el (rev' əl) *n.* noisy festivity; merrymaking. [Old French *reveler* to revolt, make merry noisily, from Latin *rēbellāre* to revolt, from *re-* again + *bellare* to make war.]

rever·ie (rev' ər ē) *n.* daydreaming of happy, pleasant things; dreaminess; meditation.

re·view (ri vū') *n.* critical summary or discussion. [French *revue* survey, critical article, magazine, from *revoir* to see again, going back to Latin *re-* again + *vidēre* to see.]

re·volt·ing (ri vōl' ting) *adj.* disgusting; offensive; loathsome.

Ri·ga (rē' gə) capital of Latvia, formerly an independent country, now a republic of the Soviet Union.

rod (rod) *n.* unit of measurement equal to 5 1/2 yards or 16 1/2 feet.

ruck·sack (ruk' sak', ru̇k' sak') *n.* knapsack. [German *Rücksack* literally, back sack.]

ruse (rüz) *n.* trick; action intended to deceive.

rush (rush) *n., pl.* **rush·es.** any of several reedy or grasslike plants found in marshy areas, having slender, often hollow stems, and clusters of small green or brown flowers.

rush

ruth·less·ness (rüth' lis nis) *n.* state of being without pity, mercy, or compassion.

S

sac·ris·tan (sak' ri stən) *n.* a person who is in charge of a sacristy, a room in a church where objects used in ceremonies are kept.

a bat, ā cake, ä father, är car, ãr dare; e hen, ē me, ėr term; i bib, ī kīte, ir clear; o top, ō rope, ô saw, oi coin, ôr fork, ou out; u sun, u̇ book, ü moon, ū cute; ə about, taken

sa·la·mi (sə lä′ mē) *n.* sausage of seasoned pork or beef. [Italian *salami,* plural of *salame,* from *salār* to salt, going back to Latin *sal* salt.]

sal·ly port (sal′ ē pôrt′) *n.* a protected gate or underground passage in a fortification through which troops may pass when making a sudden attack.

sal·u·ta·tion (sal′ yə tā′ shən) *n.* greeting; welcoming.

sand·spit (sand′ spit′) *n.* narrow point of land, consisting of sand, that extends into the sea.

sap·phire (saf′ īr) *n.* precious stone that is blue in color.

sau·cy (sô′ sē) *adj.* bold or rude; forward.

sauer·kraut (sour′ krout′) *n.* finely shredded cabbage that has been salted and fermented in its own juice. [German *Sauerkraut,* from *sauer* sour + *Kraut* cabbage.]

sce·nic (sē′ nik, sēn′ ik) *adj.* of, relating to, or full of natural scenery; picturesque.

schol·ar (skol′ ər) *n.* a person who has complete knowledge of, and is considered to be an expert in, a particular field, especially one of the humanities. [Late Latin *scholāris* relating to a school, from Latin *schola.*]

scone (skōn, skon) *n.* small biscuit, often round, usually served with butter.

Scott, Rob·ert Fal·con (skot′, rob′ ərt fal′ kən) 1868-1912, English naval officer and Antarctic explorer.

scull (skul) *n.* one of a pair of light oars used together, one on each side of a boat, by a single rower.

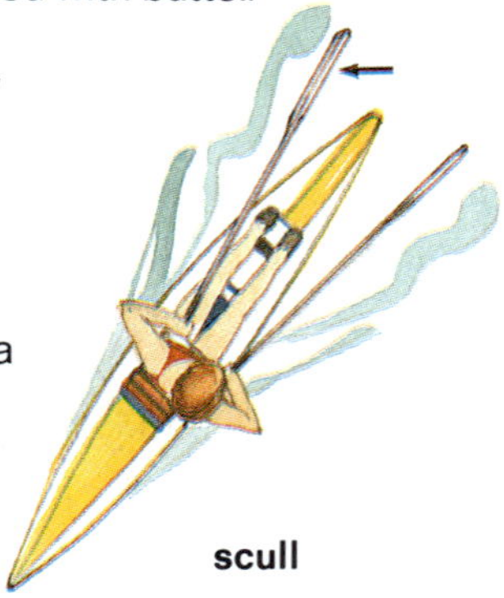

scull

scut·tle (skut′ əl) *v.* **scut·tled, scut·tling.** to cause a boat or ship to sink by cutting, boring, or uncovering an opening in the bottom, deck, or sides.

seep (sēp) *v.* to spread or flow slowly through something.

seer (sir) *n.* person who is believed to have the power of foreseeing future events; prophet; visionary.

sem·i·cir·cle (sem ē′ sėr′ kəl) *n.* half a circle, or something arranged in or resembling a half circle.

sen·es·chal (sen′ ə shəl) *n.* person in charge of a royal or noble household, especially in medieval times.

sen·ti·nel (sen′ tən əl) *n.* person stationed to keep watch and alert others of danger; guard; sentry. [French *sentinelle* sentry, from Italian *sentinella* sentry, probably going back to Latin *sentīre* to perceive, feel.]

sen·try (sen′ trē) *n., pl.* **sen·tries.** a person, especially a soldier, stationed to keep watch and alert others of danger; guard.

se·quence (sē′ kwəns) *n.* group, collection, or series of connected things. [Late Latin *sequentia* that which follows, from Latin *sequens,* present participle of *sequī* to follow.]

serf (sėrf) *n.* in the Middle Ages, a peasant bound to the land or to the service of a landlord. [French *serf* servant, from Latin *servus* slave.]

sev·er (sev′ ər) *v.* to cut apart or off. [Old French *sevrer* to separate, going back to Latin *sēparāre.*]

shag (shag) *n.* a small sea bird having webbed feet, a hooked bill, a pouch under the beak for holding fish, and a crest during the breeding season.

shil·ling (shil′ ing) *n.* coin of the United Kingdom equal to five pence or one-twentieth of a pound.

shoal (shōl) *n.* sandbank or sandbar that can be seen at low tide. [Old English *sceald* shallow.]

shunt·ing (shunt′ ing) *adj.* **1.** (of trains) switching from one track to another. **2.** moving aside or away.

siege (sēj) *n.* act or process of surrounding an enemy position in order to capture it by constant attack and by cutting off its supplies. **to lay siege to.** to try to capture by means of a siege.

sig·nif·i·cance (sig nif′ i kəns) *n.* special value or importance. [Latin *significāns* full of meaning, present participle of *significāre* to show by signs.]

sim·ple·ton (sim′ pəl tən) *n.* unwise or silly person; fool.

si·mul·ta·ne·ous·ly (sī′ məl tā′ nē əs lē) *adv.* at the same time; concurrently.

Sin·bad (sin′ bad) sailor in *The Arabian Nights* who had seven extraordinary voyages.

singed (sinjd) *adj.* burned at the ends or tips; lightly burned; scorched.

skim (skim) *v.* **skimmed, skim·ming. 1.** to take a quick glance at something. **2.** to move or glide lightly and swiftly over a surface.

slake (slāk) *v.* **slaked, slak·ing.** to relieve or satisfy; quench.

sledge (slej) *n.* sled or sleigh.

smite (smīt) *v.* **smot, smitten.** to strike hard, especially with the hand or with a weapon.

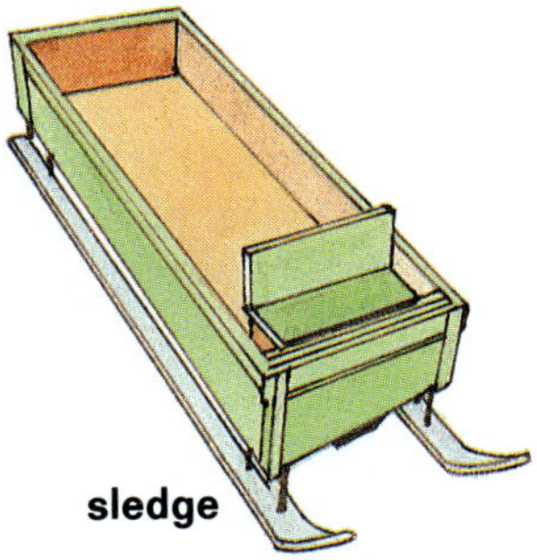

sledge

Smith·son·i·an In·sti·tu·tion (smith sōn′ ē ən in′ sti tü′ shən) U.S. national museum in Washington, D.C. Also, unofficially **Smithsonian Institute.**

snout (snout) *n.* part of an animal's head that projects forward, including the nose, mouth, and jaws.

sod·den (sod′ ən) *adj.* soaked through; waterlogged; soggy.

sol·emn (sol′ əm) *adj.* **1.** performed with formality or ceremony. **2.** having a grave or serious character. [Latin *sōllemnis* established, religious, from *sōllus* whole + *annus* year.]

so·lem·ni·ty (sə lem′ nə tē) *n., pl.* **so·lem·ni·ties.** the state or quality of being solemn; seriousness.

sol·id (sol′ id) *n. Mathematics.* figure having length, width, and thickness as a cube, sphere, or pyramid.

son·net (son′ it) *n.* a poem that has fourteen lines and a fixed pattern of rhyme.

sow (sou) *n.* an adult female pig.

spec·trum (spek′ trəm) *n., pl.* **spec·tra** or **spec·trums.** a band of colors into which white light is separated when it passes through a prism. The colors of the spectrum are red, orange, yellow, green, blue, indigo, and violet.

spectrum

square (skwãr) *n.* **1.** plane figure having four sides of equal length and four right angles. **2.** the product of a number multiplied by itself.

squire (skwīr) *n.* **1.** in the Middle Ages, a young man who, in preparation for his own knighthood, attended a knight. **2.** English country gentleman or landowner. [Old French *esquier* from Latin *scutarius* shield-bearer.]

a b**a**t, ā c**a**ke, ä f**a**ther, är c**ar**, ãr d**are**; e h**e**n, ē m**e**, ėr t**er**m; i b**i**b, ī k**i**te, ir cl**ear**; o t**o**p, ō r**o**pe, ô s**aw**, oi c**oi**n, ôr f**or**k, ou **ou**t; u s**u**n, u̇ b**oo**k, ü m**oo**n, ū c**u**te; ə **a**bout, tak**e**n

sta·lac·tite (stə lak′ tīt, stal′ ək tīt′) *n.* formation resembling an icicle, hanging down from the ceiling of a cave. It is usually composed of calcium carbonate deposited by water seeping through the rock above. [Modern Latin *stalactites*, from Greek *stalaktos* trickling, dripping; because it results from the dripping of water.]

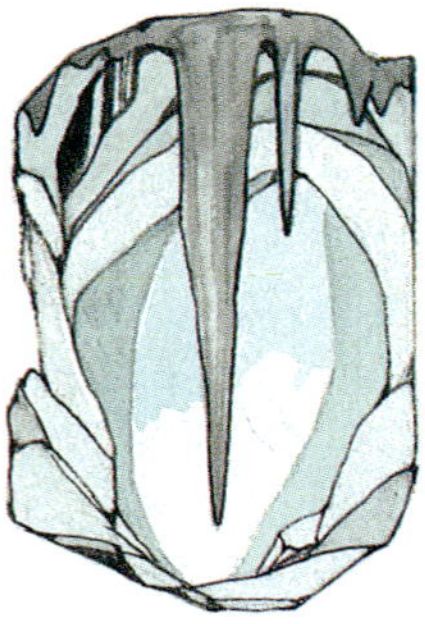
stalactite

stale·mate (stāl′ māt′) *n.* deadlock; standstill.

stark (stärk) *adj.* completely; absolutely.

sta·tus (stā′ təs, stat′ əs) *n.* **1.** relative place or rank, especially social or professional standing. **2.** state; condition.

stead·fast·ness (sted′ fast′ nis) *n.* faithfulness; firmness; constancy.

stern (stėrn) *n.* rear part of a boat or ship.

ster·oid (stãr′ oid) *n.* any of a group of organic compounds, some of which are produced naturally. Others are manufactured and used in medicines.

stew·ard (stü′ ərd, stū′ ərd) *n.* **1.** person in charge of the food and other passenger services, as on a ship, airplane, or train. **2.** one who manages or supervises another's property, finances, or affairs. [Old English *stigweard* official directing a household, from *stig* house, hall + *weard* keeper.]

stores (stôrz) *n. pl.* supplies, as of food or equipment.

strait (strāt) *n.* narrow waterway or channel connecting two larger bodies of water.

strat·a·gem (strat′ ə jəm) *n.* a scheme, trick, or maneuver designed to outwit or surprise an enemy or obtain an advantage. [French *stratageme*, from Latin *stratēgēma*, from Greek *stratēgēma*, from *stratēgos* general.]

strive (strīv) *v.* **strove** or **strived, striv·en** (striv′ ən), **striving.** to make a great effort.

strong-willed (strong′ wild′) *adj.* having a strong will; stubborn; willful; headstrong.

sub·mit (səb mit′) *v.* **sub·mit·ted, sub·mit·ting.** to put forward for consideration; turn in. [Latin *submittere* to let down, lower, put below.]

sub·se·quent (sub′ sə kwənt) *adj.* coming or happening after, or as a result. [Latin *subsequēns*, present participle of *sebsequī* to follow.]

suc·ceed (sək sēd′) *v.* to come next in the place of another.

suit·or (sü′ tər) *n.* a man who courts, or seeks to marry, a woman.

sul·fur (sul′ fər) *n.* a yellow, nonmetallic element occurring in both free and combined forms.

Su·per·in·tend·ent of Doc·u·ments, the head of the U.S. Government Printing Office.

surge (sėrj) *v.* **surged, surg·ing. 1.** to increase or rise suddenly. **2.** to move with a forceful, swelling motion, as waves. [Old French *sorgir* to rise, going back to Latin *surgere*.]

sur·vey (sər vā′) *v.* to view or examine as a whole. [Anglo-Norman *surveier* to look over, going back to Latin *super* above, over + *vidēre* to see.]

sus·pend (sə spend′) *v.* to attach from above so as to allow free movement; hang. [Latin *suspendere* to hang up.]

suspend

sus·pense (sə spens′) *n.* worry or tension resulting from being in doubt about the outcome of something. [Old French *suspens* delay, going back to Latin *suspensus* past participle *suspendere* to hang up.]

T

tap·es·try (tap′ is trē) *n., pl.* **tap·es·tries.** a heavy woven fabric decorated with designs or pictures often showing historical or mythological events. Tapestries are used as wall hangings and coverings for floors and furniture.

tap·i·o·ca (tap′ ē ō′ kə) *n.* a starchy substance obtained from the root of the cassava plant, used in cooking to make pudding and to thicken sauces and soups.

tar·ry (tãr′ ē) *v.* **tar·ried, tar·ry·ing. 1.** to remain in a place; stay, especially longer than one expected. **2.** to delay in doing something, especially in coming or going.

tech·nique (tek nēk′) *n.* a method of doing something. [French *technique* procedures and methods of an art or profession, from Greek *technikos* relating to art, skillful, from *technē* art, skill, craft.]

te·di·ous (tē′ dē əs) *adj.* causing weariness and boredom because of length or dullness; boring.

ten·ant (ten′ ənt) *n.* a person who pays rent to occupy or use the property of another as land, a house, or apartment. [Old French *tenant* one who holds or possesses, from *tenir* to hold, from Latin *tenēre.*]

ten·dril (ten′ drəl) *n.* anything, as a wispy curl of hair, that resembles a tendril, a thin, leafless, often coiling part of a climbing plant that enables the plant to cling to a wall, tree trunk, or other object for support.

thatched (thacht) *adj.* covered with straw, reeds, or rushes.

the·o·ry (thē′ ər ē, thir′ ē) *n., pl.* **the·o·ries.** an idea or ideas that explain a group of facts or an event; assumption that has been proven to be true. [Late Latin *theōria*, from Greek *theōria* a looking at, thing looked at, from *theōros* spectaton, from *thea* a sight + *horan* to see.]

ther·mal (thėr′ məl) *adj.* of or relating to heat or warmth. [Greek *thermē* heat.]

thrift shop (thrift′ shop′) *n.* a store that sells used items or other merchandise at a reduced price. [Old Norse *thrift* prosperity.]

thriv·ing (thrī′ ving) *adj.* successful; prosperous; fortunate.

throng (thrông, throng) *n.* large number of people gathered or crowded together; crowd. [Old English *gethrong* crowd.]

toi·let (toi′ lit) *n.* **1.** act or process of washing, dressing, or grooming oneself. **2.** bathroom.

to·ken (tō′ kən) *n.* sign or symbol.

tongue (tung) *n.* spoken language or dialect.

to·paz (tō′ paz) *n.* a lustrous crystalline mineral, occurring in a variety of colors and used as a gem.

top·ic (top′ ik) *n.* the subject of a speech or composition.

tour·ney (tür′ nē) *n.* **1.** formal combat between two or more mounted knights armed with lances or other weapons; tournament. **2.** series of contests involving two or more persons or teams. [Old French *tornei* tournament, from *torneier* to joust, turn round, going back to Latin *tornāre* to turn in a lathe.]

tourney

a bat, ā cake, ä father, är car, ãr dare; e hen, ē me, ėr term; i bib, ī kīte, ir clear; o top, ō rope, ô saw, oi coin, ôr fork, ou out; u sun, u̇ book, ü moon, ū cute; ə about, taken

tra·di·tion·al (trə dish′ ən əl) *adj.* coming from long-established customs or practices.

tra·gic (traj′ ik) *adj.* **1.** very sad, unfortunate or disasterous. **2.** of or relating to tragedy, especially dramatic tragedy.

trans·act (tran sakt′, tran zakt′) *v.* to conduct business.

trem·u·lous (trem′ yə ləs) *adj.* **1.** lacking firmness or courage; timid; wavering. **2.** characterized by trembling or shaking. [Latin *tremulus* trembling.]

trench (trench) *n.* **trench·es.** long, narrow ditch with the excavated earth piled up in front, used especially for the protection of soldiers in combat.

tres·tle (tres′ əl) *n.* short beam or bar supported by four diverging legs used as a support.

trig·gered (trig′ ərd) *adj.* set to go off.

triv·i·al·i·ty (triv′ ē al′ ə tē) *n., pl.* **triv·i·al·i·ties. 1.** thing or matter of little importance. **2.** quality or state of having little importance; shallowness.

troupe (trüp) *n.* group or company, especially of traveling actors, singers, or circus performers.

truce (trüs) *n.* temporary halt to fighting. [Middle Enghlish *trewes*, plural of *trewe* temporary peace, from Old English *trēow* faith, promise, compact.]

tu·nic (tü′ nik, tū′ nik) *n.* piece of clothing resembling a long shirt reaching to the knee or below.

tunic

turn·spit (tėrn′ spit′) *n.* person who turns roasting meat on a spit.

tur·ret (tėr′ it) *n.* small tower, usually forming part of a larger structure.

two·pence (tup′ əns) *n.* sum of money and coin equal to two British pennies.

U

U·gan·da (ū gan′ də, ü gän′ də) *n.* a country in east-central Africa.

un·a·dul·ter·at·ed (un′ ə dul′ tə rā′ tid) *adj.* unmixed; pure; undiluted.

underground (un′ dər ground′) *n.* railway that runs wholly or partly underground, especially one in a large city providing passenger and commuting service; subway.

un·err·ing·ly (un ãr′ ing lē) without error.

un·fore·seen (un′ fôr sēn′) *adj.* not known beforehand; unexpected; unanticipated.

u·ni·corn (ū′ nə kôrn′) *n.* legendary white horse with a long, pointed horn in the middle of its forehead, regarded as a symbol of innocence and purity. [Latin *unicornus* having one horn, from *unus* one + *cornu* horn.]

unicorn

Un·ion (ūn′ yən) *n.* the United States of America regarded as a national whole, especially those states that remained loyal to the national government during the Civil War.

ur·gent (ėr′ jənt) *adj.* demanding immediate action or attention; pressing. [Latin *urgēns*, present participle of *urgēre* to press, drive.]

ut·ter (ut′ ər) *v.* to express aloud; give voice to. [Middle Dutch *uteren* to speak, show.]

V

vague (vāg) *adj.* not precise or exact in meaning; not expressed definitely.

val·or (val′ ər) *adj.* great courage or bravery, especially in battle.

valve (valv) *n.* device used to control the flow of liquids or gases in piping and other closed systems by blocking or partially blocking passages by means of a movable part.

var·let (var′ lit) *n.* evil man; scoundrel.

vast (vast) *adj.* very great in extent, size, or amount.

ven·i·son (ven′ ə sən) *n.* the flesh of a deer, used as food. [Old French *veneisun*, from Latin *vēnātiō* hunting.]

vent (vent) *v.* to give expression to; let out. [Partly from French *vent* wind, from Latin *ventus*; partly from French *event* hole, opening, going back to Latin *ex* out + *ventus* wind.]

ven·ture (ven′ chər) *v.* **ven·tured, ven·tur·ing.** to do or undertake something in spite of risks and dangers.

ver·sion (vėr′ zhən) *n.* **1.** different or altered form of something. **2.** account or description as presented from a particular viewpoint. [Medieval Latin *versio* conversion, translation, a turning, from Latin *vertere* to turn.]

ver·tex (vėr′ teks) *n.*, *pl.* **ver·tes·es** or **ver·ti·ces.** *Geometry.* **1.** the point of a triangle, pyramid, or the like, opposite the base. **2.** the point of intersection of the sides of an angle.

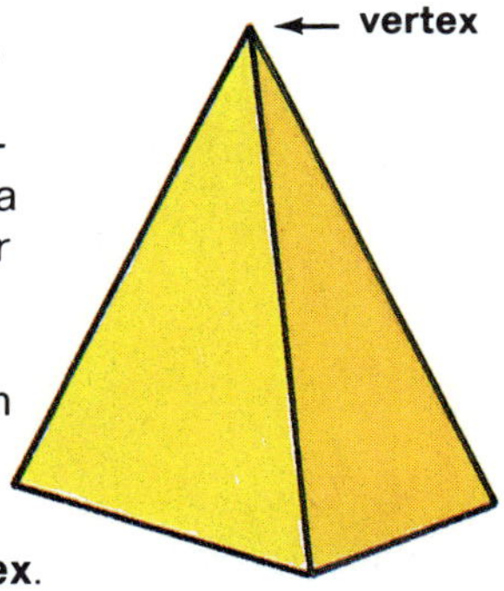

ver·ti·ces, See **vertex**.

ves·tige (ves′ tij) *n.* trace, sign, or evidence of something that once existed but no longer does; slight remnant. [French *vestige* footprint, trace, from Latin *vestīgium*.]

vic·to·ri·ous (vik tôr′ ē əs) *adj.* having achieved a victory; successful.

view·point (vū′ point′) *n.* a way of thinking; point of view; mental attitude.

vi·gil (vij′ əl) *n.* act or period of remaining awake, as to guard or observe something. [Old French *vigile* watch on the eve of a holy day, from Latin *vigilia* watching.]

vig·or·ous·ly (vig′ ər əs lē) *adv.* in a lively, energetic, or forceful way.

vil·la (vil′ ə) *n.* large and luxurious home, especially one in a country or at the seashore.

vil·lain (vil′ ən) *n.* wicked, evil, or criminal person. [Old French *vilain* peasant, churl, rustic, from Medieval Latin *villānus* serf, farm servant, from Latin *villa* farm.]

vim (vim) *n.* energy, strength or enthusiasm.

volt (vōlt) *n.* a unit for measuring the force that makes electrons move in an electric current.

vol·u·ble (vol′ yə bəl) *adj.* given to a large, smooth flow of words; talkative; fluent. [Latin *volūbilis*, from *volvere* to roll.]

vouch·safe (vouch sāf′) *v.* **vouch·safed, vouch·saf·ing.** to give or grant out of kindness. [Originally, *vouch safe* to warrant as safe, guarantee; Old French *voucher* to summon, claim, from Latin *vocare* to call.]

vow (vou) *n.* solemn promise or pledge.

vul·ner·a·ble (vul′ nər ə bəl) *adj.* capable of being hurt, wounded, or damaged; sensitive. [Late Latin *vulnerābilis* wounding, going back to *vulnus* wound.]

W

ward·er (wôr′ dər) *n.* guard; watchman.

war·y (wãr′ ē) *adj.* on the alert; watchful.

a b**a**t, ā c**a**ke, ä f**a**ther, är c**ar**, ãr d**are**; e h**e**n, ē m**e**, ėr t**er**m; i b**i**b, ī k**ī**te, ir cl**ear**; o t**o**p, ō r**o**pe, ô s**aw**, oi c**oi**n, ôr f**or**k, ou **ou**t; u s**u**n, u̇ b**oo**k, ü m**oo**n, ū c**u**te; ə **a**bout, tak**e**n

way·far·er (wā′ fãr′ ər) *n.* traveler, especially one who travels on foot.

weath·er·cock (weth′ ər kok′) *n.* weather vane having the shape of a rooster.

whith·er (hwith′ ər, with′ ər) *Archaic. adv.* to what place; where.

wick·er (wik′ ər) *n.* slender, flexible twigs woven together, used in making baskets, furniture, and the like.

wince (wins) *v.* **winced, winc·ing.** to draw back suddenly; flinch slightly.

wind·lass (wind′ ləs) *n.* a device consisting of a cylinder, rope, and crank, used chiefly to lift anchors and buckets in wells.

windlass

wist·ful·ly (wist′ fə lē) *adv.* in a sadly yearning way; thoughtfully; longingly.

work (wėrk) *v.* **worked** or **wrought, work·ing. 1.** to shape, handle, or process. **2.** to put forth mental or physical effort in order to accomplish a definite end or purpose. [Old English *weorc* act, deed, task, toil, occupation, handiwork.]

wrath·ful (rath′ fəl) *adj.* full of extreme or violent anger.

wrought (rôt) *v.* See **work.**

Y

yard-arm (yärd′ ärm′) *n.* long rod fastened across a mast, used to support a sail.

yeo·man (yō′ mən) *n., pl.* **yeo·men. 1.** in English society, a small farmer who owned and farmed a small piece of land. **2.** naval petty officer. [Middle English *yoman* servant in a royal or noble household, possibly a contraction of *yongman* young man, from Old English *geong* young + *mann* man.]

Z

Zeus (züs) *n. Greek Mythology.* the greatest of the gods, ruler of the heavens and the earth, whose chief weapon was the thunderbolt.

a bat, ā cake, ä father, är car, ãr dare; e hen, ē me, ėr term; i bib, ī kīte, ir clear; o top, ō rope, ô saw, oi coin, ôr fork, ou out; u sun, u̇ book, ü moon, ū cute; ə about, taken